T0244439

THE
50 GREATEST
PLAYERS
IN
BRAVES
HISTORY

ROBERT W. COHEN

LYONS
PRESS

ESSEX, CONNECTICUT

An imprint of Globe Pequot, the trade division of
The Rowman & Littlefield Publishing Group, Inc.
4501 Forbes Blvd., Ste. 200
Lanham, MD 20706
www.rowman.com

Distributed by NATIONAL BOOK NETWORK

British Library Cataloguing in Publication Information available

Library of Congress Cataloging-in-Publication Data

Names: Cohen, Robert W, author.
Title: The 50 greatest players in Braves history / Robert W. Cohen.
Other titles: Fifty greatest players in Braves history
Description: Essex, Connecticut: Lyons Press, [2023] | Includes bibliographical references.
Identifiers: LCCN 2022044341 (print) | LCCN 2022044342 (ebook) |
ISBN 9781493071128 (cloth) | ISBN 9781493071180 (epub)
Subjects: LCSH: Atlanta Braves (Baseball team)--Biography. | Atlanta Braves
(Baseball team)--History. | Baseball
players--Georgia--Atlanta--Biography.
Classification: LCC GV875.A8 C65 2023 (print) | LCC GV875.A8 (ebook) |
DDC 796.357/6409758231--dc23/eng/202209289
LC record available at https://lccn.loc.gov/2022044341
LC ebook record available at https://lccn.loc.gov/2022044342

♾™ The paper used in this publication meets the minimum requirements of American National Standard for Information Sciences—Permanence of Paper for Printed Library Materials, ANSI/ NISO Z39.48-1992.

CONTENTS

ACKNOWLEDGMENTS

I would like to express my gratitude to the grandchildren of Leslie Jones, who, through the Trustees of the Boston Public Library, Print Department, supplied many of the photos included in this book.

I also wish to thank Kate Yeakley of RMYAuctions.com, George A. Kitrinos, Keith Allison, Kenji Takabayashi, L. W. Yang, Jim Accordino, Ian D'Andrea, and Rich Anderson, each of whom generously contributed to the photographic content of this work.

INTRODUCTION

THE BRAVES LEGACY

The oldest continuously operating professional sports team in America, the franchise now known as the Atlanta Braves has its roots in the Boston Red Stockings, who came into being in 1871, one year after baseball's first openly all-professional team, the Cincinnati Red Stockings, disbanded. Founded by Boston businessman Ivers Whitney Adams, who owned and operated the American Net and Twine Company, and former Cincinnati player-manager Harry Wright, the Boston Red Stockings entered the world of pro baseball as one of the nine charter members of the National Association of Professional Baseball Players (NAPBBP) that served as the forerunner of the National League from 1871 to 1875.

Led by player-manager Wright, star second baseman Ross Barnes, and pitcher Albert Spalding, who compiled a remarkable overall record of 204-53 during his five seasons in Boston, the Red Stockings dominated the National Association, winning four of that league's five championships, before joining the newly formed National League when the NAPBBP dissolved following the conclusion of the 1875 campaign. Remaining a formidable squad under Wright during the new league's formative years after being purchased by wealthy businessman Arthur H. Soden in 1877, the Red Stockings, who played their home games at the Union Base Ball Grounds in Boston's South End from 1871 to 1914, won consecutive pennants in 1877 and 1878. However, they failed to perform at the same lofty level in any of the next four seasons under managers John Morrill and Jack Burdock, finishing no higher than second in any of those campaigns. Experiencing something of a resurgence in 1883, the newly named Beaneaters captured their third NL championship by compiling a record of 63-35, finishing in the process four games ahead of the runner-up Chicago White

Stockings. However, the Beaneaters contended for the title in just two of the next seven seasons, placing fifth in the eight-team circuit on four separate occasions, as Morrill, Mike "King" Kelly, Jim Hart, and Frank Selee all took turns managing the team.

Re-establishing themselves as the class of the National League under Selee during the 1890s, the Beaneaters won five more pennants, capturing three straight titles from 1891 to 1893, and another two in 1897 and 1898. Particularly outstanding in 1892, 1897, and 1898, the Beaneaters ran away with the NL flag in the first of those campaigns by posting a regular-season mark of 102-48, before defeating the second-place Cleveland Spiders 5–0–1 in an early incarnation of the World Series. Five years later, the Beaneaters edged out the Baltimore Orioles for the NL title by compiling a record of 93-39-3 that gave them a franchise-best .705 winning percentage. They followed that up by capturing their fifth pennant of the decade with a mark of 102-47-3 that enabled them to finish six games ahead of the runner-up Orioles in the standings.

Piloted by Selee throughout this period of excellence, the Beaneaters benefited greatly from their manager's ability to assess and hire talented players. A rare 19th-century major-league manager who did not double as a player or rise from the ranks of former players, Selee evaluated talent as well as anyone in the game, bringing into the fold during his time in Boston standout performers such as first baseman Fred Tenney, second baseman Bobby Lowe, third baseman Jimmy Collins, shortstop Herman Long, outfielder Hugh Duffy, whose .440 batting average in 1894 represents the highest single-season mark in baseball history, and staff ace Kid Nichols, who won 330 games and surpassed 30 victories seven times as a member of the Beaneaters.

Unfortunately, the establishment of the rival American League at the turn of the century contributed greatly to a precipitous fall from grace by the Beaneaters, who ended up losing many of their best players to the Boston Americans (Red Sox). Their roster decimated by the departures of Hall of Fame third sacker Jimmy Collins and star outfielders Buck Freeman and Chick Stahl, the Beaneaters entered into an extended period of mediocrity, posting just one winning record from 1900 to 1913, with the team finishing either last or next-to-last in the eight-team senior circuit in eight of those 14 seasons.

In addition to an overall lack of talent, the Beaneaters found themselves being hampered during the first part of the 20th century by several changes in ownership and management that prevented them from establishing any sort of continuity. With his team struggling terribly on the playing field and at the gate, longtime Beaneaters owner Arthur Soden elected to sell the ballclub to railroad magnates George and John Dovey prior to the start of the 1907 campaign. The renamed "Doves" remained under the control of the Dovey brothers for just four years, before being purchased late in 1910 by a group of investors headed by New York lawyer William Hepburn Russell. However, after spending one season playing under the sobriquet "Rustlers," the team went up for sale once again when Russell died of a heart attack on November 21, 1911. Purchased shortly thereafter by millionaire New York attorney and politician James E. Gaffney, who had strong connections to Tammany Hall, which used an Indian chief as its symbol, the franchise adopted its now-famous "Braves" moniker. Meanwhile, after Frank Selee surrendered his managerial post at the end of 1901, seven different men served as skipper in Boston over the course of the next 11 seasons, before Gaffney finally settled on former Phillies, Tigers, and New York Highlanders manager George Stallings in 1913.

After helping the Braves improve their record by 19 games the previous year, Stallings guided them on an improbable run to the NL pennant in 1914 that saw them become the only team ever to capture a league championship after being in last place on the Fourth of July. Led by star shortstop Rabbit Maranville, NL MVP Johnny Evers, and co–staff aces Dick Rudolph and Bill James, the "Miracle Braves" culminated their amazing season by sweeping Connie Mack's heavily favored Philadelphia Athletics in the World Series.

Inspired by the success his team experienced in 1914, Braves owner James Gaffney decided to build a larger, more modern ballpark at the end of the year. After spending the first few months of the 1915 campaign playing their home games at Fenway Park, the Braves christened Braves Field on August 18, 1915. Located one mile west of Fenway, the 40,000-seat stadium proved to be the largest park in the majors at the time. Easily accessible by public transportation, the fan friendly ballpark served as home to the Braves for the next 38 years, during which time it also hosted the 1915 and 1916 World Series (for the Red Sox), the 1936 MLB All-Star Game, the 1948 World Series, and multiple football games.

Remaining contenders under Stallings for two more years, the Braves finished second in the NL in 1915 and third in 1916, before beginning a dark period in franchise history that lasted nearly three decades. With ownership of the team passing from Gaffney to former Harvard football coach Percy D. Haughton (1916–1918), motion picture mogul George Washington Grant (1919–1922), Judge Emil Fuchs (1923–1935), and, finally, to former Red Sox owner Bob Quinn (1936–1944), the Braves compiled a winning record just five times from 1917 to 1945, never finishing any higher than fourth in the NL standings. Losing at least 100 games on five separate occasions, the Braves proved to be particularly awful in 1935, posting an embarrassing mark of 38-115 that gave them the second-lowest single-season winning percentage (.248) of the 20th century. Meanwhile, as the Braves, who became more commonly known as the "Bees" from 1936 to 1940, underwent frequent changes in ownership, they also suffered from a lack of stability in the dugout, with 10 different men managing them over that 29-year stretch, including shortstop Dave Bancroft (1924–1927), former Pirates and Cardinals skipper Bill McKechnie (1930–1937), and Casey Stengel (1938–1943). Nevertheless, several outstanding players graced the Braves' roster during these lean years, with Hall of Fame second baseman Rogers Hornsby leading the league with a .387 batting average in his only year with the team in 1928, center fielder Wally Berger establishing himself as one of the NL's top sluggers during the 1930s, and popular right fielder Tommy Holmes earning multiple All-Star selections and one runner-up finish in the league MVP voting during the 1940s.

With construction magnates Lou Perini, Guido Rugo, and C. Joseph Maney purchasing the shares of other stockholders early in 1944, they assumed majority control of the Braves and quickly set about righting the ship. After paying off the team's creditors, shortening the outfield dimensions at spacious Braves Field, and going through three managers their first two years in charge, Perini, Rugo, and Maney decided to entrust their team to former Braves outfielder Billy Southworth, who had guided the Cardinals to two pennants and one world championship the previous four years in St. Louis. Aided by the return from the military of star pitchers Johnny Sain and Warren Spahn, 1947 NL MVP Bob Elliott, and Tommy Holmes, who continued to perform at an elite level, Southworth helped turn the Braves into contenders before long, leading them to their first winning record in eight seasons in 1946, a third-place finish the following year, and the NL pennant in 1948. Although the Braves lost the 1948 World Series to the Cleveland Indians in six games, they remained a solid team under Southworth for two more years, before a slow start in 1951 prompted ownership to name Holmes player-manager. But, with the Braves faring no better under Holmes, former Chicago Cubs skipper Charlie Grimm assumed managerial duties early in 1952, which turned out to be the Braves' last year in the city of Boston.

With attendance at Braves Field steadily dwindling due to the growing popularity of the Ted Williams–led Red Sox, majority owner Lou Perini announced on March 13, 1953, that he planned to move the Braves to

Milwaukee. Welcomed with open arms by the state of Wisconsin, the Braves set a then-NL record by drawing 1.8 million fans to newly constructed Milwaukee County Stadium in 1953. Responding well to their new fanbase, the Braves posted a record of 92-62 their first year in Milwaukee that represented their best mark since the championship campaign of 1914, earning in the process a second-place finish in the NL standings.

Yet, even though Grimm led the Braves to strong showings in each of the next two seasons as well, ownership replaced him at the helm with former St. Louis Browns and Pittsburgh Pirates manager Fred Haney during the early stages of the 1956 campaign. Inheriting a talented squad that included an eclectic mix of veterans and emerging superstars, Haney guided the Braves to two pennants, one world championship, and a pair of close second-place finishes over the course of the next four seasons, before eventually being relieved of his duties.

After finishing just one game behind the pennant-winning Dodgers in 1956, the Braves laid claim to the NL flag the following year by compiling a record of 95-59 that left them eight games ahead of the runner-up St. Louis Cardinals in the final NL standings. They subsequently defeated the Yankees in seven games in the World Series behind the stellar pitching of Lew Burdette, who earned three complete-game victories over the AL champions. Continuing their dominance of the senior circuit in 1958, the Braves repeated as league champions, this time finishing eight games ahead of the second-place Pittsburgh Pirates, with a record of 92-62. However, after taking a three-games-to-one lead over New York in the Fall Classic, the Braves failed to repeat as world champions when the Yankees stormed back to win the final three contests. The Braves nearly earned their third straight trip to the World Series in 1959, concluding the regular season with a record of 86-68 that left them tied with the Dodgers for first place. But consecutive losses to Los Angeles in a best-of-three playoff to determine the league champion left them on the outside looking in when the Series began.

Certainly, the steady hand of manager Fred Haney contributed greatly to the success the Braves experienced during the late 1950s. But Milwaukee also had as much talent as any team in the league, from top to bottom. In addition to a deep starting rotation anchored by Lew Burdette and the ageless Warren Spahn, the Braves featured a potent lineup that included slugging first baseman Joe Adcock, perennial All-Star catcher Del Crandall, speedy center fielder Bill Bruton, and one of the most dynamic hitting tandems of all time in Eddie Mathews and Hank Aaron, who combined to hit more homers than any other pair of teammates in baseball history. In fact, Mathews is generally regarded as one of the greatest third basemen ever to play the game, while Aaron's name invariably comes up in any conversations involving the greatest player in the history of the sport.

The duo of Aaron and Mathews continued to serve as the focal point of the Braves' offense well into the 1960s, even after slugging catcher Joe Torre and hard-hitting left fielder Rico Carty joined them in the Milwaukee lineup during the early part of the decade. But even though the Braves remained one of the league's top scoring teams, their mediocre pitching allowed them to finish as high as second just once from 1960 to 1965 under managers Charlie Dressen (1960–1961), Birdie Tebbetts (1961–1962), and Bobby Bragan (1963–1965). Nevertheless, the Braves proved to be extremely competitive, compiling a winning record in each of those six seasons.

Despite the success the Braves experienced in Milwaukee, Chicago business executive William Bartholomay seemed intent on moving them to a larger television market almost as soon as he purchased the team from Lou Perini in November 1962. Attracted to the fast-growing city of Atlanta and its brand-new 52,000-seat ballpark, Bartholomay announced his plans to relocate the Braves to Georgia for the 1965 season. Forced to remain in Milwaukee for one more year by an injunction filed in Wisconsin, the Braves completed their move to Atlanta in 1966, playing their first game at Atlanta Stadium (later renamed Atlanta-Fulton County Stadium) on April 12.

Not faring particularly well their first three seasons in Atlanta under managers Bobby Bragan, Billy Hitchcock, and Lum Harris, the Braves posted just one winning record from 1966 to 1968, finishing fifth in the 10-team NL twice. But after each league expanded to 12 teams and adopted a new two-division format in 1969, the Braves advanced to the playoffs by compiling a regular-season record of 93-69 that left them three games ahead of the second-place San Francisco Giants and four games in front of the third-place Cincinnati Reds in the NL West, which they also shared with the Los Angeles Dodgers, Houston Astros, and newly formed San Diego Padres. However, the Braves failed to make it to the World Series, losing to the "Miracle Mets" in three straight games in the first-ever National League Championship Series (NLCS).

Experiencing very little success the next 12 seasons under managers Lum Harris (1968–1972), Eddie Mathews (1972–1974), Clyde King (1974–1975), Dave Bristol (1976–1977), and Bobby Cox (1978–1981), the Braves finished over .500 just three times, never seriously contending for the division title. Nevertheless, Braves fans found consolation in the achievements of Hank Aaron, who, after spending much of his career playing in virtual anonymity, finally began to receive the recognition he deserved as he moved inexorably toward breaking Babe Ruth's all-time home-run record. Pitcher Phil Niekro and outfielders Rico Carty and Ralph Garr also excelled for the team during this time, with Carty and Garr each winning a batting title. Meanwhile, after Ted Turner purchased the Braves in 1976, the team experienced an increase in popularity, with the media magnate using them as a major programming draw for his fledgling cable network, WTBS. The first franchise to have a nationwide audience and fanbase, the Braves soon found themselves being marketed as "America's Team."

Finally emerging as contenders once again under new manager Joe Torre in 1982, the Braves captured the NL West title by compiling a regular-season record of 89-73 that enabled them to edge out the second-place Dodgers by one game and the third-place Giants by two. However, just as they had done 13 years earlier, the Braves exited the postseason tournament quickly, losing to the eventual world champion St. Louis Cardinals in the NLCS in three straight games.

Performing well under Torre once again in 1983, the Braves finished second in the division, three games behind the first-place Dodgers, with a record of 88-74. But, despite the presence of two-time NL MVP Dale Murphy, the Braves subsequently entered into another period of mediocrity, failing to post a winning record in any of the next seven seasons, as Torre (1984), Eddie Haas (1985), Bobby Wine (1985), Chuck Tanner (1986–1988), and Russ Nixon (1988–1990) all took turns managing the team.

With Bobby Cox, who had spent the previous four seasons serving the Braves as general manager, returning to the dugout midway through the 1990 campaign, things began to turn around in Atlanta the following year. A shrewd judge of talent and an excellent tactician, Cox, who, in addition to managing the Braves from 1978 to 1981, had previously played third base for the Yankees for two seasons, managed in the minors for several years, and piloted the Toronto Blue Jays from 1982 to 1985, brought a newfound stability to the Braves, serving as the team's manager for the next two decades. And with newly hired GM John Schuerholz doing an expert job of running the organization, pitching coach Leo Mazzone developing the mound skills of young hurlers Tom Glavine, John Smoltz, and Steve Avery, multiple-time Cy Young Award winner Greg Maddux being acquired via free agency, third baseman Terry Pendleton providing veteran leadership, and talented players such as David Justice, Ron Gant, and Chipper Jones being promoted from the minor leagues, the Braves soon emerged as the class of the National League, winning 14 division titles, five pennants, and one World Series from 1991 to 2005.

Led by NL MVP Terry Pendleton, the Braves compiled a regular-season record of 94-68 in 1991 that enabled them to edge out the Dodgers for the NL West title by just one game. But, after laying claim to their first pennant in more than three decades by defeating the Pittsburgh Pirates in seven games in the NLCS, the Braves came up just short in the World Series, losing to the Minnesota Twins in seven games. The ensuing campaign followed a similar script, with the Braves capturing their second straight division title and winning a hard-fought seven-game NLCS over the Pirates, before once again losing the World Series, this time to the Toronto Blue Jays in six games. Their pitching staff bolstered by the offseason acquisition of Greg Maddux, the Braves posted a record of 104-58 in 1993 that placed them one game ahead of the runner-up Giants in the final NL West standings. Performing particularly well down the stretch, the Braves overcame a nine-game deficit to San Francisco on August 11 by winning 55 of their final 74 contests. However, they subsequently suffered a six-game defeat at the hands of the Philadelphia Phillies in the NLCS that prevented them from advancing to the Fall Classic for the third straight time.

With further expansion causing each league to adopt a new three-division setup in 1994, the Braves moved to the NL East, which they have spent close to 30 years sharing with the New York Mets, Philadelphia Phillies, Montreal Expos/Washington Nationals, and Florida/Miami Marlins. Although a players' strike brought the 1994 campaign to a premature end, the Braves resumed their divisional dominance the following year, capturing the first of their nine consecutive NL East titles behind the stellar pitching of Greg Maddux, who earned Cy Young honors for the fourth straight time by going 19-2 with a 1.63 ERA. This time, though, the Braves reached their ultimate goal, first disposing of the Colorado Rockies in the NLDS in four games, then sweeping the Cincinnati Reds in four straight games in the NLCS, and finally defeating the Cleveland Indians in six games in the World Series, becoming in the process the first team to win a world championship in three different cities.

Heavily favored to win the Fall Classic once again in 1996 after sweeping the Dodgers in the NLDS and overcoming a three-games-to-one deficit to the Cardinals in the NLCS by outscoring their overmatched opponents by a combined margin of 32–1 in the final three contests, the Braves grabbed a quick 2–0 lead over the Yankees in the World Series. But New York turned the tables on the Braves, denying them their second straight world championship by winning the final four games.

After spending 31 seasons playing their home games at Atlanta-Fulton County Stadium, the Braves moved into Turner Field in 1997, ironically the same year that Time Warner inherited the team after purchasing the Turner Broadcasting System from Ted Turner. Located at 755 Hank Aaron Drive, less than one block from the Braves' previous home, Turner Field had originally been built as Centennial Olympic Stadium in 1996 to serve as the centerpiece of that year's Summer Olympics. Converted into a base-ball park following the conclusion of the Olympic Games, Turner Field, which had a seating capacity of just over 52,000 for baseball, ended up serving as home to the Braves for the next 20 years, during which time it hosted the NLDS 11 times, the NLCS four times, the 1999 World Series, and the 2000 MLB All-Star Game.

Completely unaffected by the changes surrounding them, the Braves won the division title again in 1997 by amassing more than 100 victories for the first of three straight times. However, after sweeping the Houston Astros in the NLDS, they suffered a six-game defeat at the hands of the eventual world champion Florida Marlins in the NLCS. The Braves came up short in each of the next two postseasons as well, losing to the San Diego Padres in six games in the 1998 NLCS after posting a franchise-record 106 victories during the regular season, before being swept by the Yankees in four straight games in the 1999 World Series.

Although the Braves claimed the NL East title in each of the next six seasons as well, they failed to make it back to the World Series, being swept by the Cardinals in the 2000 NLDS, losing to the Arizona Diamondbacks in five games in the 2001 NLCS, suffering five-game defeats at the hands of the Giants, Cubs, and Houston Astros in the 2002, 2003, and 2004 NLDS, and losing to the Astros again in the 2005 NLDS, this time in four games.

Despite winning just one World Series from 1991 to 2005, the Braves established a standard of long-term excellence unmatched by any other team since the beginning of divisional play in 1969 by posting at least 90 victories 13 times and capturing 14 division titles. Featuring one of the NL's better offenses throughout the period, the Braves presented to the opposi-tion a lineup that included at different times outstanding performers such as hard-hitting first baseman Fred McGriff, Hall of Fame third baseman Chip-per Jones, swift shortstop Rafael Furcal, and standout outfielders David Justice, Ron Gant, and Andruw Jones. But the Braves' greatest strength proved to be their exceptional pitching, with Greg Maddux, Tom Glavine, and John Smoltz combining for nearly a decade to give them arguably the finest trio of starters ever assembled by one team. Meanwhile, under the expert tutelage of Leo Mazzone, fellow hurlers Steve Avery, Denny Neagle, and Kevin Millwood all had the finest seasons of their respective careers.

Unfortunately, all good things must come to an end, as the Braves discovered shortly after Mazzone left Atlanta to serve as pitching coach in Baltimore at the end of 2005. With both Greg Maddux and Tom Glavine having departed via free agency a few seasons earlier, Time Warner putting the team up for sale in December 2005, and John Schuerholz stepping down as general manager to assume the role of team president following the conclusion of the 2007 campaign, the Braves posted just two winning records and failed to make the playoffs four straight times from 2006 to 2009.

Purchased by Liberty Media on May 16, 2007, the Braves continued to struggle under manager Bobby Cox and new GM Frank Wren the next few seasons, before finally returning to the playoffs as a wild card in 2010. However, they exited the postseason tournament quickly, losing to the Giants in the NLDS in four games.

With Bobby Cox announcing his retirement at the end of 2010, the Braves replaced him in the dugout with former Florida Marlins skipper Fredi González, who led his new team to a record of 89-73 in 2011. Buoyed by the rapid development of first baseman Freddie Freeman and closer Craig Kimbrel into two of the game's best young players, the Braves posted more than 90 victories in each of the next two seasons, making the playoffs as a wild card in 2012, before laying claim to their 17th division title the following year. But they failed to advance beyond the first round of the postseason tournament both times, losing to the Cardinals 1–0 in the 2012 NL Wild Card Game, and falling to the Dodgers in four games in the 2013 NLDS.

After the Braves finished well out of contention in 2014, they fired general manager Frank Wren, replacing him on an interim basis with former Cleveland Indians and Texas Rangers GM John Hart, before promoting assistant general manager John Coppolella to GM on October 1, 2015. But, after an investigation conducted by Major League Baseball revealed that Coppolella had committed what the Braves termed "a breach of MLB rules regarding the international player market," he resigned his post on October 2, 2017. A little over one month later, the Braves replaced Coppolella with longtime baseball executive Alex Anthopoulos, who has continued to serve the organization as GM and executive vice president ever since. Meanwhile, with the Braves finishing with fewer than 70 victories in both 2015 and 2016, they relieved Fredi González of his managerial duties during the early stages of the 2016 campaign, replacing him at the helm with Brian Snitker, who had spent more than three decades coaching and managing at different levels of the organization.

Saying goodbye to Turner Field at the end of 2016, the Braves moved into their new home, SunTrust Park, the following year. Located in Cobb County, Georgia, some 10 miles northwest of downtown Atlanta, Sun-Trust Park, which has since been renamed Truist Park, has received positive reviews, with Woody Studenmund of the *Hardball Times* calling the 41,000-seat ballpark a "gem" and saying that "the compact beauty of the stadium and its exciting approach to combining baseball, business, and social activities" made a strong impression on him.

Faring only slightly better in their new home in 2017, the Braves finished a distant third in the NL East, with a record of 72-90. However, they have since turned things around under Snitker, capturing the division title in each of the last five seasons, advancing to the NLCS twice, and winning their fourth World Series in 2021, despite entering the postseason tournament as heavy underdogs after posting only 88 victories during the regular season. After needing just four games to dispose of the 95-win Milwaukee Brewers in the NLDS, Atlanta upset the defending world champion Los Angeles Dodgers in six games in the NLCS. The Braves subsequently laid claim to their first world championship in 26 years by defeating the Houston Astros in six games in the Fall Classic.

With team leader and Braves icon Freddie Freeman leaving Atlanta via free agency prior to the start of the 2022 campaign, the Braves got off to a slow start this past season, losing more games than they won through the end of May. However, they eventually righted themselves, overcoming a 10½-game deficit to the Mets in early June by compiling a record of 77-34 the rest of the way, earning in process their fifth straight NL East title. But the Braves subsequently came up short in the playoffs, losing to the Phillies in four games in the NLDS.

Nevertheless, with outstanding players such as Matt Olson, Ozzie Albies, Ronald Acuña Jr., Max Fried, and Austin Riley currently gracing their roster, the Braves figure to be perennial contenders for the division title and NL flag in the years ahead. Their next division championship will be their 23rd. The Braves have also won 18 pennants and four World Series.

In addition to the level of success the Braves have reached as a team over the years, a significant number of players have attained notable individual honors during their time in Boston, Milwaukee, or Atlanta. The Braves boast seven MVP winners and seven winners of the Cy Young Award. Dating back to the 19th century, they have also featured 21 home-run champions and 11 batting champions. The Braves have retired the numbers of nine players. Meanwhile, 40 members of the Baseball Hall of Fame spent at least one full season playing for the Braves, 25 of whom had several of their peak seasons in either Boston, Milwaukee, or Atlanta.

FACTORS USED TO DETERMINE RANKINGS

It should come as no surprise that selecting the 50 greatest players ever to perform for a team with the rich history of the Braves presented a difficult and daunting task. Even after I narrowed the field down to a mere 50 men, I found myself faced with the challenge of ranking the elite players that remained. Certainly, the names of Hank Aaron, Warren Spahn, Eddie Mathews, Chipper Jones, Greg Maddux, Tom Glavine, and Freddie Freeman would appear at, or near, the top of virtually everyone's list, although the order might vary somewhat from one person to the next. Several other outstanding performers have gained general recognition through the years as being among the greatest players ever to wear a Braves uniform, with Dale Murphy, Phil Niekro, John Smoltz, and Andruw Jones heading the list of other Braves icons. But how does one differentiate between the all-around brilliance of Hank Aaron and the offensive excellence of Chipper Jones; or the pitching greatness of Warren Spahn and the extraordinary hitting ability of Eddie Mathews? After initially deciding who to include on my list, I then needed to determine what criteria I should use to formulate my final rankings.

The first thing I decided to examine was the level of dominance a player attained during his time in Boston, Milwaukee, or Atlanta. How often did he lead the National League in some major offensive or pitching statistical category? How did he fare in the annual MVP and/or Cy Young voting? How many times did he make the All-Star team?

I also needed to weigh the level of statistical compilation a player achieved while wearing a Braves uniform. Where does a batter rank in team annals in the major offensive categories? How high on the all-time list of Braves hurlers does a pitcher rank in wins, ERA, complete games, innings pitched, shutouts, and saves? Of course, I also needed to consider the era in which the player performed when evaluating his overall numbers. For example, modern-day starting pitchers such as Greg Maddux and Tom Glavine were not likely to throw nearly as many complete games or shutouts as Warren Spahn, who anchored the Braves' starting rotation throughout the 1950s. And Brian McCann was likely to post better overall offensive numbers than Joe Torre, who played for the Braves during the pitching-dominated 1960s.

Other important factors I needed to consider were the overall contributions a player made to the success of the team, the degree to which he improved the fortunes of the ballclub while wearing a Braves uniform, and the manner in which he impacted the team, both on and off the field. While the number of pennants and division titles the Braves won during a particular player's years with the ballclub certainly entered into the equation, I chose not to deny a top performer his rightful place on the list if his years in Boston, Milwaukee, or Atlanta happened to coincide with a lack of overall success by the team. As a result, the names of players such as Wally Berger, Ralph Garr, and Darrell Evans will appear in these rankings.

There are two other things I wish to mention. Firstly, I only considered a player's performance while playing for the Braves when formulating my rankings. That being the case, the names of exceptional players such as Felipe Alou and Fred McGriff, both of whom had many of their best years for other teams, may appear lower on this list than one might expect. In addition, since several of the rules that governed 19th-century baseball (including permitting batters to dictate the location of pitches until 1887, situating the pitcher's mound only 50 feet from home plate until 1893, and crediting a stolen base to a runner any time he advanced from first to third base on a hit) differed dramatically from those to which we have become accustomed, I elected to include only those players who competed after 1900, which is generally considered to be the beginning of baseball's "modern era." Doing so eliminated from consideration 19th-century standouts such as Kid Nichols, Jimmy Collins, Herman Long, Hugh Duffy, and "Sliding" Billy Hamilton.

Having established the guidelines to be used throughout this book, we are ready to take a look at the 50 greatest players in Braves history, starting with number 1 and working our way down to number 50.

1

HANK AARON

Despite the pitching brilliance of Warren Spahn and Greg Maddux and the tremendous slugging of Eddie Mathews and Chipper Jones, Hank Aaron represented the only possible choice for the top spot in these rankings. Among the handful of greatest players in the history of the game, Hammerin' Hank, as he came to be known, retired as MLB's all-time leader in home runs, RBIs, and total bases, compiling the vast majority of his numbers during his 21 seasons with the Braves. The NL leader in a major statistical category an astounding 39 times, Aaron hit at least 40 homers eight times, knocked in more than 100 runs 11 times, scored more than 100 runs 15 times, and batted over .300 on 14 separate occasions, en route to setting franchise records in 10 different offensive categories. Excelling in the field and on the basepaths as well, Aaron won three Gold Gloves and stole more than 20 bases six times, with his superb all-around play earning him 21 All-Star selections, nine *Sporting News* All-Star nominations, one NL MVP award, and seven other top-five finishes in the balloting. A member of Braves teams that won two pennants and one world championship, Aaron later received the additional honors of having his #44 retired by the organization, being named to MLB's All-Century Team, being accorded a number five ranking on the *Sporting News'* 1999 list of Baseball's 100 Greatest Players, and gaining induction into the Baseball Hall of Fame the first time his name appeared on the ballot.

Born in Mobile, Alabama, on February 5, 1934, Henry Louis Aaron grew up with his seven siblings on the edge of poverty in the district of Toulminville, where he worked several odd jobs as a youngster to help support his family. With his parents unable to provide him with proper baseball equipment, Aaron learned how to play the game in a quite informal manner, recalling, "When I was growing up in Mobile, Alabama, I taught myself how to hit by swinging at bottle caps with a broomstick. When you don't have a lot, you take it upon yourself to learn how to do things, to discover what you are capable of. . . . My friend Cornelius Giles, who is no longer with us, would pitch the bottle caps to me. Or I would toss them up myself. We would do this all day long."

A gifted athlete, Aaron eventually established himself as a star in multiple sports at Central High School, excelling in both football and baseball for two years, before transferring to the private Josephine Allen Institute for the final two years of his education. Particularly outstanding on the diamond even though he employed a cross-handed batting style that he retained until his early days as a professional, Aaron played shortstop, third base, and some outfield for teams that won consecutive Mobile Negro High School Championships.

Following an unsuccessful tryout with the Dodgers at the age of 15, Aaron received permission from his mother to sign with the semipro Mobile Black Bears, on the condition that he not travel with the team and compete only in local games. After two years with the Black Bears, Aaron inked a deal with the Negro American League champion Indianapolis Clowns that paid him the then-exorbitant sum of $200 a month. Performing extremely well for the Clowns in 1952, Aaron helped lead them to the Negro League championship, prompting both the New York Giants and Boston Braves to extend him contract offers via telegram. Choosing the Braves over the Giants, Aaron later said, "I thought my chances to make the Braves were better and that they were being fairer to me, paying me more money to play in a lower classification. . . . Besides, the Giants spelled my name 'Arron' on their telegram."

After officially signing with the Braves on June 14, 1952, the 18-year-old Aaron reported to the Class C Eau Claire (Wisconsin) Bears, with whom he earned Northern League Rookie of the Year honors by batting .336, hitting nine homers, and collecting 19 doubles in only 87 games. Promoted to Jacksonville the following year, Aaron, along with Black teammates Horace Garner and Félix Mantilla, helped integrate the Sally League, earning the respect of the hometown fans and gaining recognition as the league's most valuable player by topping the circuit with a .362 batting average, 125 RBIs, 115 runs scored, 208 hits, 36 doubles, and 338 total bases.

Aaron, who played mostly second base at Jacksonville, spent the ensuing winter in Puerto Rico learning to play the outfield and working with coach Mickey Owen on his batting stance, before laying claim to the Braves' starting left field job during the early stages of the 1954 campaign. Although Aaron suffered a fractured ankle in early September that brought his season to a premature end, he had a solid rookie year, hitting 13 homers, driving in 69 runs, scoring 58 times, and batting .280, in 122 games and just over 500 total plate appearances. Moved to right field the following year, Aaron established himself as one of the best young players in the game

Hank Aaron retired as MLB's all-time leader in several statistical categories.
Courtesy of RMYAuctions.com

by hitting 27 homers, knocking in 106 runs, scoring 105 times, batting .314, finishing second in the league with 189 hits, and topping the circuit with 37 doubles, with his strong play earning him a ninth-place finish in the NL MVP voting and the first of his 21 consecutive All-Star selections. Continuing his exceptional play in 1956, Aaron began an extraordinary 12-year run during which he posted the following numbers:

YEAR	HR	RBI	RUNS	HITS	AVG	OBP	SLG	OPS
1956	26	92	106	200	**.328**	.365	.558	.923
1957	**44**	**132**	**118**	198	.322	.378	.600	.978
1958	30	95	109	196	.326	.386	.546	.931
1959	39	123	116	**223**	**.355**	.401	**.636**	**1.037**

YEAR	HR	RBI	RUNS	HITS	AVG	OBP	SLG	OPS
1960	40	**126**	102	172	.292	.352	.566	.919
1961	34	120	115	197	.327	.381	.594	.974
1962	45	128	127	191	.323	.390	.618	1.008
1963	**44**	**130**	**121**	201	.319	.391	**.586**	**.977**
1964	24	95	103	187	.328	.393	.514	.907
1965	32	89	109	181	.318	.379	.560	.938
1966	**44**	**127**	117	168	.279	.356	.539	.895
1967	**39**	109	**113**	184	.307	.369	**.573**	.943

* Please note that any numbers printed in bold throughout this book indicate that the player led the league in that statistical category that year.

Consistently ranking among the NL leaders in virtually every major statistical category throughout that 12-year period, Aaron earned six of his nine *Sporting News* All-Star nominations, 10 top-10 finishes in the NL MVP voting, and league MVP honors in 1957, when he led the Braves to their first pennant in nearly a decade and their first world championship in 43 years.

Although the right-handed-hitting Aaron possessed a wiry 6-foot, 180-pound frame his first several years in the league, before gradually increasing his weight by some 10 or 15 pounds as his career progressed, his quick and powerful wrists enabled him to generate the kind of bat speed that made him a tremendous power threat at the plate. Also blessed with outstanding hand-eye coordination, Aaron possessed the unique ability to wait on the pitcher's offering until the last possible second and literally pluck the ball from the catcher's glove. Taking note of the inability of opposing hurlers to throw the ball by his teammate, Joe Adcock stated, "Trying to throw a fastball by Henry Aaron is like trying to sneak a sunrise past a rooster."

Aaron once said, "I looked for the same pitch my whole career, a breaking ball. All the time. I never worried about the fastball. They couldn't throw it past me, none of them."

Despite the exceptional numbers Aaron posted year after year, the fact that he spent his first 12 seasons playing in Milwaukee often caused him to be overlooked by the media and the public, which typically accorded far more attention to the era's other top two players, Willie Mays and Mickey Mantle. But, in truth, Aaron took a backseat to no one in terms of his all-around playing ability. Although he lacked Mantle's awesome power and Mays's charisma, the speedy, strong-armed Aaron played the outfield exceptionally well, excelled on the basepaths, and produced at the plate more consistently than either of his contemporaries, hitting for just as high a batting average, while typically driving in more runs.

Identified by Sandy Koufax as the toughest batter he ever faced, Aaron, who the Hall of Fame southpaw nicknamed "Bad Henry," also received lofty praise from Mantle, who said, "As far as I'm concerned, Aaron is the best ballplayer of my era. He is to baseball of the last 15 years what Joe DiMaggio was before him. He never received the credit he's due."

Although Aaron posted slightly subpar numbers in 1968, concluding the campaign with 29 homers, 86 RBIs, 84 runs scored, a .287 batting average, and 28 stolen bases, he gained All-Star recognition for the 14th straight time, before earning a third-place finish in the MVP balloting the following year by hitting 44 homers, driving in 97 runs, scoring 100 times, and batting an even .300 for the NL Western Division champion Braves.

With the Braves playing in hitter-friendly Atlanta-Fulton County Stadium after relocating to Georgia a few years earlier and Aaron having reached the 500-home-run plateau, the outfielder set his sights on baseball's all-time home-run record that had been held by Babe Ruth for nearly half a century. Altering his approach at the plate somewhat in subsequent seasons, Aaron, who spent much of his career driving the ball with power to all fields, became more of a pull hitter, turning on the ball far more often than he ever did during his time in Milwaukee.

Continuing to perform at an elite level as he entered his late-30s, Aaron hit 38 homers, knocked in 118 runs, scored 103 times, and batted .298 in 1970, before earning a third-place finish in the NL MVP voting the following year by ranking among the league leaders with 47 homers, 118 RBIs, and a .327 batting average, while also topping the circuit with a slugging percentage of .669 and an OPS of 1.079.

With Aaron closing in on Ruth's record, he finally began to receive the recognition he deserved for being one of the greatest players ever. But fame has its price, as Aaron discovered when, after hitting 34 homers in 1972 and another 40 the following season, he stood just one home run shy of Ruth's cherished mark of 714 round-trippers. Sadly, the thought of a Black man breaking the record of a white American hero brought out the worst in many people, preventing Aaron from enjoying what should have been a glorious time in his life. Although the reserved and dignified Aaron never let on how much the thousands of insulting letters and death threats he received heading into the 1974 campaign bothered him, they left a bitter taste in his mouth, causing him to later write in his 1991 autobiography,

I Had a Hammer, "I thought I had earned the right to be treated like a human being in the city that was supposed to be too busy to hate. The way I saw it, the only thing Atlanta was too busy for was baseball. It didn't seem to give a damn about the Braves, and it seemed like the only thing that mattered about the home run record was that a nigger was about to step out of line and break it."

And when Aaron finally hit his record-setting home run on April 8, 1974, instead of experiencing exultation over his tremendous achievement, he felt relieved, afterward telling the assembled mass, "I'm glad it's all over."

Aaron remained in Atlanta until the end of the year, hitting another 18 homers, before being traded to the Milwaukee Brewers for veteran out-fielder Dave May and minor-league pitcher Roger Alexander on November 2, 1974. Leaving the Braves with career totals of 733 home runs, 2,202 RBIs, 2,107 runs scored, 3,600 hits, and 600 doubles, Aaron continues to rank first in franchise history in each of those categories. He also holds franchise records for highest slugging percentage (.567) and OPS (.944), and most total bases (6,591), extra-base hits (1,429), sacrifice flies (113), games played (3,076), plate appearances (13,090), and at-bats (11,628). Meanwhile, Aaron ranks extremely high in team annals in batting average (.310), triples (96), walks (1,297), and stolen bases (240).

After leaving Atlanta, Aaron spent two seasons serving the Brewers almost exclusively as a designated hitter, before announcing his retirement following the conclusion of the 1976 campaign with career totals of 755 home runs, 2,297 RBIs, 2,174 runs scored, 3,771 hits, 624 doubles, 98 triples, and 240 stolen bases, a .305 batting average, a .374 on-base percentage, and a .555 slugging percentage. Still MLB's all-time leader in RBIs, extra-base hits (1,477), and total bases (6,856), Aaron also continues to rank among the game's all-time leaders in home runs, runs scored, hits, doubles, games played (3,298), plate appearances (13,941), at-bats (12,364), and putouts and assists by a right fielder.

After retiring as an active player, Aaron, who Muhammad Ali once called "The only man I idolize more than myself," returned to Atlanta as vice president of player development for the Braves, a position he held for 13 years before settling into a largely ceremonial role as senior vice president and assistant to the president in 1989. Aaron also briefly worked for Turner Broadcasting, opened a chain of fast-food restaurants, and established an auto dealership in Atlanta he called Hank Aaron BMW.

Elected to the Baseball Hall of Fame by the members of the BBWAA in 1982, Aaron later received the additional honors of having an award named after him that each league presents annually to its top offensive performer, being named to MLB's All-Century Team, receiving the Presidential Citizens Medal from President Clinton in 2001, and receiving the Presidential Medal of Freedom from President Bush one year later.

Although Aaron typically shunned the spotlight during and after his playing career, he made one notable public appearance in 2007, when a juiced-up Barry Bonds hit his 756th career home run, breaking in the process Aaron's long-standing major-league record. Appearing on the JumboTron scoreboard in San Francisco, Aaron graciously offered his congratulations to Bonds, saying, "I would like to offer my congratulations to Barry Bonds on becoming baseball's career home run leader. It is a great accomplishment which required skill, longevity, and determination. Throughout the past century, the home run has held a special place in baseball, and I have been privileged to hold this record for 33 of those years. I move over now and offer my best wishes to Barry and his family on this historical achievement. My hope today, as it was on that April evening in 1974, is that the achievement of this record will inspire others to chase their own dreams."

Henry Aaron lived another 14 years, before dying in his sleep two weeks shy of his 87th birthday, on January 22, 2021. Upon learning of his passing, Chipper Jones issued a tweet that read: "I can't imagine what Hank Aaron went through in his lifetime. He had every right to be angry or militant . . . but never was! He spread his grace on everything and everyone he came in contact with. Epitome of class and integrity. RIP Henry Aaron!"

Meanwhile, President Biden released a statement that read: "When I watched Henry Aaron play baseball, I knew I was watching someone special. It wasn't just about watching a gifted athlete master his craft on the way to a Hall of Fame career as one of the greatest to ever play the game. It was that each time Henry Aaron rounded the bases, he wasn't just chasing a record, he was helping us chase a better version of ourselves."

BRAVES CAREER HIGHLIGHTS

Best Season

There are so many great seasons from which to choose, with the 1957, 1960, 1961, 1962, 1963, and 1971 campaigns all ranking among Aaron's finest. But, even though Aaron somehow failed to earn NL MVP honors in 1959, finishing third in the balloting behind Ernie Banks and teammate Eddie Mathews, he turned in the finest all-around performance of his career, leading the league with a batting average of .355, 223 hits, 400 total bases, a slugging percentage of .636, and an OPS of 1.037, finishing second in the circuit with 46 doubles and an on-base percentage of .401, placing third with 39 homers and 123 RBIs, and ranking fourth with 116 runs scored, while also winning the second of his three Gold Gloves.

Memorable Moments/Greatest Performances

Aaron hit the first home run of his storied career off veteran right-hander Vic Raschi during a 7–5 win over the Cardinals on April 23, 1954.

Aaron clinched the pennant for the Braves when he hit a two-run homer off Billy Muffett in the bottom of the 11th inning that gave them a 4–2 win over the Cardinals on September 23, 1957.

Aaron subsequently performed brilliantly during the Braves' seven-game win over the Yankees in the 1957 World Series, batting .393, with three homers, seven RBIs, and five runs scored.

Aaron helped lead the Braves to a 10–6 win over the Dodgers on June 29, 1958, by going 4-for-5, with a homer and five RBIs, with his sixth-inning grand slam off Don Drysdale breaking the game open.

Aaron led the Braves to a lopsided 13–3 victory over the Giants on June 21, 1959, by homering three times and knocking in six runs, with his homers coming off three different pitchers.

Aaron punctuated a 4-for-5 performance against the Cardinals on July 12, 1962, with a grand slam homer off ace reliever Lindy McDaniel in the bottom of the ninth inning that gave the Braves an 8–6 win.

Aaron helped lead the Braves to a 13–5 victory over the Astros on June 27, 1967, by homering twice and knocking in six runs, with one of his homers coming with the bases loaded.

Aaron became a member of the 500 Home Run Club on July 14, 1968, when he homered off Mike McCormick with two men on base in the top of the third inning of a 4–2 win over the Giants.

Aaron led the Braves to an 8–2 win over the Pirates on August 28, 1969, by knocking in six runs with a pair of homers, breaking the game open with a seventh-inning grand slam off Bruce Dal Canton.

Aaron homered and singled twice during a 15-inning, 7–6 loss to the Reds on May 17, 1970, with his first-inning RBI single off Wayne Simpson making him the first player ever to reach the dual milestones of 3,000 hits and 500 home runs.

Aaron reached another milestone when he hit his 600th career homer off Gaylord Perry during a 6–5 loss to the Giants on April 27, 1971.

Aaron led the Braves to an 8–5 win over the Cardinals on August 21, 1971, by homering twice off Steve Carlton and knocking in six runs.

Aaron gave the Braves a 7–5 victory over the Giants on September 10, 1971, when he homered with two men aboard in the bottom of the 11th inning.

Aaron gave the Braves a 6–5 win over the Mets on June 13, 1972, when he hit a solo home run off Danny Frisella with one man out in the bottom of the 10th inning.

Although the Braves suffered a 7–6 Opening Day loss to the Reds on April 4, 1974, Aaron tied Babe Ruth's career home run record when he homered off Jack Billingham in the bottom of the first inning on his very first swing of the season.

Aaron experienced the most memorable moment of his career four days later, on April 8, 1974, when, in the fourth inning of a nationally televised game against the Dodgers in Atlanta, he hit his record-setting 715th home run off Al Downing. Describing the events as they transpired, Braves announcer Milo Hamilton told the radio audience, "Henry Aaron, in the second inning walked and scored. He's sittin' on 714. Here's the pitch by Downing. Swinging. There's a drive into left-center field. That ball is gonna be-eee . . . Outta here! It's gone! It's 715! There's a new home run champion of all time, and it's Henry Aaron!" Meanwhile, as Aaron circled the bases, accompanied part of the way by a pair of excited college students who had sprinted onto the field, legendary Dodgers radio announcer Vin Scully captured the moment thusly: "What a marvelous moment for baseball; what a marvelous moment for Atlanta and the state of Georgia; what a marvelous moment for the country and the world. A black man is getting a standing ovation in the Deep South for breaking a record of an all-time baseball idol. And it is a great moment for all of us, and particularly for Henry Aaron. . . . And for the first time in a long time, that poker face of Aaron shows the tremendous strain and relief of what it must have been like to live with for the past several months."

Notable Achievements

- Hit at least 30 home runs 15 times, surpassing 40 homers on eight occasions.
- Knocked in more than 100 runs 11 times, topping 120 RBIs on seven occasions.
- Scored more than 100 runs 15 times, surpassing 120 runs scored twice.
- Batted over .300 14 times, topping the .320-mark on eight occasions.

- Surpassed 200 hits three times.
- Finished in double digits in triples three times.
- Surpassed 30 doubles 10 times, topping 40 two-baggers twice.
- Stole more than 20 bases six times, topping 30 thefts once.
- Compiled on-base percentage over .400 three times.
- Posted slugging percentage over .500 18 times, topping .600-mark on six occasions.
- Compiled OPS over 1.000 five times.
- Hit three home runs in one game vs. San Francisco Giants on June 21, 1959.
- Led NL in home runs four times, RBIs four times, runs scored three times, batting average twice, hits twice, doubles four times, total bases eight times, extra-base hits five times, slugging percentage four times, and OPS three times.
- Led NL outfielders in double plays turned three times.
- Led NL right fielders in putouts five times, assists twice, double plays turned five times, and fielding percentage once.
- Holds MLB records for most RBIs (2,297) and most total bases (6,856).
- Ranks among MLB all-time leaders with 755 home runs (2nd), 2,174 runs scored (4th), 3,771 hits (3rd), 4,161 putouts by a right fielder (4th), 179 assists by a right fielder (10th), 3,298 games played (3rd), 13,941 plate appearances (3rd), and 12,364 at-bats (2nd).
- Holds Braves single-season records for most total bases (400) and most extra-base hits (92).
- Holds Braves career records for most home runs (733), RBIs (2,202), runs scored (2,107), hits (3,600), doubles (600), total bases (6,591), extra-base hits (1,429), sacrifice flies (113), games played (3,076), plate appearances (13,090), and at-bats (11,628), and highest slugging percentage (.567), and OPS (.944).
- Ranks among Braves career leaders with .310 batting average (10th), 96 triples (2nd), 1,297 walks (3rd), and 240 stolen bases (6th).
- Two-time NL champion (1957 and 1958).
- 1957 world champion.
- Two-time NL Player of the Month.
- Three-time Gold Glove Award winner (1958, 1959, and 1960).
- 1970 Lou Gehrig Memorial Award winner.
- 1957 NL MVP.
- Finished in top five of NL MVP voting seven other times.
- 20-time NL All-Star selection (1955–1974).

- Nine-time *Sporting News* All-Star selection (1956, 1958, 1969, 1963, 1965, 1967, 1969, 1970, and 1971).
- Two-time *Sporting News* NL Player of the Year (1956 and 1963).
- #44 retired by Braves.
- Member of Braves Hall of Fame.
- Member of MLB All-Century Team.
- Number five on the *Sporting News'* 1999 list of Baseball's 100 Greatest Players.
- Elected to Baseball Hall of Fame by members of BBWAA in 1982.

2

_____ ## WARREN SPAHN _____

Considered by many baseball historians to be the greatest left-handed pitcher to ever toe the rubber, Warren Spahn posted more victories over the course of his Hall of Fame career than any other southpaw. The winner of 20 or more games 13 times, Spahn, who helped lead the Braves to three pennants and one world championship during his 21 years in Boston and Milwaukee, also compiled an ERA under 3.00 nine times, threw more than 250 innings 16 times, and tossed more than 20 complete games on 12 separate occasions, earning in the process 14 All-Star selections, four top-five finishes in the NL MVP voting, four *Sporting News* NL Pitcher of the Year nominations, and one Cy Young Award. The holder of franchise records for most wins, shutouts, and innings pitched, Spahn ranks among MLB's all-time leaders in each of those categories as well, with his magnificent pitching earning him a place on MLB's All-Century Team and a number 21 ranking on the *Sporting News'* 1999 list of Baseball's 100 Greatest Players. Further honored by having his #21 retired by the Braves, Spahn amazingly accomplished all he did after spending three years serving his country during World War II and surviving the Battle of the Bulge.

Born in Buffalo, New York, on April 23, 1921, Warren Edward Spahn owed his name to President Warren G. Harding and his father, Edward, a former semipro baseball player who supported his family by earning $27 a week selling wallpaper. Growing up with very little, young Warren found a temporary escape from the worries brought on by the poverty that gripped him and his family through baseball, which he learned from his dad at an early age.

A lefty thrower and batter, Warren enjoyed playing first base and pitching, recalling that his father stressed to him the importance of having control while working with him from a makeshift mound he built in the backyard. Stating that he also developed his signature high leg kick while working with his dad, Spahn remembered, "He insisted that I throw with a fluid motion, and the high leg kick was part of the deception to the hitter. Hitters said the ball seemed to come out of my uniform."

Spahn continued, "He taught me how to follow through with my shoulder and body, how to throw without any strain, how to get the most out of my pitch and out of my weight even when I was a skinny kid. He taught me how to roll a curveball, how to let it go off my fingers at the last moment. He taught me how to pass my knee by my right elbow. . . . I thought it was a lot of drudgery. It was lots more fun just to pick up the ball and throw, but Dad wouldn't let me play catch unless I did it correctly."

After getting his start in organized ball with the Lake City Social Club midgets at the age of nine, Spahn graduated to American Legion ball three years later, spending his first few years in the game playing first base almost exclusively. Moving to the mound after he enrolled at South Park High School, Spahn led his school to two city championships by going undefeated his final two seasons, prompting the Boston Braves to sign him for $80 a month early in 1940.

Experiencing bad luck the next two years, Spahn missed virtually all of 1940 with torn tendons in his left shoulder, before a teammate inadvertently broke his nose with an errant throw during spring training the following year. Prior to having his nose broken, though, Spahn made an extremely favorable impression on Braves manager Casey Stengel, who said, "He's only 20 years old and needs work. But mark my word, if nothing happens to the kid, he can be a great one. Someday he's going to be one of the best left-handers in the league."

Returned to the minors for more seasoning after recovering from his injury, Spahn went on to have an excellent year for Evansville of the Three-I League, leading the circuit in wins (19), winning percentage (.760), ERA (1.83), and shutouts (7), with his strong performance earning him a promotion to the parent club in 1942. But after Spahn appeared in just four games with the Braves during the early stages of the campaign, Stengel demoted him to the minors for refusing to brush back Pee Wee Reese of the Dodgers, later calling the move the worst mistake he ever made. Spahn subsequently spent the rest of the year at Hartford, going 17-12 with a 1.96 ERA, before entering the military on December 3, 1942.

Away from baseball for much of the next three years, Spahn briefly pitched for the Army's 1850th Service Unit baseball team while stationed at Camp Chaffee, Arkansas, before seeing active duty in Europe with the 1159th Engineer Combat Group's 276th Engineer Combat Battalion. Recalling how he had to change his personality somewhat to fit in with the rest of the unit, Spahn said, "Let me tell you, that was a tough bunch of guys. We had people that were let out of prison to go into the service. So,

Warren Spahn won more games than any other left-handed pitcher in baseball history.
Courtesy of RMYAuctions.com

those were the people I went overseas with, and they were tough and rough, and I had to fit that mold."

Thrust into the middle of the conflict, Spahn remembered, "We were surrounded in the Hurtgen Forest and had to fight our way out of there. Our feet were frozen when we went to sleep, and they were frozen when we woke up. We didn't have a bath or change of clothes for weeks."

In addition to surviving the Battle of the Bulge, Spahn fought in the battle for the Ludendorff Bridge at Remagen, Germany, where he was wounded in the foot by shrapnel. Ultimately awarded a Purple Heart and a battlefield commission as a second lieutenant, Spahn finally returned to the States after he received his discharge early in 1946.

Rejoining the Braves a few months later with a new attitude, Spahn recalled, "I think I was better equipped to handle major league hitters at 25 than I was at 22. . . . After what I went through overseas, I never thought of anything I was told to do in baseball as hard work. You get over feeling like that when you spend days on end sleeping in frozen tank tracks in enemy threatened territory. The Army taught me something about challenges and about what's important and what isn't."

Spending his first full season in Boston assuming the role of a spot starter, Spahn compiled a record of 8-5 and an ERA of 2.94, telling the Associated Press in August 1946, "Before the war, I didn't have anything that slightly resembled self-confidence. Then, I was tight as a drum and worrying about every pitch. But nowadays, I just throw them up without the slightest mental pressure."

Establishing himself as one of the NL's best pitchers in 1947, Spahn earned All-Star honors by going 21-10, throwing 22 complete games, and leading the league with a 2.33 ERA, seven shutouts, 289 2/3 innings pitched, and a WHIP of 1.136. Although somewhat less effective in 1948, Spahn contributed to the Braves' successful run to the NL pennant by winning 15 games, compiling an ERA of 3.71, and ranking among the league leaders with 16 complete games and 257 innings pitched. Returning to top form in 1949, Spahn earned his second All-Star nomination and a seventh-place finish in the NL MVP voting by going 21-14, with a 3.07 ERA, four shutouts, and a league-leading 151 strikeouts, 25 complete games, and 302 1/3 innings pitched. Continuing to perform at an elite level the next two seasons, Spahn finished 21-17, with a 3.16 ERA, 25 complete games, 293 innings pitched, and a league-high 191 strikeouts in 1950, before compiling a record of 22-14 and an ERA of 2.98, throwing 310 2/3 innings, and leading all NL hurlers with 164 strikeouts, seven shutouts, and 26 complete games the following year.

After going just 14-19 with a 2.98 ERA for the seventh-place Braves in 1952, Spahn re-established himself as arguably the senior circuit's finest pitcher when the Braves moved to Milwaukee in 1953, beginning an exceptional 11-year run during which he posted the following numbers:

YEAR	W-L	ERA	SO	SHO	CG	IP	WHIP
1953	23-7	2.10	148	5	24	265.2	1.058
1954	21-12	3.14	136	1	23	283.1	1.228

YEAR	W-L	ERA	SO	SHO	CG	IP	WHIP
1955	17-14	3.26	110	1	16	245.2	1.278
1956	20-11	2.78	128	3	20	281.1	1.070
1957	21-11	2.69	111	4	18	271	1.177
1958	22-11	3.07	150	2	23	290	1.148
1959	21-15	2.96	143	4	21	292	1.205
1960	21-10	3.50	154	4	18	267.2	1.225
1961	21-13	3.02	115	4	21	262.2	1.142
1962	18-14	3.04	118	0	22	269.1	1.125
1963	23-7	2.60	102	7	22	259.2	1.117

In addition to leading all NL hurlers in wins six times and complete games seven times during that period, Spahn consistently ranked among the league leaders in ERA, WHIP, shutouts, and innings pitched, topping the circuit in each of those categories on multiple occasions as well. An NL All-Star in all but two of those seasons, Spahn also earned four *Sporting News* NL Pitcher of the Year nominations, four top-five finishes in the league MVP balloting, one Cy Young Award, and four other top-three finishes in the voting.

Employing a silky-smooth delivery that placed a minimum amount of stress on his left arm, the 6-foot, 180-pound Spahn managed to stay injury-free for virtually his entire career despite the heavy workload he assumed each year. Claiming that his high leg kick contributed greatly to his extraordinary durability, Spahn stated, "I wasn't a big guy. My dad said to get all the momentum you could. So, I kept my weight back, transferred it from my back leg to my front leg, and I think that's why I didn't hurt my arm."

Spahn added, "A sore arm is like a headache or a toothache. It can make you feel bad, but if you just forget about it and do what you have to do, it will go away. If you really like to pitch and you want to pitch, that's what you'll do."

Prior to delivering the ball to home plate, Spahn leaned forward, almost bowing to the hitter, before rocking back and raising his right leg above his head in what Dave Kindred of the *Sporting News* called a "five-minutes-to-six" position. Since he threw his curveball, change of pace, and fastball with the same overhand motion, the batter had no idea what to expect.

Commenting on his longtime batterymate's unusual pitching motion, Del Crandall said, "Nobody else could pitch like that, but his delivery was so much a part of his success. The higher he kicked, the better he pitched. Of course, if he had kicked any higher, he might have fallen over backwards."

Meanwhile, Spahn's biographer Al Silverman wrote, "He was all grace, kicking his right leg high in the air, his left elbow passing his right knee, just as his dad had taught him, then uncoiling and the ball snapping to the plate out of flapping sleeves and trousers, the ball streaking in and on the batter almost before he could measure it, blazing in like a freight train coming out of the darkness."

An extremely hard worker, Spahn, who threw frequently between starts and reported to spring training in excellent condition each year after spending the winters working on his ranch, also proved to be a cerebral pitcher, studying the tendencies of opposing hitters and rarely giving them the same pitches from one year to the next. And as Spahn grew older, he compensated for the diminishing velocity on his fastball by adding a screwball and slider to his repertoire of pitches.

Praising the ace of his pitching staff for his wisdom and dedication to his profession, Braves manager Fred Haney stated, "The things he can remember about pitching just amaze me. Spahnie studies. He can pitch to a certain hitter in a certain way and get him out. Another pitcher can't. The thing that impresses me most about him, though, is his spirit. He's the oldest guy on the club, but he works the hardest."

Casey Stengel also had kind words for the man he once demoted to the minor leagues, saying, "He's beyond comparison with any modern left-hander. He has beaten every handicap— the live ball, second division teams. No one can ever say anything to deny his greatness."

Yet, despite his greatness and the many accolades he received during his career, Spahn remained an insecure man who never forgot the poverty of his youth, once revealing to Dave Kindred that he didn't inform anyone when he ripped cartilage in his knee during spring training in 1953, telling the *Sporting News* writer, "I was one of the senior men on the club, and they'd have let me go in a minute if I went on the disabled list."

Spahn also chose not to be labeled a hero, stating, "The guys who died over there [in Europe during the war] were heroes." And, as for the notion that he would have won many more games had he not served in the military, Spahn said, "I matured a lot in those years. If I had not had that maturity, I wouldn't have pitched until I was 45."

Finally beginning to show his age in 1964, Spahn compiled a record of just 6-13 and an ERA of 5.29. Sold to the Mets at the end of the year, Spahn split the 1965 campaign between the league's worst team and the San Francisco Giants, going a combined 7-16, before announcing his retirement at season's end, later saying, "I didn't retire from baseball. Baseball retired me."

Ending his career with a record of 363-245, an ERA of 3.09, a WHIP of 1.195, 2,583 strikeouts in 5,243 2/3 innings of work, 382 complete games, 63 shutouts, and 28 saves, Spahn won 356 games, threw 63 shutouts, and tossed 5,046 innings as a member of the Braves, with each of those marks representing the highest figure in franchise history. A good-hitting pitcher, Spahn also hit 35 homers and knocked in 189 runs in just under 2,000 total plate appearances.

Following his playing days, Spahn remained in the game for several more years, managing in the minor leagues and coaching pitchers at both the minor-and major-league levels, before retiring from baseball for good after the 1981 season. Settling with his half-Cherokee wife, LoRene, in Hartshorne, Oklahoma, Spahn subsequently grew rich running a 2,000-acre cattle ranch and leasing some of his land for gas wells.

Suffering from several physical maladies in his later years that included a punctured lung, internal bleeding, and fluid buildup in his lungs, Spahn remained confined to a wheelchair until he passed away at the age of 82 on November 24, 2003, some three months after the Braves unveiled a statue of him kicking high outside Turner Field in Atlanta.

Upon learning of his former teammate's passing, Del Crandall said, "He's the modern-day king. I really don't think he gets the credit he deserves."

Meanwhile, fellow Hall of Fame hurler and World War II vet Bob Feller stated, "In my mind, he was the greatest left-hander of all time. . . . He was a war hero. Who knows how many games he would have won if it wasn't for World War II."

BRAVES CAREER HIGHLIGHTS

Best Season

Although Spahn performed brilliantly in several other years as well, he had the greatest season of his career in 1953, when, despite pitching in pain all year after tearing cartilage in his knee during spring training, he earned one of his four top-five finishes in the NL MVP voting by going 23-7, leading the league with an ERA of 2.10 and a WHIP of 1.058, and finishing second in the circuit with five shutouts, 24 complete games, and 265 2/3 innings pitched.

Memorable Moments/Greatest Performances

Spahn yielded only a pair of harmless singles during a 7–0 shutout of the Phillies on April 28, 1948.

Spahn threw another two-hit shutout on September 21, 1950, allowing just a second-inning single by first baseman Ed Mickelson and a fifth-inning single by third baseman Eddie Kazak during a 5–0 win over the Cardinals.

In addition to allowing just five hits and recording eight strikeouts during a 9–0 shutout of the Cubs on June 20, 1951, Spahn went 3-for-4 at the plate, with a homer, double, three RBIs, and two runs scored.

Spahn allowed just two men to reach base during a 2–0 shutout of the Cardinals on September 13, 1951, surrendering only a walk and a sixth-inning single by opposing pitcher Al Brazle.

Although Spahn yielded 10 hits during a 15-inning, 3–1 loss to the Cubs on June 14, 1952, he recorded a career-high 18 strikeouts.

Spahn allowed just one baserunner during a 5–0 shutout of the Phillies on August 1, 1953, surrendering only a fourth-inning single to Hall of Fame center fielder Richie Ashburn.

Spahn gave the Braves a 3–1 lead over the Yankees in the 1958 World Series by tossing a two-hit shutout in Game 4, surrendering just a fourth-inning triple by Mickey Mantle and a seventh-inning single by Bill Skowron during a 3–0 victory.

Spahn threw two no-hitters during his career, the first of which came on September 16, 1960, when he yielded just two walks and recorded 15 strikeouts during a 4–0 win over the Phillies.

Spahn accomplished the feat again on April 28, 1961, when, just five days after celebrating his 40th birthday, he allowed just two walks during a 1–0 win over the Giants.

Spahn followed that up with another brilliant outing, recording nine strikeouts and surrendering just two hits and two walks during a 4–1 win over the Dodgers on May 3, 1961, while also going 3-for-4 at the plate, with a double and two runs scored.

Spahn became a member of the select 300 Win Club when he allowed just six hits during a complete-game 2–1 victory over the Cubs on August 11, 1961.

Spahn hooked up with San Francisco's Juan Marichal in one of the most famous pitching duels in baseball history on July 2, 1963, eventually losing a 1–0 decision to the "Dominican Dandy" when Willie Mays homered with one man out in the bottom of the 16th inning.

Notable Achievements

- Won more than 20 games 13 times.
- Posted winning percentage over .600 12 times, topping .700-mark twice.
- Compiled ERA under 3.00 nine times, posting mark under 2.50 twice.
- Threw more than 300 innings twice, tossing more than 250 frames 14 other times.
- Threw more than 20 complete games 12 times.
- Threw 27.2 consecutive scoreless innings in 1963.
- Threw two no-hitters (one vs. Philadelphia Phillies on September 16, 1960, and one vs. San Francisco Giants on April 28, 1961).
- Led NL pitchers in wins eight times, winning percentage once, ERA three times, WHIP four times, strikeouts four times, shutouts four times, innings pitched four times, complete games nine times, assists three times, and starts twice.
- Ranks among MLB all-time leaders in wins (6th), shutouts (6th), and innings pitched (8th).
- Holds Braves career records for most wins (356), shutouts (63), innings pitched (5,046), and starts (635).
- Ranks among Braves career leaders in strikeouts (3rd), complete games (2nd), WHIP (12th), pitching appearances (2nd), and games started (6th).
- Three-time NL champion (1948, 1957, and 1958).
- 1957 world champion.
- Two-time NL Player of the Month.
- 1961 Lou Gehrig Memorial Award winner.
- 1957 Cy Young Award winner.
- Finished second in Cy Young voting three times and third once.
- Finished in top five of NL MVP voting four times.
- 14-time NL All-Star selection (1947, 1949–1954, 1956–1959, and 1961–1963).
- Five-time *Sporting News* All-Star selection (1953, 1957, 1958, 1960, and 1961).

- Four-time *Sporting News* NL Pitcher of the Year (1953, 1957, 1958, and 1961).
- #21 retired by Braves.
- Member of Braves Hall of Fame.
- Member of MLB All-Century Team.
- Number 21 on the *Sporting News'* 1999 list of Baseball's 100 Greatest Players.
- Elected to Baseball Hall of Fame by members of BBWAA in 1973.

3

GREG MADDUX

Arguably the finest pitcher of his time, Greg Maddux proved to be a study in consistency over the course of his 23-year big-league career, winning at least 15 games a record 17 straight times, en route to amassing more victories than any other hurler whose career began after 1950. A member of the Braves for 11 seasons, Maddux performed especially well during his time in Atlanta, leading all NL hurlers in virtually every major statistical category on multiple occasions, with his extraordinary mound work earning him six All-Star selections, three *Sporting News* NL Pitcher of the Year nominations, two top-five finishes in the NL MVP voting, and three of his four Cy Young awards. A huge contributor to Braves teams that won three pennants and one world championship, Maddux also earned Gold Glove honors 10 times, before receiving the additional honors of having his #31 retired by the team, being inducted into the Braves Hall of Fame, and having Cooperstown open its doors to him.

Born in San Angelo, Texas, on April 14, 1966, Gregory Alan Maddux spent much of his childhood in Madrid, Spain, where the US Air Force stationed his father. Although Greg and his older brother, Mike, also played football and basketball as youngsters, they developed a particularly strong affinity for baseball while competing in a sanctioned Little League, with their mother, Linda, recalling, "Kids would come home from practice in the hot sun, and the first thing they would do is head outside into the yard to play more baseball in the hot sun. Finally, I came to the realization that they were doing what they wanted to do. And they all survived."

With Maddux's father, Dave, being transferred back to the States during the late 1970s, the family settled in Las Vegas, where Greg attended Valley High School. A star pitcher at Valley High, Maddux helped lead the school to the state championship his junior year, with the help of Ralph Medar, a former major-league scout who oversaw workouts and organized pickup games in the area on Sunday mornings. Recalling the lessons he learned from Medar, Maddux told *Baseball Digest*, "Ralph was the first pitching coach I ever had. He worked with me when I was 15 years old, and he taught me that movement was more important than velocity. He helped me make the ball move and sink, as opposed to seeing how hard I could throw it. I think I was fortunate to learn that lesson at such a young age."

Offered a baseball scholarship to the University of Arizona, Maddux planned to play for the Wildcats until the Chicago Cubs selected him in the second round of the June 1984 MLB Draft, on the recommendation of scout Doug Mapson, who wrote of the 6-foot, 170-pound right-hander in his report to the ballclub, "I really believe this boy would be the number one player in the country if only he looked a bit more physical." After signing with the Cubs, Maddux spent most of the next three seasons in the minor leagues, receiving a brief callup late in 1986, before joining the parent club for good the following year. After struggling in his first full season in Chicago, Maddux established himself as one of the NL's top hurlers over the course of the next five seasons, gaining All-Star recognition twice by compiling an overall record of 87-57, while also winning the first three of his record 18 Gold Gloves. Having mastered his craft, particularly the art of starting his offering toward the batter's waist before having it break back over the inside part of the plate, Maddux performed especially well in 1992, earning Cy Young honors for the first of four straight times by going 20-11, with a 2.18 ERA, 199 strikeouts, and a league-leading 268 innings pitched.

A free agent after the 1992 season, Maddux ultimately chose to sign with the Braves for five years and $28 million, with Houston Astros general manager Gerry Hunsicker later calling him "the greatest free-agent signing in baseball history."

Joining a starting rotation in Atlanta that already included standouts Tom Glavine and John Smoltz, Maddux combined with his fellow future Hall of Famers the next several years to give the Braves the greatest trio of pitchers ever assembled by one team, compiling the following numbers over the course of the next 10 seasons:

YEAR	W-L	ERA	SO	SHO	CG	IP	WHIP
1993	20-10	2.36	197	1	8	267	1.049
1994	16-6	1.56	156	3	10	202	0.896
1995	19-2	1.63	181	3	10	209.2	0.811
1996	15-11	2.72	172	1	5	245	1.033
1997	19-4	2.20	177	2	5	232.2	0.946

Greg Maddux won three of his four Cy Young awards as a member of the
Braves.
Courtesy of George A. Kitrinos

1998	18-9	**2.22**	204	**5**	9	251	**0.980**
1999	19-9	3.57	136	0	4	219.1	1.345
2000	19-9	3.00	190	**3**	6	249.1	1.071
2001	17-11	3.05	173	**3**	3	233	1.060
2002	16-6	2.62	118	0	0	199.1	1.199

Consistently ranking among the league leaders in each category, Maddux earned six All-Star selections, three *Sporting News* NL Pitcher of the Year nominations, and two top-five finishes in the NL MVP voting. Meanwhile, in addition to winning the Cy Young Award in each of the first three seasons, Maddux continued his string of 13 straight seasons in which he earned Gold Glove honors. More importantly, the Braves won the division title in all but one of those seasons, advancing to the World Series three times, and winning one world championship.

Although the right-handed-throwing Maddux, who stood 6-feet tall and weighed close to 190 pounds, possessed neither an overpowering fastball nor a particularly sharp-breaking curveball, he established himself as one of the game's great pitchers by making excellent use of his pinpoint control, outstanding ball movement, and cerebral approach to his craft, which usually enabled him to anticipate the opposing hitter's thought process.

Marveling at Maddux's ability to get inside the head of the opposing batter, Wade Boggs stated, "It seems like he's inside your mind with you. When he knows you're not going to swing, he throws a straight one. He sees into the future. It's like he has a crystal ball hidden inside his glove."

John Smoltz said of his teammate, "Every pitch has a purpose. Sometimes he knows what he's going to throw two pitches ahead. I swear, he makes it look like guys are swinging foam bats against him."

Hall of Fame outfielder Tony Gwynn discussed the strategy Maddux used to baffle opposing hitters, commenting, "He's like a meticulous surgeon out there. He puts the ball where he wants to. You see a pitch inside and wonder, 'Is it the fastball or the cutter?' That's where he's got you."

Meanwhile, Bob Nightengale of *USA Today* explained how Maddux managed to dominate opposing lineups without being a power pitcher: "Maddux, whose fastball is routinely clocked at only 88 mph, remarkably throws more fastballs than any established pitcher in the game. The difference is control and movement. He can throw the fastball with nearly pinpoint control, while the ball darts and spins as if he's controlling it like a yo-yo."

Relying primarily on a sinker, circle changeup, cutter, and two-and four-seam fastball, Maddux told WSCR's Matt Spiegel, "It's not a speed contest, it's a pitching contest. . . . I always relied on locating my fastball and changing speeds when I had to. That was my way. . . . I could probably throw harder if I wanted, but why? When they're in a jam, a lot of pitchers try to throw harder. Me, I try to locate better."

Further expounding on his approach to pitching, Maddux said during a 2001 interview with Bob Nightengale, "The best pitch in baseball is a located fastball. That will always be the best pitch. You can set up every-thing you want off that."

Maddux continued, "Don Sutton used to always say to make sure all your pitches look the same when they're five feet out of your hand. Then find ways to make the ball end up in different places and at different speeds. The more ways you can put it in more places at more speeds, the better. That's pitching."

Also known for his intense study of hitters and their tendencies, Maddux made a strong impression with his excellence in that area on Javy López, who said, "He studied hitters days before his starts. He would sit down in the video room and study everything about the hitters, including their mechanics. He would do that for days."

Tom Glavine added, "I think the hitters think he can go back and recall every pitch he has ever thrown. That's not the case, but I think he's probably better at remembering things than most people are. He's definitely better in the course of the game at making adjustments on a hitter based on what he's seen, whether it's one swing or a guy's last at-bat."

Maddux's mastery of the art of pitching earned him the admiration and respect of everyone in the game, including one of the sport's other top hurlers, Randy Johnson, who suggested, "Greg Maddux is probably the best pitcher in all of baseball, along with Roger Clemens. He's much more intel-ligent than I am because he doesn't have a 95 or 98 mph fastball. I would tell any pitcher who wants to be successful to watch him, because he's the true definition of a pitcher."

Expressing similar sentiments in an article that appeared in a 1995 edi-tion of *Sports Illustrated*, Tom Verducci wrote, "His career is a masterpiece, available for all to see every fifth day or so as he works atop the pitching mounds of National League ballparks. The rest of us, should we recognize our good fortune, could be eyewitnesses to genius. Did you see van Gogh paint? No, you could respond, but I saw Greg Maddux pitch."

Some three years later, Rob Neyer stated on ESPN Sportszone, "We've never seen the likes of Maddux before, and chances are most of us won't live long enough to see the likes of him again."

Although Maddux won 16 games for the Braves in 2003, he posted an inordinately high ERA of 3.96 that signaled the end of his period of dom-inance. A free agent again at season's end, the 37-year-old Maddux elected to rejoin the Cubs, leaving the Braves having compiled an overall record of 194-88, an ERA of 2.63, and a WHIP of 1.051 as a member of the team, while also throwing 61 complete games, tossing 21 shutouts, recording 1,828 strikeouts, and issuing just 383 bases on balls in 2,526 2/3 innings of work.

Maddux ended up spending most of the next three seasons in Chicago, posting a composite mark of 38-37 for the Cubs, before splitting his final two-plus years between the Dodgers and Padres. Choosing to announce his retirement following the conclusion of the 2008 campaign, Maddux ended his career with a record of 355-227 that gives him the second-most victories of any pitcher who made his debut following the advent of the so-called Live Ball Era in 1920, with only Warren Spahn's 363 wins surpassing his total. Maddux also compiled an ERA of 3.16 and a WHIP of 1.143, recorded 3,371 strikeouts, and threw 35 shutouts, 109 complete games, and 5,008 1/3 innings.

Since retiring as an active player, Maddux has remained close to the game as a coach and a consultant, assuming front office positions with the Cubs, Rangers, and Dodgers, before spending four years serving as pitching coach for the University of Nevada.

Inducted into the Braves Hall of Fame during a special ceremony held at Atlanta's Omni Hotel on July 17, 2009, Maddux received the following words of praise from his longtime manager Bobby Cox during the banquet festivities: "I get asked all the time was he the best pitcher I ever saw. Was he the smartest pitcher I ever saw? The most competitive I ever saw. The best teammate I ever saw. The answer is yes to all of those."

BRAVES CAREER HIGHLIGHTS

Best Season

Although Maddux also performed brilliantly during the strike-shortened 1994 campaign, the 1995 season would have to be considered the finest of his career. In addition to compiling a record of 19-2 that gave him an extraordinary winning percentage of .905, Maddux led all NL hurlers with an ERA of 1.63, a WHIP of 0.811, 10 complete games, three shutouts, and 209 2/3 innings pitched, earning in the process a third-place finish in the NL MVP balloting and Cy Young and *Sporting News* NL Pitcher of the Year honors for the fourth consecutive time.

MEMORABLE MOMENTS/GREATEST PERFORMANCES

Maddux dominated San Francisco's lineup on April 14, 1994, recording nine strikeouts and allowing just three hits and one unearned run during a complete-game 6–1 Braves win.

Maddux hurled another gem 10 days later, surrendering just three hits, striking out 11 batters, and issuing no walks during a 3–0 shutout of the Pirates on April 24, 1994.

In addition to tossing another three-hit shutout on August 11, 1994, Maddux went 3-for-5 at the plate and knocked in two runs during a 13–0 win over the Colorado Rockies.

Maddux surrendered just one hit during a 3–1 complete-game victory over the Astros on May 28, 1995, allowing just one walk and an eighth-inning homer by Jeff Bagwell.

Maddux recorded nine strikeouts and issued no walks during a 1–0, two-hit shutout of the Cardinals on August 20, 1995, yielding just a fifth-inning single by Brian Jordan and a sixth-inning double by catcher Danny Sheaffer.

Maddux pitched magnificently in Game 1 of the 1995 World Series, allowing just two hits and two unearned runs during a complete-game 3–2 win over the hard-hitting Cleveland Indians.

Maddux turned in another brilliant performance against the Yankees in Game 2 of the 1996 World Series, scattering six hits over the first eight innings of a 4–0 Braves win.

Maddux threw 40 1/3 straight scoreless innings from September 2 to September 28, 2000, tossing consecutive four-hit shutouts against the Arizona Diamondbacks on September 7 and the Florida Marlins on September 13. Maddux also allowed just two hits and recorded 13 strikeouts over the first seven innings of a 10–0 win over the Montreal Expos on the 23rd of the month, before turning the game over to the Braves bullpen.

Maddux turned in perhaps his most dominant performance as a member of the Braves on May 2, 2001, when he surrendered just two hits, walked one batter, and recorded a career-high 14 strikeouts during a 1–0 shutout of the Milwaukee Brewers.

Notable Achievements

- Won at least 15 games 11 straight times, posting 20 victories once and 19 victories four other times.
- Posted winning percentage over .600 nine times, topping .700-mark on four occasions.
- Compiled ERA under 3.00 seven times, posting mark under 2.00 twice.
- Posted WHIP under 1.000 four times.
- Struck out more than 200 batters once.

- Threw more than 250 innings twice.
- Threw 40.1 consecutive scoreless innings in 2000.
- Led NL pitchers in wins twice, winning percentage twice, ERA four times, WHIP four times, shutouts five times, innings pitched three times, complete games three times, putouts three times, assists seven times, and starts three times.
- Ranks among MLB all-time leaders in wins (8th), strikeouts (10th), and games started (4th).
- Holds Braves single-season records for lowest ERA (1.56 in 1994) and WHIP (0.811 in 1995).
- Ranks among Braves career leaders in wins (6th), winning percentage (2nd), ERA (7th), WHIP (2nd), strikeouts (5th), strikeouts-to-walks ratio (2nd), shutouts (10th), innings pitched (8th), pitching appearances (10th), and games started (6th).
- Three-time NL champion (1995, 1996, and 1999).
- 1995 world champion.
- Six-time NL Player of the Week.
- Eight-time NL Pitcher of the Month.
- 10-time Gold Glove Award winner (1993–2002).
- Three-time NL Cy Young Award winner (1993, 1994, and 1995).
- Finished in top five of NL Cy Young voting four other times, placing second once.
- Finished in top five of NL MVP voting twice, placing as high as third in 1995.
- Six-time NL All-Star selection (1994, 1995, 1996, 1997, 1998, and 2000).
- Four-time *Sporting News* All-Star selection (1993, 1994, 1995, and 2000).
- Three-time *Sporting News* NL Pitcher of the Year (1993, 1994, and 1995).
- #31 retired by Braves.
- Member of Braves Hall of Fame.
- Number 39 on the *Sporting News'* 1999 list of Baseball's 100 Greatest Players.
- Elected to Baseball Hall of Fame by members of BBWAA in 2014.

4
EDDIE MATHEWS

The only man to play for the Braves in Boston, Milwaukee, and Atlanta, Eddie Mathews established himself as one of the game's great sluggers and the premier third baseman of his time over the course of his career, which he spent almost entirely with the team that signed him right out of high school. A member of the Braves from 1952 to 1966, Mathews combined with Hank Aaron to form the greatest home-run-hitting tandem in baseball history, surpassing 30 homers 10 times himself, while also driving in more than 100 runs five times, scoring more than 100 runs eight times, and batting over .300 on three separate occasions. A two-time NL home run champion, Mathews hit more homers than anyone else in team annals, aside from Aaron, retiring with the sixth-most round-trippers in the history of the game. A solid and dependable fielder as well, Mathews led all NL third basemen in putouts twice, assists three times, and fielding percentage once, with his outstanding all-around play earning him two runner-up finishes in the league MVP voting, nine All-Star selections, and four *Sporting News* All-Star nominations. Yet, even though Mathews earned the additional honors of having his #41 retired by the Braves, being ranked number 63 on the *Sporting News'* 1999 list of Baseball's 100 Greatest Players, and gaining induction into the Baseball Hall of Fame, he remains one of the most overlooked and underappreciated truly great players in the history of the game.

Born in Texarkana, Texas, on October 13, 1931, Edwin Lee Mathews grew up in Santa Barbara, California, after moving there with his family at the age of four. Inheriting his passion for baseball from his father, a Western Union telegraph operator and former semipro athlete, and his mother, Mathews recalled years later, "My mother used to pitch to me, and my father would shag balls. If I hit one up the middle close to my mother, I'd have some extra chores to do. My mother was instrumental in making me a pull hitter."

A star in multiple sports at Santa Barbara High School, Mathews excelled on both the diamond and gridiron, receiving several scholarship offers in football, before ultimately signing with the Boston Braves on the night of his graduation.

Beginning his professional career at only 17 years of age, Mathews batted .363 and hit 17 home runs for High Point-Thomasville of the North Carolina State League during the second half of the 1949 campaign, earning him a promotion to Double-A Atlanta the following year. Continuing his prodigious slugging in Atlanta, Mathews hit 32 homers, knocked in 106 runs, and batted .272, gaining him general recognition as the best hitting prospect in all of baseball, with the legendary Ty Cobb stating after witnessing him on one occasion, "I've only known three or four perfect swings in my time. This lad has one of them."

Subsequently drafted into the military, Mathews spent the first few months of the 1951 campaign in the Navy, before receiving a hardship discharge because of his father's illness and his status as the sole financial supporter of his family. After finishing out the year with the Braves' top farm club, the Milwaukee Brewers, Mathews arrived in Boston in 1952, laying claim to the team's starting third base job shortly thereafter.

Performing fairly well in his first big-league season, Mathews earned a third-place finish in the NL Rookie of the Year voting by hitting 25 homers, driving in 58 runs, and scoring 80 times, although he also batted just .242 and topped the senior circuit with 115 strikeouts. Maturing into one of baseball's top sluggers after the Braves moved to Milwaukee in 1953, Mathews began an exceptional five-year run during which he posted the following numbers:

YEAR	HR	RBI	RUNS	AVG	OBP	SLG	OPS
1953	**47**	135	110	.302	.406	.627	1.033
1954	40	103	96	.290	.423	.603	1.026
1955	41	101	108	.289	.413	.601	1.014
1956	37	95	103	.272	.373	.518	.892
1957	32	94	109	.292	.387	.540	.927

In addition to ranking among the NL leaders in home runs, on-base percentage, slugging percentage, and walks all five seasons, Mathews placed near the top of the league rankings in RBIs and runs scored four times each, earning in the process four All-Star selections, two *Sporting News* All-Star nominations, and two top-10 finishes in the NL MVP voting. Particularly outstanding in 1953, Mathews finished in the league's top five in seven

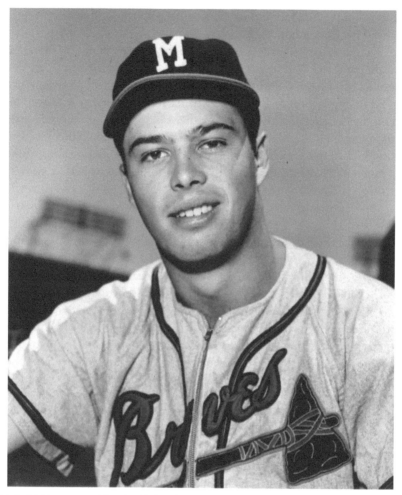

Eddie Mathews combined with Hank Aaron to hit more home runs than any other duo in baseball history.
Courtesy of RMYAuctions.com

different offensive categories, topping the circuit in homers and placing second in RBIs, slugging percentage, and total bases (363), with his fabulous performance earning him a runner-up finish to Roy Campanella in the MVP balloting. More importantly, Mathews's exceptional play helped lead the Braves to one pennant and three second-place finishes during that five-year period.

A dead-pull hitter, the left-handed-swinging Mathews, who stood 6'1" and weighed close to 200 pounds, possessed tremendous power at the plate, often drawing comparisons to AL counterpart Mickey Mantle for his proficiency in that area. In comparing the two sluggers, Warren Spahn said, "Mathews is just as strong as Mantle. They don't hit the same—Mantle gets all of his weight into his swing; Mathews uses his wrists more."

Mathews also displayed a keen batting eye and great patience at the plate, drawing more than 100 bases on balls six times, and leading the league in that category on four separate occasions.

Meanwhile, as Mathews emerged as one of the game's top sluggers, he improved his defense dramatically, with longtime teammate Johnny Logan recalling, "Eddie was a below-average fielder when he came up, but he made himself into a good third baseman. Connie Ryan, one of our coaches, would hit 50 to 100 groundballs to Eddie every day in spring training. He'd knock them down with his chest and pick them up. He broke his nose three times fielding balls."

Also known for his mental and physical toughness, Mathews earned the respect of players throughout the league with his fighting prowess and willingness to stand up for himself and his teammates. After Brooklyn's Clem Labine hit Braves first baseman Joe Adcock in the head with a fastball on August 1, 1954, Mathews nearly came to blows with Jackie Robinson, although cooler heads ultimately prevailed. Three years later, a beanball war with the Dodgers ended up with Mathews pummeling 6'5" Brooklyn right-hander Don Drysdale. And, after being slammed into at third base by a hard-sliding Frank Robinson during an August 1960 meeting with the Reds, Mathews landed several blows to the face of the future Hall of Famer, with Warren Spahn recalling years later, "Eddie hit him with three punches that not even Muhammad Ali could have stopped. Eddie was a tough competitor and a tough guy. He didn't back down from anybody."

Former Braves teammate Lew Burdette added, "With Eddie, you never worried about anything. If somebody charged the mound when you were pitching, you knew he was going to be there. Eddie used to tell me, 'Let the son of a gun charge you and get the hell out of the way.'"

Aside from his occasional altercations, though, Mathews rarely displayed any emotion on the field, once saying, "I'm not the type to make a big production out of everything I do. I think it's a joke when a guy strikes out and throws his bat. If I have to do that to show the fans I'm mad, to heck with it. I shouldn't have to fling bats or kick water coolers."

Although Mathews batted just .251 for the pennant-winning Braves in 1958, he earned his fifth All-Star selection by finishing third in the league with 31 homers and 85 walks, driving in 77 runs, and scoring 97 times. Mathews followed that up with two of his most productive seasons, earning a runner-up finish in the 1959 NL MVP balloting by leading the league with 46 homers, knocking in 114 runs, scoring 118 times, and batting a career-high .306, before batting .277 and placing near the top of the league rankings with 39 homers, 124 RBIs, 108 runs scored, 111 walks, and an OPS of .948 in 1960.

Despite his outstanding production, the fact that Mathews played in Milwaukee and had to share the limelight with Hank Aaron prevented him from receiving as much notoriety as he deserved. Yet even though the two stars had to vie for the limited amount of media attention the city offered, they got along extremely well, with Aaron remembering, "We weren't jealous of each other at all. That's one reason we were so successful."

Mathews continued his string of eight straight All-Star selections in 1961 and 1962, hitting 32 homers, knocking in 91 runs, scoring 103 times, and batting .306 in the first of those campaigns, before reaching the seats 29 times, driving in 90 runs, scoring 106 others, and batting .265 in the second. However, even though Mathews remained a dangerous hitter for three more years, his batting average and overall production fell off dramatically after he tore the ligaments in his right shoulder while swinging at a high pitch thrown by Houston's Dick Farrell in 1962.

After hitting 32 homers, driving in 95 runs, scoring 77 times, and batting .251 in 1965, Mathews hit just 16 homers and knocked in only 53 runs when the Braves moved to Atlanta the following year, prompting the team to trade him to the Houston Astros for two nondescript players on December 31, 1966. Mathews, who, in his 15 years with the Braves, hit 493 homers, drove in 1,388 runs, scored 1,452 times, collected 2,201 hits, 338 doubles, and 70 triples, stole 66 bases, drew 1,376 bases on balls, struck out 1,387 times, batted .273, compiled an on-base percentage of .379, and posted a slugging percentage of .517, ended up splitting the next two seasons between the Astros and Tigers, assuming a backup role for both teams, before announcing his retirement when the Tigers released him less than three weeks after they won the 1968 World Series. During his time in Houston, Mathews became the seventh member of baseball's 500-homer club. And, while playing for the Tigers, Mathews hit the 511th and 512th home runs of his career, passing in the process Mel Ott for sixth place on the all-time list.

Following his playing days, Mathews briefly entered the business world, before returning to the Braves as a coach in 1971. Eventually replacing Luman Harris as manager of the team during the latter stages of the 1972 campaign, Mathews remained in that post until July 1974, when ownership relieved him of his duties.

After leaving baseball, Mathews experienced several health problems, developing a serious case of pneumonia in 1982 that forced him to spend months in the hospital. During a cruise to the Cayman Islands 14 years later, Mathews slipped while boarding a boat, fell into the water, and fractured his pelvis when he became wedged between the vessel and the pier. Failing to fully recover from his accident, Mathews spent the next few years in discomfort, before dying of complications from pneumonia at a hospital in La Jolla, California, at the age of 69, on February 18, 2001.

Upon learning of his longtime teammate's passing, Hank Aaron, who combined with Mathews to hit a record 863 home runs, said, "He could hit them just as well as I could. I was there to shake his hand quite a few times when he crossed home plate. . . . He was a better hitter than a lot of people gave him credit for. He was a good fielder and ran the bases very well, too. He was a great teammate, and a great family man."

Former Braves shortstop Johnny Logan stated, "I think he was one of the greatest third basemen of all time. He had one of the sweetest swings I ever saw."

Joe Torre, who joined the Braves in 1961, said, "Eddie Mathews was my hero. He was captain, and I always called him that. He never backed off, never was tentative."

Meanwhile, MLB commissioner Bud Selig, who grew up in Milwaukee rooting for the Braves, stated, "It's a sad day. I loved Eddie Mathews. When you saw him play, you knew you were seeing greatness."

BRAVES CAREER HIGHLIGHTS

Best Season

Although Mathews had several outstanding years for the Braves, he turned in the finest performance of his career in 1953, when, at the tender age of 22, he hit 47 homers, knocked in 135 runs, scored 110 times, batted .302, collected 175 hits, 31 doubles, and 8 triples, amassed 363 total bases, and compiled an OPS of 1.033.

Memorable Moments/Greatest Performances

Mathews led the Braves to an 11–3 win over the Dodgers on September 27, 1952, by hitting three home runs, with two of his homers coming off starter Joe Black and the other off reliever Ben Wade.

Mathews contributed to a 15–6 victory over the Cubs on April 22, 1953, by knocking in six runs with a double and a pair of homers.

Mathews proved to be a one-man wrecking crew on June 30, 1953, going 5-for-5, with two homers, four RBIs, and three runs scored during a 6–4 win over the Reds, with his two-run homer in the top of the 10th inning providing the margin of victory.

Mathews gave the Braves a 6–5 win over the Pirates on June 30, 1957, when he homered off reliever Luis Arroyo with one man aboard in the bottom of the 13th inning.

Mathews experienced perhaps the most memorable moment of his career when he gave the Braves a 7–5 win over the Yankees in Game 4 of the 1957 World Series by hitting a two-run homer off Bob Grim in the bottom of the 10th inning.

Mathews led the Braves to a 10–7 victory over the Reds on April 24, 1959, by homering twice, driving in five runs, and scoring four times, with his eighth-inning grand slam off lefty Jim O'Toole providing the winning margin.

Mathews proved to be the difference in an 8–5 victory over the Astros on August 8, 1965, driving in six runs with a double and a pair of homers.

Mathews again knocked in six runs during a 10–8 win over the Cardinals on August 16, 1965, driving home Felipe Alou and Hank Aaron with the winning runs with a two-run single in the top of the ninth inning after homering and hitting safely two other times earlier in the game.

Notable Achievements

- Hit more than 30 home runs 10 times, surpassing 40 homers on four occasions.
- Knocked in more than 100 runs five times, topping 120 RBIs twice.
- Scored more than 100 runs eight times.
- Batted over .300 three times.
- Surpassed 30 doubles once.
- Drew more than 100 bases on balls five times.
- Compiled on-base percentage over .400 four times.
- Posted slugging percentage over .500 eight times, topping .600-mark on three occasions.
- Posted OPS over 1.000 three times.
- Hit three home runs in one game vs. Brooklyn Dodgers on September 27, 1952.

- Led NL in home runs twice, bases on balls four times, and on-base percentage once.
- Finished second in NL in RBIs twice, runs scored once, total bases twice, bases on balls three times, slugging percentage once, and OPS twice.
- Led NL third basemen in putouts twice, assists three times, double plays turned once, and fielding percentage once.
- Ranks among Braves career leaders in home runs (2nd), RBIs (3rd), runs scored (3rd), hits (3rd), triples (10th), doubles (4th), extra-base hits (3rd), total bases (3rd), bases on balls (2nd), slugging percentage (tied for 5th), OPS (3rd), sacrifice flies (4th), games played (3rd), plate appearances (3rd), and at-bats (3rd).
- Two-time NL champion (1957 and 1958).
- 1957 world champion.
- September 1959 NL Player of the Month.
- Finished second in NL MVP voting twice (1953 and 1959).
- Nine-time NL All-Star selection (1953, 1955, 1956, 1957, 1958, 1959, 1960, 1961, and 1962).
- Four-time *Sporting News* All-Star selection (1955, 1957, 1959, and 1960).
- #41 retired by Braves.
- Member of Braves Hall of Fame.
- Number 63 on the *Sporting News'* 1999 list of Baseball's 100 Greatest Players.
- Elected to Baseball Hall of Fame by members of BBWAA in 1978.

5

CHIPPER JONES

A huge contributor to Braves teams that won 11 consecutive division titles, three pennants, and one World Series, Chipper Jones spent his entire career in Atlanta, establishing himself as one of the greatest third basemen and switch-hitters in MLB history. A member of the Braves for parts of 19 seasons, Jones ended his career among the franchise's all-time leaders in virtually every major offensive category, with his 1,512 walks representing the highest total in team annals. An eight-time NL All-Star, Jones also earned two Silver Sluggers, one MVP award, and five other top-10 finishes in the balloting by hitting more than 30 homers six times, driving in more than 100 runs nine times, batting over .300 10 times, and posting an OPS over 1.000 on five separate occasions. One of only nine players to have his number retired by the team, Jones received the additional honors of being inducted into the Braves Hall of Fame and voted into the Baseball Hall of Fame the very first time his name appeared on the ballot.

Born in DeLand, Florida, on April 24, 1972, Larry Wayne Jones Jr. grew up in nearby Pierson, where he became more commonly known as "Chipper" after a relative suggested that his physical resemblance to his father made him a "chip off the old block." Raised on a 10-acre leatherleaf fern farm in a small, blue-collar town known as the "Fern Capital of the World," Jones learned how to play baseball from his father, a math teacher and varsity baseball coach at Taylor High School. However, he acquired his confident attitude from his mother, Lynne, a professional equestrienne, recalling, "Our den was full of her trophies. She had that little strut about her, that little look in her eye."

A natural right-handed hitter, Jones developed his left-handed swing while competing against his father in one-on-one games played in the backyard of his mom's horse farm. With his father playing such an integral role in his early development, Jones often turned to him for advice during his career, once saying, "Nobody knew my swing inside and out like my dad.

He built it. . . . It got to be almost comical how hot I got every time Dad came to town. The Braves should have put him on the payroll."

Emerging as a standout on the diamond by the time he reached his early teens, Jones spent one year at Taylor High School, before transferring to The Bolles School, a prestigious private academy located some 100 miles away in Jacksonville. Claiming that she and her husband decided to send their son to a different school because his athletic prowess allowed him to receive favorable treatment at Taylor High, Jones's mom said, "He was making straight A's and he never cracked a book."

Although Jones eventually grew more comfortable at Bolles, he initially found the change in atmosphere overwhelming, recalling, "I went from a one-stoplight town to a big city, pulling into a parking lot full of better cars than I drove, and a lot of rich kids. It was tough, a big growing-up process."

A two-sport star at Bolles, Jones excelled in baseball and football, performing well enough at quarterback on the gridiron to be offered scholarships to USC and the University of Florida. Even more outstanding on the diamond, Jones earned Florida State Player of the Year honors as a senior by batting .488 as a switch-hitting shortstop, while also compiling a record of 7-3 and an ERA of 1.00 as a pitcher. Choosing baseball over football, Jones decided to sign with the Braves when they selected him with the first overall pick of the June 1990 MLB Draft.

After getting his start in pro ball at the Braves' rookie-league camp in Bradenton, Florida, Jones spent the 1991 season at Class A Macon, where he excelled at the bat, hitting 15 home runs and batting .326, but struggled with the glove, committing 56 errors in 135 games at shortstop. Jones subsequently split the 1992 campaign between High-A Durham and Double-A Greenville, performing well at both stops, before helping Triple-A Richmond advance to the International League playoffs in 1993 by hitting 13 homers, driving in 89 runs, and batting .325. Promoted to the Braves late in the year, Jones appeared in eight games with the parent club, collecting two hits in three official at-bats, before missing the entire 1994 regular season with a tear of the anterior cruciate ligament in his left knee he suffered during spring training.

Fully recovered by the start of the 1995 campaign, Jones joined the Braves for good, replacing Terry Pendleton as the team's starting third baseman. Performing well in his first full season, Jones earned a runner-up finish to Dodger pitcher Hideo Nomo in the NL Rookie of the Year voting by hitting 23 homers, driving in 86 runs, scoring 87 times, and batting .265. Continuing to excel at the plate during the postseason, Jones helped lead the Braves to their first world championship in 38 years by batting a

Chipper Jones ranks second only to Hank Aaron in franchise history in most offensive categories.
Courtesy of Keith Allison

composite .364, with three homers, eight RBIs, and 10 runs scored. Emerging as one of the league's best players the following season, Jones began an exceptional eight-year run during which he posted the following numbers:

YEAR	HR	RBI	RUNS	AVG	OBP	SLG	OPS
1996	30	110	114	.309	.393	.530	.923
1997	21	111	100	.295	.371	.479	.850

1998	34	107	123	.313	.404	.547	.951
1999	45	110	116	.319	.441	.633	1.074
2000	36	111	118	.311	.404	.566	.970
2001	38	102	113	.330	.427	.605	1.032
2002	26	100	90	.327	.435	.536	.972
2003	27	106	103	.305	.402	.517	.920

By driving in more than 100 runs in eight consecutive seasons, Jones became the first player in franchise history to accomplish the feat. Jones also joined Hank Aaron as the only players in team annals to score as many as 100 runs in a season six straight times. In addition to consistently ranking among the NL leaders in runs scored and OPS, Jones finished third in the league in homers and walks (126) in 1999. An NL All-Star in five of those eight seasons, Jones also earned three *Sporting News* All-Star nominations, two Silver Sluggers, and five top-10 finishes in the league MVP voting, winning the award in 1999. More importantly, the Braves finished first in the NL East each season and advanced to the World Series in both 1996 and 1999.

Extremely impressed by Jones's 1996 performance, noted baseball analyst Peter Gammons called the 24-year-old third baseman "clearly the foundation of the next generation."

Meanwhile, Phillies outfielder Lenny Dykstra stated, "I think Chipper Jones is not human. I think he's been created by Ted Turner and some scientists."

An exceptional all-around hitter, the 6'4", 210-pound Jones possessed outstanding power and a keen batting eye from both sides of the plate, hitting more than 20 homers 14 straight times from 1995 to 2008, while also drawing more than 100 bases on balls on three separate occasions. Primarily a gap-to-gap hitter, Jones drove the ball well to all parts of the ballpark, enabling him to also amass more than 30 doubles nine times. Displaying very few weaknesses as a hitter, Jones had only one bad habit—that being his tendency to "step in the bucket" toward third base while batting right-handed. To counteract that, Jones added a toe tap before starting his swing as a way of keeping his timing and balance intact.

Less proficient in the field, Jones struggled somewhat with the glove his first few years in the league, once committing as many as 25 errors at the hot corner, before gradually turning himself into a solid third baseman. Still, Jones never truly distinguished himself in that phase of the game, even moving to left field for two seasons to make room at third for the recently acquired Vinny Castilla prior to the start of the 2002 campaign. Although initially somewhat reluctant to switch positions, Jones later said, "I used to spend so much mental preparation on defense, either working on it or worrying about it. I'm sure it took away from my offense."

Jones's All-American image and outstanding play his first few seasons in Atlanta made him the darling of Braves fans, who showered him with affection every time he stepped to the plate. However, a revelation made by Jones during the 1998-99 offseason caused the public to view him in a somewhat different light in future years. With his marriage to his first wife, Karin, falling apart, Jones admitted during an interview to having multiple affairs and fathering a child with a waitress from a Hooters restaurant whom he had met during spring training, saying, "I've messed up royally. I wish you were allowed one mulligan in life. To be able to rewind two years and play it all over again, I'd do it in a heartbeat."

Subsequently jeered by fans throughout the league for his illicit behavior, Jones often had to resort to stuffing cotton in his ears to muffle the boos he received at opposing ballparks. Always hated in New York for the damage he did every time the Braves faced the Mets, Jones found the reception he received at Shea Stadium particularly objectionable, with the fans adding to their previous chants of "Lar-ry! Lar-ry!" reminders of his infidelity.

Ironically, it took the tragic events of September 11, 2001, to reduce the enmity that existed between Jones and the fans of New York, with the compassion that he and his Braves teammates showed toward the city creating a sort of mutual respect that lasted the remainder of his career. In fact, Jones, who named one of his sons "Shea" because of the tremendous success he experienced at the Mets home ballpark, later said, "I didn't mean my son's name to be a slap in the face to the fans of New York. I enjoyed playing on that stage. Other than Atlanta, there's nowhere else I wanted to play more than New York."

Moved back to third base in 2004, Jones hit 30 homers and knocked in 96 runs, but scored only 69 times and batted just .248 while missing three weeks with a strained right hamstring. Jones missed a significant amount of playing time in each of the next two seasons as well, being limited to just 109 games in 2005 by a torn ligament in his left foot and 110 contests the following year by a series of nagging injuries that continued to plague him for the rest of his career. Nevertheless, Jones posted good overall numbers, hitting 21 homers, driving in 72 runs, and batting .296 in the first of those campaigns, before homering 26 times, knocking in 86 runs, and batting .324 in the second.

Despite appearing in only 134 games in 2007, Jones had one of his finest seasons, earning a sixth-place finish in the NL MVP voting by hitting 29 homers, driving in 102 runs, scoring 108 times, finishing second in the league with a .337 batting average, and topping the circuit with an OPS of 1.029. Although plagued by a sore shoulder that limited him to just 128 games the following year, Jones continued his exceptional hitting, homering 22 times, knocking in 75 runs, and leading the league with a .364 batting average and .470 on-base percentage.

Signed by the Braves to a four-year, $61 million contract extension prior to the start of the 2009 season, Jones said at the time, "I've been good to the Braves, but they've been better to me. They never even let me get to a free-agency year. The money I've made in the game is ridiculous, but I'd like to think it hasn't changed me."

Jones spent one more year starting at third base full-time for the Braves, hitting 18 homers, driving in 71 runs, scoring 80 others, and batting .264 in 2009, before assuming a somewhat diminished role the next three seasons after tearing the ACL in his left knee once again in 2010. After briefly considering retirement two years earlier, Jones announced prior to the start of the 2012 campaign that he planned to retire at the end of the year. Remaining true to his word, Jones hung up his spikes at season's end, concluding his career with 468 home runs, 1,623 RBIs, 1,619 runs scored, 2,726 hits, 549 doubles, 38 triples, 150 stolen bases, a .303 batting average, a .401 on-base percentage, and a .529 slugging percentage. The only switch-hitter in major-league history with more than 1,000 plate appearances to compile a .300 batting average, .400 on-base percentage, and .500 slugging percentage, Jones is also the only player to bat over .300 from both sides of the plate.

Following his playing days, Jones remained away from the game until 2016, when he returned to the Braves as a special assistant to baseball operations. After spending five years working primarily as an instructor during spring training, scout, and minor-league player evaluator, Jones joined the Braves coaching staff on a part-time basis in 2021 as an assistant hitting consultant.

Jones, who spends much of the year living on his Texas ranch with his third wife, former model Taylor Higgins, holds nothing but fond memories of the time he spent in Atlanta, stating, "I never wanted to play anywhere else. I'm a Southern kid, and I wanted to play in a Southern town where I felt comfortable. And I felt comfortable from day one in the Braves organization."

CAREER HIGHLIGHTS

Best Season

Although Jones remained an extremely productive hitter well into his 30s, he had most of his finest seasons earlier in his career, performing especially well in his MVP campaign of 1999, when he led the Braves to the pennant by hitting a career-high 45 homers, driving in 110 runs, scoring 116 others, stealing 25 bases, batting .319, and compiling a career-best OPS of 1.074.

Memorable Moments/Greatest Performances

Jones gave the Braves an 8–7 win over the Florida Marlins on May 20, 1995, by homering off ace reliever Robb Nen with one man out in the bottom of the ninth inning.

After homering earlier in the contest, Jones delivered the decisive blow of a 5–4 win over the Colorado Rockies in Game 1 of the 1995 NLDS when he homered again with two men out and no one on in the top of the ninth inning.

Jones led the Braves to a 14–7 win over the Mets on June 25, 1997, by homering twice, knocking in five runs, and scoring four times, with his fifth-inning grand slam off Bobby Jones breaking the game open.

Jones, who feasted on Mets pitching throughout his career, torched New York hurlers for four homers and seven RBIs during a three-game sweep of Atlanta's fiercest rival in late-September of 1999 that virtually clinched the NL East title for the Braves.

Jones contributed to a 9–0 victory over the Arizona Diamondbacks on April 27, 2001, by going 5-for-5, with a homer, double, and three runs scored.

After homering the previous inning, Jones gave the Braves a 7–6 win over Colorado on August 19, 2002, by following a game-tying solo home run by Gary Sheffield in the bottom of the ninth with a solo blast of his own.

Jones proved to be the difference in a 6–4 win over the Cubs in Game 4 of the 2003 NLDS, homering twice and knocking in four runs, with his two-run shot off Mark Guthrie in the top of the eighth inning providing the margin of victory.

Jones gave the Braves a 6–4 win over the Marlins on May 17, 2006, when he homered with two men aboard in the bottom of the 11th inning.

Jones led the Braves to a lopsided 10–4 victory over the Nationals on August 14, 2006, by hitting three homers and knocking in five runs, with his homers coming off three different pitchers.

Jones gave the Braves a 15–13 win over the Phillies on May 2, 2012, when he hit a two-run homer off Brian Sanches in the bottom of the 13th inning.

Jones made the last home run of his career a memorable one, giving the Braves an 8–7 win over the Phillies on September 2, 2012, by homering off closer Jonathan Papelbon with two men aboard in the bottom of the ninth inning.

Notable Achievements

- Hit more than 20 home runs 14 straight times, topping 30 homers six times and 40 homers once.
- Knocked in more than 100 runs nine times.
- Scored more than 100 runs eight times.
- Batted over .300 10 times, topping the .330-mark on three occasions.
- Surpassed 30 doubles 10 times, amassing more than 40 two-baggers on three occasions.
- Stole at least 20 bases twice.
- Drew more than 100 bases on balls three times.
- Compiled on-base percentage over .400 10 times.
- Posted slugging percentage over .500 11 times, topping .600-mark on three occasions.
- Posted OPS over 1.000 five times.
- Hit three home runs in one game vs. Washington Nationals on August 14, 2006.
- Led NL in batting average once, on-base percentage once, and OPS once.
- Finished second in NL in batting average once and OPS once.
- Holds Braves career record for most bases on balls (1,512).
- Ranks among Braves career leaders in home runs (3rd), RBIs (2nd), runs scored (2nd), hits (2nd), doubles (2nd), extra-base hits (2nd), total bases (2nd), on-base percentage (2nd), slugging percentage (3rd), OPS (2nd), sacrifice flies (2nd), games played (2nd), plate appearances (2nd), and at-bats (2nd).
- Three-time NL champion (1995, 1996, and 1999).
- 1995 world champion.
- Four-time NL Player of the Week.

- Two-time Silver Slugger Award winner (1999 and 2000).
- 1999 NL MVP.
- Finished in top 10 of NL MVP voting five other times, placing as high as fourth in 1996.
- Eight-time NL All-Star selection (1996, 1997, 1998, 2000, 2001, 2008, 2011, and 2012).
- Three-time *Sporting News* All-Star selection (1999, 2000, and 2001).
- #10 retired by Braves.
- Member of Braves Hall of Fame.
- Elected to Baseball Hall of Fame by members of BBWAA in 2018.

6

TOM GLAVINE

Known for his calm demeanor, ability to expand the strike zone, and cerebral approach to his craft, Tom Glavine spent parts of 17 seasons in Atlanta, recording the fourth-most wins, strikeouts, and innings pitched of any hurler in franchise history. One of the NL's premier pitchers for more than a decade, the left-handed-throwing Glavine won at least 20 games five times and compiled an ERA under 3.00 on six separate occasions, earning in the process eight All-Star selections, two Cy Young awards, and four other top-five finishes in the voting. A member of Braves teams that won five pennants and one World Series, Glavine also gained recognition as the *Sporting News* NL Pitcher of the Year twice, before being further honored by having his #47 retired by the Braves and being inducted into the Baseball Hall of Fame in his first year of eligibility.

Born in Concord, Massachusetts, on March 25, 1966, Thomas Michael Glavine grew up with his three siblings in the Boston suburb of Billerica, in a home built by his father, Fred, who ran his own construction company. Although Tom worked for his father's company when he got older, pouring the foundations for houses and building swimming pools, he spent most of his free time as a youth playing hockey and baseball, later admitting that the former remained his first love throughout his teenage years.

Eventually lettering in both sports at Billerica High School, Glavine starred on the ice at center, leading the region in scoring his senior year with 44 goals and 41 assists. Also excelling as a pitcher on the diamond, Glavine led Billerica to the Eastern Massachusetts baseball championship that same year. An outstanding student as well, Glavine initially signed a letter of intent to attend the University of Lowell after the school offered him the opportunity to compete in both sports. But he changed his mind when the Braves selected him in the second round of the June 1984 MLB Draft and the Los Angeles Kings picked him in the fourth round of that year's NHL Draft just five days later. Choosing to sign with the Braves after the team's scouting director, Paul Snyder, offered him an $80,000 bonus,

Glavine headed to the Gulf Coast League, where he began his pro career as a member of the Bradenton Braves.

After one year at Bradenton, Glavine split the next three seasons between Class A Sumter in the South Atlantic League, Double-A Greenville in the Southern League, and Triple-A Richmond in the International League, performing especially well at Greenville after he added a changeup to his assortment of pitches. Promoted to the Braves during the latter stages of the 1987 campaign, Glavine struggled over the final month of the season, compiling a record of 2-4 and an ERA of 5.54 in his nine starts, while issuing 33 walks in just over 50 innings of work. Although Glavine performed somewhat better after he became a regular member of the starting rotation the following year, lowering his ERA by nearly one run and improving his control, he went just 7-17 for a Braves team that finished last in the NL West with a record of 54-106.

Pitching for losing teams in each of the next two seasons as well, Glavine posted a composite mark of 24-20, before emerging as one of baseball's top hurlers in 1991, when he helped lead the Braves to their first division title in nine years by going 20-11, with a 2.55 ERA and a career-high 192 strikeouts, 246 2/3 innings pitched, and nine complete games. Named the winner of the NL Cy Young Award at the end of the year, Glavine said at the time, "I'm not going to say I'm the best pitcher, but I've always felt I had the ability to be considered one of the better pitchers. It was just a matter of developing the ability I had. I'm not cocky, but I think I'm a confident person. When I go out there, I'm confident in my ability to win."

Expressing similar confidence in the ace of the Braves pitching staff, teammate Ron Gant stated, "We know when we walk on the field with Glavine in there, all we need is two or three runs."

Continuing his exceptional work in 1992, Glavine earned his second consecutive All-Star nomination and a runner-up finish to future Braves teammate Greg Maddux in the Cy Young voting by going 20-8, with a 2.76 ERA and league-leading five shutouts. Glavine followed that up with another outstanding season, gaining All-Star recognition once again and a third-place finish in the Cy Young balloting by compiling a record of 22-6 and an ERA of 3.20.

Though not a large man, the 6-foot, 180-pound Glavine proved to be a hard thrower early in his career, sporting a good fastball made more effective by the way it moved as it approached home plate. Glavine's pitching repertoire also included a circle changeup that he typically located off the outside corner, plus-curveball, tailing two-seam fastball, slider, and straight change. Although Glavine gradually lost velocity on his fastball as his career

Tom Glavine won two Cy Young Awards during his time in Atlanta.

progressed, his excellent control, deception, and ability to change speeds, paint the outside corner with pitch after pitch, and expand the strike zone ever so slightly during games enabled him to remain an effective pitcher well into his 30s. Refusing to give in to batters, Glavine continued to pound the corners when behind in the count rather than throw the ball down the middle of the plate, causing him to issue 1,500 bases on balls over the course of his career.

Extremely popular with Braves fans after posting three consecutive 20-win seasons, Glavine suddenly found himself being maligned by the hometown patrons due to his role in the 1994 players' strike. The Braves' player representative, Glavine expressed his frustration with team owners during negotiations, at one point telling the press, "These guys (owners) are getting more than they ever thought they were going to get. So why is it so hard to get a deal? The answer to that question is, they've always wanted more. More to the point where they have total control over players' careers. . . ."

With the fans ready to criticize any player, they took exception to Glavine's remarks, with Braves president Stan Kasten later saying, "He was vilified as the leader of the union. The fans' anger was misplaced. He was just doing his job and exhibiting the same determination and passion that makes us love him on the mound."

Although Glavine eventually won back the support of the fans with his superb pitching, Greg Maddux established himself as the ace of the Braves pitching staff shortly after he arrived in Atlanta in 1993. Nevertheless, Glavine continued to perform at an elite level the rest of the decade, winning at least 15 games five more times, en route to earning another four All-Star nominations. Particularly outstanding in 1998, Glavine won his second Cy Young Award by compiling a record of 20-6, registering 157 strikeouts, and ranking among the league leaders with a 2.47 ERA, three shutouts, and four complete games. After leading all NL hurlers with 21 victories in 2000, Glavine had two more good years for the Braves, winning 16 games in 2001 and another 18 the following year.

But, with the Braves having recently signed John Smoltz to a three-year, $30 million contract extension, they chose not to extend a similar offer to Glavine when he became a free agent at the end of 2002, prompting him to ink a three-year, $35 million deal with the Mets that included a vesting option for a fourth year. Glavine ended up spending the next five seasons in New York, posting an overall record of 61-56 for the Braves' archrivals, before returning to Atlanta at the age of 42 in 2008. However, after appearing in only 13 games with the Braves, Glavine sustained the first major arm injury of his career, forcing him to undergo season-ending surgery on his shoulder and elbow. An unsuccessful comeback attempt the following year ended with the Braves releasing Glavine on June 3, 2009.

Announcing his retirement shortly thereafter, Glavine ended his career with a record of 305-203, an ERA of 3.54, a WHIP of 1.314, 56 complete games, 25 shutouts, and 2,607 strikeouts in 4,413 1/3 innings pitched. As a member of the Braves, he went 244-147, with a 3.41 ERA, 1.296 WHIP, 52 complete games, 22 shutouts, and 2,091 strikeouts in 3,408 innings of work. A good-hitting pitcher, Glavine also won four Silver Sluggers during his time in Atlanta.

Praising his longtime teammate for the guile, intelligence, and composure he displayed on the mound during their many years together, Chipper Jones said, "It doesn't take a rocket scientist to figure out that his kind of poise, his mentality, his way of going about his business, well, that's what won him over 300 games."

Inducted into the Braves Hall of Fame during a special ceremony held at Turner Field on August 6, 2010, that also saw the team retire his #47, Glavine told the fans in attendance, "I hope at the end of the day, whether you watched the game here at the stadium or on TV, when you saw number 47 walk to the mound, you knew I was going to give you everything I had."

Remaining with the Braves following his retirement as an active player, Glavine accepted a position in the front office as a special assistant to team president John Schuerholz. Glavine also spent more than a decade serving as a guest analyst on Braves telecasts shown on Fox Sports South and Fox Sports Southeast, before leaving his post prior to the start of the 2022 season following the death of his father. However, Glavine, who lives in Santa Rosa Beach, Florida, left the door open to possibly returning to broadcasting Braves games in 2023, stating, "I'm not walking away permanently. We have talked about certainly revisiting things at the end of this season for the following season."

BRAVES CAREER HIGHLIGHTS

Best Season

Although Glavine also performed magnificently for the Braves in 1992 and 1998, he proved to be a bit more dominant in 1991, when, en route to earning Cy Young and *Sporting News* NL Pitcher of the Year honors, he led the league with 20 wins and nine complete games, finished second in the circuit with 246 2/3 innings pitched, and placed third with an ERA of 2.55, a WHIP of 1.095, and 192 strikeouts, establishing in the process career-best marks in four different categories.

Memorable Moments/Greatest Performances

Glavine turned in the first dominant pitching performance of his career on September 7, 1988, when he surrendered just three hits and two walks during a 4–1 complete-game win over the Giants.

Glavine allowed only two hits during a 3–0 shutout of the Phillies on May 4, 1989, yielding just a fourth-inning single to second baseman Tommy Herr and a fifth-inning triple to catcher Darren Daulton.

In addition to recording a career-high 12 strikeouts and allowing just four hits and two unearned runs over the first eight innings of a 9–2 win over the Phillies on June 19, 1991, Glavine went 3-for-4 at the plate with two RBIs.

Glavine recorded nine strikeouts, issued two walks, and yielded just a pair of harmless singles during a 2–0 shutout of the Astros on April 7, 1992.

Glavine tossed another two-hit shutout on April 27, 1992, surrendering just a sixth-inning single by shortstop Shawon Dunston and a seventh-inning single by Ryne Sandberg during a 5–0 win over the Cubs.

Glavine outdueled Jack Morris in Game 1 of the 1992 World Series, allowing just four hits, issuing no walks, and recording six strikeouts during a 3–1 complete-game victory over Toronto.

Although Glavine didn't figure in the decision, he hit the only home run of his career during a 2–1 win over the Reds on August 10, 1995, taking John Smiley deep in the bottom of the sixth inning.

Glavine earned 1995 World Series MVP honors by winning both his starts against Cleveland, allowing just two runs and four hits in 14 innings of work. Particularly outstanding in the Game 6 clincher, Glavine recorded eight strikeouts, surrendered just one hit, and walked three batters over the first eight innings of a 1–0 victory.

Glavine also excelled during the 1996 postseason, yielding just one run on five hits over the first 6 2/3 innings of a 5–2 win over the Dodgers in Game 3 of the NLDS, before surrendering just three hits over the first seven innings of a 15–0 rout of the Cardinals in Game 7 of the NLCS, while also knocking in three runs with a first-inning triple.

Notable Achievements

- Won at least 20 games five times, surpassing 16 victories on three other occasions.
- Posted winning percentage over .600 11 times, topping .700-mark on four occasions.
- Compiled ERA under 3.00 six times, posting mark under 2.50 once.
- Led NL pitchers in wins five times, shutouts once, complete games once, assists once, and starts six times.
- Ranks among Braves career leaders in wins (4th), strikeouts (4th), shut outs (tied for 8th), innings pitched (4th), pitching appearances (6th), and games started (3rd).
- Five-time NL champion (1991, 1992, 1995, 1996, and 1999).
- 1995 world champion.
- Three-time NL Player of the Week.
- Four-time NL Pitcher of the Month.
- Four-time Silver Slugger Award winner.
- 1995 World Series MVP.
- Two-time NL Cy Young Award winner (1991 and 1998).

- Finished in top five of NL Cy Young voting four other times, placing second twice and third twice.
- Eight-time NL All-Star selection (1991, 1992, 1993, 1996, 1997, 1998, 2000, and 2002).
- Four-time *Sporting News* All-Star selection (1991, 1992, 1998, and 2000).
- Two-time *Sporting News* NL Pitcher of the Year (1991 and 2000).
- #47 retired by Braves.
- Member of Braves Hall of Fame.
- Elected to Baseball Hall of Fame by members of BBWAA in 2014.

7

FREDDIE FREEMAN

Once described by manager Brian Snitker as "my rock" and "everything that the Braves stand for," Freddie Freeman proved to be the heart and soul of the Braves for more than a decade. One of the most beloved players in franchise history, Freeman spent parts of 12 seasons in Atlanta, serving as the face and voice of the ballclub virtually that entire time. An exceptional on-field performer as well, Freeman hit more than 20 homers eight times, knocked in more than 100 runs twice, and batted over .300 seven times, while also leading all NL first basemen in putouts four times and double plays turned on three separate occasions. A huge contributor to Braves teams that won five division titles, one pennant, and one World Series, Freeman earned three Silver Sluggers, one Gold Glove, five All-Star selections, one NL MVP award, and five other top-10 finishes in the balloting, before differences with ownership over a new contract led to his departure from Atlanta prior to the start of the 2022 campaign.

Born in Villa Park, California, on September 12, 1989, Frederick Charles Freeman grew up in nearby Fountain Valley, where he spent his youth competing with and against Little Leaguers much older than himself. A citizen of both the United States and Canada since his parents emigrated to this country from north of the border, Freeman spent his formative years rooting for the Los Angeles Angels, before laying the foundation for a career in baseball as a third baseman and pitcher at El Modena High School. Performing exceptionally well at both positions as a senior, Freeman batted .417 and won six of his seven mound decisions, prompting the *Orange County Register* to name him its 2007 Player of the Year. Offered an athletic scholarship to California State University, Fullerton, Freeman initially signed a letter of intent to play college baseball for the Titans, before changing his mind when the Braves selected him in the second round of the June 2007 MLB Draft, with the 78th overall pick.

After signing with the Braves for $409,500, Freeman spent the next four seasons advancing through their farm system, performing well at six different stops, before being called up to the parent club for the first time in September 2010. Named the team's starting first baseman prior to the start of the ensuing campaign, Freeman acquitted himself extremely well in his first full season, earning a runner-up finish to teammate Craig Kimbrel in the NL Rookie of the Year voting by hitting 21 homers, driving in 76 runs, scoring 67 times, batting .282, and compiling an OPS of .795. Although Freeman batted just .259 the following year, he increased his overall offensive production, concluding the campaign with 23 homers, 94 RBIs, and 91 runs scored, while also leading all players at his position in putouts and double plays.

Establishing himself as one of the NL's finest all-around hitters in 2013, Freeman hit 23 homers, scored 89 runs, finished second in the league with 109 RBIs, placed third in the circuit with a .319 batting average, and compiled an OPS of .897, earning in the process his first All-Star nomination and a fifth-place finish in the NL MVP voting. After two more solid seasons, Freeman began an outstanding six-year run during which he posted the following numbers:

YEAR	HR	RBI	RUNS	AVG	OBP	SLG	OPS
2016	34	91	102	.302	.400	.569	.968
2017	28	71	84	.307	.403	.586	.989
2018	23	98	94	.309	.388	.505	.892
2019	38	121	113	.295	.389	.549	.938
2020	13	53	**51**	.341	.462	.640	1.102
2021	31	83	**120**	.300	.393	.503	.896

In addition to leading the NL in runs scored twice, Freeman topped the senior circuit in hits once and doubles twice, with his league-leading 191 safeties and 44 two-baggers in 2018 both representing career-high marks. Freeman also consistently ranked among the league leaders in RBIs, batting average, total bases, bases on balls, on-base percentage, and slugging percentage, placing near the top of the league rankings in the last two categories in 2017 despite missing seven weeks with a fractured wrist. Furthermore, Freeman led all NL first basemen in putouts in each of the last three seasons, with his exceptional all-around play earning him three more All-Star selections, three Silver Sluggers, one Gold Glove, five top-10 finishes in the NL MVP voting, and MVP honors during the pandemic-shortened 2020 campaign. More importantly, the Braves finished first in the NL East in each of the last four seasons, also winning the World Series in 2021.

Freddie Freeman earned NL MVP honors in 2020.
Courtesy of Keith Allison

Freeman, who stands a towering 6'5" and weighs 220 pounds, possesses outstanding plate coverage, exceptional hand-eye coordination, and a powerful left-handed swing that has been described as "unorthodox" due to his tendency to move his shoulders slightly before he lowers his hands. Capable of driving the ball out of any part of the park, Freeman uses the entire field, making him a difficult hitter for opposing teams to defense. A patient hitter, Freeman also possesses a keen batting eye, although his fierce swing makes him susceptible to the strikeout. Excellent with the glove as well, Freeman has soft hands and is surprisingly quick around the bag, making him extremely adept at fielding grounders hit to either side and completing the 3-6-3 double play.

One of Freeman's greatest assets, though, is his tremendous leadership ability, which has made him one of the most respected players in the league over the course of his career. Gradually emerging as the unquestioned leader of the Braves, Freeman assumed the role of "big brother" to many of his teammates, who often used him as a sounding board. Freeman also served as a mentor to the team's younger players, advising them on the proper way to conduct themselves, both on and off the playing field.

Declared a free agent at the end of 2021 after rejecting a five-year, $125 million offer made by the Braves before the trade deadline, Freeman expressed his desire to remain in Atlanta for the rest of his career, stating before Game 3 of the World Series, "I haven't envisioned playing anywhere else because I haven't gotten to that point yet. I've put on this uniform— since 2007, I got to put on a Braves uniform with the (minor league) Gulf Coast League team. It's all I've ever known. . . . I think everyone in this room knows I want to stay here."

However, after Freeman's agent insisted on a sixth year when the Braves reportedly increased their long-standing offer to five years and $140 million during the offseason, negotiations grew increasingly contentious between the two sides, prompting ownership to work out a trade with the Athletics on March 14, 2022, that brought slugging first baseman Matt Olson to Atlanta for four prospects. With the Braves essentially shutting the door on a return by Freeman by signing Olson to an eight-year contract shortly thereafter, Freeman issued a statement to the fans of Atlanta through Twitter that read:

> I don't even know where to begin. For the past 15 years I got to be a part of your organization. It was truly an honor. We went through the very highs together and some lows, but those lows are what made last year so special. You watched me grow up from a baby-faced kid to marrying my love @chelseafreeman5 and seeing us bring 3 beautiful boys into this world. I'm so glad my family got to be a part of yours! To Snit, my coaches, teammates, training staff, clubhouse staff, and everyone who made Turner Field and Truist Park so special for my family and I over the years, thank you from the bottom of my heart. It has been a blast to have you cheer for me, and I hope I was able to bring smiles to a lot of your homes over the years. I gave everything I had day in and day out and I hope you guys saw that as well. Although our time has come to an end, I look forward to seeing and playing in front of you all

again. When that time comes, I hope you remember all the wonderful memories we made together. I love you Braves Country! Champions Forever!

Stunned by the news of Freeman's impending departure, Braves shortstop and Atlanta area native Dansby Swanson said, "The easiest thing to say is that (Freeman's) number 5 should never be worn again."

Braves second baseman Ozzie Albies stated, "He's one of the guys we're never going to forget here."

Meanwhile, manager Brian Snitker tried to make the best of a sad situation, saying, "We hate that Freddie is not going to be here—me especially. He was a big part of things when I came in here. There's no doubt we're all going to miss him. But we've got pretty good players."

Freeman, who lived with his wife, Chelsea, and their three young sons in Atlanta during the baseball season but spent his offseasons back in Southern California, subsequently signed a six-year, $162 million contract with the Los Angeles Dodgers that officially ended his lengthy association with the Braves. In his 11-plus years in Atlanta, Freeman hit 271 homers, knocked in 941 runs, scored 969 times, collected 1,704 hits, 367 doubles, and 25 triples, stole 53 bases, batted .295, compiled an on-base percentage of .384, and posted a slugging percentage of .509.

Continuing to perform at an elite level his first year in Los Angeles, Freeman earned his sixth All-Star nomination by hitting 21 homers, driving in 100 runs, batting .325, and leading the league with 117 runs scored, 199 hits, 47 doubles, and a .407 on-base percentage, in helping the Dodgers compile the best regular-season record in baseball. However, his season ended in disappointment when the Dodgers lost to the Padres in the NLDS.

BRAVES CAREER HIGHLIGHTS

Best Season

Although Freeman earned NL MVP honors in 2020, he posted the best overall numbers of his career in 2019, when he batted .295, collected 34 doubles, and ranked among the league leaders with 38 homers, 121 RBIs, 113 runs scored, a .389 on-base percentage, and a .938 OPS.

Memorable Moments/Greatest Performances

Freeman delivered the decisive blow of a 6–3 victory over the Mets on September 23, 2015, when he homered off Jeurys Familia with two men on in the top of the ninth inning.

Freeman has hit for the cycle twice in his career, accomplishing the feat for the first time during a 9–8 win over the Reds on June 25, 2016.

Freeman hit safely in 30 consecutive games from August 24 to September 28, 2016, a period during which he went 43-for-112 (.384) with seven homers, 11 doubles, 27 RBIs, and 26 runs scored.

Freeman helped lead the Braves to a 9–2 win over the Marlins on May 10, 2018, by going 5-for-5, with a homer and two RBIs.

Freeman provided most of the offensive firepower during a 5–3 win over the White Sox on September 1, 2019, driving in all five runs with a single and a pair of homers.

Freeman contributed to a 29–9 rout of the Marlins on September 9, 2020, by homering twice, doubling, and knocking in a career-high six runs.

Freeman gave the Braves an 8–7 win over the Red Sox on September 25, 2020, when he hit a pinch-hit two-run homer in the bottom of the 11th inning.

Freeman came through in the clutch again in the 2020 NL Wild Card Game, giving the Braves a 1–0 victory over the Reds when he delivered an RBI single to center field in the bottom of the 13th inning.

Freeman hit for the cycle for the second time in his career on August 18, 2021, when he went 4-for-5, with two RBIs and four runs scored during an 11–9 win over the Marlins.

Freeman experienced two memorable moments during the Braves' successful postseason run to the 2021 world championship, the first of which came when he delivered the decisive blow of a 5–4 victory over the Milwaukee Brewers in Game 4 of the NLDS by hitting a solo homer off Josh Hader in the bottom of the eighth inning.

Freeman also put the finishing touches on the Braves' 7–0 win over Houston in the Game 6 World Series clincher when he homered to left-center field off Ryne Stanek in the top of the seventh inning.

Notable Achievements

- Hit more than 20 home runs eight times, topping 30 homers on three occasions.
- Knocked in more than 100 runs twice, topping 120 RBIs once.

- Scored more than 100 runs three times, scoring 120 runs once.
- Batted over .300 seven times, topping .340-mark once.
- Surpassed 30 doubles seven times, amassing more than 40 two-baggers three times.
- Compiled on-base percentage over .400 four times.
- Posted slugging percentage over .500 eight times, topping .600-mark once.
- Posted OPS over .900 five times, topping 1.000-mark once.
- Hit in 30 consecutive games in 2016.
- Hit for the cycle twice (vs. Cincinnati Reds on June 15, 2016, and vs. Miami Marlins on August 18, 2021).
- Led NL in runs scored twice, hits once, extra-base hits twice, doubles twice, sacrifice flies once, and games played twice.
- Finished second in NL in RBIs three times, batting average once, hits once, doubles twice, total bases twice, on-base percentage once, slugging percentage once, and OPS once.
- Led NL first basemen in putouts four times and double plays turned three times.
- Ranks among Braves career leaders in home runs (6th), RBIs (7th), runs scored (10th), hits (7th), doubles (3rd), extra-base hits (6th), total bases (6th), bases on balls (5th), on-base percentage (10th), slugging percentage (10th), OPS (5th), sacrifice flies (tied for 7th), games played (9th), plate appearances (9th), and at-bats (9th).
- 2021 NL champion.
- 2021 world champion.
- Five-time NL Player of the Week.
- Two-time NL Player of the Month.
- 2020 NL Hank Aaron Award winner.
- Three-time Silver Slugger Award winner (2019, 2020, and 2021).
- 2018 Gold Glove Award winner
- Two-time Wilson Defensive Player of the Year (2018 and 2019).
- 2020 NL MVP.
- Finished in top 10 of NL MVP voting five other times, placing in top five twice.
- Five-time NL All-Star selection (2013, 2014, 2018, 2019, and 2021).
- 2020 All-MLB First-Team selection.
- Two-time All-MLB Second-Team selection (2019 and 2021).

8

JOHN SMOLTZ

The only player to serve as a member of all 14 division-championship teams the Braves fielded from 1991 to 2005, John Smoltz spent two decades in Atlanta, excelling on the mound as both a starter and a reliever. The winner of at least 15 games on six separate occasions, Smoltz also recorded more than 40 saves three times, earning in the process eight All-Star selections, one Cy Young Award, and two other top-five finishes in the voting. The franchise's all-time leader in strikeouts, Smoltz also ranks extremely high in team annals in wins, saves, innings pitched, pitching appearances, and games started. A tremendous postseason performer as well, Smoltz helped lead the Braves to five pennants and one world championship with his ability to excel under pressure, which contributed greatly to the team's decision to retire his #29 and his induction into the Baseball Hall of Fame the first time his name appeared on the ballot.

Born in Detroit, Michigan, on May 15, 1967, John Andrew Smoltz grew up with his two younger siblings some 90 miles northwest, in Lansing, Michigan. Although his parents stressed God, family, and schoolwork over athletics, John became obsessed with baseball early in life, telling his mother at the age of seven that he planned to become a professional baseball player.

Eventually emerging as a standout athlete at Waverly High School, Smoltz earned a scholarship to Michigan State University by excelling in both baseball and basketball. However, rather than enrolling at MSU, Smoltz chose to sign with the Detroit Tigers when they selected him in the 22nd round of the June 1985 MLB Draft. Smoltz subsequently spent most of the next two seasons in the Detroit farm system, receiving very little instruction from the organization's roving minor-league pitching coaches, before being dealt to the Braves for veteran hurler Doyle Alexander on August 12, 1987.

Recalling his feelings at the time, Smoltz said, "I was very disappointed. I thought, 'I'm going to the worst team in baseball.' Then I switched my thoughts, realizing I can get to the big leagues quicker and help turn this franchise around, which has been a great story."

Sent to the Braves' Triple-A affiliate in Richmond, Smoltz flourished under the tutelage of pitching coach Leo Mazzone, who, rather than tampering with his delivery, which he later called "one of the most beautiful I'd ever seen," focused on improving his curve and slider. Vastly improving his performance under Mazzone, Smoltz compiled a record of 10-5 and an ERA of 2.79 over the first few months of the 1988 campaign, prompting the parent club to summon him to the big leagues in late July. Failing to make much of an impression in his 12 starts with the Braves the rest of the year, Smoltz won just two of his nine decisions and posted an ERA of 5.48. However, after being inserted into the starting rotation full-time in 1989, Smoltz earned his first All-Star selection by going 12-11 with a 2.94 ERA and 168 strikeouts for a Braves team that finished last in the NL West for the second of three straight times.

Although somewhat less effective in 1990, Smoltz posted respectable numbers, concluding the campaign with a record of 14-11, an ERA of 3.85, and a team-high 170 strikeouts. But Smoltz subsequently suffered through a miserable first half of 1991, performing so poorly the first three months of the season that Braves GM John Schuerholz suggested he see a psychologist.

Recalling his mental state at the time, Smoltz, who had a record of 2-11 and an ERA of 5.16 at the All-Star break, stated, "Anytime things started to get a little hairy, I would begin to unravel. . . . It became a foregone conclusion in my mind that, once runners were on, they were going to score."

However, after a few sessions of therapy, Smoltz straightened himself out by viewing before each start a video showing some of his best performances, later saying, "Remembering my little highlight reel helped me break out of it and banish the negative thoughts from my head."

Compiling a record of 12-2 and an ERA of 2.63 the rest of the year, Smoltz finished the season 14-13 with a 3.80 ERA, before helping the Braves advance to the World Series by defeating the Pirates twice in the NLCS. An All-Star in each of the next two seasons, Smoltz went 15-12, with a 2.85 ERA, 246 2/3 innings pitched, nine complete games, and a league-leading 215 strikeouts in 1992, before compiling a record of 15-11 and an ERA of 3.62, throwing 243 2/3 innings, and finishing second in the league with 208 strikeouts the following year.

Plagued by pain in his pitching arm that began bothering him two years earlier, Smoltz went just 6-10 with a 4.14 ERA over the first three months of the 1994 campaign, before undergoing elbow surgery to remove

John Smoltz excelled for the Braves as both a starter and a reliever.

a bone spur and chips just before a players' strike brought the season to a premature end.

Rejoining the Braves in 1995, Smoltz helped them capture the NL East title by going 12-7 with a 3.18 ERA, while also striking out 193 batters in the same number of innings. Reaching the zenith of his career the following year, Smoltz earned Cy Young honors and his fourth All-Star selection by compiling a record of 24-8, leading the league with 276 strike-outs and 253 2/3 innings pitched, and ranking among the leaders with an ERA of 2.94, a WHIP of 1.001, six complete games, and two shutouts. Although the Braves subsequently came up just short in the postseason, suffering a six-game defeat at the hands of the Yankees in the World Series, Smoltz did everything he could to bring them their second straight world championship, going a combined 4-1 with an ERA just under 1.00 in his five postseason starts.

Expressing his satisfaction after being named the winner of the Cy Young Award, Smoltz said, "Everybody felt I needed this to be on par with Greg [Maddux] and Tommy [Glavine]. At least winning the award takes the pressure off of that. I know down the road I'll be honored to have played with those two guys."

Meanwhile, Braves pitching coach Leo Mazzone stated, "John Smoltz was as awesome and dominant a pitcher as I've ever seen."

Although the 6'3", 210-pound Smoltz, whose right-handed offerings included an impressive fastball, a slider that veered away from right-handed batters, and a splitter that broke down to left-handed hitters, often found himself being overshadowed by Maddux and Glavine, he "had the best stuff of all of them," according to Mazzone, who went on to say, "Greatest slider I've ever seen from a right-handed pitcher. Powerful fastball. A nasty split-finger. A changeup. And a curveball."

Mazzone added, "John has a good knowledge of pitching. When you're looking at film, if there's a mechanical flaw, he understands. He's not just a thrower. There might be a misconception there as far as his being a thrower and not a pitcher. But he is a pitcher. He knows what he wants to do, and when he executes it consistently, nobody can touch him."

Displaying no animosity toward Maddux and Glavine for their loftier status in the Braves' hierarchy of starting pitchers, Smoltz acknowledged, "My sense is that I was the guy riding in the backseat most of the time. As good as Greg was, Tom was right up there with him."

After signing a four-year contract extension with the Braves worth $7.75 million per year at the end of 1996, Smoltz continued to perform at an elite level the next two seasons, going 15-12 with a 3.02 ERA, 241 strikeouts, and a league-leading 256 innings pitched in 1997, before compiling a record of 17-3 and an ERA of 2.90 in the ensuing campaign despite missing a significant amount of time with elbow soreness. Smoltz, who underwent a second arthroscopic surgery on his elbow at the end of 1997, later described the discomfort he felt the following year, saying, "I am absolutely serious when I say that I pitched some of my greatest games in some of my worst conditions."

Continuing to ignore the team doctor's suggestion that he undergo Tommy John surgery, Smoltz compiled a record of 11-8 and an ERA of 3.19 in 1999, telling a reporter in August, "I'm at the point right now where I just don't know how long it's going to last. It's pitch to pitch, start to start now."

To relieve the pain, Smoltz gave up throwing overhand and adopted a three-quarters, almost sidearm, delivery, saying, "I basically taught myself how to pitch a whole new way. Nobody knew how hard it was. I was trying to fake it."

Finally forced to go under the knife when his elbow gave out during spring training in 2000, Smoltz missed the entire year, and part of 2001 as well, before moving to the bullpen when he returned to action. Performing well as a reliever much of the season, Smoltz concluded the 2001 campaign with a record of 3-3, an ERA of 3.36, and 10 saves in 11 opportunities.

A free agent at season's end, Smoltz seriously considered signing with another team so that he might return to his favored role of starting pitcher. But even though the Braves wanted him back only as a reliever, Smoltz ultimately chose to return to Atlanta, later saying, "I looked at the total picture. Family, lifestyle, my charity and community work, financial, friends and family. And baseball."

Transitioning seamlessly into the role of full-time closer, Smoltz performed magnificently over the course of the next three seasons, earning two All-Star nominations and one third-place finish in the Cy Young voting by amassing a total of 144 saves, with his league-leading 55 saves in 2002 establishing a single-season franchise record that still stands. Even more dominant the following year, Smoltz collected 45 saves in 49 opportunities, compiled an ERA of 1.12, and struck out 73 batters in 64 1/3 innings of work.

Yet, with Smoltz eventually concluding that throwing all-out all the time made closing more dangerous than starting, he convinced GM John Schuerholz and manager Bobby Cox to return him to the starting rotation in 2005. Smoltz subsequently spent the next three years serving as the Braves' most reliable starter, earning another two All-Star selections by posting a composite record of 44-24, with his 16 victories in 2006 tying him for the league lead. However, after winning another 14 games the following year, Smoltz missed most of 2008 with shoulder pain that forced him to undergo arthroscopic surgery in June.

With the Braves offering the 42-year-old Smoltz an incentive-laden contract for 2009 based on his health and performance, he elected to sign with the Red Sox, prompting longtime teammate Chipper Jones to say, "I lost a brother. If he's retiring, that's one thing. But for him to be playing somewhere else is unacceptable."

Smoltz, who left Atlanta with an overall record of 210-147, an ERA of 3.26, a WHIP of 1.170, 53 complete games, 16 shutouts, 154 saves, and 3,011 strikeouts in 3,395 innings pitched, ended up splitting the 2009 campaign between the Red Sox and Cardinals, compiling a record of 3-8 and an ERA of 6.35 in his 15 starts, before announcing his retirement at the end of the year. In addition to his 213 regular-season victories, Smoltz won another 15 postseason contests, ending his career with a playoff and World Series record of 15-4 and an ERA of 2.67. In discussing his ability to perform well under pressure, Smoltz said, "I just relished it. I could not wait for the big moment, the big game."

Since retiring as an active player, Smoltz has remained in the public eye by serving as a baseball analyst, first for TBS, the television home of the Braves, and later, for both Fox Sports and the MLB Network.

Inducted into the Baseball Hall of Fame in 2015, one year after Greg Maddux and Tom Glavine joined the game's immortals, Smoltz received the following words of praise at the time from Bobby Cox, who said, "When John was on the mound, you always thought you were going to win a ballgame."

As for how he would like to be remembered, Smoltz said, "My legacy will be however someone wants to view it. Certainly, I'm proud of it. I don't even know if I have a word for it. I mean, I literally gave everything I had every single time I went out there."

BRAVES CAREER HIGHLIGHTS

Best Season

Despite his exceptional work out of the bullpen, Smoltz is remembered far more as a starter, with his finest season while serving in that capacity coming in 1996, when he earned NL Cy Young honors and an 11th-place finish in the MVP voting by leading all NL hurlers with 24 wins, a .750 winning percentage, 276 strikeouts, and 253 2/3 innings pitched, finishing second in WHIP (1.001), complete games (6), and shutouts (2), and placing fourth in ERA (2.94).

Memorable Moments/Greatest Performances

Smoltz recorded eight strikeouts and allowed just two hits during a 6–1 complete-game victory over Philadelphia on May 27, 1990, holding the Phillies hitless until the ninth inning, when they scored their only run on a one-out double by Lenny Dykstra and a two-out single by Von Hayes.

Smoltz won both his starts in the 1991 NLCS, performing especially well in the Game 7 clincher, when he shut out the Pirates, 4–0, on six hits.

Smoltz recorded a career-high 15 strikeouts during a 2–1 complete-game victory over the Montreal Expos on May 24, 1992.

Smoltz turned in a dominant performance on June 24, 1992, recording 10 strikeouts, issuing two walks, and yielding just a pair of singles to Jack Clark during a 5–0 shutout of the Giants.

Smoltz earned 1992 NLCS MVP honors by going 2-0 with a 2.66 ERA during the Braves' seven-game victory over Pittsburgh. Particularly outstanding in Game 1, Smoltz allowed just four hits and one run over the first eight innings of a 5–1 Braves win.

Smoltz dominated the San Diego lineup on April 14, 1996, recording 13 strikeouts and allowing just one hit and one walk over the first eight innings of a 4–0 Braves win.

Smoltz hurled another gem on May 29, 1996, surrendering just four hits, walking two batters, and recording 13 strikeouts during a 2–0 shutout of the Cubs.

In addition to recording 10 strikeouts and surrendering just five hits, two walks, and two runs over the first eight innings of an 8–2 win over the Expos on September 22, 1996, Smoltz drove in three runs with a sixth-inning homer.

Smoltz continued his outstanding postseason pitching in 1996, earning a 2–1 victory over the Dodgers in Game 1 of the NLDS by allowing just one run, four hits, and two walks over the first nine innings, before Javy López homered in the top of the 10th. Smoltz subsequently won both his starts against St. Louis in the NLCS, compiling an ERA of 1.20 by surrendering just two runs in 15 innings of work, before allowing just six hits and one earned run in 14 innings against the Yankees in the World Series.

Smoltz again displayed his ability to excel under pressure when he struck out 11 and yielded just three hits during a 4–1 complete-game win over Houston in Game 3 of the 1997 NLDS.

Smoltz allowed only two men to reach base when he shut out the Reds, 3–0, on April 30, 1999, yielding just one walk and a fifth-inning single by catcher Ed Taubensee.

Notable Achievements

- Won more than 20 games once, surpassing 15 victories on five other occasions.
- Saved more than 40 games three times, surpassing 50 saves once.

- Posted winning percentage over .600 eight times, topping .700-mark twice.
- Compiled ERA under 3.00 seven times, posting mark under 2.00 once.
- Posted WHIP under 1.000 once.
- Recorded more than 200 strikeouts five times.
- Threw more than 250 innings twice.
- Threw 30 consecutive scoreless innings in 1992.
- Led NL pitchers in wins twice, winning percentage twice, strikeouts twice, innings pitched twice, saves once, and starts three times.
- Holds Braves single-season record for most saves (55 in 2002).
- Holds Braves career record for most strikeouts (3,011).
- Ranks among Braves career leaders in wins (5th), saves (2nd), WHIP (9th), innings pitched (5th), strikeouts-to-walks ratio (7th), pitching appearances (3rd), and games started (5th).
- Five-time NL champion (1991, 1992, 1995, 1996, and 1999).
- 1995 world champion.
- Three-time NL Player of the Week.
- Three-time NL Pitcher of the Month.
- 1992 NLCS MVP.
- 1997 Silver Slugger Award winner.
- 1996 NL Cy Young Award winner.
- Finished in top five of NL Cy Young voting two other times.
- Finished eighth in 2002 NL MVP voting.
- 2002 NL Fireman of the Year.
- 2002 NL Rolaids Relief Man of the Year.
- Eight-time NL All-Star selection (1989, 1992, 1993, 1996, 2002, 2003, 2005, and 2007).
- 1996 *Sporting News* All-Star selection.
- 1996 *Sporting News* NL Pitcher of the Year.
- #29 retired by Braves.
- Member of Braves Hall of Fame.
- Elected to Baseball Hall of Fame by members of BBWAA in 2015.

9

DALE MURPHY

O ne of the most popular players in franchise history, Dale Murphy established himself as the face of the Braves during his 15 years in Atlanta.
Clean-cut and well-mannered, Murphy didn't smoke, drink, or curse,
enabling him to acquire a reputation as a boy scout who set an example
for the nation's youth. Meanwhile, on the playing field, Murphy proved to
be one of the finest all-around players of his generation, driving in more
runs, scoring more times, and amassing more hits, extra-base hits, and total
bases than anyone else in the NL during the 1980s. A tremendous force on
offense, Murphy hit more than 30 homers six times, knocked in more than
100 runs five times, and batted over .300 on three separate occasions, earning in the process four Silver Sluggers. An exceptional defensive outfielder
as well, Murphy won five Gold Gloves, with his outstanding all-around play
earning him two MVP awards, seven NL All-Star selections, four *Sporting
News* All-Star nominations, and a place in the Braves Hall of Fame.

Born in Portland, Oregon, on March 12, 1956, Dale Bryan Murphy
attended Woodrow Wilson High School, where he starred on the diamond
as a catcher, compiling a batting average of .465 his senior year. After initially accepting a baseball scholarship to Arizona State University, Murphy
chose to sign with the Braves when they made him the fifth overall pick of
the 1974 MLB Amateur Draft.

Murphy subsequently spent the next four years advancing through
the Braves' farm system, earning a brief callup to the parent club in 1976,
before being returned to the minors the following year, when he batted
.305, hit 22 homers, and knocked in 90 runs at Triple-A Richmond. But,
while Murphy excelled at the plate for the Braves' top minor-league affiliate,
he developed a throwing problem that manifested itself with consistently
errant throws to second base, often bouncing the ball in front of the pitching mound or tossing it into the outfield.

Called up by the Braves once again in September of 1977, Murphy
performed well on offense, homering twice, batting .316, and knocking in

14 runs in just 76 plate appearances. But he continued to struggle with his throwing, committing six errors in only 17 games behind the plate.

Convinced that a change in positions was in order, the Braves handed Murphy a first baseman's glove when he reported to spring training in 1978. Remaining at that post for much of the year after he earned a spot in the starting lineup, Murphy performed erratically in the field, committing a total of 23 errors. However, he displayed potential at the plate, hitting 23 homers and driving in 79 runs, despite batting only .226 and leading the NL with 145 strikeouts. Splitting his time between first base and catcher the following year, Murphy failed to improve at either position. But he showed some growth as a hitter, cutting down on his strikeouts, batting .276, homering 21 times, and knocking in 57 runs, even though he appeared in just 104 games due to cartilage damage in his left knee that forced him to undergo arthroscopic surgery.

Moved to the outfield in 1980, Murphy spent most of the season patrolling center field for the Braves, taking an immediate liking to his new position. Meanwhile, Murphy developed into one of the more formidable batsmen in the senior circuit, earning the first of his seven All-Star nominations by batting .281, knocking in 89 runs, and ranking among the league leaders with 33 homers, 98 runs scored, and a .510 slugging percentage. Failing to perform at the same level during the strike-shortened 1981 campaign, Murphy hit just 13 homers, drove in only 50 runs, and batted just .247. But he rebounded the following season to begin an outstanding four-year run during which he posted the following numbers:

YEAR	HR	RBI	RUNS	AVG	OBP	SLG	OPS
1982	36	**109**	113	.281	.378	.507	.885
1983	36	**121**	131	.302	.393	**.540**	**.933**
1984	36	100	94	.290	.372	**.547**	.919
1985	37	111	**118**	.300	.388	.539	.927

In addition to finishing either first or second in the NL in home runs all four years, Murphy placed at, or near, the top of the league rankings in RBIs, runs scored, total bases, slugging percentage, and OPS each season. Murphy also stole 30 bases in 1983, making him a member of the then-select "30-30" club. Awarded a Silver Slugger and a Gold Glove at the end of each season, Murphy earned four straight All-Star selections and four consecutive top-10 finishes in the NL MVP voting as well, winning the award in both 1982 and 1983. More importantly, the Braves ended a

Dale Murphy won consecutive NL MVP awards as a member of the Braves during the early 1980s.

long drought by winning the division title in 1982, before finishing a close second in the NL West the following year.

Standing 6'4" and weighing 210 pounds, the right-handed-hitting Murphy possessed tremendous power to all fields, frequently driving pitches on the outside part of the plate over the right field wall. Capable of turning on inside offerings as well, Murphy presented a dilemma to opposing pitchers, with San Diego Padres right-hander LaMarr Hoyt saying, "The only way to stop him is to throw balls. Throw away, away, away. Even then he might hurt you."

Cincinnati Reds pitcher Mario Soto added, "I don't challenge Murphy, even if he's 0-for-20. Not him, not ever."

Murphy's only real weakness as a hitter proved to be his penchant for striking out (he fanned more than 100 times in every full season he played from 1978 to 1990). However, he also gradually developed a keen batting eye and more patience at the plate, consistently ranking among the NL leaders in bases on balls from 1982 to 1988.

Establishing himself over time as one of the senior circuit's finest defensive outfielders, Murphy did an excellent job in center field for the Braves, before being shifted to right in 1987 to save wear and tear on his knees. Applauding Murphy for his successful transition to the outfield, Andre Dawson said, "If you can't be impressed by Murph, you can't be impressed. What really impresses me is how he started out as a catcher a few years back and ends up in center field with a Gold Glove. You've got to appreciate that kind of talent."

An outstanding baserunner as well, Murphy received praise for his proficiency in that area from Hank Aaron, who stated, "What's really special about him is that he knows how to run the bases. He gets up his speed, and he knows what his capabilities are. If he tries for a base, you know he's going to make it."

Murphy's exceptional all-around play earned him the admiration of Nolan Ryan, who commented after he won his second MVP award, "I can't imagine Joe DiMaggio was a better all-around player than Dale Murphy."

Joe Torre spoke of the totality of Murphy's game when he stated, "You can put him in a class with a Mays and an Aaron because he can beat you with his glove, and he can beat you with a home run."

Chicago Cubs pitching coach Billy Connors expressed similar sentiments when he said, "He's the best I've ever seen, and I've seen Willie Mays. I've seen Murphy win games every way there is, a base hit in the ninth, a home run, a great catch, beating the throw to first on a double play. I've never seen anything like him before in my life."

In addition to his excellence on the ballfield, Murphy earned the respect and admiration of everyone in the game with his model behavior, unassuming nature, and humility, which he exhibited when he accepted his first MVP award, saying at the time, "There are so many people responsible for what happened this year with the Braves. I keep thinking about Jerry Royster, who carried us for the last month, and Terry Harper, who carried us for the last week. It's hard to pick an MVP on a winning team."

After winning the award again the following year, Murphy stated, "It doesn't really sink in. . . . It hasn't really hit home. I just still feel like one of the guys on the team. I don't feel any different, and I don't feel I should. I don't want to feel this award—two, or however many—puts me at a higher level than anybody else."

Developing a deep fondness for Murphy during their time together in Atlanta, former Braves manager Joe Torre said, "If you're a coach, you want him as a player. If you're a father, you want him as a son. If you're a woman, you want him as a husband. If you're a kid, you want him as a father. What else can you say about the guy?"

Choosing to take a less serious approach to the almost saintly qualities of his teammate, Braves pitcher Terry Forster commented, "Just look at him over there. Doesn't drink, doesn't smoke, doesn't take greenies, nicest guy you'd ever want to meet, hits the hell out of the ball, hustles like crazy, plays a great center field, and isn't trying to get anything from anybody . . . doesn't he just make you sick?"

With the Braves finishing last in the NL West in 1986, Murphy received very little support from his teammates on offense, causing him to "slump" to 29 homers, 83 RBIs, 89 runs scored, and a .265 batting average. But even though the Braves performed no better the following year, Murphy managed to hit a career-high 44 homers, drive in 105 runs, score 115 times, and compile a batting average of .295, earning in the process his last All-Star selection and an 11th-place finish in the NL MVP voting.

Unfortunately, the 1987 campaign proved to be Murphy's last as an elite player. Experiencing a precipitous decline in offensive production the next two seasons, Murphy hit 24 homers, knocked in 77 runs, and batted just .226 in 1988, before homering 20 times, driving in 84 runs, and batting only .228 the following year.

In trying to explain his fall from grace years later, Murphy said, "I think I got into some bad habits. I wasn't hitting the ball the other way. I got a little pull happy. Part of that is mental too—you start thinking you've got to overcompensate, might be losing a little bit of your swing. It's what happens as you approach your mid-30s, usually."

With Murphy no longer performing at the same level he did earlier in his career, the Braves spent much of 1988 and 1989 fielding trade offers for him, although they never actually made a move. However, Murphy finally took matters into his own hands midway through the 1990 campaign when he expressed his willingness to leave Atlanta to Braves GM/manager Bobby Cox, recalling, "I went into Bobby's office . . . and told him of my decision. I told him, 'Bobby, I'm going to move on after the season, going to be a free agent.' I said if there's a trade that looks like it could work, I'd be interested."

Subsequently included in a five-player trade the Braves completed with the Philadelphia Phillies on August 3, 1990, that netted them little in return, Murphy remembered, "It was such a sudden thing for fans, and even teammates."

Murphy, who left Atlanta with career totals of 371 home runs, 1,143 RBIs, 1,103 runs scored, 1,901 hits, 306 doubles, 37 triples, and 160 stolen bases, a .268 batting average, a .351 on-base percentage, and a .478 slugging percentage, ended up starting for the Phillies in right field for just one full season, hitting 18 homers, driving in 81 runs, and batting .252 in 1991, before being released just prior to the start of the 1993 campaign after missing most of the previous year with a left knee injury. A victim of bad timing, Murphy left Atlanta just before the Braves established themselves as the class of the National League and departed Philadelphia two days before the Phillies began their successful run to the 1993 NL pennant.

After being released by the Phillies, Murphy spent the first two months of the 1993 season assuming a backup role with the expansion Colorado Rockies, batting just .143 in 26 games, before announcing his retirement in late May. Over parts of 18 big-league seasons, Murphy hit 398 homers, knocked in 1,266 runs, scored 1,197 times, collected 2,111 hits, 350 doubles, and 39 triples, stole 161 bases, batted .265, compiled an on-base percentage of .346, and posted a slugging percentage of .469.

On June 20, 1994, the Braves honored Murphy by retiring his jersey #3 at Atlanta-Fulton County Stadium. Speaking afterward of what the ceremony meant to him, Murphy said, "This was saying goodbye. When I retired, I never had the chance to tell people here. This is kind of final."

Since retiring from baseball, Murphy has dedicated himself to his religion and to contributing to society through various charitable causes. From 1997 to 2000, Murphy served as president of the Boston Mission of The Church of Jesus Christ of Latter-day Saints, in which role he supervised nearly 200 Mormons who were working on two-year stints as missionaries in Massachusetts. In 2005, Murphy founded "I Won't Cheat," an organization that promotes honesty to young athletes and stresses the dangers of taking performance-enhancing drugs. Murphy has also served as a member of the National Advisory Board for the charity Operation Kids, and remains active in raising money for the charity Operation Smile, a nonprofit organization that performs surgery on children born with a cleft palate.

Murphy, who, in 2017, opened Murph's restaurant in Atlanta and currently resides with his family in Alpine Valley, Utah, continues to hold the Braves and the city of Atlanta close to his heart after all these years, saying, "We'll always be Braves. All of our kids were born in Atlanta. We're always thankful for that association and what I was able to accomplish there because of the Braves and (former general manager) Bill Lucas and because of Bobby (Cox) getting me to the outfield."

BRAVES CAREER HIGHLIGHTS

Best Season

Although Murphy posted comparable numbers in 1982, 1984, 1985, and 1987, his second MVP campaign of 1983 proved to be his finest all-around season. In addition to leading the league with 121 RBIs, a slugging percentage of .540, and an OPS of .933, Murphy finished second in home runs (36), runs scored (131), and total bases (318), third in on-base percentage (.393), fourth in walks (90), and sixth in batting average (.302) and hits (178).

Memorable Moments/Greatest Performances

Murphy led the Braves to an 8–7 win over the Padres on September 15, 1977, by homering twice and knocking in four runs, with his leadoff homer off Rollie Fingers in the top of the 10th inning providing the margin of victory.

Murphy helped lead the Braves to a 9–7 win over the Giants on July 2, 1978, by knocking in six runs with a homer and single, delivering the game's big blow in the bottom of the fifth inning when he homered off Vida Blue with the bases loaded.

Murphy hit three homers and knocked in five runs during a 6–4 win over the Giants on May 18, 1979, victimizing Vida Blue twice and Tom Griffin once.

Murphy contributed to a 10–7 victory over the Padres on September 14, 1979, by going 5-for-5, with two homers, a triple, three RBIs, and three runs scored.

Murphy provided most of the offensive firepower during a 6–4 win over the Giants on August 11, 1983, knocking in five runs with a single and a pair of homers.

Murphy gave the Braves a 7–4 win over the Phillies on July 12, 1985, by homering with two men aboard in the bottom of the ninth inning.

Murphy led the Braves to a 12–4 rout of the Mets on April 12, 1987, by knocking in five runs with a double and a pair of homers.

Murphy highlighted a 10-run sixth-inning rally by the Braves that resulted in a 10–1 victory over the Giants on July 27, 1989, by hitting a pair of three-run homers.

Notable Achievements

- Hit at least 20 home runs 11 times, topping 30 homers six times and 40 homers once.
- Knocked in more than 100 runs five times, topping 120 RBIs once.
- Scored more than 100 runs four times.
- Batted over .300 three times.
- Surpassed 30 doubles three times.
- Stole more than 20 bases twice, topping 30 thefts once.
- Drew more than 100 bases on balls once.
- Compiled on-base percentage over .400 once.
- Posted slugging percentage over .500 seven times.
- Posted OPS over .900 four times.
- Hit three home runs in one game vs. San Francisco Giants on May 18, 1979.
- Led NL in home runs twice, RBIs twice, runs scored once, extra-base hits once, total bases once, bases on balls once, slugging percentage twice, OPS once, games played four times, and plate appearances once.
- Led NL center fielders in assists once and double plays turned twice.
- Led NL right fielders in putouts twice, assists once, and double plays turned once.
- Ranks among Braves career leaders in home runs (4th), RBIs (4th), runs scored (6th), hits (6th), doubles (6th), extra-base hits (5th), total bases (4th), bases on balls (4th), sacrifice flies (5th), games played (4th), plate appearances (4th), and at-bats (4th).
- Four-time NL Player of the Week.
- Six-time NL Player of the Month.
- Four-time Silver Slugger Award winner (1982, 1983, 1984, and 1985).
- Five-time Gold Glove Award winner (1982, 1983, 1984, 1985, and 1986).
- Two-time NL MVP (1982 and 1983).
- Finished in top 10 of NL MVP voting two other times (1984 and 1985).
- Seven-time NL All-Star selection (1980, 1982, 1983, 1984, 1985, 1986, and 1987).
- Four-time *Sporting News* All-Star selection (1982, 1983, 1984, and 1985).
- #3 retired by Braves.
- Member of Braves Hall of Fame.

10
PHIL NIEKRO

One of only 13 pitchers to win as many as 300 games since the so-called Dead Ball Era ended some 100 years ago, Phil Niekro spent parts of 21 seasons with the Braves, appearing in more games than any other hurler in franchise history. Ranking extremely high in team annals in virtually every pitching category, Niekro, who became known to his teammates as "Knucksie" due to his reliance on his patented knuckleball, won at least 20 games three times, compiled an ERA under 3.00 seven times, recorded more than 200 strikeouts on three separate occasions, and threw more than 300 innings and 20 complete games four times each during his time in Milwaukee and Atlanta, before spending most of his last four years in the majors competing in the AL. A four-time NL All-Star, Niekro also earned three top-five finishes in the Cy Young voting, one top-10 finish in the MVP balloting, and five Gold Gloves, before being further honored by having his #35 retired by the Braves and gaining induction into the Baseball Hall of Fame.

Born in Blaine, Ohio, on April 1, 1939, Philip Henry Niekro Jr. grew up in nearby Lansing, where he learned how to throw the knuckleball from his father, a coal miner and former semiprofessional pitcher. The grandson of Polish Russian immigrants, Niekro became close childhood friends with future NBA star John Havlicek, who often helped him practice the knuckler in his backyard by serving as his catcher.

Looking back on his early years, Niekro said, "I had a great connection with my family. My father was a coal miner. He took me fishing and hunting. There was a lot of love in our family. We went to church every Sunday together. I went to play bingo with my mother on Fridays. We did everything as a group. They supported me every step along the way."

Niekro added, "My father taught the knuckleball to me in the backyard. I didn't know what it was or anything, he showed me how to hold it, and we'd just play knuckleball in the backyard."

Eventually developing into a standout athlete at Bridgeport High School, Niekro played varsity baseball, basketball, and football, excelling in particular on the diamond, where he won 17 of his 18 mound decisions. Offered numerous athletic scholarships, Niekro chose instead to pitch for several local teams in the hope that he might be discovered by a major-league scout. Finally taking matters into his own hands, Niekro attended a Milwaukee Braves tryout camp in nearby Bellaire, Ohio, where he performed well enough to receive a contract offer worth $275 a month.

Revealing that his father handled all contract negotiations for him, Niekro stated, "My dad said, 'It's nice you want my son to play professional baseball, but before he does, we have to sit down here and make a little deal.' I got $500 as a signing bonus. . . . My greatest thrill in baseball was signing my first major-league contract in our kitchen, with my father and mother, my brother Joe, and my sister Phyllis present. July 19, 1958—I became a professional."

Beginning his pro career with Class D Wellsville (New York) in the spring of 1959, Niekro struggled early on, prompting manager Harry Minor to call him into his office one day and inform him that the club planned to release him. Recalling his thoughts at the time, Niekro said, "The first thing I thought about was that I was going to end up like my dad, in a coal mine. Or in a steel mill. I had my chance, and I screwed it up. So, I just sat there and finally said, 'I'm not going! Harry, I need to play, I just need to play!'"

Meanwhile, John Havlicek remembered, "He didn't want to go back to the mines, he didn't want to disappoint his dad. Phil says he'll shine shoes, cut grass, clean bases, anything to stay with the club. And the manager agreed to give Phil a second chance."

Sent to one of the Braves' other Class D teams, Niekro began a long climb up the organizational ladder that included stops at Jacksonville, Austin, and Louisville, performing well in each city, before spending the 1963 season pitching for the Fort Knox Army team while serving in the military. Finally arriving in Milwaukee in 1964, Niekro appeared in 10 games with the Braves during the early stages of the campaign, before being sent down to Triple-A Denver, where, for the first time as a professional, he assumed the role of a starter.

Oddly enough, when Niekro rejoined the Braves in 1965, he spent almost all his time working out of the bullpen, compiling a record of 2-3 and an ERA of 2.89 in 41 appearances and 75 innings of work. Niekro subsequently split the ensuing campaign between the Braves and their Triple-A affiliate in Richmond, going 4-3 with a 4.11 ERA for the parent club,

Phil Niekro appeared in more games than any other pitcher in franchise history.
Courtesy of RMYAuctions.com

before arriving in Atlanta to stay in 1967. Performing extremely well for the Braves as both a starter and a reliever, Niekro compiled a record of 11-9, completed 10 of his 20 starts, saved nine games, struck out 129 batters in 207 innings, and led all NL hurlers with an ERA of 1.87.

Inserted into the Braves' starting rotation full-time in 1968, Niekro had a solid season, going 14-12, with a 2.59 ERA, five shutouts, 15 complete games, and 140 strikeouts in 256 2/3 innings of work. Niekro followed that up by compiling a record of 23-13, an ERA of 2.56, and a WHIP of 1.027, striking out 193 batters, and throwing 21 complete games and 284 1/3 innings for the division-winning Braves in 1969, earning in the process his first All-Star selection and a runner-up finish to Tom Seaver in the NL Cy Young voting.

Pitching for mostly mediocre Braves teams the next few years, Niekro typically lost nearly as many games as he won, posting an overall record of

56-54 from 1970 to 1973. However, Niekro re-established himself as one of the NL's elite pitchers in 1974, earning a third-place finish in the Cy Young balloting by going 20-13, with a 2.38 ERA, 195 strikeouts, six shutouts, and a league-leading 18 complete games and 302 1/3 innings pitched.

Employing a sidearm motion, the right-handed-throwing Niekro, who stood 6'1" and weighed close to 190 pounds, depended almost exclusively on the knuckleball to retire opposing batters, once saying, "I never knew how to throw a fastball, never learned how to throw a curveball, a slider, split-finger, whatever they're throwing nowadays. I was a one-pitch pitcher."

Yet, with Niekro's signature pitch fluttering toward home plate in an unpredictable manner that confounded even the league's best hitters, it proved to be enough to allow him to navigate his way through opposing lineups.

In trying to describe the movement of Niekro's knuckler, Willie Stargell said, "Phil Niekro's knuckleball is like a butterfly with hiccups."

Claiming that facing Niekro completely upset his timing at the plate, Pete Rose stated, "I work for three weeks to get my swing down pat, and Phil messes it up in one night. . . . Trying to hit that thing is a miserable way to make a living."

Meanwhile, Don Zimmer said of the pitch that forced catchers to wear an oversized mitt, "It's pretty hard to hit a ball that the catcher can't even catch."

With the Braves posting just one winning record from 1975 to 1981, Niekro did not fare much better, compiling a composite mark of just 110-109 during that same period. Nevertheless, he pitched better than his overall record would seem to indicate, earning two more All-Star selections and two sixth-place finishes in the NL Cy Young voting. Particularly effective in 1976 and 1978, Niekro finished 17-11 with a 3.29 ERA for the last-place Braves in the first of those campaigns, before ranking among the NL leaders with 19 wins and 248 strikeouts, while also leading the league with 22 complete games and 334 1/3 innings pitched two years later. One of the game's most durable pitchers, Niekro led the NL in complete games and innings pitched three straight times from 1977 to 1979, completing more than 20 of his starts and throwing more than 330 innings in each of those seasons.

Pitching for a contending team once again in 1982, Niekro helped the Braves capture the NL West title by going 17-4 with a 3.61 ERA, although, at 43 years of age, he proved to be less of a workhorse, throwing "just" 234 1/3 innings and four complete games. Less effective in 1983, Niekro won just 11 of his 21 decisions, compiled an ERA of 3.97, threw only 201 2/3 innings, recorded fewer strikeouts, and issued more bases on balls, causing an article to appear in the *Atlanta Constitution* a few days after the season ended claiming that the Braves intended to part ways with the game's oldest player.

Elaborating further on the team's plans, *Constitution* sports editor Jesse Outlar wrote, "When [Joe] Torre came back to manage the team that Niekro also would have liked to manage, there was speculation of friction. Though Niekro resented being pulled in the late innings by Torre, there was no verbal clash between them."

In a follow-up story the next day, Chris Mortensen wrote, "Niekro confirmed that he had been encouraged to retire. He declined and was granted a request to put him on waivers for the purpose of giving him his unconditional release. While the decision had been unanimous at a September 25 staff meeting that Niekro should retire, it was primarily the decision of Torre and Bob Gibson, his pitching coach."

Braves owner Ted Turner, a longtime supporter of Niekro, gave his pitcher the option of returning to the team. But Niekro decided that the time had come for him to leave Atlanta, telling Turner, "I can't go back to the Braves under those conditions," and informing the press, "It was a wonderful marriage for 24 years, but now we are divorced and neither one of us is unhappy. In brief, the Braves wanted me to retire, but I want to pitch another season or so."

Recalling his feelings at the time, Niekro later said, "I was born a Brave, and I wanted to die a Brave. I had my mind set on that. And that was the longest damn day I had in my life. The most depressing day in my life was that day."

Niekro subsequently signed with the Yankees, with whom he spent the next two seasons posting a total of 32 victories, the last of which made him a member of the select 300 Win Club. Meanwhile, on August 6, 1984, an off day for the Yankees, the Braves honored Niekro with a 40-minute pregame ceremony during which they retired his #35 and presented him with a replica of the statue of himself that they planned to erect outside Atlanta-Fulton County Stadium.

Released by the Yankees prior to the start of the 1986 campaign, Niekro spent most of the next two seasons with the Cleveland Indians, winning another 18 games, before signing a $1 contract with the Braves on September 23, 1987, that allowed him to officially retire as a member of the team. Over parts of 24 big-league seasons, Niekro started 716 contests, compiled a record of 318-274, an ERA of 3.35, and a WHIP of 1.268, threw 245 complete games and 45 shutouts, struck out 3,342 batters in 5,404 innings of work, and collected 29 saves, with his 716 starts, 5,404 innings pitched, and 3,342 strikeouts all placing him among MLB's all-time leaders. An outstanding fielder who won five Gold Gloves over the course of his career, Niekro also amassed the fourth-most putouts of any pitcher in MLB history. In addition to holding the Braves career record for most pitching appearances (740), Niekro, who compiled an ERA of 3.20 and a WHIP of 1.229 as a member of the team, ranks among the franchise's all-time leaders in wins (268), strikeouts (2,912), shutouts (43), innings pitched (4,622 1/3), complete games (226), and starts (595).

Some six years after Niekro retired as an active player, he began a four-year stint as manager of the Colorado Silver Bullets, an all-women's baseball team. While serving in that capacity, Niekro gained induction into the Baseball Hall of Fame, being voted in by the members of the BBWAA in 1997, his fifth year of eligibility. One of the more active and visible Hall of Fame members in the years that followed, Niekro served on the Hall's Board of Directors and as a member of the Veterans Committee until a diagnosis of cancer forced him to adopt a more sedentary lifestyle. Finally losing his battle with the dreaded disease on December 27, 2020, Niekro passed away at his home in Flowery Branch, Georgia, at the age of 81.

Following his passing, the Braves issued a press release that read: "We are heartbroken on the passing of our treasured friend, Phil Niekro. Knucksie was woven into the Braves fabric, first in Milwaukee and then in Atlanta. Phil baffled batters on the field and later was always the first to join in our community activities. It was during those community and fan activities where he would communicate with fans as if they were long lost friends. He was a constant presence over the years, in our clubhouse, our alumni activities, and throughout Braves Country, and we will forever be grateful for having him be such an important part of our organization."

BRAVES CAREER HIGHLIGHTS

Best Season

Although Niekro pitched exceptionally well for the Braves in 1969, he performed slightly better in 1974, when he earned a third-place finish in the Cy Young voting by leading all NL hurlers with 20 victories, 18 complete games, and 302 1/3 innings pitched, while also finishing second in ERA (2.38), WHIP (1.115), and shutouts (6), and fourth in strikeouts (195).

Memorable Moments/Greatest Performances

Niekro outdueled Philadelphia's Rick Wise on June 13, 1967, allowing just two hits and three walks during a 1–0 Braves win.

Niekro allowed just two men to reach base during an 11–2 win over the Cincinnati Reds on September 5, 1969, recording 10 strikeouts and retiring every batter he faced after Alex Johnson walked and Tony Pérez homered in the bottom of the first inning.

Niekro hurled another gem on April 26, 1970, striking out seven, issuing one walk, and yielding just a seventh-inning single to Manny Sanguillén and an eighth-inning single to Matty Alou during a 2–0 shutout of the hard-hitting Pittsburgh Pirates.

Niekro tossed another two-hit shutout on July 25, 1970, recording eight strikeouts and allowing just a pair of harmless singles by Billy Williams during a 9–0 win over the Cubs.

Niekro threw a no-hitter on August 5, 1973, walking three batters and recording four strikeouts during a 9–0 win over the San Diego Padres.

Although Niekro issued five bases on balls during a 3–0 shutout of the Reds on October 2, 1976, he also recorded nine strikeouts and allowed just one hit, holding the Big Red Machine hitless until the bottom of the ninth inning, when César Gerónimo doubled to left with one man out.

Niekro turned in another dominant performance on June 9, 1977, yielding just four hits, walking one batter, and recording a career-high 13 strikeouts during a 3–0 shutout of the Phillies.

Niekro surrendered just two hits, struck out seven, and issued one walk during an 8–0 shutout of the Pirates on July 23, 1979, allowing only a first-inning single by Dave Parker and an eighth-inning double by catcher Steve Nicosia.

Niekro again yielded just two hits during a 2–0 shutout of the Astros on July 14, 1980, surrendering only a third-inning double by J. R. Richard and a ninth-inning single by Joe Morgan, while also recording 11 strikeouts and walking three batters.

Niekro threw another two-hit shutout on May 12, 1981, yielding just a pair of harmless singles to second baseman Phil Garner and catcher Tony Peña during a 2–0 win over the Pirates.

In addition to allowing just three hits during a 4–0 win over the Padres on October 1, 1982, Niekro homered with one man aboard in the top of the eighth inning.

Notable Achievements

- Won at least 20 games three times, surpassing 17 victories on three other occasions.
- Posted winning percentage over .600 four times, topping .800-mark once.
- Compiled ERA under 3.00 seven times, posting mark under 2.00 once.
- Recorded more than 200 strikeouts three times.
- Threw more than 300 innings four times, tossing more than 250 frames seven other times.
- Threw at least 20 complete games four times.
- Threw 30.2 consecutive scoreless innings in 1974.
- Threw no-hitter vs. San Diego Padres on August 5, 1973.
- Led NL pitchers in wins twice, winning percentage once, ERA once, strikeouts once, innings pitched four times, complete games four times, putouts three times, and starts four times.
- Ranks among MLB all-time leaders in strikeouts (11th), innings pitched (4th), and starts (5th).
- Holds Braves career record for most pitching appearances (740).
- Ranks among Braves career leaders in wins (3rd), strikeouts (2nd), shutouts (3rd), innings pitched (2nd), complete games (tied for 5th), and games started (2nd).
- Three-time NL Player of the Week.
- Five-time Gold Glove Award winner.
- Finished in top five of NL Cy Young voting three times, placing as high as second in 1969.
- Finished ninth in 1969 NL MVP voting.
- Four-time NL All-Star selection (1969, 1975, 1978, and 1982).
- #35 retired by Braves.
- Member of Braves Hall of Fame.
- Elected to Baseball Hall of Fame by members of BBWAA in 1997.

11

ANDRUW JONES

dentified by longtime Braves manager Bobby Cox and Hall of Fame pitchers John Smoltz and Tom Glavine as the best defensive player any of them ever saw, Andruw Jones spent parts of 12 seasons patrolling center field for the Braves, performing so brilliantly in the field that he often drew comparisons to Willie Mays. The winner of 10 consecutive Gold Gloves for his magnificent play in center, Jones used his speed and superb instincts to lead all NL outfielders in putouts six times, making several spectacular catches along the way that left opponents shaking their heads. An extremely capable hitter as well, Jones hit more than 30 homers seven times, knocked in more than 100 runs five times, and batted over .300 once, with his 51 homers in 2005 setting a single-season franchise record that still stands. Also an excellent baserunner early in his career, Jones scored more than 100 runs and stole at least 20 bases four times each, with his outstanding all-around play earning him five NL All-Star selections, two *Sporting News* All-Star nominations, and two top-10 finishes in the league MVP voting. A member of teams that won 10 division titles and two pennants, Jones later received the additional honor of being inducted into the Braves Hall of Fame.

Born in Willemstad, Curacao, on April 23, 1977, Andruw Rudolf Jones grew up on the tiny island nation, which is part of the Kingdom of the Netherlands, some 37 miles off the northern coast of Venezuela and about 70 miles east of Aruba. Jones, whose father, Henry, had been one of the island's best baseball players during the 1960s and 1970s, displayed a similar affinity for the sport at an early age, excelling on a youth team that traveled to Japan for a tournament shortly after he celebrated his 11th birthday.

After spending his formative years catching and playing third base, Jones moved to the outfield as a teenager, establishing himself before long as the most talented player on the island. Often competing against grown men, Jones more than held his own, even playing for Curacao's national team in the Latin American Games. Signed by the Braves as a free agent at only 16 years of age in 1993, Jones spent just one month with their minor-league affiliate in West Palm Beach, Florida, before being promoted to Danville of the Appalachian League. Named the number two prospect in the Appy League by *Baseball America* after batting .336 and stealing 16 bases in 36 games and 143 at-bats with Danville, Jones subsequently spent the 1995 campaign with Macon in the South Atlantic League, for whom he hit 25 homers, collected 41 doubles, stole 56 bases, and batted .277, while also earning the title of Best Defensive Outfielder in the circuit.

While at Macon, Jones made an extremely favorable impression on his manager, Nelson Norman, who told *Baseball America*, "He (Jones) just has so much natural ability. There is something there that you don't see at his age. You look at him and you can see something there that other players don't have."

Ranked as the number one prospect in all of baseball by that same publication heading into 1996, Jones proved himself worthy of that distinction by performing exceptionally well while advancing through three levels of the Braves' farm system. Perhaps Jones surprised even himself, though, when, after posting a composite batting average of .339 and totaling 34 homers, 92 RBIs, 115 runs scored, and 30 steals while splitting the season's first few months between High-A Durham, Double-A Greenville, and Triple-A Richmond, he received his first callup to the parent club in mid-August. Making his big-league debut just four months past his 19th birthday, Jones struggled somewhat at the plate over the season's final six weeks, batting just .217, although he managed to hit five homers and drive in 13 runs in only 31 games. But Jones then gave a preview of what lay ahead, when, after homering once and driving in three runs during Atlanta's seven-game victory over St. Louis in the NLCS, he reached the seats twice, knocked in six runs, and batted .400 against the Yankees in the World Series.

Named the Braves' starting right fielder prior to the start of the 1997 campaign, Jones spent much of the year manning that post, before moving to center field full-time during the season's second half. Posting respectable numbers on offense, Jones earned a fifth-place finish in the NL Rookie of the Year voting by hitting 18 homers, driving in 70 runs, scoring 60 times, stealing 20 bases, and batting .231.

Emerging as one of the premier players at his position the following year, Jones hit 31 homers, knocked in 90 runs, scored 89 others, stole 27 bases, batted .271, and compiled an OPS of .836, although his 40 walks and 129 strikeouts left something to be desired. Meanwhile, Jones won the first of his 10 consecutive Gold Gloves by leading all NL outfielders in

Andruw Jones's 51 homers in 2005 represent a single-season franchise record.
Courtesy of Kenji Takabayashi

putouts for the first of five straight times and collecting a league-high 20 outfield assists. Jones performed well once again in 1999, concluding the campaign with 26 homers, 84 RBIs, 97 runs scored, 24 steals, a batting average of .275, and an OPS of .848, before beginning an outstanding seven-year run during which he posted the following numbers:

YEAR	HR	RBI	RUNS	AVG	OBP	SLG	OPS
2000	36	104	122	.303	.366	.541	.907
2001	34	104	104	.251	.312	.461	.772
2002	35	94	91	,.264	.366	.513	.878
2003	36	116	101	.277	.338	.513	.851

2004	29	91	85	.261	.345	.488	.833
2005	**51**	**128**	95	.263	.347	.575	.922
2006	41	129	107	.262	.363	.531	.894

In addition to surpassing 30 homers in all but one of those seasons, Jones topped 100 RBIs five times and 100 runs scored four times, earning in the process five All-Star selections and two top-10 finishes in the NL MVP voting. Particularly outstanding in 2005 after increasing his workout regimen and following the advice of Willie Mays, who suggested that he widen his batting stance, Jones became the first player in franchise history to reach the 50-homer plateau, with his strong performance earning him a close second-place finish to Albert Pujols in the MVP balloting. Meanwhile, the Braves won the division title in each of the first six seasons, although they advanced beyond the opening round of the postseason tournament just once.

The right-handed-hitting Jones, who possessed a lean 6'1" frame when he first arrived in Atlanta, gradually bulked up to 225 pounds, allowing him to increase his power at the plate. Although Jones possessed good power to all fields, he pulled the ball most of the time, choosing to sacrifice contact and a higher batting average for greater home-run production. Somewhat of a free-swinger, Jones drew as many as 70 bases on balls just five times his entire career, while striking out more than 100 times on 11 separate occasions. And, as Jones grew in size, he lost some of his speed, never again finishing in double-digits in stolen bases after swiping more than 20 bags in each of his first four seasons.

Nevertheless, Jones retained his extraordinary ball-hawking skills, establishing himself as the finest defensive player in the game at his position, as Houston Astros slugger Lance Berkman acknowledged when he said, "I don't think there's any argument—he's the best center fielder in the game."

Expressing similar sentiments, Tom Glavine stated, "With all due respect to Willie Mays, who I never saw play, Andruw Jones is the best defensive center fielder of our generation."

Capable of running down balls hit to the outfield gaps or tracking down long flyballs hit well over his head, Jones gathered in virtually everything hit in the air to center field, prompting Braves teammate Greg Maddux to suggest, "Andruw has got to save each starter 10 runs a year."

In discussing Jones's ability to go back on a ball, former announcer Tim McCarver stated, "You cannot hit a ball over his head. If the ball's over his head, it's out of the ballpark."

Although Jones hit 26 homers, knocked in 94 runs, and won his 10th consecutive Gold Glove in 2007, he batted just .222, beginning in the process a dramatic decline in overall production that defined the rest of his career. A free agent at season's end, Jones signed a two-year, $36 million deal with the Dodgers, ending his lengthy association with the Braves. During his time in Atlanta, Jones hit 368 homers, knocked in 1,117 runs, scored 1,045 times, collected 1,683 hits, 330 doubles, and 34 triples, stole 138 bases, batted .263, compiled a .342 on-base percentage, and posted a .497 slugging percentage.

Despite being only 31 years of age when he joined the Dodgers, Jones never came close to living up to the terms of his contract. Hampered by two sore knees and a 25-pound increase in weight, Jones spent just one season in Los Angeles, hitting three homers, driving in 14 runs, and batting an embarrassing .158 in a part-time role, before being released at the end of the year. Jones subsequently split the next four seasons between the Rangers, White Sox, and Yankees, failing to hit more than 19 homers or bat any higher than .247 while serving all three teams as a part-time player. A free agent at the end of 2012, Jones signed with the Tohoku Rakuten Golden Eagles of the Japan Pacific League, with whom he spent the next two seasons, before announcing his retirement following a pair of unsuccessful comeback attempts in the States. Prior to departing for Japan, though, Jones ran afoul of the law, being arrested for battery on the morning of Christmas Day, 2012, after police officers responded to a domestic disturbance call made by his wife, Nicole, who filed for divorce shortly thereafter.

Jones, who, over parts of 17 big-league seasons, hit 434 homers, knocked in 1,289 runs, scored 1,204 times, collected 1,933 hits, 383 doubles, and 36 triples, stole 152 bases, batted .254, compiled an on-base percentage of .337, and posted a slugging percentage of .486, returned to Atlanta following the conclusion of his playing career to serve the Braves as a special assistant to baseball operations, a position he currently holds.

BRAVES CAREER HIGHLIGHTS

Best Season

Although Jones established career-high marks with 122 runs scored, 199 hits, 36 doubles, and a batting average of .303 in 2000, he had what is generally considered to be his signature season in 2005, when he gained recognition from the *Sporting News* as that publication's Major League Player of the Year and earned a second-place finish in the NL MVP balloting by leading the league with 51 homers and 128 RBIs, scoring 95 runs, batting .263, and ranking among the circuit leaders with 337 total bases and a .575 slugging percentage.

Memorable Moments/Greatest Performances

Jones became the youngest player ever to hit a home run in the World Series when he homered twice, knocked in five runs, and scored three times during a 12–1 rout of the Yankees in Game 1 of the 1996 Fall Classic. By homering in each of his first two plate appearances, Jones also joined Oakland's Gene Tenace (1972) as the only players to accomplish the feat in World Series play.

Jones helped lead the Braves to a 20–5 mauling of the Colorado Rockies on April 18, 1999, by going 5-for-6, with a homer, triple, six RBIs, and two runs scored.

After hitting a solo home run earlier in the contest, Jones delivered the decisive blow of a 10–7 win over the Yankees on July 16, 1999, when he homered off Mariano Rivera in the top of the ninth inning with two men out and two men on.

Jones led the Braves to a 7–1 victory over the Phillies on September 25, 2002, by homering three times and driving in four runs, reaching the seats twice against starter Brett Myers and once against righty reliever Jose Santiago.

Jones contributed to a lopsided 14–5 victory over the Cardinals on July 18, 2006, by going 5-for-5, with two homers, a double, six RBIs, and three runs scored.

Jones gave the Braves a 5–2 win over the Phillies on April 30, 2007, when he homered off Antonio Alfonseca with two men on base in the bottom of the ninth inning

Notable Achievements

- Hit more than 20 home runs 10 times, topping 30 homers seven times and 40 homers twice.
- Knocked in more than 100 runs five times, topping 120 RBIs twice.
- Scored more than 100 runs four times.
- Batted over .300 once.
- Surpassed 30 doubles five times.
- Stole at least 20 bases four times.

- Posted slugging percentage over .500 six times.
- Posted OPS over .900 twice.
- Hit three home runs in one game vs. Philadelphia Phillies on September 25, 2002.
- Led NL with 51 home runs and 128 RBIs in 2005.
- Led NL outfielders in putouts six times, assists once, and double plays turned once.
- Led NL center fielders in putouts six times, assists three times, and double plays turned twice.
- Holds Braves single-season record for most home runs (51 in 2005).
- Ranks among Braves career leaders in home runs (5th), RBIs (5th), runs scored (7th), hits (9th), doubles (5th), extra-base hits (4th), total bases (5th), bases on balls (7th), sacrifice flies (3rd), games played (6th), plate appearances (8th), and at-bats (8th).
- Two-time NL champion (1996 and 1999).
- Four-time NL Player of the Week.
- Two-time NL Player of the Month.
- 2005 Silver Slugger Award winner.
- 10-time Gold Glove Award winner (1998, 1999, 2000, 2001, 2002, 2003, 2004, 2005, 2006, and 2007).
- Finished in top 10 of NL MVP voting twice, placing second in 2005.
- Five-time NL All-Star selection (2000, 2002, 2003, 2005, and 2006).
- Two-time *Sporting News* All-Star selection (2005 and 2006).
- 2005 *Sporting News* Major League Player of the Year.
- Member of Braves Hall of Fame.

12

WALLY BERGER

One of the National League's top sluggers for much of the 1930s, Wally Berger spent parts of eight seasons in Boston, proving to be a one-man wrecking crew during that time. Playing for mostly losing ballclubs, Berger typically hit nearly half the home runs the Braves managed as a team, annually ranking among the league leaders in that category. A complete hitter, Berger, who surpassed 30 homers on three separate occasions, also knocked in more than 100 runs and batted over .300 four times each, despite receiving very little protection from the rest of the Braves' lineup. A good defensive outfielder as well, Berger did an excellent job for the Braves in center field, with his outstanding all-around play earning him four All-Star nominations and two top-10 finishes in the NL MVP voting, before an ailing shoulder brought his days as a dominant hitter to a premature end.

Born in Chicago, Illinois, on October 10, 1905, Walter Anton Berger grew up in the Mission District of San Francisco after his family moved there in 1910. The son of German immigrants, Berger displayed an affinity for baseball at an early age, excelling on the local sandlots, before starring at third base for Mission High School. Although Berger dropped out of school after his junior year to help support his family, he retained his interest in baseball, recalling in his posthumously published 1993 memoir, *Freshly Remember'd*, "I was out of school but still very much interested in baseball. I decided I wanted to be a ball player, but I also believed I should go to work to help out with my family. I was reading about all those 16-and 17-year-old kids signing up."

Assuming numerous jobs the next few years, Berger worked as a carpenter's helper, a cargo stenciler at Pier 42 on the San Francisco waterfront, a truck driver, and a glass door glazer for the Nicolai Door Company. All the while, though, Berger continued to prepare himself for an eventual career in baseball by competing in several local semipro leagues, playing at different times for the San Carlos Athletic Club, the Woodmen of America,

Wally Berger carried the Braves' offense for much of the 1930s.
Courtesy of Boston Public Library, Leslie Jones Collection

and the Bertillion Hatters. Finally choosing to turn pro in 1926, Berger turned down a promotion to shipping clerk at Nicolai that would have paid him $45 a week, so that he might report to spring training with the San Francisco Seals of the Pacific Coast League.

After one year in San Francisco, Berger spent most of 1927 with Pocatello of the Utah-Idaho League, for whom he batted .385 and hit 24 home runs in only 92 games while transitioning to the outfield. Returning to the PCL the following year, Berger spent the next two seasons starring for the Los Angeles Angels, performing especially well in 1929, when he hit 40 homers, drove in 166 runs, scored 170 times, collected 249 hits, and batted .335. Nevertheless, with the Cubs owning his rights and boasting a starting outfield that included perennial .300 hitter Riggs Stephenson and future Hall of Famers Hack Wilson and Kiki Cuyler, Berger did not receive an opportunity to compete at the major-league level until the Braves sent pitcher Art Delaney, outfielder George Harper, and cash to Los Angeles in exchange for his services.

Tendered a $4,500 contract for 1930 by the Braves, Berger chose not to sign at first, remembering, "I held out immediately. They said, 'We're giving you the standard increase over your minor league salary. You come up and show us what you can do and then we'll talk about what you can get the second year.' I finally agreed. They said I'd have to prove myself, so, with that thought in mind, I went to spring training."

Proving his worth to the Braves after laying claim to the team's starting left field job, Berger took the NL by storm, setting major-league rookie records that stood for years by hitting 38 homers and driving in 119 runs, with his 38 round-trippers representing an astounding 58 percent of his team's total. Berger also finished his debut season with 98 runs scored, 14 triples, a .310 batting average, an OPS of .990, and more putouts than any other player at his position. With the NL's experimentation with a livelier ball ending in 1931, Berger, as was the case with virtually every other player in the league, compiled less impressive power numbers. Nevertheless, after moving to center field, he had another extremely productive season, finishing third in the circuit with 19 homers, driving in 84 runs, scoring 94 times, and establishing career-high marks with 199 hits, 44 doubles, a batting average of .323, and an on-base percentage of .380. Berger followed that up by hitting 17 homers, knocking in 73 runs, scoring 90 times, and batting .307 in 1932, before beginning an outstanding four-year run during which he posted the following numbers:

YEAR	HR	RBI	RUNS	AVG	OBP	SLG	OPS
1933	27	106	84	.313	.365	.566	.932
1934	34	121	92	.298	.352	.546	.899
1935	34	130	91	.295	.355	.548	.903
1936	25	91	88	.288	.361	.483	.844

In addition to consistently ranking among the NL leaders in homers and RBIs, Berger annually placed near the top of the league rankings in doubles, total bases, slugging percentage, and OPS. Berger also twice led all NL center fielders in putouts, with his outstanding all-around play earning him four consecutive All-Star selections and two top-10 finishes in the NL MVP balloting.

The right-handed-hitting Berger, who stood 6'2" and weighed 200 pounds, possessed a muscular physique and powerful forearms that enabled him to drive the ball deep to all parts of the ballpark, making him one of the most feared sluggers in the senior circuit. More than just a home-run hitter, Berger proved to be a veritable "doubles machine," amassing at least 34 two-baggers five straight times from 1931 to 1935, while also accumulating more than 300 total bases on four separate occasions. Making the numbers Berger compiled that much more impressive is the fact that he had virtually no protection in the batting order, allowing opposing pitchers to frequently pitch around him. Indeed, from 1930 to 1935, Berger hit 45 percent of the home runs the Braves collected as a team.

In discussing the degree to which Berger carried the Braves' offense during his time in Boston, noted sportswriter and author Al Hirshberg stated, "For four years, Wally Berger had been the Braves' only claim to fame. Berger could do everything, but his real strength was his big bat . . . no matter how badly the Braves were doing, Berger, single-handed, could keep some customers coming in."

Unfortunately, Berger suffered an injury to his shoulder in 1936 that limited him to 138 games and ultimately ended his period of dominance. Able to appear in only 30 games the first two months of the ensuing campaign, Berger hit just five homers and knocked in only 22 runs, before being dealt to the Giants on June 15, 1937, for pitcher Frank Gabler and $35,000. Berger, who left the Braves having hit 199 homers, driven in 746 runs, scored 651 times, collected 1,263 hits, 248 doubles, and 52 triples, batted .304, compiled an on-base percentage of .362, and posted a slugging percentage of .533 as a member of the team, homered more times (105) in Braves Field than any other player in history.

Unable to regain his stroke after leaving Boston, Berger spent the next three-and-a-half years assuming part-time roles with the Giants, Reds, and Phillies, experiencing his greatest success in Cincinnati in 1938, when, in 99 games, he hit 16 homers, knocked in 56 runs, and batted .307. Released by the Phillies midway through the 1940 campaign, the 34-year-old Berger briefly played for Indianapolis in the American Association, before retiring as an active player after spending part of 1941 with his former Pacific Coast League team, the Los Angeles Angels. Reflecting back on his final days in the game, Berger said, "My heart wasn't in it anymore after being in the big leagues. Going up was fine, but going down, no."

Berger, who over the course of his major-league career, hit 242 homers, knocked in 898 runs, scored 809 times, collected 1,550 hits, 299 doubles, and 59 triples, batted an even .300, compiled an on-base percentage of

.359, and posted a slugging percentage of .522, subsequently spent nearly four years serving as a baseball coach at the Naval Air Training Station in San Diego during World War II, before scouting for the Giants and Yankees for a few years following his discharge in October 1945.

Leaving baseball for good in 1950, Berger returned to Manhattan Beach, California, where he spent several years handling disposition of aircraft parts for the Norair Division of Northrop Corporation. He also later served as a staff member of the Aviation Technician's School at Northrop Institute of Technology in Inglewood, California. Retiring to private life in 1970, Berger subsequently devoted most of his time to speaking engagements and baseball ceremonials, before passing away at the age of 83 on November 30, 1988, shortly after suffering a stroke.

Summing up Berger's career in his introduction to *Freshly Remember'd*, George Morris Snyder wrote: "Berger was modest, quiet, hard-working, conscientious, and disciplined. He didn't kick dirt on umpires, become engaged in scandal, or engage in wacky behavior. He didn't make good copy for the boys in the press box. In his prime, he played in a 'pitchers park' with a team that never came close to winning all the marbles. It was a club out of the mainstream. It was inadequately financed, poorly administered, and usually overmatched on the field. Despite all this, the Braves were always an interesting team, a team that had its great moments. They were led by the best manager of the times and supported by devoted and hopeful fans. And for seven seasons their most brilliant, courageous, and persevering player was Walter Anton Berger."

BRAVES CAREER HIGHLIGHTS

Best Season

Berger played at a Hall of Fame level much of his time in Boston, hitting more than 30 homers three times, while also driving in more than 100 runs and batting over .300 four times each. But, forced to identify one season as the finest of his career, I elected to go with 1935, since Berger earned a sixth-place finish in the NL MVP voting by batting .295, scoring 91 runs, leading the league with 34 homers and 130 RBIs, ranking among the leaders with 39 doubles, 323 total bases, a slugging percentage of .548, and an OPS of .903, and amassing more putouts (458) than any other outfielder in the senior circuit.

Memorable Moments/Greatest Performances

Berger made the first home run of his career a memorable one, homering with the bases loaded off starter Watty Clark in the seventh inning of a 7–2 win over Brooklyn on April 20, 1930.

Berger tied a major-league record by collecting four outfield assists during a 2–0 win over the Phillies on April 27, 1931.

Berger had the only five-hit game of his career on September 11, 1931, when he went 5-for-5, with one RBI and three runs scored during a 6–3 win over the Cardinals.

Berger helped lead the Braves to a 6–3 victory over the Phillies on April 29, 1933, by homering twice and driving in four runs, with his three-run blast in the bottom of the eighth inning providing the winning margin.

Berger knocked in all four runs the Braves scored during a 4–3 win over the Cardinals on August 23, 1933, with a pair of homers off St. Louis starter Tex Carleton.

Berger delivered the big blow of a 4–1 win over the Phillies on October 1, 1933, when he hit a pinch-hit grand slam home run in the bottom of the seventh inning.

Berger helped lead the Braves to an 8–6 win over the Phillies on May 29, 1935, by driving in a career-high six runs with a first-inning bases loaded single and a second-inning grand slam.

Berger proved to be the difference in an 8–3 win over the Reds on June 17, 1935, breaking the game open with a two-run homer in the bottom of the seventh inning, before reaching the seats again with two men aboard in the ensuing frame.

Berger continued his assault on Cincinnati pitching on July 23, 1935, homering twice and knocking in five runs during a 7–6 Braves win, with his solo blast in the top of the 12th inning providing the margin of victory.

Notable Achievements

- Hit more than 20 home runs five times, topping 30 homers on three occasions.
- Knocked in more than 100 runs four times, topping 120 RBIs twice.
- Batted over .300 four times.
- Finished in double digits in triples once.
- Surpassed 30 doubles five times, amassing more than 40 two-baggers once.

- Posted slugging percentage over .500 five times, topping .600-mark once.
- Posted OPS over .900 three times.
- Led NL with 34 home runs and 130 RBIs in 1935.
- Finished second in NL in home runs once, RBIs once, doubles once, extra-base hits three times, total bases once, slugging percentage once, and OPS once.
- Led NL outfielders in putouts once and fielding percentage once.
- Led NL center fielders in putouts twice, double plays turned twice, and fielding percentage once.
- Led NL left fielders in putouts once and double plays turned once.
- Ranks among Braves career leaders in home runs (10th), RBIs (12th), doubles (9th), extra-base hits (7th), total bases (10th), slugging percentage (2nd), and OPS (4th).
- Finished in top 10 of NL MVP voting twice, placing as high as third in 1933.
- Four-time NL All-Star selection (1933, 1934, 1935, and 1936).
- 1933 *Sporting News* All-Star selection.

13

BOB ELLIOTT

T he heart and soul of the Braves' 1948 NL pennant-winning ballclub, Bob Elliott proved to be such an integral part of the team's lineup during his five years in Boston that he earned the nickname "Mr. Team." An extremely consistent line-drive hitter who also possessed good power and a keen batting eye at the plate, Elliott batted over .300 twice and surpassed 20 homers and 100 RBIs three times each as a member of the Braves, after previously spending eight seasons starring for the Pittsburgh Pirates. Elliott, who knocked in more runs during the 1940s than any other player in the major leagues, excelled in the field as well, leading all NL third basemen in every major defensive category at one time or another, with his excellent all-around play in Boston earning him three All-Star selections and one league MVP trophy.

Born in San Francisco, California, on November 26, 1916, Robert Irving Elliott grew up some 600 miles southeast, in El Centro, California, where he played football and baseball at Union High School and El Centro Junior College. Recalling that he got his start in organized baseball at the age of 17, Elliott said, "Jack Stark ran a semipro club at El Centro . . . and recommended me to [former major leaguer George] Cutshaw. Cutshaw, in turn, told Mr. (William) Benswanger of the Pirates about me. Oscar Vitt, managing Oakland, offered me a contract, but George said, 'You stick with me. I can get you to Pittsburgh.' He was doing some scouting for that club. I figured that with a direct line to the National League, I would have a better chance, so I stuck with Cutshaw, who landed me with the Pirates."

After beginning his pro career with Savannah of the Class B South Atlantic League in 1936, Elliott gradually rose through the Pirates' farm system, finally arriving in Pittsburgh during the latter stages of the 1939 campaign. Starting 30 games in center field for the Pirates the last month of the season, Elliott batted .333, hit three homers, knocked in 19 runs, and scored 18 others. Elliott, who lacked superior running speed but possessed a strong throwing arm, subsequently spent the next two seasons starting in

Bob Elliott helped lead the Braves to the NL pennant in 1948, one year after he earned league MVP honors.
Courtesy of Boston Public Library, Leslie Jones Collection

right field for the Pirates, earning one All-Star nomination, before moving to third base in 1942.

Exempt from military service due to head injuries he sustained when struck with a batted ball early in 1943, Elliott established himself as one of the NL's most productive hitters during the "war years" of 1942 to 1945, driving in more than 100 runs three times and batting over .300 once, en route to earning two All-Star selections and three top-10 finishes in the league MVP voting. Praising Elliott for his superior play at one point during the 1943 season, the Pirates published a profile of him that stated, "His power, speed, fielding skill, and spirit make him look so much like a natural that there is hardly any question that he is destined to rank eventually with the greatest of his time."

Nevertheless, after Elliott posted less impressive numbers in 1946, the Pirates elected to include him in a six-player trade they completed with the Braves the day after the regular season ended. Happy to be leaving Pittsburgh and the spacious left field at Forbes Field, which greatly hampered his home-run output the previous eight years, the right-hand-ed-hitting Elliott received the following words of motivation from Braves manager Billy Southworth upon his arrival in Boston: "You're a very fine ball player, Bob. You can make all the plays you're supposed to at third base. You have an excellent arm. You run the bases well and are a dangerous long-ball hitter. All you need to achieve true greatness is the added sparkle of more hustle. If you hustle, I'm absolutely convinced that you will win the most valuable player award this season."

Proving his new skipper prophetic, Elliott earned NL MVP honors his first year in Boston by hitting 22 homers, scoring 93 runs, and rank-ing among the league leaders with 113 RBIs, 35 doubles, a .317 batting average, a .410 on-base percentage, and a .517 slugging percentage, with his exceptional play helping the Braves compile a record of 86-68 that rep-resented their best mark in 31 years. Elliott followed that up by hitting 23 homers, driving in 100 runs, scoring 99 others, batting .283, and drawing a league-leading 131 bases on balls for the Braves' 1948 pennant-winning team, earning in the process his second consecutive All-Star nomination and a 13th-place finish in the MVP balloting.

Described by longtime *Boston Globe* columnist Harold Kaese as "a rugged young man, blond, blue-eyed, and wearing a chin like a chisel," the 6-foot, 190-pound Elliott possessed a solid build that enabled him to drive the ball with power to all fields. More of a gap-to-gap, line-drive hitter than a pure slugger, Elliott did an excellent job of working the count, proving to be one of the senior circuit's most patient hitters. A good baserunner as well, especially after his talk with Southworth, Elliott got the most out of his merely average speed, with White Sox GM Frank Lane once calling him "one of the greatest hustlers I ever saw," and adding, "Bob played every game as if the championship hinged on it."

Commenting on the totality of Elliott's game, Frankie Frisch, his for-mer manager in Pittsburgh, stated, "He could play third base or the outfield as good as anybody. Any manager would want him on his ballclub. He played mad all the time. Baseball could use a few more Bob Elliotts."

Meanwhile, Billy Southworth expressed his appreciation for everything Elliott brought to the Braves when he said, "The ball games he won for me, or the home runs and extra-base hits he got to put us in the game are too numerous to mention. He was one of the elite. He was a fellow that carried a lot of the club. The other players looked up to him. He was the core of the ballclub."

Although the Braves finished well out of contention in each of the next three seasons, Elliott continued to perform at a high level, averaging 19 home runs, 84 RBIs, and 81 runs scored from 1949 to 1951, while also compiling a composite batting average of .291. Particularly outstanding in 1950, Elliott hit a career-high 24 homers, ranked among the league leaders with 107 RBIs and a .305 batting average, scored 94 runs, and compiled an OPS of .898.

But, with Eddie Mathews set to join the parent club in 1952, the Braves traded Elliott to the Giants just prior to the start of the regular season for relief pitcher Sheldon Jones and $50,000. Praising Elliott for the quality of his character prior to his departure for New York, *Boston Daily Record* columnist Dave Egan wrote, "Bob Elliott has been a big leaguer off the field and on it for 13 years. . . . He has been a man of decency and integrity."

Elliott ended up spending just one year with the Giants, hitting only 10 homers and batting just .228 in a part-time role, before asking for his release at season's end. After splitting the 1953 campaign between the St. Louis Browns and Chicago White Sox, Elliott announced his retirement, ending his career with 170 home runs, 1,195 RBIs, 1,064 runs scored, 2,061 hits, 382 doubles, 94 triples, 60 stolen bases, a .289 batting average, a .375 on-base percentage, and a .440 slugging percentage. In his five years with the Braves, Elliott hit 101 homers, knocked in 466 runs, scored 436 times, collected 763 hits, 145 doubles, and 22 triples, stole 13 bases, batted .295, compiled an on-base percentage of .398, and posted a slugging percentage of .485.

After leaving the big leagues, Elliott returned to his native California, where he spent one season playing for the San Diego Padres in the Pacific Coast League, before beginning a brief managerial career during which he piloted the Padres (1955–1957), Sacramento Solons (1959), and American League's Kansas City Athletics (1960). Retiring from baseball altogether after serving as a coach for the expansion Los Angeles Angels in 1961, Elliott went to work for a beer distributor in Indio, California, retaining his position there until the spring of 1966, when he suffered a ruptured windpipe. Despite receiving several blood transfusions and undergoing surgery for hemorrhaging in his stomach and lower esophagus, Elliott died at San Diego's Mercy Hospital on May 4, 1966, at only 49 years of age.

BRAVES CAREER HIGHLIGHTS

Best Season

Although Elliott also posted excellent numbers for the Braves in 1948 and 1950, he had the finest season of his career in 1947, when he earned NL MVP honors by hitting 22 homers, knocking in 113 runs, scoring 93 times, finishing second in the league with a .317 batting average and 35 doubles, and compiling an OPS of .927.

Memorable Moments/Greatest Performances

Elliott came back to haunt his former team on August 19, 1947, when he gave the Braves a dramatic 7–5 victory over the Pirates by hitting a two-out, three-run homer off Al Lyons in the bottom of the ninth inning.

Elliott starred during an 11–6 win over the Phillies on July 3, 1948, hitting a pair of homers, tripling, driving in five runs, and scoring four times.

After driving in two runs earlier in the contest with a double and single, Elliott delivered the decisive blow of an 8–6 win over the Cardinals on July 25, 1948, when he homered with two men aboard in the top of the ninth inning.

Elliott gave the Braves all the runs they needed to clinch at least a tie for the NL pennant on September 26, 1948, when he homered off Larry Jansen with two men aboard in the bottom of the first inning of a 3–2 victory over the Giants. Recalling his three-run blast years later, Elliott said, "I caught this one hard. It was off to right center. I didn't think it would make it. . . . It went right over the visiting bullpen. We were ahead 3–0." Elliott then added that manager Billy Southworth told him, "That's the best base hit you ever got in your life, Bob."

Although the Braves lost the 1948 World Series to the Cleveland Indians in six games, Elliott performed exceptionally well in his only postseason appearance, batting .333 with two homers, five RBIs, and an OPS of 1.010. Particularly outstanding in Game 5, which the Braves won, 11–5, Elliott homered twice off Bob Feller, knocked in four runs, and scored three times.

Elliott led the Braves to a 6–4 win over the Giants on September 24, 1949, by hitting three homers and knocking in five runs.

Elliott contributed to an 11–6 victory over the Pirates on July 21, 1951, by going 4-for-5, with a homer, double, walk, three RBIs, and career-high five runs scored.

Notable Achievements

- Hit more than 20 home runs three times.
- Knocked in more than 100 runs three times.
- Batted over .300 twice.
- Surpassed 30 doubles once.
- Drew more than 100 bases on balls once.
- Compiled on-base percentage over .400 twice.
- Posted slugging percentage over .500 twice.
- Posted OPS over .900 once.
- Hit three home runs in one game vs. New York Giants on September 24, 1949.
- Led NL with 131 walks in 1948.
- Finished second in NL in batting average once, on-base percentage once, and doubles once.
- Led NL third basemen in putouts once and fielding percentage once.
- Holds Braves single-season record for most bases on balls (131 in 1948).
- Ranks among Braves career leaders in on-base percentage (3rd) and OPS (11th).
- 1948 NL champion.
- 1947 NL MVP.
- Three-time NL All-Star selection (1947, 1948, and 1951).
- 1948 *Sporting News* All-Star selection.

14

CRAIG KIMBREL

The NL's premier closer during the early stages of his career, Craig Kimbrel spent five years with the Braves, leading the league in saves in four of those. Just the second pitcher to top the senior circuit in saves in four consecutive seasons, Kimbrel proved to be practically unhittable during his time in Atlanta, consistently compiling an ERA under 2.00 and striking out nearly half the batters he faced. A member of Braves teams that advanced to the playoffs three times and won one division title, Kimbrel amassed more saves than anyone else in franchise history, earning in the process four All-Star selections and two top-five finishes in the Cy Young voting. Yet, despite his dominant pitching, the Braves parted ways with Kimbrel just prior to the start of the 2015 campaign, including him in a blockbuster trade they completed with the San Diego Padres that netted them four players and one draft pick.

Born in Huntsville, Alabama, on May 28, 1988, Craig Michael Kimbrel got his start in baseball at the age of four with a local civic league team, before advancing to the Babe Ruth leagues some eight years later. A third baseman and outfielder during his formative years, Kimbrel moved to the mound after enrolling at Lee High School, where he spent three seasons excelling on the diamond and as a quarterback on the gridiron. Offered a scholarship to Wallace State Community College in Hanceville, Alabama, Kimbrel assumed the dual role of closer and spot-starter his freshman year at WSCC, compiling a record of 8-0 and an ERA of 1.99, with his strong performance prompting the Braves to select him in the 33rd round of the June 2007 MLB Draft. However, Kimbrel decided to return to college for his sophomore year, during which time he went 9-3, with a 2.88 ERA and 123 strikeouts in 81 innings pitched, while working primarily out of the bullpen. Having improved his draft stock, Kimbrel signed with the Braves when they selected him again, this time in the third round of the June 2008 MLB Draft.

Kimbrel subsequently spent the next two years in the minor leagues, impressing everyone with whom he came into contact while advancing through seven levels of the Braves' farm system. Speaking glowingly of the 21-year-old right-hander after watching him dominate the opposition at Triple-A Gwinnett early in 2010, one scout likened him to then-Braves closer, Billy Wagner, saying, "It's Wagner's body, similar arm action, he uses his legs like Wagner, and he has the same explosive fastball and wipeout slider. He's over-the-top competitive, pitches with no fear, and seems to amp up his stuff when the game is on the line, and I love to see that. . . . Once his command arrives consistently, he's legit. When all is said and done, he's a big-league closer, and a well above-average one for me."

Called up by the parent club twice in 2010, Kimbrel performed magnificently in his 21 relief appearances, compiling a record of 4-0 and an ERA of 0.44, recording the first save of his career, and striking out 40 batters in just over 20 innings of work. Picking up right where he left off after joining the Braves for good the following year, Kimbrel earned NL Rookie of the Year honors and the first of his four consecutive All-Star nominations by going 4-3 with a 2.10 ERA, establishing a new rookie record by registering a league-leading 46 saves, and striking out 127 batters over 77 innings, while allowing just 48 hits.

Awed by his young teammate's weaponry, veteran right-hander Tim Hudson stated late in the year, "If he stays healthy, I think he has the potential to be one of the best closers ever. He throws 100 mph and he's got an 88-mph breaking ball that breaks like a 78-mph slider. It's a big break, but it's hard. The potential is there for him to be great, not just really good. He's the best closer I've played with."

Continuing to perform at an elite level the next three seasons, Kimbrel posted the following numbers:

YEAR	W-L	ERA	SAVES	SO	BB	HITS	IP	WHIP
2012	3-1	1.01	**42**	116	14	27	62.2	0.654
2013	4-3	1.21	**50**	98	20	39	67	0.881
2014	0-3	1.61	**47**	95	26	30	61.2	0.908

In addition to leading the league in saves, compiling an ERA under 2.00, and registering a WHIP under 1.000 each year, Kimbrel posted a strikeouts-to-walks ratio of better than three to one and allowed fewer than six hits per nine innings pitched each season. Meanwhile, by recording 116 strikeouts in 62 2/3 innings of work in 2012, Kimbrel became the first

Craig Kimbrel holds the franchise record for most career saves.
Courtesy of L.W. Yang

pitcher ever to strike out at least half the batters he faced during a season. Two years later, Kimbrel became just the third pitcher to register at least 40 saves in four consecutive seasons and the first NL hurler since Bruce Sutter to lead the league in saves four straight times. Named the NL Rolaids Reliever of the Year in 2012 and 2014, Kimbrel also gained recognition as the *Sporting News* NL Fireman of the Year in 2012 and that same publication's NL Pitcher of the Year in 2013 and 2014.

Blessed with overpowering stuff, the 6-foot, 215-pound Kimbrel relied primarily on a four-seam fastball that registered close to 100 mph on the radar gun and a mid-to-upper-80s curveball thrown with a "spike" grip to retire opposing batters. Kimbrel also employed a rather unusual pre-pitch stance that saw him stare in for the catcher's signs from a hunched-over position, with his pitching elbow extended outward.

Although Kimbrel registered saves at a record-setting pace his first few years in Atlanta, the Braves' poor showing as a team in 2014 and desire to sever ties with overpaid and underachieving outfielder Melvin Upton

Jr. prompted them to complete a trade with the Padres on April 5, 2015, that sent the ace reliever and Upton to San Diego for outfielders Cameron Maybin and Carlos Quentin, prospects Matt Wisler and Jordan Paroubeck, and the 41st overall pick in the 2015 MLB Draft, which they used to select Austin Riley.

Revealing that he agonized over making the trade, Braves GM John Hart said, "It was a luxury for us to have Craig. I love him. It was a painful trade. It was painful for me, and it was painful for the fans. Craig is everything that's good about the game."

Kimbrel, who left Atlanta with an overall record of 15-10, an ERA of 1.43, a WHIP of 0.903, 186 saves, and 476 strikeouts in 289 innings of work, ended up spending just one year in San Diego, saving 39 games for the Padres in 2015, before being dealt to the Red Sox for four players at season's end. After earning three straight All-Star selections with the Red Sox by amassing a total of 108 saves, Kimbrel signed with the Cubs as a free agent in 2019. However, since leaving Boston, Kimbrel has struggled to regain his earlier form, performing well only in 2021, when he gained All-Star recognition for the eighth time by collecting 23 saves and compiling a 0.49 ERA for the Cubs. After finishing out the season with the crosstown rival Chicago White Sox, Kimbrel spent 2022 with the Los Angeles Dodgers, for whom he went 6-7, with a 3.75 ERA and 22 saves. Kimbrel, who will turn 35 years of age two months into the 2023 campaign, will enter the season with a career record of 41-36, an ERA of 2.31, a WHIP of 0.985, 394 saves, and 1,098 strikeouts in 668.1 innings pitched, with his 394 saves representing the seventh-highest total in MLB history.

BRAVES CAREER HIGHLIGHTS

Best Season

Although Kimbrel performed magnificently his entire time in Atlanta, he proved to be most dominant in 2012, when he earned a fifth-place finish in the NL Cy Young voting and an eighth-place finish in the MVP balloting by leading the league with 42 saves, winning three of his four decisions, compiling an ERA of 1.01 and a career-best WHIP of 0.654, and striking out 116 batters in only 62 2/3 innings of work.

Memorable Moments/Greatest Performances

En route to earning NL Rookie of the Year honors, Kimbrel threw 39 consecutive scoreless innings from June 11 to September 9, 2011, establishing along the way a number of rookie records, including most saves (27) prior to the All-Star break and most saves in a season (41).

Kimbrel reached several milestones during his time in Atlanta, with one of those coming during a 2–1 win over the Nationals on August 18, 2013, when he recorded his 28th consecutive save opportunity, breaking in the process John Smoltz's previous franchise record of 27.

Kimbrel became just the 11th pitcher in major-league history to record 50 saves in a season when he closed out a 1–0 win over the Phillies on September 27, 2013.

Kimbrel surpassed John Smoltz as the franchise's all-time saves leader on June 6, 2014, when he closed out a 5–2 win over the Arizona Diamondbacks, giving him a career total of 155 saves.

Notable Achievements

- Saved more than 40 games four times, amassing 50 saves once.
- Posted winning percentage over .700 twice.
- Compiled ERA under 2.00 four times, posting mark under 1.00 once.
- Posted WHIP under 1.000 three times.
- Struck out more than 100 batters twice.
- Posted strikeouts-to-walks ratio of better than three to one four times.
- Threw 39 consecutive scoreless innings in 2011.
- Led NL pitchers in saves four straight times.
- Holds Braves career record for most saves (186).
- Two-time NL Rookie of the Month.
- 2011 NL Rookie of the Year.
- Finished in top five of NL Cy Young voting twice.
- Four-time NL All-Star selection (2011, 2012, 2013, and 2014).
- Two-time NL Rolaids Relief Man of the Year (2012 and 2014).
- Two-time *Sporting News* NL Fireman of the Year (2011 and 2012).
- Two-time *Sporting News* NL Pitcher of the Year (2013 and 2014).

15
LEW BURDETTE

Acquired by the Braves during the latter stages of the 1951 campaign for $50,000 and an aging Johnny Sain, Lew Burdette went on to establish himself as one of the most successful pitchers in franchise history over the course of the next 13 seasons, winning 20 games twice and surpassing 17 victories four other times. Combining with Warren Spahn from 1953 to 1961 to form the finest and most durable pitching tandem in the game, Burdette also compiled an ERA under 3.00 three times and threw more than 250 innings on six separate occasions, earning in the process two All-Star selections and a future place in the Braves Hall of Fame. Yet, despite his many other accomplishments, Burdette will always be remembered primarily for his magnificent pitching performance in the 1957 World Series that enabled the Braves to win their first world championship in more than four decades.

Born in Nitro, West Virginia, on November 22, 1926, Selva Lewis Burdette spent much of his youth playing baseball on the local sandlots, before focusing exclusively on football at Nitro High School, which did not have a baseball team. Returning to his first love following his graduation from high school in 1944, Burdette took a job as a message boy at a local American Viscose Rayon plant, for whose baseball team he also pitched. Competing against other Industrial League teams in the Viscose Athletic Association, Burdette compiled a record of 12-2, before his entrance into the Air Corps Reserve in April 1945 forced him to temporarily put his baseball career on hold.

Released from active duty after just six months, Burdette subsequently enrolled at the University of Richmond, where his exceptional mound work began to draw the attention of major-league scouts, including one from the Boston Braves who told him, "I don't like the way you pitch. You may as well forget about baseball."

Ultimately signed by the Yankees in 1947 for $200 a month, Burdette ended up spending the next four years advancing through their farm system, before finally being called up to the majors toward the end of 1950. After pitching poorly in his two appearances in New York, Burdette spent much of the ensuing campaign with the San Francisco Seals in the Pacific Coast League, compiling a record of 14-12 over the first five months of the season, before receiving his big break on August 29, 1951, when the Yankees sent him and $50,000 to the Braves for Johnny Sain to help them with their push for the postseason.

After making three relief appearances with the Braves at the end of 1951, Burdette spent most of the following year working out of the bull-pen, going just 6-11 with a 3.61 ERA and seven saves. But, after joining the starting rotation during the second half of the 1953 season, Burdette earned the trust of manager Charlie Grimm by finishing the year with a record of 15-5, an ERA of 3.24, and six complete games, while also recording nine saves and throwing 175 innings.

A full-time starter by 1954, Burdette emerged as one of the NL's most reliable pitchers, going 15-14, finishing second in the league with a 2.76 ERA and four shutouts, and throwing 13 complete games and 238 innings. After a slightly subpar 1955 season in which he went 13-8 with a 4.03 ERA, Burdette began an outstanding six-year run during which he posted the following numbers:

YEAR	W-L	ERA	SHO	CG	IP	WHIP
1956	19-10	**2.70**	**6**	16	256.1	1.116
1957	17-9	3.72	1	14	256.2	1.243
1958	20-10	2.91	3	19	275.1	1.195
1959	**21-15**	4.07	**4**	20	289.2	1.208
1960	19-13	3.36	4	**18**	275.2	1.132
1961	18-11	4.00	3	14	**272.1**	1.204

Although the right-handed-throwing Burdette spent the entire period pitching in the shadow of the great Warren Spahn, he proved to be nearly the equal of his Hall of Fame teammate, ranking among the NL leaders in wins, innings pitched, and complete games each season, while also leading the league in ERA once and consistently placing near the top of the league rankings in shutouts and WHIP. An NL All-Star in 1957 and 1959, Burdette also earned MVP consideration four times and one third-place finish in the Cy Young voting. Meanwhile, the Braves finished either first or second in the league in five of those six seasons, winning two pennants and

Lew Burdette defeated the Yankees three times in the 1957 World Series.

one world championship, with Burdette's three victories and two shutouts in the 1957 World Series earning him series MVP honors.

The 6'2", 190-pound Burdette, who relied on a sinking fastball, slider, and changeup to retire opposing batters, did not throw particularly hard, never recording more than 113 strikeouts in any single season. But whatever Burdette lacked in velocity, he made up for with exceptional control and outstanding movement on his pitches, particularly his sinking fastball, which many opposing managers and players claimed to be a spitball.

In discussing Burdette's signature pitch, Jackie Robinson stated, "He's got the best spitter I ever saw. They call it a sinker, but I never saw a sinker act like that. Why, he struck me out once on a pitch that must have broken a foot. I missed it by eight inches."

Extremely nervous and fidgety on the mound, Burdette helped arouse suspicion as to the legality of his pitches with his many mannerisms and gestures that included fixing his jersey and hat, wiping his forehead, touching his lips, and talking to himself. Learning how to use his idiosyncrasies to his advantage, Burdette explained, "I think there's a lot of psychology going for me. I fidget when I'm getting ready to pitch. Batters get it into their heads that I'm doing something tricky to the ball. So, they're more than half convinced that I'm throwing a spitter or something like that. The result is, I get guys out on balls that merely may be rather ordinary sinkers."

Braves manager Fred Haney supported Burdette's contention that he did nothing illegal to the baseball, stating, "He's just a fidgety guy on the mound."

Burdette's period of excellence came to an end in 1962, when he compiled a record of 10-9 and an ERA of 4.89 ERA, completed just six of his starts, and threw only 143 2/3 innings. After Burdette went 6-5 with a 3.64 ERA over the first 10 weeks of the ensuing campaign, the Braves traded him to the Cardinals for pitcher Bob Sadowski and utilityman Gene Oliver on June 15, 1963. Burdette, who during his time in Boston and Milwaukee, compiled a record of 179-120, an ERA of 3.53, and a WHIP of 1.234, struck out 923 batters in 2,638 innings of work, completed 146 of his 330 starts, threw 30 shutouts, and recorded 24 saves, subsequently split the next four years between the Cardinals, Cubs, Phillies, and Angels, assuming the role of a spot-starter/long reliever for all four teams, before announcing his retirement during the latter stages of the 1967 campaign. Over parts of 18 big-league seasons, Burdette posted an overall record of 203-144, compiled an ERA of 3.66 and a WHIP of 1.243, recorded 1,074 strikeouts in 3,067 1/3 innings of work, threw 158 complete games and 33 shutouts, and collected 32 saves.

After retiring as an active player, Burdette briefly worked as a scout for the Central Scouting System and coached pitchers in the Gulf Coast League and in his hometown of Sarasota, Florida, where he also owned a gas station and a nightclub at different times. Returning to the game in 1972, Burdette became pitching coach for the Braves, saying upon rejoining the organization with which he experienced his greatest triumphs, "They've always been my club. Everything good happened when I was with the Braves. They've been my life."

However, Burdette lasted just two seasons in Atlanta, leaving baseball for good at the end of 1973 and subsequently working in public relations for a Milwaukee brewery and then in cable television in Florida for 20 years, before retiring to private life. Stricken with lung cancer in his later years, Burdette lived until February 6, 2007, when he died at the age of 80 in Winter Garden, Florida.

Upon learning of his former Cardinals teammate's passing, Dick Groat stated, "He was a great, great competitor. He was a marvelous pitcher who won big game after big game. It was fun to play behind Lew. He knew how to pitch everybody, and he wouldn't beat himself with bases on balls. He also pitched the way he said he was going to pitch before the game and made us better infielders because there were never any surprises. We knew how to position ourselves."

Meanwhile former Braves shortstop Johnny Logan summed up the career and personality of his longtime teammate by saying, "I don't know if he threw a spitter or not. His ball would really sink. He was a hell of a battler. Whatever Spahnie did, Lew wanted to do better. They had that competition between them. Lew was a big star, but he always gave Spahnie the credit."

BRAVES CAREER HIGHLIGHTS

Best Season

Despite his heroic World Series performance in 1957, Burdette pitched slightly better during the regular season in both 1956 and 1958, with the second of those campaigns proving to be the finest of his career. In addition to compiling a record of 20-10 in 1958 that gave him a league-best .667 winning percentage, Burdette ranked among the NL leaders with a 2.91 ERA, a 1.195 WHIP, three shutouts, 275 1/3 innings pitched, and 19 complete games, earning in the process a third-place finish in the Cy Young voting and an 11th-place finish in the NL MVP balloting.

Memorable Moments/Greatest Performances

Burdette allowed just one hit and two walks during a complete-game 5–1 win over the Dodgers on May 12, 1954, with Brooklyn scoring its only run on a fifth-inning homer by Gil Hodges.

Burdette helped his own cause on August 13, 1957, by homering twice, knocking in four runs, and scoring three times during a complete-game 12–4 win over the Reds.

Burdette experienced his finest moment in the 1957 World Series, when he led the Braves to a seven-game victory over the Yankees by winning all three of his starts, surrendering in the process just two runs in 27 innings of work. Particularly dominant in Games 5 and 7, Burdette tossed a pair of shutouts, with his 5–0 win in the Series finale coming on just two days' rest. Recalling his former teammate's heroic performance in Game 7, Johnny Logan said, "He was a tiger. This was his dream. It didn't matter that he had only two days' rest. His adrenalin was flowing. He loved to compete. And, this was the Yankees, the team that had traded him. He pitched with emotion. He wanted and got revenge."

Burdette beat the Dodgers with both his arm and his bat on July 10, 1958, homering twice and knocking in five runs during an 8–4 Braves win, hitting one of his homers with the bases loaded.

Burdette punctuated a 4–0 shutout of the Dodgers on August 21, 1958, by hitting a two-run homer off Sandy Koufax in the top of the fourth inning.

Burdette continued his dominance of the Yankees in Game 2 of the 1958 World Series, earning a complete-game 13–5 victory, while also hitting a three-run homer.

Burdette locked up with Pittsburgh's Harvey Haddix in a memorable pitching duel on May 26, 1959, working 13 scoreless innings, before Haddix allowed his first baserunner and lost a 1–0 decision to Burdette and the Braves in the bottom of the 13th.

After working three scoreless innings in relief, Burdette gave the Braves an 8–7 win over the Dodgers on July 30, 1960, by homering off reliever Larry Sherry in the top of the 11th.

Burdette threw 33 consecutive scoreless innings from August 10 to August 27, 1960, a period during which he tossed three straight shutouts. The highlight of the streak came on August 18, when Burdette threw a 1–0 no hitter against the Phillies, allowing only one man to reach base via a hit-batsman.

Burdette outdueled Sandy Koufax on June 16, 1961, surrendering just five hits during a 2–1 complete-game victory over the Dodgers, and hitting a solo homer off the Hall of Fame southpaw in the top of the fifth inning.

Burdette turned in his last dominant performance for the Braves on June 12, 1963, surrendering just three hits and one walk during a 9–0 complete-game win over the hapless Mets.

Notable Achievements

- Won at least 20 games twice, surpassing 17 victories four other times.
- Posted winning percentage over .600 six times, topping .700-mark once.
- Compiled ERA under 3.00 three times.
- Threw more than 250 innings six times.
- Completed 20 of his starts once.
- Threw 33 consecutive scoreless innings in 1960.
- Threw no-hitter vs. Philadelphia Phillies on August 18, 1960.
- Won three games and tossed two shutouts in 1957 World Series.
- Led NL pitchers in wins once, winning percentage once, ERA once, shutouts twice, innings pitched once, complete games once, putouts twice, assists once, and starts once.
- Ranks among Braves career leaders in wins (7th), strikeouts (11th), shutouts (4th), innings pitched (6th), complete games (12th), pitching appearances (7th), and games started (7th).
- Two-time NL champion (1957 and 1958).
- 1957 world champion.
- 1957 World Series MVP.
- August 1958 NL Player of the Month.
- Finished third in 1958 Cy Young voting.
- Two-time NL All-Star selection (1957 and 1959).
- Member of Braves Hall of Fame.

16

RABBIT MARANVILLE

Known for his quickness in the field and eye-popping basket catches, Rabbit Maranville overcame his diminutive stature to establish himself as one of the finest middle infielders of his time. Spending most of his 23-year big-league career at shortstop, Maranville recorded more putouts at that post than any other player who ever manned the position, while also amassing the most assists of any player in MLB history. A member of the Braves for parts of 15 seasons, Maranville contributed to the team on offense as well in his two tours of duty with the club, stealing more than 20 bases four times and finishing in double digits in triples on five separate occasions, with his outstanding all-around play earning him two top-five finishes in the NL MVP voting and a plaque in Cooperstown.

Born in Springfield, Massachusetts, on November 11, 1891, Walter James Vincent Maranville first fell in love with the game of baseball while attending the Charles Street and Chestnut Street grammar schools. Getting his start in organized ball as a catcher for Springfield Technical High, Maranville spent one year behind the plate, before quitting school at the age of 15 to learn how to become a pipe fitter and tinsmith. However, Maranville ended his apprenticeship before long, choosing instead to pursue a career in baseball. Discovered while playing shortstop for a semipro team in 1911, Maranville signed with the New Bedford Whalers of the New England League, for whom he batted just .227 and committed 61 errors in 117 games at short in his first year as a professional. Improving his performance dramatically in 1912, Maranville batted .283 and tightened up his defense somewhat, prompting the Braves to purchase his contract for $1,000.

Although Maranville spent less than two full seasons at New Bedford, it was during his time there that he acquired his distinctive nickname, recalling years later, "I was very friendly with a family by the name of Harrington. One night, I was down to their house having dinner with them when Margaret, the second oldest daughter, asked me if I could get two passes for the next day's game, as she wanted to take her seven-year-old sister to see me play. I said, 'Sure, I'll leave them in your name at the Press Gate.' She said, 'And come down to dinner after the game.' I left the two passes as I promised, and, after the game, I went down to their house for dinner. I rang the doorbell and Margaret came and opened the door and said, 'Hello Rabbit.' I said, 'Where do you get that Rabbit stuff?' She said, 'My little seven-year-old sister named you that because you hop and bound around like one.'"

After making his major-league debut with the Braves on September 10, 1912, Maranville struggled at the plate during the season's final month, batting just .209 in his 26 starts at shortstop. Yet even though he committed 11 errors in the field, Maranville garnered attention for his tremendous range and unique method of catching popups, recalling, "The fall of 1912, my fielding was above the average, but my hitting was not so good. However, I was the talk of the town because of my peculiar way of catching a fly ball. They later named it the 'Vest-Pocket Catch.' Boston wasn't drawing any too good, but it seemed like everyone that came out to the park came to see me make my peculiar catch or get hit on the head."

In an earlier version of the basket catch later immortalized by Willie Mays, Maranville casually settled himself under popups with his arms resting at his side, before suddenly bringing his hands together at waist level and allowing the ball to fall seamlessly into the pocket of his glove. In discussing his distinctive maneuver, Maranville stated, "Many of the players passed different remarks about my catch which wouldn't go in print. I do, however, remember what Jimmy Sheckard said: 'I'll bet you he doesn't drop three balls in his career, no matter how long or short he may be in the game. Notice the kid is perfectly still, directly under the ball, and in no way is there any vibration to make the ball bounce out of his glove.'"

Laying claim to the Braves' starting shortstop job in 1913, Maranville posted relatively modest offensive numbers, concluding the campaign with two homers, 48 RBIs, 68 runs scored, 25 stolen bases, and a batting average of .247. Nevertheless, Maranville's spirited play and strong defense earned him a third-place finish in the NL MVP balloting. Although Maranville batted just .246 the following year, he compiled better overall numbers, finishing the season with four homers, 78 RBIs, 74 runs scored, and 28 steals, while also leading all NL shortstops in putouts, assists, and double plays turned. And, with the Braves winning the pennant, Maranville finished second in the NL MVP voting to teammate and double-play partner Johnny Evers, who the team had purchased from the Cubs the previous winter.

Rabbit Maranville recorded more assists than any other player in major-league history.

Combining with Evers to give the Braves the best middle infield in baseball, Maranville later said, "It was just Death Valley, whoever hit a ball down our way. Evers, with his brains, taught me more baseball than I ever dreamed about. He was psychic. He could sense where a player was going to hit if the pitcher threw the ball where he was supposed to."

While Maranville credited Evers for much of his success, Braves manager George Stallings heaped praise on his shortstop following the team's stunning upset win over the Philadelphia Athletics in the 1914 World Series, saying at the time, "Maranville is the greatest player to enter baseball since Ty Cobb arrived. I've seen 'em all since 1891, in every league around the south, north, east, and west, but Maranville is the peer of them all. He came into the league under a handicap—his build. He was too small to be a big leaguer in the opinion of critics. I told him he was just what I wanted: a small fellow for shortstop. All he had to do was to run to his left or right, or come in, and size never handicapped speed in going after the ball."

Standing just 5'5" and weighing considerably less than his listed playing weight of 155 pounds, the right-handed-hitting Maranville compensated for his lack of size by doing all the "little things" to help his team win. In addition to covering a tremendous amount of ground in the field, Maranville moved runners along, stole bases, and kept his teammates loose with his zany antics, both on and off the playing field. A noted practical joker, Maranville often mocked umpires and mimicked the actions of hitters or pitchers who took an especially long time to get ready. Fueled by alcohol, Maranville was also known to stroll across building ledges, throw firecrackers, swallow goldfish, and dive into swimming pools from his hotel room.

After turning down a lucrative offer to play for the Chicago Whales of the rival Federal League following the Braves' victory over Philadelphia in the 1914 World Series, Maranville spent the next six seasons in Boston, although he missed most of the 1918 campaign while serving as a gunner in the Navy during World War I. But, after Maranville batted .266 and scored only 48 runs in 1920, the Braves traded him to the Pirates for three players and a sum of money said to be $15,000 on January 23, 1921.

With the NL instituting the use of a livelier ball during the 1920s, Maranville ended up having four of his most productive offensive seasons for the Pirates, while splitting his time between shortstop and second base. Performing especially well in 1921 and 1922, Maranville batted .294, knocked in 70 runs, scored 90 times, and collected 180 hits in the first of those campaigns, before establishing career-high marks with 115 runs scored, 198 hits, and a .295 batting average the following year.

However, plagued by an addiction to alcohol, Maranville eventually wore out his welcome in Pittsburgh, causing him to live a nomadic existence from 1925 to 1928, a period during which he served as a part-time player for the Cubs (1925), Dodgers (1926), and Cardinals (1927–1928). Finally swearing off alcohol after being demoted to the minor leagues at one point in 1927, Maranville returned to Boston for a second tour of duty with his original team two years later, beginning in the process an extremely successful five-year stint during which he earned MVP consideration four times. Starting at shortstop for the Braves the first three seasons before moving to second base in 1932, Maranville concluded the 1929 campaign with a batting average of .284, 87 runs scored, and a total of 536 assists that placed him second among players who manned his position. He followed that up by batting .281, scoring 85 times, and leading all NL shortstops in fielding percentage in 1930, before experiencing a gradual decline in production over the course of the next three seasons.

After batting just .218 and scoring only 46 runs in 1933, Maranville broke his ankle in a collision at home plate the following spring, forcing him to miss the entire season. Although the 43-year-old Maranville attempted a comeback in 1935, he appeared in only 23 games, before announcing his retirement at the end of the year with career totals of 28 home runs, 884 RBIs, 1,256 runs scored, 2,605 hits, 380 doubles, 177 triples, and 291 stolen bases, a batting average of .258, an on-base percentage of .318, and a slugging percentage of .340. As a member of the Braves, Maranville hit 23 homers, knocked in 558 runs, scored 802 others, collected 1,696 hits, 244 doubles, and 103 triples, stole 194 bases, batted .252, compiled an on-base percentage of .313, and posted a slugging percentage of .329, with his 103 three-baggers representing the highest total in franchise history.

In discussing his career in 1936, Maranville wrote, "For a quarter of a century, I've been playing baseball for pay. It has been pretty good pay, most of the time. The work has been hard, but what of it? It's been risky. I've broken both my legs. I've sprained everything I've got between my ankles and my disposition. I've dislocated my joints and fractured my pride. . . . I've lost a lot of teeth and square yards of hide. But I've never lost my self-respect, and I've kept what I find in few men of my age—my enthusiasm."

After retiring as an active player, Maranville managed in the minor leagues for a few years, before beginning a career as a youth instructor that took him to Rochester, Detroit, and, finally, New York City. As director of the New York *Journal-American* sandlot baseball school after World War II, Maranville taught thousands of youngsters how to play the game in clinics held at Yankee Stadium and the Polo Grounds, with his most notable pupil being Hall of Fame pitcher Whitey Ford. Maranville lived until January 5, 1954, when he died at the age of 62 of coronary sclerosis, just a few weeks before the members of the BBWAA elected him to the Baseball Hall of Fame.

Once described by legendary sportswriter Grantland Rice as "the link between the old days and the new in baseball," Maranville also found himself being depicted by Rice in the following manner: "He broke in with the hard-bitten crew in Boston and wasn't exactly a sissy, reveling in the atmosphere in which he found himself. For years he was a turbulent figure on the field, fighting enemy ball players and umpires—and even the players on his own team when he found it necessary."

Meanwhile, author Gary Caruso wrote in his 1995 book, *Braves Encyclopedia*, "After the Braves' 1914 World Series victory, George Stallings said Maranville was 'the greatest player to come to the majors since Ty Cobb.' Though that statement proved to be a bit much, Rabbit was one of the game's most highly regarded players in his era. . . . Make no mistake, Rabbit was one of the greatest defensive infielders of all time."

BRAVES CAREER HIGHLIGHTS

Best Season

Although Maranville posted better offensive numbers in two or three other seasons, he made his greatest overall impact in 1914, when he helped lead the Braves to the NL pennant by topping the senior circuit in games played, ranking among the leaders in plate appearances and at-bats, driving in a career-high 78 runs, scoring 74 times, stealing 28 bases, and leading all players at his position in putouts and assists, with his solid all-around play earning him a second-place finish in the NL MVP voting.

Memorable Moments/Greatest Performances

After singling twice and stealing two bases earlier in the contest, Maranville gave the Braves a 5–4 victory over the Pirates on August 6, 1914, when he hit a solo homer off Pittsburgh starter Babe Adams in the bottom of the 10th inning. Recalling his game-winning blast years later, Maranville, who delivered the blow while nursing a severe hangover, said, "Truthfully, I never did see the ball I hit, and years later Babe Adams, who was the pitcher that day, asked me if it was a curve or a fastball I hit over the fence. I told him I never saw it and he said, 'I know darn well you never did.'"

Maranville contributed to a 13–0 rout of the Giants on June 29, 1917, by going 5-for-5, with a homer, stolen base, four RBIs, and two runs scored.

Maranville helped lead the Braves to a 9–1 win over the Phillies on July 1, 1919, by knocking in five runs and homering twice in one game for the only time in his career.

Maranville starred during a 7–6 victory over the Pirates on June 9, 1920, going 5-for-5, with a pair of doubles, one RBI, and two runs scored.

Maranville again went 5-for-5 during a 10–9 win over the Pirates on July 29, 1929, also finishing the game with two RBIs and two runs scored.

Maranville helped lead the Braves to a 13–4 thrashing of the Cardinals on June 10, 1931, by collecting four hits, drawing two bases on balls, and scoring a career-high five runs.

Notable Achievements

- Finished in double digits in triples five times.
- Stole more than 20 bases four times, topping 30 thefts once.
- Led NL in assists twice and games played once.
- Led NL shortstops in putouts five times, assists twice, double plays turned three times, and fielding percentage twice.
- Led NL second basemen in putouts once and fielding percentage once.
- Holds MLB career records for most putouts by a shortstop (5,139) and most assists by any player (8,967).
- Ranks fifth in MLB history in assists by a shortstop (7,354).
- Holds Braves career record for most triples (103).
- Ranks among Braves career leaders in runs scored (12th), hits (8th), doubles (10th), total bases (9th), bases on balls (10th), stolen bases (9th), sacrifice hits (2nd), games played (5th), plate appearances (6th), and at-bats (6th).
- 1914 NL champion.
- 1914 world champion.
- Finished in top five of NL MVP voting twice, placing third in 1913 and second in 1914.
- Member of Braves Hall of Fame.
- Elected to Baseball Hall of Fame by members of BBWAA in 1954.

17

TOMMY HOLMES

An outstanding contact hitter who batted over .300 five straight times for the Braves, Tommy Holmes spent 10 seasons in Boston, proving to be the most difficult player in the game to strike out during that time. Fanning only 122 times in more than 5,500 plate appearances over the course of his career, Holmes compiled an at-bats per strikeout ratio of 40.9 that ranks as the seventh-best mark in major-league history. Also capable of delivering the long ball, Holmes hit more than 20 homers and knocked in more than 100 runs once each, while also amassing more than 40 doubles on two separate occasions. A solid defender as well, Holmes led all NL right fielders in putouts twice, double plays turned three times, and fielding percentage twice, with his excellent all-around play earning him two All-Star selections, one runner-up finish in the league MVP voting, and a place in the Braves Hall of Fame.

Born in Brooklyn, New York, on March 29, 1917, Thomas Francis Holmes grew up in the Borough Park section of his hometown, where he spent much of his youth training to be a boxer. A fan of the Brooklyn Dodgers during his formative years, Holmes turned his attention to baseball when his father forbade him to pursue a career in boxing. Developing into a star first baseman at Brooklyn Technical High School, Holmes, who batted and threw left-handed, began to make a name for himself his final two years by posting batting averages of .585 and .613.

Later crediting Brooklyn Tech head coach Anthony Tarrantino for much of the success he experienced on the diamond, Holmes said, "He was the John McGraw of the high schools. In the winter months, he used to have me eat my lunch up in the gymnasium. He would draw home plate on the floor, and then we would talk about hitting. He'd show me parts of the plate, zoning and so forth. He was telling me how to reach the outside of the plate, how to reach the inside, and what to look for from a pitcher. He also taught me to have the courage to hit to opposite fields."

Tommy Holmes batted over .300 five straight times for the Braves.
Courtesy of Boston Public Library, Leslie Jones Collection

Competing semiprofessionally as well while in high school, Holmes recalled, "We grew up playing ball, or watching it, all the time. Right in Brooklyn, we had the Parade Grounds, which had about 21 fields. One big half-mile square filled with diamonds, and we played there every Sunday."

Hoping to land a job with one of the two local semipro teams that drew the attention of major-league scouts, Holmes approached Bay Parkway manager Harry Hess following his graduation from Brooklyn Tech, remembering, "Hess told me I was just a kid, but then one day a guy didn't show up and he said, 'Can you play left field?' I said sure, even though I had never played left field in my life. I was a first baseman. Well, I got a couple hits, and the next Tuesday night an owner of the Bushwicks—there were two brothers, Joe and Max Rosner, who owned both clubs—he called and asked me if I would play at Dexter Park for him against Josh Gibson, Satchel Paige, and all of those great Negro League players. I told him sure.

I batted against Satchel Paige; I didn't know who he was, but I got a couple of hits."

Discovered by Yankees scout Paul Krichell while competing against Paige and Gibson's Pittsburgh Crawfords, Holmes signed with New York, after which he spent the next five years in the minors, performing well at every stop, but finding himself unable to make the big-league roster due to the presence of star outfielders Joe DiMaggio, Tommy Henrich, and Charlie Keller. Holmes finally received his big break, though, on December 9, 1941, when, just two days after the Japanese attack on Pearl Harbor, the Braves acquired him from the Yankees for first baseman Buddy Hassett and outfielder Gene Moore, in what ranks as one of the finest trades in franchise history.

Named the Braves' starting center fielder shortly after he arrived in Boston, the 25-year-old Holmes made an immediate impact as a rookie, with the help of veteran teammate Paul Waner, then in the latter stages of his Hall of Fame career. Recalling the advice he received from Waner, Holmes said, "He used to tell me, 'Look, there are three men in the outfield. Why should we hit it where they are?' He used to preach shooting for the foul lines. If you missed, he said, it was just a foul ball; if you got it in, it was a double. 'And if it goes in the stands,' he said, 'don't worry. We don't pay for the baseballs.' If they tried to cover the lines on him, then they were opening gaps in right-and left-center, and he would put the ball out there. This is what he taught me. And while I wasn't a power hitter, I used to get around 35 or 40 doubles a year from following Paul's advice."

Hitting out of the leadoff spot in the batting order for most of his rookie season, Holmes hit four homers, knocked in 41 runs, scored 56 others, batted .278, and compiled an on-base percentage of .353, while also drawing 64 bases on balls and striking out just 10 times in 633 plate appearances. Unable to serve in the military during World War II due to a severe sinus condition, Holmes remained with the Braves in 1943, improving upon his numbers slightly, before emerging as one of the NL's better players the following year. Having added some muscle onto his lean 5'10", 180-pound frame by working in the Brooklyn shipyards during the previous offseason, Holmes began to display more power at the plate in 1944, more than doubling his home-run output by reaching the seats 13 times. Assuming the third spot in the Braves' batting order, Holmes also knocked in 73 runs, scored 93 times, batted .309, and finished third in the league with 195 hits and 42 doubles.

After moving to right field in 1945, Holmes had the finest offensive season of his career, earning his first All-Star selection and a runner-up finish to Chicago's Phil Cavarretta in the NL MVP balloting by leading the majors with 28 homers, 47 doubles, 224 hits, 367 total bases, a .577 slugging percentage, and an OPS of .997, while also ranking among the leaders with 117 RBIs, 125 runs scored, and a .352 batting average. Holmes, who amazingly struck out just nine times in 714 plate appearances, made history by becoming the first man ever to lead the major leagues in home runs and fewest strikeouts in the same season.

Holmes further distinguished himself in 1945 by hitting safely in 37 consecutive games from June 6 to July 12, breaking in the process Rogers Hornsby's previous NL mark of 33 straight contests with at least one hit. Looking back on his extraordinary achievement years later, Holmes said, "It wasn't until after I'd broken the record that I realized how much tension and pressure I'd been under. A sigh of relief went out of me so huge that I felt like a collapsing balloon. Up until that moment, it had never bothered me; but, boy, it had been building."

The left-handed-hitting Holmes certainly benefited greatly from management's decision to shorten the distance to the right field fence at Braves Field by 20 feet prior to the start of the 1945 campaign. Nevertheless, the cavernous ballpark remained a challenging one for even the league's top sluggers, making Holmes's home-run total that much more impressive.

Meanwhile, as Holmes established himself as one of the senior circuit's top offensive performers, he continued to build on his tremendous popularity with the hometown fans that he enjoyed his entire time in Boston. Endearing himself to the fans in Beantown with his hustle, excellent all-around play, and affable personality, Holmes shared an especially cordial relationship with the denizens of the 1,500-seat, stand-alone bleachers situated behind the area he patrolled in right field. Dubbed the "Jury Box" by a local sportswriter, the section with its wooden benches was filled during the club's contending years of 1946 to 1948 with a crew of regulars who developed a friendly give-and-take with their hero. "How many hits you gonna get today, Tommy?" a patron might yell, and Holmes would either offer a verbal response or hold up however many fingers he deemed appropriate.

Although Holmes never again reached the heights he attained in 1945 after the game's best players returned from the war, he continued to perform at an extremely high level from 1946 to 1948, batting well over .300 all three seasons, leading the league with 191 hits in 1947, and earning his second All-Star nomination the following year by collecting 190 hits and batting .325 for the pennant-winning Braves. Nevertheless, with Holmes turning 32 years of age just prior to the start of the 1949 campaign, he assumed a somewhat diminished role in each of the next two seasons, occasionally being benched against left-handed pitching. Still, he managed to bat .298, hit nine homers, and drive in 51 runs, in only 105 games and 322 official at-bats in 1950.

Named player-manager of the Braves' Class A Hartford Chiefs farm club prior to the start of the 1951 season, Holmes continued to function in that dual role until he returned to Boston later in the year to replace fired manager Billy Southworth and serve the team as a pinch-hitter. Holmes then led the Braves to an overall record of 61-69 over parts of the next two seasons, before being relieved of his duties on May 31, 1952. Choosing to take the high road when asked about his dismissal, Holmes said, "They are wonderful people. They probably hated twice as much telling me I was fired as I disliked hearing it. And it's no disgrace to be replaced by Charlie Grimm."

Many years later, though, Holmes told the *Boston Herald*, "It broke my heart when they let me go. I was ready to have a home built up there. That was going to be my home. It was a shock. It was like losing your family. I don't think I ever got over that, even yet."

After being let go by the Braves, Holmes spent the rest of 1952 serving the Dodgers almost exclusively as a pinch-hitter, before announcing his retirement at the end of the year with career totals of 88 home runs, 581 RBIs, 698 runs scored, 1,507 hits, 292 doubles, 47 triples, and 40 stolen bases, a batting average of .302, an on-base percentage of .366, and a slugging percentage of .432. Holmes also walked 480 times, giving him a nearly four to one walks-to-strikeouts ratio for his career.

Following his playing days, Holmes spent five years managing in the Braves' and Dodgers' farm systems, before becoming in 1959 director of the *New York Journal-American*'s sandlot baseball program, a position he maintained for more than three decades. Beginning in 1973, Holmes also spent 30 years serving as director of amateur baseball relations for the New York Mets, remaining in that position until finally retiring in 2003, at the age of 86. Holmes lived five more years, enjoying his retirement until he died of natural causes at an assisted living facility in Boca Raton, Florida, on April 14, 2008, two weeks after celebrating his 91st birthday.

Claiming some years earlier that the fans seated behind him in the "Jury Box" provided him with his greatest baseball memories, Holmes stated, "Williams, DiMaggio, Musial—they never had what I did. The other 29,000 fans, if they wanted to give me a boo or two, go ahead. But not if you sat behind me in the Jury Box, I'll tell you that. They were always hollering at me, 'Keep your eye on the ball, Tommy! Try and wait for a good one, Tommy!' Tommy this, and Tommy that."

BRAVES CAREER HIGHLIGHTS

Best Season

With many of the game's best players serving in the military, Holmes compiled easily the most impressive numbers of his career in 1945, earning a second-place finish in the NL MVP voting and his lone *Sporting News* All-Star nomination by leading the league with 28 homers, 224 hits, 47 doubles, 367 total bases, a .577 slugging percentage, and an OPS of .997, while also finishing second in batting average (.352) and RBIs (117), third in runs scored (125), and fourth in on-base percentage (.420) and stolen bases (15). Recalling his magical season years later, Holmes, who batted .408 in his home ballpark and incredibly struck out only nine times all year, said, "Everything I tried, everything I did, worked out."

Memorable Moments/Greatest Performances

Holmes starred in defeat on May 15, 1945, going a perfect 5-for-5 at the plate, with three doubles, three RBIs, and two runs scored during an 8–7 loss to the Cardinals.

Some three weeks later, on June 6, 1945, Holmes began a 37-game hitting streak that lasted until July 8, setting in the process a modern NL record that stood until Pete Rose hit safely in 44 consecutive games 33 years later. During his streak, Holmes went 66-for-156 (.423), with nine homers, three triples, 10 doubles, 41 RBIs, 43 runs scored, 18 walks, and just two strikeouts.

Holmes contributed to a lopsided 9–0 victory over the Reds on June 7, 1947, by going 5-for-5, with a double, three RBIs, and three runs scored.

Holmes had another big day against the Reds on July 10, 1947, hitting a pair of solo homers and scoring four runs during a 6–4 Braves win.

Holmes drove home the only run scored in Game 1 of the 1948 World Series when he singled to left field with two men out and two men on base in the bottom of the eighth inning, making a winner out of Johnny Sain, who outdueled Bob Feller, 1–0.

Notable Achievements

- Hit more than 20 home runs once.
- Knocked in more than 100 runs once.
- Scored more than 100 runs once.

- Batted over .300 five times.
- Surpassed 200 hits once.
- Finished in double digits in triples once.
- Surpassed 30 doubles six times, topping 40 two-baggers twice.
- Compiled on-base percentage over .400 once.
- Posted slugging percentage over .500 once.
- Posted OPS over .900 once.
- Led NL in home runs once, hits twice, doubles once, total bases once, slugging percentage once, OPS once, and at-bats once.
- Led NL right fielders in putouts twice, double plays turned three times, and fielding percentage twice.
- Led NL center fielders in double plays turned once and fielding percentage twice.
- Holds franchise record for longest hitting streak (37 games in 1945).
- Ranks among Braves career leaders in doubles (8th), hits (12th), extra-base hits (tied for 10th), total bases (12th), plate appearances (12th), and at-bats (11th).
- 1948 NL champion.
- Finished second in 1945 NL MVP voting.
- Two-time NL All-Star selection (1945 and 1948).
- 1945 *Sporting News* All-Star selection.
- 1945 *Sporting News* NL Player of the Year.
- Member of Braves Hall of Fame.

18

JOHNNY SAIN

An outstanding right-handed pitcher who relied primarily on guile and his exceptional breaking ball to retire opposing batters, Johnny Sain spent parts of seven seasons in Boston, combining with Warren Spahn to give the Braves the most formidable pitching duo in baseball. Although Sain did not begin his major-league career in earnest until after he celebrated his 28th birthday due to time spent in the military during World War II, he won at least 20 games, threw more than 250 innings, and tossed more than 20 complete games four times each, earning in the process two All-Star selections and a pair of top-five finishes in the NL MVP voting. A huge contributor to Boston's 1948 pennant-winning ballclub, Sain later received the additional honor of being named to the Braves Hall of Fame. Nevertheless, Sain is largely remembered today for his inclusion in one of the most celebrated refrains in sports history.

Born in Havana, Arkansas, on September 25, 1917, John Franklin Sain acquired a love of the game of baseball at an early age from his father, an automobile mechanic and former pitcher at the amateur level who taught him how to throw a curveball, vary his pitching motion, and change speeds on his pitches. Eventually emerging as a standout hurler at Havana High School, Sain became determined to pursue a career on the diamond, even though others often discouraged him, claiming that he lacked the velocity on his fastball to succeed as a professional.

Signed by the Red Sox following his graduation from Havana High in 1935, Sain began a long six-year journey that included stints in the farm systems of the Red Sox, St. Louis Browns, Detroit Tigers, and Brooklyn Dodgers. Pitching his best ball during that period for Newport in 1938 and 1939, Sain compiled a record of 16-4 and an ERA of 2.72 in the first of those campaigns, before going 18-10 with a 3.27 ERA in the second.

Ultimately purchased by the Braves from the Dodgers' minor-league affiliate in Nashville on April 8, 1942, Sain spent most of the season in Boston, going 4-7 with a 3.90 ERA and six saves, while working primarily

Johnny Sain, seen here with Boston manager Casey Stengel, combined with Warren Spahn during the late 1940s to give the Braves a dynamic pitching tandem.
Courtesy of Boston Public Library, Leslie Jones Collection

out of the bullpen. However, after enlisting for aviation training in the Navy during the latter stages of the campaign, Sain ended up missing the next three seasons while serving his country during World War II. After completing his preliminary ground training at Amherst College, Sain was transferred to Chapel Hill, North Carolina, where he received his preflight instruction. A few months later, Sain moved on to Corpus Christi Naval Air Training Base, from which he graduated as an ensign in August 1944. Sain subsequently spent the rest of the war teaching flying at Corpus Christi, before receiving his discharge on November 25, 1945.

Rejoining the Braves in 1946, Sain established himself as the ace of their pitching staff, compiling a record of 20-14, finishing second in the league with a 2.21 ERA, placing third in the circuit with 265 innings pitched and 129 strikeouts, and leading the league with 24 complete games, with his exceptional mound work earning him a fifth-place finish in the NL

MVP voting. Later crediting his maturation into one of the league's best pitchers to his time spent in the military, Sain said, "I think learning to fly an airplane helped me as much as anything. I was 25 years old. Learning to fly helped me to concentrate and restimulated my ability to learn."

During his three years away from the game, Sain also came to realize that, even though he stood 6'2" and weighed close to 200 pounds, he needed to change his approach on the mound since he lacked high-end velocity, later explaining, "I lacked the velocity to throw the ball past hitters, so I had to depend on the mechanics. Variation of delivery, motion, various speeds, movement on the ball. I hurt my elbow the second year and after that I threw 90 percent breaking pitches."

Nicknamed the "Man of a Thousand Curves," Sain turned his breaking ball into easily his most effective weapon after the war, claiming that the knowledge of aerodynamics he had absorbed as a pilot helped him perfect his primary offering.

Although Sain pitched somewhat less effectively in 1947, concluding the campaign with an ERA of 3.52, he still gained All-Star recognition by compiling a record of 21-12 and ranking among the league leaders with 22 complete games, 266 innings pitched, and 132 strikeouts. Returning to top form in 1948, Sain helped lead the Braves to their first pennant in 34 years by going 24-15, with a 2.60 ERA and a league-leading 28 complete games and 314 2/3 innings pitched, earning in the process his second consecutive All-Star selection and a runner-up finish in the NL MVP balloting.

Becoming in 1948 a part of one of baseball's most fabled pitching tandems, Sain combined with teammate Warren Spahn to post 43 percent of Boston's 91 victories. And, with Sain and Spahn winning 11 games between them in the month of September as the Braves moved inexorably toward the league championship, Boston sportswriter Gerald Hern penned the following poem that remains a part of both men's legacy:

First, we'll use Spahn,
Then we'll use Sain,
Then an off day,
Followed by rain.

Back will come Spahn
Followed by Sain
And followed,
We Hope,
By two days of rain.

Unfortunately, with Sain suffering from a sore shoulder he blamed on his experimenting with a screwball during spring training, he failed to perform at the same lofty level in 1949, finishing the season just 10-17 with an abnormally high 4.81 ERA. However, he rebounded the following year to go 20-13, compile an ERA of 3.94, and rank among the league leaders with 25 complete games and 278 1/3 innings pitched.

The 1950 campaign proved to be Sain's last full season in Boston. After his ailing right shoulder caused Sain to get off to a poor start the following year, the Braves traded him to the Yankees on August 29, 1951, for $50,000 and a young pitcher named Lew Burdette who would figure prominently in their fortunes for the next decade. Sain left the Braves having compiled an overall record of 104-91, an ERA of 3.49, and a WHIP of 1.319 as a member of the team. He also struck out 698 batters in 1,624 1/3 innings of work, threw 121 complete games, tossed 15 shutouts, and saved 11 contests. An excellent-hitting pitcher, Sain also batted .242, hit two homers, knocked in 74 runs, and struck out only 13 times in 594 official at-bats during his time in Boston.

After finishing out the 1951 season in New York, Sain underwent a new radiation therapy from a doctor in Dallas for his aching right shoulder at the end of the year that helped him resurrect his career as a relief pitcher and spot starter for the Yankees the next few seasons. Contributing significantly to teams that won three pennants and three world championships from 1951 to 1954, Sain posted an overall record of 33-20 and saved 41 games for the Yankees, before being dealt to the Kansas City Athletics during the early stages of the 1955 campaign. Released by the Athletics on July 16, 1955, Sain subsequently announced his retirement, ending his career with a record of 139-116, an ERA of 3.49, a WHIP of 1.300, 910 strikeouts in 2,125 2/3 innings pitched, 140 complete games, and 16 shutouts.

After retiring as an active player, Sain returned to Arkansas, where he spent the next few years raising his children and running the Chevrolet dealership he had owned since 1952, before beginning an extremely successful career as a pitching coach. Serving as a member of the coaching staffs of the Athletics, Yankees, Braves, Twins, White Sox, and Tigers at different times, Sain helped develop 20-game winners Jim Kaat, Jim "Mudcat" Grant, Wilbur Wood, Mickey Lolich, Denny McLain, and Jim Bouton, with Bouton saying of his mentor, "He got pitchers to believe in themselves," and calling him "the greatest pitching coach who ever lived."

Retiring from baseball for good in 1987, Sain settled down to a quiet life in the Chicago suburb of Downers Grove, Illinois, where he remained until November 7, 2006, when he died at the age of 89 after suffering a stroke four years earlier.

BRAVES CAREER HIGHLIGHTS

Best Season

Although Sain also performed exceptionally well two years earlier, he pitched his best ball for the Braves in 1948, when he gained recognition as the *Sporting News* NL Pitcher of the Year and earned a runner-up finish to Stan Musial in the NL MVP balloting by leading the league in wins (24), complete games (28), innings pitched (314 2/3), and starts (39), while also finishing second in shutouts (4), third in ERA (2.60) and strikeouts (137), and fourth in WHIP (1.208).

Memorable Moments/Greatest Performances

Sain excelled both on the mound and at the plate on June 9, 1946, earning a 14–3 complete-game win over the Reds, while also going 4-for-5 with a triple and five RBIs.

Sain turned in the most dominant performance of his career on July 12, 1946, when he issued no bases on balls and yielded just a first-inning bloop double by third baseman Grady Hatton during a 1–0, one-hit shutout of the Reds.

Sain hurled another gem on September 1, 1946, surrendering just four hits and no walks during an 8–0 shutout of the Phillies.

Sain got the better of Cleveland's Bob Feller in Game 1 of the 1948 World Series, allowing just four hits, issuing no walks, and recording six strikeouts during a 1–0 pitchers' duel. Looking back on his superb outing years later, Sain said, "I always try to minimize the importance of a game. But it was a thrill of a lifetime to beat a guy like Bob Feller."

Sain punctuated a complete-game 13–3 win over the Pirates on June 12, 1951, by hitting one of his three career home runs.

Notable Achievements

- Won at least 20 games four times.
- Posted winning percentage over .600 three times.

- Compiled ERA under 3.00 twice, finishing with mark under 2.50 once.
- Threw more than 300 innings once, tossing more than 250 frames three other times.
- Threw more than 20 complete games four times.
- Led NL pitchers in wins once, innings pitched once, complete games twice, putouts twice, assists once, and starts once.
- Finished second in NL in wins three times, ERA once, shutouts once, complete games twice, and starts twice.
- Finished in top five of NL MVP voting twice, placing as high as second in 1948.
- 1948 NL champion.
- Two-time NL All-Star selection (1947 and 1948).
- 1948 *Sporting News* All-Star selection.
- 1948 *Sporting News* NL Pitcher of the Year.
- Member of Braves Hall of Fame.

19

BRIAN MCCANN

A good-hitting catcher who also provided the Braves with solid defense behind the plate and outstanding leadership, Brian McCann spent 10 seasons in Atlanta, serving as the team's primary backstop in nine of those. The NL's top offensive performer at his position for nearly a decade, McCann hit at least 20 homers seven times, batted over .300 twice, and knocked in more than 90 runs three times, winning in the process five Silver Sluggers. A capable defender as well, McCann led all NL receivers in putouts, fielding percentage, and runners caught stealing once each, with his strong all-around play earning him seven NL All-Star selections and three *Sporting News* All-Star nominations.

Born in Athens, Georgia, on February 20, 1984, Brian Michael McCann grew up around baseball, with his father, Howard, serving as an assistant coach under Steve Webber at the University of Georgia before becoming head coach at Marshall University, and his older brother, Brad, often taking him to Braves games at Atlanta-Fulton County Stadium. Looking back on how his early years helped shape his future, McCann said, "We were always at the field. My childhood memories, a big portion of those, are watching my dad coach. I just loved to be around the game. I loved everything about it."

Settling with his family near Atlanta at the age of 12 after his father left Marshall and opened a baseball academy, Brian spent most of his time on the diamond playing second base, before transitioning to catcher in high school. Excelling behind the plate for Duluth High School, McCann received a number 26 ranking from *Baseball America* on that publication's 2002 list of the nation's top high school prospects, prompting the University of Alabama to offer him a baseball scholarship. However, after initially committing to Alabama, McCann changed his plans when the Braves selected him in the second round of the June 2002 MLB Draft.

McCann subsequently spent the next two-and-a-half years advancing through the Braves' farm system, before joining the parent club in June

2005. Appearing in 59 games over the season's final four months, the 21-year-old McCann batted .278, hit five homers, and knocked in 23 runs, in just over 200 total plate appearances.

Although McCann spent most of the following spring listening to others rave about top catching prospect Jarrod Saltalamacchia, he made a strong impression on former catcher and Braves coach Eddie Pérez, who recalled, "Everybody was talking about Saltalamacchia. When I saw Mac, I said, 'Well, he's O.K.' But when I started to know him and talk to him, I said, 'This kid's going to be good, because he wants to get better, he wants to learn.' He was 21 or 22, but he was ready to go, and he was asking questions: 'What do I need to do to get better?' Something the other guy never had. I never saw that from anybody, especially another catcher."

Outplaying Saltalamacchia during the preseason, McCann laid claim to the Braves' starting catcher's job, after which he went on to earn his first Silver Slugger and the first of his six consecutive All-Star nominations by hitting 24 homers, driving in 93 runs, batting .333, and compiling an OPS of .961. McCann followed that up with another solid year, concluding the 2007 campaign with 18 homers, 92 RBIs, and a .270 batting average, while finishing second among NL receivers in putouts, although he also committed 13 errors in the field, which ranked as the second-highest total of any backstop. McCann posted excellent numbers in each of the next two seasons as well, hitting 23 homers, driving in 87 runs, and batting .301 in 2008, before reaching the seats 21 times, knocking in 94 runs, and batting .281 the following year, when he began using glasses for the first time after undergoing LASIK surgery two years earlier.

An extremely productive hitter, the left-handed-swinging McCann, who stood 6'3" and weighed 225 pounds, possessed an excellent power stroke that made him a threat to drive the ball over the right field wall at Turner Field. Aided by Chipper Jones, who taught him to tap his front toes twice before starting his swing, McCann also developed into a smart hitter who had the ability to slash the ball to all fields, although he pulled most of his homers to right.

Impressed with the skill that McCann displayed in the batter's box, fellow catcher Russell Martin said, "He just has so much plate coverage. He doesn't really have a go-to spot where you can get him out."

Somewhat less proficient defensively his first few years in the league, McCann led all NL catchers in errors twice and passed balls once, while also allowing more stolen bases than any other receiver in 2010. However, after shedding 15 pounds prior to the start of the 2011 season, McCann became more mobile and much quicker behind the plate, enabling him to

Brian McCann hit at least 20 homers for the Braves seven times.
Courtesy of Keith Allison

lead all players at his position in putouts once, fielding percentage once, and range factor twice.

With McCann having improved his defense, Eddie Pérez called him the finest all-around catcher in the game after he also totaled 45 homers and 148 RBIs from 2010 to 2011, stating, "I'd take my guy first. I know Joe Mauer's one of the best in the game, but Mac is right there with him. To me, right now, he is the best catcher in the big leagues."

An outstanding leader as well, McCann earned the respect of everyone in the locker room with the serious approach he took to his craft, with Chipper Jones saying of his teammate, "Everybody respects what he has to say because he brings it every day. You know that when he's saying something, he's not blowing smoke. I think the guys really respond to him."

After hitting 20 homers, driving in 67 runs, and batting just .230 in 2012, McCann earned his final All-Star selection the following year, despite being limited by injuries to only 102 games, 20 home runs, 57 RBIs, and a .256 batting average. A free agent at season's end, McCann signed with the Yankees for five years and $85 million, ending in the process his nine-year stint in Atlanta.

Upon inking his deal with New York, McCann received praise from Yankees manager Joe Girardi, who said, "A catcher who's a capable defender and threat at the plate is hard to find. He's an offensive catcher who really has the ability to work a pitching staff. He's a complete catcher. He's a middle-of-the-order hitter. His power in this ballpark should work very well."

Although McCann compiled a batting average of just .232 in each of his first two seasons in New York, he proved to be a productive hitter for the Yankees, hitting 23 homers and driving in 75 runs in 2014, before homering 26 times and knocking in 94 runs the following year. But, with McCann slumping to 20 homers and 58 RBIs in 2016 and the Yankees seeking to get younger, they traded the veteran receiver to Houston for a pair of pitching prospects at season's end. McCann ended up spending the next two years assuming a part-time role with the Astros, providing veteran leadership to a team that won two division titles and one World Series, before becoming a free agent again at the end of 2018.

Choosing to return home, McCann signed a one-year, $2 million contract with the Braves on November 26, 2018, that allowed him to fulfill his dream of ending his career in the same place it started that he first revealed during a 2017 interview with the *Atlanta Journal-Constitution*, when he told that publication, "This is my home. I played close to 10 years here. This organization is really, really, really close to my heart. . . . I'll always be an Atlanta Brave. So, we'll see what happens in the future."

McCann, who lived with his wife, Ashley, in Atlanta, added, "This is our home. This is where we both grew up and went to high school, and we'll live here forever. This is where our roots are, and we'll always come back here."

Sharing playing time with Tyler Flowers in 2019, McCann hit 12 homers, knocked in 45 runs, and batted .249, before announcing his retirement shortly after the St. Louis Cardinals eliminated the Braves from the postseason tournament with a victory in Game 5 of the NLDS. Over parts of 15 big-league seasons, McCann hit 282 homers, knocked in 1,018 runs, scored 742 times, collected 1,590 hits, 294 doubles, and five triples, batted .262, compiled a .337 on-base percentage, and posted a .452 slugging percentage. In his 10 years with the Braves, McCann hit 188 homers, knocked in 706 runs, scored 492 others, amassed 1,139 hits, 236 doubles, and two triples, batted .275, compiled a .348 on-base percentage, and posted a .469 slugging percentage.

Expressing his admiration for McCann upon learning of his decision to retire, Dansby Swanson said, "He's been one of the best teammates I've ever had from the baseball experience to the clubhouse. Just being around him every day, he has the unique ability to pull the best out in everybody. So, I'm extremely grateful, and I know all of us are that he chose to come back home and be a part of this."

Ronald Acuña Jr. added through an interpreter, "I grew up watching the Atlanta Braves, we all did, and I was fortunate enough to watch his career. What else is there to say about him? Veteran, superstar, the tremendous seasons he had. Just a perfect career. He has a tremendous impact for your organization."

BRAVES CAREER HIGHLIGHTS

Best Season

McCann's first full season in Atlanta proved to be his finest. In addition to hitting 24 homers, driving in 93 runs, and collecting 34 doubles in 2006, McCann established career-high marks with a batting average of .333, an on-base percentage of .388, and a slugging percentage of .572, earning in the process his first All-Star selection.

Memorable Moments/Greatest Performances

McCann became the first player in Braves history to hit a home run in his first postseason at-bat when he homered off Roger Clemens with two men on base in the bottom of the second inning of a 7–1 win over the Astros in Game 2 of the 2005 NLDS.

After hitting a home run earlier in the contest, McCann highlighted a seven-run ninth-inning rally by the Braves on July 25, 2008, that resulted in an 8–2 win over the Phillies by homering off Brad Lidge with the bases loaded.

McCann capped off a six-run rally in the top of the 10th inning that gave the Braves an 8–2 win over the Astros on August 11, 2010, by hitting a pinch-hit grand slam homer off Jeff Fulchino.

McCann gave the Braves a 7–6 victory over the Marlins on August 29, 2010, when he hit a solo home run off Juan Carlos Oviedo with two men out in the bottom of the ninth inning.

McCann provided further heroics on May 17, 2011, when, after tying the game with a pinch-hit home run off Mark Melancon with two men out in the bottom of the ninth inning, he gave the Braves a 3–1 win over the Astros by homering off Jeff Fulchino with one man on in the 11th.

McCann delivered the decisive blow of a 7–6 win over the Toronto Blue Jays on May 28, 2013, when he hit his second home run of the game off Thad Weber in the top of the 10th inning.

Notable Achievements

- Hit at least 20 home runs seven times.
- Batted over .300 twice.
- Surpassed 30 doubles four times, amassing more than 40 two-baggers once.
- Posted slugging percentage over .500 twice.
- Posted OPS over .900 once.
- Led NL catchers in putouts once, double plays turned twice, runners caught stealing once, and fielding percentage once.
- Ranks among Braves career leaders in home runs (11th), doubles (12th), extra-base hits (tied for 10th), intentional bases on balls (9th), and sacrifice flies (9th).
- 2010 All-Star Game MVP.
- July 7, 2013, NL Player of the Week.
- Five-time Silver Slugger Award winner (2006, 2008, 2009, 2010, and 2011).
- Seven-time NL All-Star selection (2006, 2007, 2008, 2009, 2010, 2011, and 2013).
- Three-time *Sporting News* All-Star selection (2006, 2010, and 2011).

20

FRED TENNEY

An excellent defensive first baseman whose work around the bag greatly influenced future generations of players who manned the position, Fred Tenney spent 15 years in Boston, establishing himself during that time as one of the finest first sackers of the Dead Ball Era. Considered the originator of the 3-6-3 double play, Tenney also developed the style of playing deep and well off the bag, enabling him to amass more assists than any other first baseman at the time of his retirement. A solid offensive performer as well, Tenney batted over .300 seven times and scored more than 100 runs on three separate occasions, with his strong all-around play making him a key contributor to Boston teams that won two NL pennants. And more than a century after he appeared in his last game, Tenney continues to rank among the franchise's all-time leaders in several offensive categories, with his 244 sacrifice bunts representing the highest total in team annals.

Born in Georgetown, Massachusetts, on November 26, 1871, Frederick Tenney displayed a creative side to his personality at an early age, excelling in drawing and sketching in grammar school. The son of a Civil War veteran who nearly died during the conflict due to what he later described as "intense suffering," Tenney received his introduction to baseball at the age of nine. Eventually emerging as a standout left-handed-throwing catcher during his teenage years, Tenney starred behind the plate for two seasons at Brown University, performing so well that Boston Beaneaters manager Frank Selee contacted him the night of his senior dinner to ask him to briefly fill in at catcher for his team due to a rash of injuries to the club's regular backstops.

Sustaining an injury himself in his very first game as a major leaguer on June 16, 1894, Tenney had to be removed from the contest in the fifth inning after a foul tip fractured a finger on his throwing hand. Nevertheless, the 22-year-old receiver made enough of an impression on team brass in his first foray into pro ball that Beaneaters owner James Billings subsequently offered him a contract worth $300.

Returning to action later in the year after his finger healed, Tenney batted .395 and scored 23 runs in just 27 games with the Beaneaters, before assuming a part-time role with the club in each of the next two seasons. Performing well at the plate both years, Tenney batted .272 and scored 35 runs in 49 games in 1895, before batting .336, compiling an on-base percentage of .400, and scoring 64 times in 88 games the following season. However, Tenney's erratic throwing arm prevented him from laying claim to the starting catcher's job, forcing him to split his time between catcher and the outfield, before finally finding a permanent home at first base in 1897.

Replacing veteran Tommy Tucker as Boston's starter at that position, Tenney concluded the 1897 campaign with one homer, 85 RBIs, 125 runs scored, 34 stolen bases, a batting average of .318, and an on-base percentage of .376. He followed that up with two more outstanding seasons, batting .328, driving in 62 runs, and scoring 106 others in 1898, before knocking in 67 runs, scoring 115 times, and ranking among the league leaders with 209 hits, 17 triples, a .347 batting average, and a .411 on-base percentage the following year.

Employing the same strategy at the plate as Hall of Fame outfielder "Wee" Willie Keeler, the left-handed-hitting Tenney, who typically assumed either the first or second spot in the Boston batting order, excelled at "hitting 'em where they ain't," establishing himself before long as one of the league's best place hitters. Although, at just 5'9" and 155 pounds, Tenney possessed very little power, he did an expert job of driving the ball past opposing infielders and using his quickness to turn singles into doubles and doubles into triples, with his 74 three-baggers representing the sixth-highest total in franchise history. A superb bunter as well, Tenney consistently ranked among the NL leaders in sacrifice hits, topping the circuit with 29 in 1902.

Despite his offensive prowess, though, Tenney built his reputation primarily on his defense. In addition to being credited with popularizing the 3-6-3 double play, Tenney ignored the conventional wisdom of the day by playing deep and off the first-base bag to give him increased opportunities to make plays in the field. Furthermore, perhaps because of his smallish frame, Tenney invented the first baseman stretch, with a *Chicago News* reporter writing in 1897, "Tenney's way is far different from that of other first basemen. He reaches his hands far out for the ball and stretches his legs, so that he is further out from the bag on every throw than any other first baseman in the league."

Extremely competitive and feisty, Tenney engaged in a pair of memorable confrontations during his career, one of which involved Pittsburgh

Fred Tenney excelled for the Braves at first base during the Dead Ball Era.
Courtesy of Boston Public Library

Pirates player/manager Fred Clarke. Recalling his skirmish with the Hall of Fame outfielder, which resulted in a 10-game suspension for both men, Tenney said, "Clarke called me names, then I twisted his nose, and he kicked me in the stomach."

Tenney also became involved with umpire Bill Klem on August 7, 1906, with the two men making front-page news with their fracas over unused baseballs. Although accounts of the altercation vary somewhat, it seems that Klem declined to return extra balls after the game, prompting Tenney to begin searching his pockets. The two men subsequently exchanged punches, leading to what *Sporting Life* called "the most turbulent scene ever witnessed on a Boston ballfield."

Nevertheless, Tenney, who became known as the "Soiled Collegian" for his willingness to pursue a career in baseball after attending college, possessed a highly intellectual side to his persona, painting and sketching during the offseason, while also serving as a journalist for the *Boston Post*, the *New York Times*, and *Baseball Magazine* at different times. In explaining his decision to play major-league baseball, Tenney once stated, "I have often been asked why I chose to be a ballplayer when I had several professions open to me. Some seem to think it is a downward to branch out into professional baseball. I always answer by saying that doctors, lawyers, bankers, and writers are plentiful, but, in the entire United States, there are not more than 200 first-rank ballplayers. They have scraped this country from Canada to the Gulf— even to the coal mines—with a fine-tooth comb, but they can find no more."

Tenney continued, "What profession can we find that is better for a man than baseball? It is both honorable and profitable, and that is why I am a professional ballplayer. . . . Yes, I am a college graduate. I won my diploma from Brown University. I entered the national game knowing full well what I was doing, and I have never had a cause to regret it. The profession is not only honorable and profitable, but it is healthful. I have a little home at Winthrop, Massachusetts, just outside of Boston, and to be there with my wife and little girls after the season, I assure you, is a most happy existence."

With the foul strike rule (making balls batted into foul territory strikes for the first time) being introduced to the game at the turn of the century, Tenney never again posted the lofty numbers he compiled from 1897 to 1899. Still, he remained a productive offensive player and one of the league's better hitters from 1900 to 1907. Performing especially well in 1902 and 1903, Tenney batted .315, scored 88 runs, and finished second in the circuit with a .409 on-base percentage in the first of those campaigns, before batting .313, compiling an on-base percentage of .415, and scoring 79 runs the following year, when he assumed the role of team captain. Meanwhile, Tenney continued to excel in the field, leading all NL first basemen in assists seven times and putouts twice during that eight-year stretch.

After being named manager in 1905, Tenney remained in Boston for three more years, guiding the Beaneaters to an overall record of just 158-295, before being relieved of his duties and included in an eight-player trade with the Giants on December 3, 1907. Tenney ended up spending two seasons in New York, playing his best ball for the Giants in 1908, when he led the NL with 101 runs scored, finished second in the circuit with 72 walks, and led all major-league first basemen with a career-high 1,624 putouts. Commenting on the overall impact that Tenney made in his first year with the Giants, W. S. Farnsworth wrote in the New York *Evening Journal*, "He is like wine—he improves with age. He is not only playing a grand game, but his coaching is making the youngsters, (Al) Bridwell and

(Larry) Doyle, the spiciest pair ever to cavort around the keystone corner of an infield. And his great ability to 'stretch' has given [third baseman] Arthur Devlin the greatest fielding season he has had since joining the Giants. With his swat-stick too, Tenney has a record to be proud of."

However, after Tenney scored only 43 runs and batted just .235 in 1909, the Giants released him at the end of the year. Tenney subsequently spent the ensuing campaign playing in the New England League, before returning to Boston, where he spent the 1911 season serving the Braves as a player/manager. Fired and released once again after leading the team to a record of just 44-107, Tenney announced his retirement, ending his career with 22 home runs, 688 RBIs, 1,278 runs scored, 2,231 hits, 270 doubles, 77 triples, 285 stolen bases, a .294 batting average, a .371 on-base percentage, and a .358 slugging percentage. Tenney also recorded 1,363 assists and 17,903 putouts at first base, with the first figure representing the highest total compiled by any player who manned the position for another two decades.

After retiring from baseball, Tenney partnered with Henry Spinney in forming the Tenney-Spinney Shoe Company. He also worked for the Equitable Life Insurance Society for more than three decades and continued writing for the *New York Times*. Tenney lived until July 3, 1952, when he died at the age of 80 following a long illness.

BRAVES (BEANEATERS) CAREER HIGHLIGHTS

Best Season

A strong case could be made that Tenney had his finest season in 1902, when, relative to the rest of the league, his .315 batting average, .409 on-base percentage, .785 OPS, and 88 runs scored measured up quite well to the numbers he posted from 1897 to 1899. Nevertheless, with the rules governing the game just prior to the turn of the century greatly increasing offensive production, Tenney compiled easily the most impressive numbers of his career, performing especially well in 1899, when he batted .347, compiled an on-base percentage of .411 and an OPS of .851, drove in 67 runs, scored 115 others, and collected 209 hits and 17 triples.

Memorable Moments/Greatest Performances

Tenney made history on June 14, 1897, when he started what may have been the first-ever 3-6-3 double play during a 5–3 win over the Cincinnati Reds. Recalling the play years later, Tenney said, "We were playing Cincinnati in Boston when the batter hit the ball over first. I grabbed it and threw to (shortstop Herman) Long, then hurried to the bag and took Long's throw for a double play. It seemed that you could have heard a pin drop for 10 seconds, and then the crowd just let out a roar. It had seen something new."

Tenney gave the Beaneaters a 5–4 win over the Giants on May 29, 1902, when he hit a two-run homer off New York starter Tully Sparks with two men out in the bottom of the ninth inning.

Tenney proved to be the difference in a 3–1 win over the Cubs on July 4, 1902, stealing two bases and driving in all three runs with a pair of singles.

Tenney contributed to a 10–5 victory over the Reds on August 8, 1902, by going 4-for-5 at the plate, with two doubles, three RBIs, and two runs scored.

Tenney starred during a 9–5 victory over the Phillies on July 1, 1905, collecting four hits, driving in three runs, and scoring twice.

Tenney had another big day against the Phillies on May 3, 1911, going a perfect 5-for-5 at the plate, with two doubles, one run scored, and a stolen base during a 4–3 win.

Notable Achievements

- Scored more than 100 runs three times.
- Batted over .300 seven times.
- Surpassed 200 hits once.
- Finished in double digits in triples once.
- Stole more than 20 bases five times, topping 30 thefts once.
- Compiled on-base percentage over .400 five times.
- Posted slugging percentage over .500 once.
- Posted OPS over 1.000 once.
- Led NL in sacrifice hits once, plate appearances once, and at-bats once.
- Finished second in NL with .409 on-base percentage in 1902.
- Led NL first basemen in putouts twice, assists eight times, double plays turned once, and fielding percentage once.
- Holds franchise career record for most sacrifice hits (244).

- Ranks among Braves career leaders in runs scored (5th), hits (4th), triples (6th), doubles (11th), total bases (8th), bases on balls (6th), stolen bases (tied for 4th), games played (7th), plate appearances (5th), and at-bats (7th).
- Two-time NL champion (1897 and 1898).

21

JOE TORRE

When Joe Torre gained admission to the Baseball Hall of Fame in 2014, he did so largely on the strength of the 10 division titles, six AL pennants, and four World Series he won as manager of the New York Yankees from 1996 to 2007. However, Torre previously merited serious consideration for induction into Cooperstown by excelling for three different teams at catcher, third base, and first base during an outstanding playing career that covered parts of 18 seasons. Playing his best ball for the Braves and Cardinals from 1961 to 1974, Torre earned one MVP award and nine All-Star nominations, being named to the NL squad five times as a member of the Braves, with whom he spent eight full seasons. An exceptional hitter and solid defensive catcher, Torre hit more than 20 homers four times, knocked in more than 100 runs twice, batted over .300 twice, and led all players at his position in fielding percentage twice during his time in Milwaukee and Atlanta, establishing himself in the process as the senior circuit's top receiver. Transitioning to the infield after being traded to the Cardinals following the conclusion of the 1968 campaign, Torre spent his nine remaining big-league seasons manning either first or third base, before embarking on a lengthy managerial career during which he served as skipper for five different teams.

Born in Brooklyn, New York, on July 18, 1940, Joseph Paul Torre grew up with his four older siblings in the borough's Marine Park section, where he suffered through a difficult childhood. The son of Italian immigrants, young Joseph often watched as his father, Joe Sr., who worked as a plainclothes officer in the New York City Police Department, physically abused his mother until they finally divorced in 1951. Frequently targeted by his father as well, Torre revealed years later, "Although he never physically hurt me, he verbally abused me often."

Holding much fonder memories of his mother, Margaret, Torre described her as "a loving, stabilizing influence who always was there for me."

With Torre receiving virtually no support from his father, he later identified his older brother, Frank, who went on to play first base for the Braves for five seasons in Milwaukee, as the person who impacted him the most during his formative years, recalling, "Frank was the kick in the butt I needed to amount to anything in life. It was Frank who toughened me up, Frank who turned me into a catcher, Frank who put me through high school, Frank who used to send me spending money, even when he was off fighting in Korea, and Frank who was everything I ever wanted to be. He was a ballplayer. I may not have had a father in my life then, but I sure as hell had a hero."

The younger Torre, who ironically grew up rooting for the New York Giants instead of the Dodgers, eventually established himself as a star on the diamond at Saint Francis Prep High School after he converted to catcher on the advice of his brother, Frank. While in high school, Torre also played for the Brooklyn Cadets of the All-American Amateur Baseball Association, performing well enough as a member of the team to receive a contract offer from Braves scout Honey Russell on August 24, 1959.

After signing with the Braves for $22,500, Torre began his professional career at Class C Eau Claire, hitting 16 home runs and batting .344 in 1960, with his strong play earning him a late-season callup to the parent club. Returned to the minors the following year, the 20-year-old Torre batted .342 and knocked in 24 runs in just 27 games with Triple-A Louisville, before being summoned to Milwaukee by the Braves in early June when starting catcher Del Crandall injured his throwing arm. Despite his lack of experience, Torre acquitted himself extremely well the rest of the year, hitting 10 homers, driving in 42 runs, and batting .278 in 113 games and just over 400 official at-bats, earning in the process a runner-up finish to Cubs outfielder Billy Williams in the NL Rookie of the Year voting.

With Crandall returning to action in 1962, Torre assumed a backup role, hitting five homers, knocking in 26 runs, and batting .282 in just 220 official at-bats, before displacing Crandall as the Braves' starting receiver the following year, when he earned his first All-Star selection by hitting 14 homers, driving in 71 runs, and batting .293. Also starting 35 games at first base, Torre impressed Braves manager Bobby Bragan with his defensive work around the bag, with Bragan noting, "He's got good hands, and he goes to his right very well. I've never seen a young right-handed first baseman make that tough first-to-second-to first double play as well."

Splitting his time between catcher and first base in 1964, Torre had his finest season to date, earning the second of his five straight All-Star nominations and a fifth-place finish in the NL MVP balloting by hitting 20 homers

Joe Torre earned five All-Star nominations as a member of the Braves.

and ranking among the league leaders with 109 RBIs, 193 hits, 36 doubles, and a .321 batting average. Torre followed that up with another excellent year, concluding the 1965 campaign with 27 homers, 80 RBIs, and a .291 batting average, while also winning the only Gold Glove of his career.

The right-handed-swinging Torre, who stood 6'2" and weighed close to 230 pounds his first several years in the league, proved to be one of the NL's most consistent and productive hitters for most of his career, with Jim Kaat saying, "Talk about a pure hitter—he [Torre] was an RBI guy, a production guy, almost like [Orlando] Cepeda." A line-drive hitter who also had the ability to deliver the long ball, Torre earned every hit he got since he lacked the foot speed to leg out infield singles. Meanwhile, Torre, who typically manned either the fourth or fifth spot in the Braves' batting order, did an excellent job of providing protection in the middle of the lineup for sluggers Hank Aaron and Eddie Mathews.

Taking full advantage of the friendly confines at Atlanta Stadium when the Braves moved south in 1966, Torre had one of his finest offensive seasons, hitting a career-high 36 homers, knocking in 101 runs, and batting .315. However, after beginning the 1967 campaign in similar fashion, Torre tore ligaments in his ankle while chasing Philadelphia's Clay Dalrymple in a rundown, forcing him to miss a month of action, and limiting him to just 20 homers, 68 RBIs, and a .277 batting average for the season. Experiencing more misfortune in 1968, Torre suffered a broken finger in April and a broken cheekbone and nose later in the year when a pitch thrown by Cubs right-hander Chuck Hartenstein struck him in the face. Able to appear in only 115 games, Torre finished the season with just 10 homers, 55 RBIs, and a .271 batting average.

With Torre seeking a salary of $77,000 heading into 1969 and the Braves countering with an offer of $60,000, the two parties became involved in a bitter dispute exacerbated by the catcher's recent role as the team's union representative during a threatened players' strike. Displaying his unhappiness over Torre's spring training holdout, Braves vice president Paul Richards told the media that, based on his performance the past two seasons, the catcher "could hold out until Thanksgiving" as far as he was concerned. In response, Torre asked that the Braves not only meet his salary demands, but also that he receive an apology from Richards.

With the two sides eventually reaching an impasse, the Braves traded Torre to the St. Louis Cardinals for slugging first baseman Orlando Cepeda on March 17, 1969. While Cepeda went on to have a couple of productive years for the Braves, Torre, who left Atlanta with career totals of 142 home runs, 552 RBIs, 470 runs scored, 1,087 hits, 154 doubles, and 21 triples, a .294 batting average, a .356 on-base percentage, and a .462 slugging percentage, ended up having three exceptional seasons in St. Louis before his skills began to erode.

After hitting 18 homers, driving in 101 runs, and batting .289 while manning first base for the Cardinals in 1969, Torre split the ensuing campaign between catcher and third base, earning All-Star honors for the first of four straight times by hitting 21 homers, knocking in 100 runs, and placing near the top of the league rankings with 203 hits and a .325 batting average. Then, after shedding more than 20 pounds the following offseason to get down to a playing weight of close to 200, Torre spent most of 1971 at third base, where he had the greatest season of his career. In addition to hitting 24 homers, scoring 97 runs, and compiling an OPS of .976, Torre led the NL with 137 RBIs, 230 hits, and a .363 batting average, earning in the process league MVP honors.

Although Torre never again reached such heights, he remained a consistent performer for the Cardinals for three more years, gaining All-Star recognition another two times, before being dealt to the New York Mets at the end of 1974. Torre spent the next two-plus seasons assuming a part-time role with his hometown team, before retiring as an active player when the ballclub appointed him its new manager in June 1977. Torre, who ended his playing career with 252 home runs, 1,185 RBIs, 996 runs scored, 2,342 hits, 344 doubles, 59 triples, a .297 batting average, a .365 on-base percentage, and a .452 slugging percentage, subsequently spent most of the next five seasons managing the Mets to an overall record of 286-420, before being fired at the end of the strike-shortened 1981 campaign. Returning to Atlanta following his dismissal, Torre managed the Braves from 1982 to 1984, guiding them to an overall winning record and one division title. But when they finished two games under .500 in 1984, Torre received his walking papers, leading to a six-year stint as a broadcaster for the California Angels. Torre then piloted the St. Louis Cardinals for parts of six seasons, experiencing only a moderate amount of success, before being named manager of the Yankees in 1996 after being relieved of his duties in St. Louis.

Considered only a mediocre manager prior to his return to New York, Torre created a new legacy for himself by leading the Yankees to six pennants and four world championships over the next 12 seasons, establishing himself along the way as one of the most respected figures in the game with his expert handling of a talented roster and unpredictable owner (George Steinbrenner) known for his impulsive nature. In discussing the qualities that made Torre such an effective skipper, Yankees third baseman Scott Brosius stated, "He's a great manager. There is more to managing than who to pitch and play. It's managing people, the press . . . and Joe does that all great. Players follow the tone set by the manager, and Joe is the calming influence of this team."

Meanwhile, noted author David Halberstam once described Torre as "a man secure in his knowledge of who he is and secure in his faith. Though he would prefer to win, rather than to lose, how he behaves as a man and how he sees himself is not based on his career winning percentage. The key to Torre is that he is a good baseball man, but he also knows there is much more to life than baseball, and that, finally, it is how you behave, more obviously when things are not going well, that defines you."

Finally leaving the Yankees at the end of 2007, Torre spent the next three years guiding the Los Angeles Dodgers to two division titles, before retiring from managing following the conclusion of the 2010 campaign. Over parts of 29 seasons as a major-league manager, Torre led his teams to 13 division titles, six pennants, four world championships, and an overall record of 2,326-1,997.

After leaving the Dodgers at the end of the 2010 season, Torre accepted a position in the Office of the Commissioner of Baseball as executive vice president of baseball operations that he retained until February 2020, when he became a special assistant to the commissioner. Away from baseball, the 82-year-old Torre continues to assist those many unfortunate individuals affected by domestic violence through his Safe at Home Foundation that he first created in 2002.

BRAVES CAREER HIGHLIGHTS

Best Season

Although Torre also performed exceptionally well for the Braves in 1964, he had his finest all-around season for them in 1966, when he ranked among the NL leaders in seven different offensive categories, including home runs (36), RBIs (101), batting average (.315), on-base percentage (.382), and slugging percentage (.560).

Memorable Moments/Greatest Performances

Torre led the Braves to a 7–3 win over the Reds on May 20, 1964, by driving in five runs with a homer, double, and single, with his bases loaded home run off Joey Jay in the top of the ninth inning proving to be the game's decisive blow.

Torre touched up Hall of Fame right-hander Juan Marichal for two homers and five RBIs during a 10–4 win over the Giants on May 26, 1965.

Torre homered twice and knocked in three runs during a 5–4 win over the Reds on July 24, 1966, with his leadoff homer off reliever Billy McCool in the top of the 10th inning providing the margin of victory.

Torre gave the Braves a 6–5 win over the Houston Astros on August 11, 1967, when he led off the bottom of the 16th inning with a home run off right-handed reliever Barry Latman.

Notable Achievements

- Hit at least 20 home runs four times, topping 30 homers once.
- Knocked in more than 100 runs twice.
- Batted over .300 twice.
- Surpassed 30 doubles once.
- Posted slugging percentage over .500 once.
- Posted OPS over .900 once.
- Led NL catchers in fielding percentage twice, caught stealing percentage once, and runners caught stealing once.
- May 1965 NL Player of the Month.
- 1965 Gold Glove Award winner.
- Finished fifth in 1964 NL MVP voting.
- Five-time NL All-Star selection (1963, 1964, 1965, 1966, and 1967).
- Three-time *Sporting News* All-Star selection (1964, 1965, and 1966).
- Elected to Baseball Hall of Fame by members of Veterans Committee in 2014.

22

JOE ADCOCK

A hard-hitting first baseman who possessed prodigious power at the plate, Joe Adcock spent 10 seasons in Milwaukee, establishing himself during that time as one of the most feared sluggers in the National League. Serving as a perfect complement to Hank Aaron and Eddie Mathews in the middle of the Braves' batting order, Adcock surpassed 30 homers and 100 RBIs twice each, batted over .300 once, and posted a slugging percentage over .500 eight times, despite being hampered by injuries and often being platooned. A solid fielder as well, Adcock led all NL first sackers in putouts twice and fielding percentage four times, with his strong all-around play making him a key contributor to Braves teams that won two pennants and one World Series.

Born in Coushatta, Louisiana, on October 30, 1927, Joseph Wilbur Adcock grew up with his younger sister on the family farm, where he began assisting with the chores associated with farming at the age of seven. The son of Ray Adcock, a businessman, farmer, and longtime sheriff of Red River County, and Helen (Lyles) Adcock, a schoolteacher, Joseph received no exposure to baseball during his formative years, recalling, "There was no town team, no school team, not even a diamond. I'd hit a rock with a stick out by the roadside down home, and I'd knock corncobs up on the barn roof with a broomstick. But as far as playing baseball, that was just something I heard my dad talk about."

Always big for his age, Adcock naturally gravitated toward basketball, eventually becoming a star on the court while attending Coushatta High School, which he led to the state Class B finals as a senior in 1944. Offered a basketball scholarship to Louisiana State University, Adcock initially focused on furthering his skills on the court at LSU, before being recruited for the baseball team as well despite his lack of experience. Recalling his initial foray into the national pastime, Adcock said, "I was all hit and no field. I'd never worn spikes. I'd never had a uniform. I never played a game with nine men on a side."

Although basketball remained Adcock's first love, he eventually developed into a top slugger and capable defensive first baseman at LSU, prompting Cincinnati Reds scout Paul Florence to sign him to a contract after he helped lead the Tigers to the Southeastern Conference championship as a junior in 1947. Adcock subsequently spent the next three years in the minor leagues, before joining the Reds in 1950 after hitting 19 homers and batting .298 at Tulsa the previous year. Platooned in left field for most of the next three seasons due to the presence of slugging first baseman Ted Kluszewski, the right-handed-hitting Adcock received limited playing time, even though he proved to be a productive hitter whenever he found his name entered on the lineup card.

Finally afforded the opportunity to play full-time after the Braves acquired him from the Reds as part of a complicated four-team trade on February 16, 1953, Adcock laid claim to the starting first base job immediately upon his arrival in Milwaukee, after which he went on to hit 18 homers, drive in 80 runs, score 71 times, collect 33 doubles, and compile a batting average of .285. Adcock also performed well in the field and provided leadership in the clubhouse, prompting Braves manager Charlie Grimm, a former first baseman himself, to say, "Adcock is my kind of player—a holler guy. . . . He has a good pair of hands and shifts well."

Despite missing the final three weeks of the ensuing campaign after having his right thumb broken by a Don Newcombe pitch, Adcock increased his offensive output, earning an eighth-place finish in the NL MVP voting by hitting 23 homers, knocking in 87 runs, scoring 73 others, batting .308, and ranking among the league leaders with a slugging percentage of .520 and an OPS of .885. The 1955 season also ended prematurely for Adcock, who sat out the final two months with a broken right hand after being struck on the wrist by an offering from Jim Hearn of the Giants.

A classic pull hitter who crowded the plate and strode into the ball, leaving him somewhat vulnerable to inside pitches, Adcock often found himself being targeted by opposing pitchers, who followed the scouting report on him, as sportswriter Red Smith suggested when he wrote, "National League strategy insists that he can't pull the ball if it's close to his wrists."

Nevertheless, Adcock never considered altering his approach at the plate, once telling Smith, "That's how I earn my living. Hitting, I mean. You've got to make up your mind—do you run away from pitches or stay in there and hit? There are a dozen different stances, but I've got to use the one that's natural for me and stay in there."

One would have a difficult time finding fault with Adcock's approach since he gradually emerged as one of the most feared hitters in the

Joe Adcock surpassed 20 homers and 100 RBIs twice each for the Braves.

game. Standing 6'4" and weighing somewhere in the vicinity of 210 pounds, Adcock possessed tremendous power to all fields, hitting several tape-measure home runs over the course of his career. The first player to hit a ball into the revamped center field bleachers at the Polo Grounds, Adcock also became the first man to hit a ball over the 83-foot-high grand-stand onto the double-deck roof in left-center field at Ebbets Field and the first right-handed batter to drive a ball over the 64-foot-high scoreboard in right-center field at Philadelphia's Connie Mack Stadium.

Fully recovered by the start of the 1956 campaign, Adcock ended up having a huge year for the Braves, finishing second in the NL with 38 home runs, 103 RBIs, and a .597 slugging percentage, while also batting .291 and compiling an OPS of .934 that placed him third in the league rankings. However, after getting off to a torrid start in 1957, Adcock suffered a dev-astating injury to his right knee in late May that ended up limiting him to just 65 games, 12 home runs, and 38 RBIs. Although Adcock courageously played through pain the following year, he found his performance being adversely affected by his still-ailing knee, later saying, "I couldn't swing a bat right. Whenever I put pressure on my back leg, out would go the knee. I didn't play a game when my leg didn't lock up on me six to eight times."

Still, despite his injury and an unwanted platoon he shared with Frank Torre, Adcock managed to hit 19 homers, drive in 54 runs, and bat .275, in helping the Braves capture their second consecutive NL pennant. Sharing playing time with Torre once again in 1959 after holding out for more money during spring training, Adcock hit 25 homers, knocked in 76 runs, and batted .292, in 115 games and just over 400 official at-bats. Expressing his dissatisfaction at one point during the season over being platooned, Adcock said, "I don't like playing one day and sitting on the bench the next. I can't do either myself or the team justice."

With Chuck Dressen replacing Fred Haney as Braves manager in 1960, Adcock became a full-time player once again, allowing him to post some of the most impressive numbers of his career the next two seasons. After earning his lone All-Star nomination in 1960 by hitting 25 homers, driving in 91 runs, and batting .298, Adcock homered 38 times, knocked in 108 runs, and batted .285 the following year, before age and injuries began to take their toll on him. Limited by his aching knee to only 112 starts at first base in 1962, the 34-year-old Adcock batted just .248, although he still managed to hit 29 homers and drive in 78 runs.

Sadly for Adcock, the 1962 campaign proved to be his last in Milwaukee. Included in a multiplayer trade the Braves completed with the Indians the following offseason, Adcock voiced his displeasure upon learning of the deal, saying, "The front office took things for granted too much with guys who won the pennant. They figured they'd keep going. Maybe they sat too long, but then they moved too fast, panicky."

Adcock, who left the Braves having hit 239 homers, driven in 760 runs, scored 564 times, collected 1,206 hits, 197 doubles, and 22 triples, batted .285, compiled an on-base percentage of .343, and posted a slugging percentage of .511 as a member of the team, ended up serving the Indians as a part-time player in 1963, before assuming a similar role with the California Angels the next three years. While in Cleveland, though, Adcock received the following words of praise from Indians skipper Birdie Tebbetts, who also managed him his last year in Milwaukee: "He never once quit on me in Milwaukee. I admire Adcock because he's one of the few players I have ever seen who never has taken a short step . . . I have never seen him dog it even once."

Choosing to announce his retirement following the conclusion of the 1966 campaign, Adcock ended his playing career with 336 home runs, 1,122 RBIs, 823 runs scored, 1,832 hits, 295 doubles, 35 triples, a batting average of .277, an on-base percentage of .337, and a slugging percentage of .485. An underrated fielder, Adcock also retired with the third-highest fielding percentage (.994) at first base in major-league history.

Following his playing days, Adcock spent one season managing the Indians, before spending another piloting the Triple-A Seattle Angels in the Pacific Coast League. After being relieved of his duties in Seattle, Adcock retired to his hometown of Coushatta, where he farmed and became a successful breeder of thoroughbred racehorses, being named Louisiana's top breeder on 10 separate occasions.

Described by his son, Jay, as "the sort of person who never met a stranger. Everyone was his friend. He was comfortable with anyone on any level in any walk of life," Adcock remained a friend to everyone he met until May 3, 1999, when he died on his farm in Coushatta at the age of 71 after spending the previous few years suffering from Alzheimer's disease.

Upon learning of his former teammate's passing, Hank Aaron said, "I had the pleasure of knowing Joe as a teammate and a friend for many years. I learned a lot from him as a player, but, as good a player as he was, he was an even better human being."

BRAVES CAREER HIGHLIGHTS

Best Season

Although Adcock gained All-Star recognition for the only time in 1960, he had his finest all-around season in 1956, when he earned an 11th-place finish in the NL MVP voting by hitting 38 homers, driving in 103 runs, scoring 76 times, batting .291, and compiling a career-best OPS of .934, while also leading all NL first basemen in fielding percentage for the first of four times.

Memorable Moments/Greatest Performances

Adcock hit a mammoth two-run homer into the center field bleachers at New York's Polo Grounds during a 3–2 win over the Giants on April 29, 1953, becoming in the process the first player ever to drive a ball into that section of the ballpark (Hank Aaron and Lou Brock later accomplished the feat as well).

Adcock flexed his muscles again on July 31, 1954, when he became just the seventh player in major-league history to hit four home runs in one game during a 15–7 win over the Dodgers at Brooklyn's Ebbets Field. Adcock, who homered off four different pitchers en route to going 5-for-5 with seven RBIs and five runs scored, barely missed a fifth home run when he doubled off the top of the left field wall in the third inning, with his 18 total bases setting an MLB record that stood for 48 years.

Adcock helped lead the Braves to a 13–3 thrashing of the Giants on July 19, 1956, by going 4-for-4 at the plate, with two homers, a double, and a career-high eight RBIs, homering once with the bases loaded and once with two men aboard.

Adcock is perhaps remembered most for delivering the blow that ended the epic pitching duel between Lew Burdette and Pittsburgh's Harvey Haddix on May 26, 1959. With the contest remaining scoreless heading into the bottom of the 13th inning and Haddix not having allowed a single baserunner up to that point, Félix Mantilla reached base on an error, prompting the Pirates left-hander to walk Hank Aaron intentionally after Eddie Mathews sacrificed Mantilla to second. Adcock subsequently drove a ball into the stands in right-center field for an apparent game-winning three-run homer, but ultimately was credited with just an RBI double after Aaron, having seen the runner ahead of him cross home plate, walked back to the dugout, causing Adcock to be called out for passing him on the basepaths.

Adcock gave the Braves a 10–6 victory over the Dodgers on May 4, 1961, when he homered off reliever Jim Golden with the bases loaded in the bottom of the 10th inning.

Notable Achievements

- Hit more than 20 home runs six times, topping 30 homers twice.
- Knocked in more than 100 runs twice.
- Batted over .300 once.
- Surpassed 30 doubles once.
- Posted slugging percentage over .500 eight times.
- Posted OPS over .900 once.
- Hit four home runs in one game vs. Brooklyn Dodgers on July 31, 1954.
- One of only three players to homer into center field bleachers in New York's Polo Grounds.

- Finished second in NL with 38 home runs, 103 RBIs, and .597 slugging percentage in 1956.
- Led NL first basemen in putouts twice and fielding percentage four times.
- Ranks among Braves career leaders in home runs (7th), RBIs (11th), extra-base hits (9th), total bases (11th), and slugging percentage (9th).
- Two-time NL champion (1957 and 1958).
- 1957 world champion.
- Finished eighth in 1954 NL MVP voting.
- 1960 NL All-Star selection.

23

DEL CRANDALL

Known for his quick release and catlike movements, Del Crandall established himself as one of the finest defensive catchers of his era over the course of his career, which he spent almost entirely in Boston and Milwaukee. A member of the Braves for parts of 13 seasons, Crandall served as their primary starter behind the plate from 1953 to 1962, a period during which he led NL receivers in putouts three times, assists six times, and fielding percentage on four separate occasions. The winner of four Gold Gloves, Crandall also proved to be an extremely capable hitter, swatting more than 20 homers three times, with his excellent all-around play and outstanding leadership ability making him a huge contributor to teams that won two pennants and one World Series. An eight-time NL All-Star, Crandall later received the additional honor of being named to the Braves Hall of Fame.

Born in Ontario, California, on March 5, 1930, Delmar Wesley Crandall moved with his family at the age of six to the city of Fullerton, where he grew up some 25 miles east of Los Angeles. The son of Richard and Nancy Crandall, both of whom worked in the citrus-packaging industry, Crandall began playing baseball at the age of nine, before receiving his introduction to catching two years later, recalling, "I became a catcher when I was in fifth grade. I was a pudgy little kid and not a very good athlete, but I was enthusiastic. Art Johnson, a coach, came to my elementary school, Maple School. He looked at me with a mask and a catcher's glove and I told him I can catch. That was the first challenge in my young life."

Aided immeasurably by Pop Lemon, a former minor-league catcher who ran the local recreation department and managed the semipro Fullerton Merchants, Crandall soon learned the art of catching and how to throw and release the ball, stating, "Everything I learned was from Pop Lemon. He was the most influential man in my baseball career."

Developing into a standout receiver at Fullerton Union High School following a growth spurt that transformed him from a stubby 5-foot freshman into a slender, 6'1" senior, Crandall began drawing the attention of

Del Crandall (left), pictured here with backup catcher Paul Burris, proved to be one of the finest defensive receivers of his era.
Courtesy of Boston Public Library, Leslie Jones Collection

major-league scouts, with the Dodgers, Yankees, Cardinals, and Braves all expressing interest in him. After turning down a $20,000 offer from the Dodgers because he felt they already had too many prospects in their farm system, Crandall ultimately chose to sign a two-year, $4,000 contract with the Braves' top farm team, the Milwaukee Brewers, later saying, "That was more money than my parents or I had ever seen."

Beginning his pro career at only 17 years of age, Crandall struggled at the plate at first, prompting the organization to demote him to Class C Leavenworth (Kansas). While at Leavenworth, Crandall, who had been a weak hitter in high school, began to find his stroke with the help of manager Harold "Dutch" Hoffman, who suggested that he cut down on his swing. Recalling the advice he received from Hoffman, Crandall said, "Dutch told me that I have to hit pepper every day, so I did with Joe Nezgoda. After three or four weeks, I started to hit. I was able to do the same things in a game that I did in pepper."

Crandall ended up spending just a year-and-a-half in the minor leagues, before being called up by the Braves midway through the 1949 campaign. Appearing in 67 games the rest of the year after making his big-league debut on June 17, 1949, Crandall became, at just over four months past his 19th birthday, the youngest starting catcher in major-league history. Despite his lack of experience, Crandall acquitted himself extremely well over the final three-and-a-half months of the season, earning a runner-up finish in the Rookie of the Year voting by batting .263, hitting four homers, and driving in 34 runs, in only 228 official at-bats.

Sidelined by a broken finger for much of 1950, Crandall appeared in only 79 games, batting just .220 with four homers and 37 RBIs. He then missed the next two seasons while serving in the Army during the Korean War, seeing active duty in Japan for part of his stint.

Returning to the States in 1953, Crandall joined the Braves at their new home in Milwaukee, where he soon emerged as one of the finest all-around receivers in the game. Gaining All-Star recognition four straight times from 1953 to 1956, Crandall averaged close to 20 home runs and 60 RBIs over that four-year stretch, proving to be especially productive in 1955, when, despite batting just .236, he hit a career-high 26 homers and knocked in 62 runs. Predominantly a pull hitter, the right-handed-swinging Crandall, who stood 6'1" and weighed close to 190 pounds, possessed good power and rarely struck out, fanning only 477 times in almost 5,600 career plate appearances.

Known more for his defense, though, Crandall, who assumed the role of team captain in 1954, helped usher in a new style of aggressive play behind the plate. More athletic than most of the short and stocky catchers of his time, the tall and muscular Crandall used his quickness and flexibility to hold runners on by throwing to all three bases, a practice that irritated some veteran players, as he revealed when he said, "When I got to the big leagues, picking off guys was not done that much. Fielders were just not used to a catcher throwing to pick off a runner. Certainly, the manager did not encourage the first or third baseman to cover the bag."

A master at recognizing hitters' weaknesses and understanding his pitchers' tendencies, Crandall also took a backseat to no one in terms of calling a game, with Warren Spahn telling the *Sporting News*, "I think he knows more about what I can do in a game situation than I do."

An expert handler of pitchers, Crandall did a superb job of bringing out the best in Spahn and Lew Burdette, Milwaukee's other top starter, although he chose not to take much of the credit for the success that the former experienced on the mound, once saying, "Spahn had such great control and was so good—great delivery, deception, and concentration—he'd just hit your glove. He developed a screwball when he couldn't throw as hard anymore."

On the other hand, Crandall admitted that he had to take a far more active role in the handling of the nervous, fidgety, and temperamental Burdette, stating, "I think I made a contribution with Burdette. I think he relied on me to do things. Sometimes he'd go into his windup before I even gave him a sign. He'd say, 'I knew what you'd call.' We had a close relationship. He trusted me."

In discussing his philosophy of catching, Crandall said, "I always looked at myself as a defensive catcher first. I think it was the enthusiasm I had playing the game. I didn't get tired and tried to be alert to anything that happened on the field. Hitting did not detract from my catching."

Although Crandall posted slightly subpar offensive numbers in 1957, finishing the season with 15 homers, 46 RBIs, and a .253 batting average, his leadership, outstanding defense, and deft handling of the pitching staff proved to be key factors in the Braves' successful run to the pennant. And when the Braves repeated as NL champions the following year, Crandall earned his fifth All-Star selection and a 10th-place finish in the league MVP voting by hitting 18 homers, driving in 63 runs, and batting .272, while also leading all NL receivers in putouts, assists, and fielding percentage. Continuing his outstanding play in 1959 and 1960, Crandall earned All-Star honors and MVP consideration both years by hitting 21 homers, knocking in 72 runs, and batting .257 in the first of those campaigns, before homering 19 times, batting .294, and establishing career-high marks with 77 RBIs and 81 runs scored in the second.

Impressed with Crandall's solid hitting and exceptional defense, Pirates general manager Joe L. Brown proclaimed, "Crandall is the best all-around catcher in the league."

Crandall also later drew praise from former Dodger receiver John Roseboro, who commented, "I think the most complete catcher during my time in the league was Del Crandall. He was sound defensively. He could catch the bad pitch and block the plate. He didn't have a strong arm, but he made up for it with a quick release and accuracy."

Meanwhile, Hank Aaron once said of his longtime teammate, "When he was healthy, there was nobody better than Campanella as both a catcher and a hitter. But I played with Del Crandall a long time and he was a match for anybody defensively."

After missing most of the 1961 season with a sore arm, Crandall shared catching duties with Joe Torre when he returned to the Braves the following year, performing well enough in a part-time role (he batted a career-high .297) to be named to his eighth All-Star team and win the last of his four Gold Gloves. But, when new manager Bobby Bragan installed Torre as the primary catcher in 1963, Crandall struggled at the plate, hitting just three homers, knocking in only 28 runs, and batting a career-low .201. Furthermore, Crandall did not see eye to eye with his new skipper on many issues, later saying, "It became increasingly obvious that Bobby Bragan and I did not get along. We had big disagreements, and it led to bad feelings. I told him (Bragan) that I thought it was time for him to trade me."

Subsequently included in a seven-player trade that the Braves completed with the Giants on December 3, 1963, that netted them outfielder Felipe Alou, Crandall left Milwaukee feeling somewhat betrayed, stating years later, "You take 10 years of being important to a ballclub and suddenly, in the next year, you are not important. That changes your view of the club."

Crandall, who left the Braves having hit 170 homers, driven in 628 runs, scored 552 times, collected 1,176 hits, 167 doubles, and 17 triples, batted .257, compiled an on-base percentage of .313, and posted a slugging percentage of .412 as a member of the team, spent just one year with the Giants, before splitting his final two seasons between the Pirates and Indians, serving as a part-time player with all three clubs. Choosing to announce his retirement following the conclusion of the 1966 campaign, Crandall ended his career with 179 home runs, 657 RBIs, 585 runs scored, 1,276 hits, 179 doubles, 18 triples, a .254 batting average, a .312 on-base percentage, and a .404 slugging percentage.

Following his playing days, Crandall briefly owned and operated a restaurant in Fullerton, California, before returning to baseball in a managerial capacity. After spending four seasons managing in the Dodgers' farm system, Crandall piloted the Milwaukee Brewers from 1972 to 1975 and the Seattle Mariners from 1983 to 1984, also coaching for the California Angels and the Dodgers at the Triple-A level in between managerial stints.

Retiring to Fullerton after leaving baseball for good in 1984, Crandall remained there with his wife, Frances, until August 2013, when she died after spending the previous few years suffering from dementia. Eventually moving into an assisted-living facility in Mission Viejo after developing Parkinson's disease, Crandall lived until May 5, 2021, when he passed away at the age of 91.

In discussing his former teammate, Joe Torre told the 2021 Baseball Hall of Fame yearbook, "I patterned myself after Del Crandall. Del didn't have a strong arm, so he had to get rid of the ball quickly. I watched the way he caught and released the ball, and that had a big influence on me."

BRAVES CAREER HIGHLIGHTS

Best Season

Although Crandall hit more home runs in three other seasons, he posted the best overall numbers of his career in 1960, earning All-Star honors, a spot on the *Sporting News* All-Star team, and a 13th-place finish in the NL MVP voting by hitting 19 homers, driving in 77 runs, scoring 81 times, and batting .294, while also leading all NL catchers in putouts and assists.

Memorable Moments/Greatest Performances

Crandall led the Braves to a 5–4 win over the Reds on September 4, 1954, by homering twice and knocking in three runs, with his solo blast in the top of the 11th inning providing the margin of victory.

Crandall gave the Braves a 5–4 win over the Phillies on September 11, 1955, when he homered off starter Herm Wehmeir with the bases loaded and two men out in the bottom of the ninth inning.

Crandall's two solo homers off starter Al Worthington enabled the Braves to eke out a 3–2 victory over the Giants on May 19, 1956.

Crandall gave the Braves an 8–7 win over the Cardinals on April 24, 1957, when he homered off Willard Schmidt with no one aboard in the bottom of the ninth inning.

Crandall helped lead the Braves to a 6–4 win over the Phillies on July 16, 1960, by going 4-for-4 with a pair of homers off Robin Roberts.

Crandall led the Braves to a 7–0 win over the Cardinals on June 1, 1962, by driving in five runs with a homer and two singles.

Notable Achievements

- Hit more than 20 home runs three times.
- Led NL with 12 sacrifice flies in 1960.
- Led NL catchers in putouts three times, assists six times, double plays turned twice, runners caught stealing five times, and fielding percentage four times.

- Ranks among Braves career leaders in home runs (12th), intentional bases on balls (6th), sacrifice flies (tied for 7th), and games played (11th).
- Two-time NL champion (1957 and 1958).
- 1957 world champion.
- Four-time Gold Glove Award winner (1958, 1959, 1960, and 1962).
- Eight-time NL All-Star selection (1953, 1954, 1955, 1956, 1958, 1959, 1960, and 1962).
- Three-time *Sporting News* NL All-Star selection (1958, 1960, and 1962).
- Member of Braves Hall of Fame.

24

TERRY PENDLETON

A winner wherever he went, Terry Pendleton proved to be a key figure in the Braves' return to prominence during the early 1990s, helping to lead them to four division titles and three league championships, after previously making significant contributions to two pennant-winning ballclubs in St. Louis. Having most of his finest seasons for the Braves from 1991 to 1994, Pendleton hit more than 20 homers twice, knocked in more than 100 runs once, and batted over .300 twice as a member of the team, earning in the process one NL MVP award and one second-place finish in the balloting. The slick-fielding Pendleton, who led all NL third basemen in putouts and assists twice each, also won the third Gold Glove of his career during his time in Atlanta. But Pendleton perhaps made his greatest impact on the Braves with his exceptional leadership ability, serving as the emotional leader of an extremely talented, but young and inexperienced team.

Born in Los Angeles, California, on July 16, 1960, Terry Lee Pendleton developed a chip on his shoulder while growing up in his South-Central neighborhood, recalling, "I was always the smallest kid on the block. I was always the last guy picked to play basketball or the last picked to play kickball, or whatever it was."

After moving with his family at the age of nine some 70 miles northwest, to Oxnard, California, Pendleton received his introduction to organized baseball in the Eastside Little League, where he failed to display the skills that would eventually allow him to pursue a career on the diamond, saying years later, "I was the worst. I was the kid playing right field for two innings."

Improving himself dramatically by spending all his free time bouncing balls off brick walls and working on his swing at the plate, Pendleton went on to play for his Channel Islands High School team in Oxnard, where, after spending his freshman year sitting on the bench, he batted close to .500 as a senior. Nevertheless, with the thick-legged Pendleton lacking superior athletic ability and standing only 5'7" at the time, he received few scholarship offers, forcing him to attend nearby Oxnard College, a community school with limited athletic facilities.

Transferring to Fresno State University after two years at Oxnard, Pendleton recalled feeling lonely and out of place at his new school, saying, "Basically, I was a black man living in a white man's world at Fresno State, and there were times when I was really down."

However, with the help of Mike Rupcich, an assistant coach who took him under his wing, Pendleton persevered through the difficult times, remembering, "He kept me sane. Coach Rupcich always had something to say, always tried to pep me up and get me rolling again."

Rupcich also helped the right-handed-swinging Pendleton become a switch-hitter, with the latter recalling, "Practice started at 2:15. So, every day the entire winter, he and I were in the cage. Every single day."

Despite all his hard work, Pendleton had his partial scholarship revoked after his junior year by head baseball coach Bob Bennett, who accused him of not hustling. After considering leaving school, Pendleton adhered to the wishes of his father, who told him, "You are going to work and pay your way through school."

Displaying his mettle, Pendleton not only returned to Fresno State for his senior year, but also earned Third-Team All-America honors as a second baseman by batting .397 and setting a school record by collecting 98 hits.

Subsequently selected by the Cardinals in the seventh round of the 1982 MLB Amateur Draft, Pendleton ended up spending two years advancing through the St. Louis farm system, transitioning to third base during that time, before being summoned to the big leagues midway through the 1984 campaign. Acquitting himself extremely well over the final 10 weeks of the season, Pendleton batted .324, homered once, knocked in 33 runs, and stole 20 bases as the Cardinals starting third baseman. Although Pendleton provided the Cardinals with strong defense and a fairly productive bat the next two seasons, driving in a total of 128 runs, he proved to be somewhat inconsistent at the plate, posting batting averages of just .240 and .239. However, Pendleton had his finest offensive season to date in 1987, helping the Cardinals capture their second pennant in three years by hitting 12 homers, knocking in 96 runs, and batting .286, while also leading all NL third sackers in assists for the second straight time.

Although Pendleton put up decent numbers in 1989, hitting 13 homers, driving in 74 runs, scoring 83 others, and batting .264, his overall offensive production fell off considerably the next three seasons, causing the Cardinals to allow him to leave via free agency at the end of 1990. Offered a four-year contract worth $10.2 million by the Braves, Pendleton

Terry Pendleton helped lead the Braves to four division titles and three
pennants.
Courtesy of George A. Kitrinos

chose to go to Atlanta, even though the Yankees offered him more money.
In explaining his decision years later, Pendleton said, "I told my wife, 'Well,
here's our two choices: We've got New York . . . and we've got Atlanta.' She
responded, 'I'm going to tell you, you go to New York, you're going by
yourself.'"

   With some members of the local media questioning the signing of
Pendleton to such a then-exorbitant deal, Braves GM John Schuerholz
stated, "On cold statistics, there might be some concern. But he's a good,
solid ballplayer who makes us a much better team. He plays a position we
felt was very important to strengthen ourselves."

Proving that Schuerholz made a wise decision, Pendleton blossomed into a star in Atlanta, serving as the Braves' offensive catalyst while leading them to the NL pennant just one year after they finished last in their division. In addition to hitting 22 homers, driving in 86 runs, and scoring 94 times, Pendleton ranked among the league leaders with a .517 slugging percentage and topped the circuit with a .319 batting average, 187 hits, and 303 total bases, earning in the process NL MVP and Comeback Player of the Year honors. Performing especially well down the stretch, Pendleton hit six homers, knocked in 19 runs, and batted .336 during the month of September, with his strong finish and outstanding leadership enabling the Braves to edge out the Dodgers for the NL West title by one game.

Looking back at the Braves unexpected run to the division title years later, Pendleton stated, "It was something that was unbelievable. To watch us start a season and 10 or 15 thousand fans at games in the first couple of months, unsure of what we might do, and then the last two months, you can't find a seat outside the stadium, let alone inside."

Despite being plagued by a severe abdominal injury and losing one of his newborn twin sons early in the year, Pendleton performed brilliantly once again in 1992, leading the Braves to their second straight division title and league championship by hitting 21 homers, batting .311, and establishing career highs with 105 RBIs, 98 runs scored, 39 doubles, and a league-leading 199 hits. Also excelling in the field, Pendleton led all NL third basemen in both putouts and assists, en route to winning the third and final Gold Glove of his career, his only trip to the All-Star Game, and a runner-up finish in the MVP voting.

Praising his former teammate for his outstanding play under such adverse conditions, Tom Glavine said, "Terry, we knew he played hurt. We also knew that he was going to go out there every day . . . to have that presence on the field offensively and defensively was huge for us, even if it was at only 80 percent."

Standing just 5'9" and weighing only about 180 pounds, Pendleton displayed a huge heart that belied his somewhat smallish frame. Always giving 100 percent of himself on the playing field, Pendleton developed into a true team leader in Atlanta, later saying, "I knew I had leadership skills. I knew I had to be selfless. The times to teach were rewarding. And the things I learned in St. Louis were what helped me in Atlanta."

Claiming that Pendleton earned NL MVP honors in 1991 largely on the strength of the intangible qualities he brought to Atlanta, baseball historian John Thorn stated, "If you look at Pendleton's numbers, they may not have been the best in the National League, but he got the award because the writers perceived he was the glue of that team. And I think that's correct."

Although Pendleton never hit more than 22 home runs in a season, he drove the ball well to all fields from both sides of the plate, enabling him to amass more than 30 doubles on four separate occasions. An excellent clutch hitter and deceptively good baserunner as well, Pendleton delivered many key hits over the course of his career and stole more than 20 bases twice. Pendleton, though, perhaps made his greatest impact with his glove, using his superior range, quick reflexes, and powerful throwing arm to help keep opposing teams off the scoreboard.

Pendleton had one more productive year for the Braves, hitting 17 homers, driving in 84 runs, scoring 81 times, and batting .272 in 1993, before age and injuries began to take their toll on him. Limited by a bad back to only 77 games during the strike-shortened 1994 campaign, Pendleton batted just .252, with seven homers and 30 RBIs. Nevertheless, he remained a leader in the Braves clubhouse, serving as a mentor to young third baseman Chipper Jones, who later singled him out during his Hall of Fame induction speech for showing him how to play the game the right way.

With Jones ready to take over at third base in Atlanta, the Braves did not attempt to re-sign Pendleton when he became a free agent at the end of 1994, prompting him to ink a one-year deal with the Florida Marlins. Performing well for the Marlins in 1995, Pendleton hit 14 homers, knocked in 78 runs, and batted .290, before being reacquired by the Braves for the stretch run during the latter stages of the ensuing campaign. Although Pendleton ended up batting just .204 in his 42 games with the Braves in 1996, he again provided them with veteran leadership, helping them capture their fourth pennant in six years.

A free agent once again at the end of 1996, Pendleton signed with the Cincinnati Reds after the Braves failed to offer him a new deal. Pendleton subsequently split the next two seasons between the Reds and Kansas City Royals, serving both teams as a part-time player, before announcing his retirement following the conclusion of the 1998 campaign, saying at the time, "It's time for me to be home with my family. I think it's where the good Lord wants me."

Pendleton, who ended his career with 140 homers, 946 RBIs, 851 runs scored, 1,897 hits, 356 doubles, 39 triples, 127 stolen bases, a .270 batting average, a .316 on-base percentage, and a .391 slugging percentage, hit 71 homers, knocked in 322 runs, scored 319 times, collected 669 hits, 130 doubles, and 13 triples, batted .287, compiled an on-base percentage of .327, and posted a slugging percentage of .445 as a member of the Braves.

After remaining away from the game for two years, Pendleton returned to the Braves as hitting coach in 2001, continuing to serve in that capacity until 2010, when he assumed the role of first base coach. Named bench coach under new Braves manager Brian Snitker in 2016, Pendleton remained in that position for just one year, before sliding into the role of minor-league hitting instructor in 2017. In his current position, Pendleton, who resides with his wife of more than 40 years in Duluth, Georgia, travels between Georgia, Mississippi, Virginia, and Florida helping individual players improve their batting skills. Describing the joy he derives from his work, Pendleton says, "To watch these kids grow and have fun . . . it's a great feeling. You know you're doing something positive in their lives."

BRAVES CAREER HIGHLIGHTS

Best Season

Pendleton's first two seasons with the Braves proved to be easily the finest of his career, and either would make an excellent choice here. I ultimately chose to go with 1991 since, in addition to hitting 22 homers, driving in 86 runs, scoring 94 times, and leading the league with 187 hits and a .319 batting average, Pendleton provided outstanding leadership to a young Braves team that captured the NL pennant, with his overall impact on the club enabling him to edge out Barry Bonds for league MVP honors.

Memorable Moments/Greatest Performances

Pendleton led the Braves to a 10–6 win over the Giants on August 6, 1991, by going 4-for-4 at the plate, with two homers, a double, four RBIs, and four runs scored.

Pendleton helped the Braves remain just one game behind the first-place Dodgers in the NL West by going 4-for-5, with a homer and two RBIs during a 7–6 win over the Reds on October 1, 1991.

Pendleton contributed to a lopsided 10–4 victory over the San Diego Padres on April 20, 1992, by driving in a career-high six runs with a single and a pair of doubles.

Pendleton gave the Braves a dramatic 7–5 victory over the Reds on August 4, 1992, when he homered off reliever Norm Charlton in the bottom of the ninth inning with two men out and one man on base.

Pendleton helped lead the Braves to an 18–5 rout of the Montreal Expos on September 21, 1993, by homering twice and knocking in four runs.

Pendleton starred in defeat on September 14, 1996, going 5-for-5 at the plate, with a double, walk, stolen base, and three runs scored during a 6–5 loss to the Mets in 12 innings.

Notable Achievements

- Hit more than 20 home runs twice.
- Knocked in more than 100 runs once.
- Batted over .300 twice.
- Surpassed 30 doubles three times.
- Posted slugging percentage over .500 once.
- Led NL in batting average once, hits twice, and total bases once.
- Finished second in NL with 105 RBIs in 1992.
- Led NL third basemen in putouts twice, assists twice, and double plays turned once.
- Three-time NL champion (1991, 1992, and 1996).
- Three-time NL Player of the Week.
- 1992 Gold Glove Award winner.
- 1991 NL Comeback Player of the Year.
- 1991 NL MVP.
- Finished second in 1992 NL MVP voting.
- 1991 *Sporting News* All-Star selection.
- 1992 NL All-Star selection.
- Member of Braves Hall of Fame.

25

FRED MCGRIFF

The first player to hit 30 or more home runs for five different teams, and the first 20th-century player to lead both the AL and NL in homers, Fred McGriff hit 493 long balls and knocked in 1,550 runs during an extremely distinguished 19-year career that has yet to land him in Cooperstown. Playing some of his best ball for the Braves from 1993 to 1997, McGriff, who ESPN sportscaster Chris Berman nicknamed "Crime Dog" after McGruff, the cartoon dog used by police to raise children's awareness on crime prevention, proved to be a huge contributor to teams that won two pennants and one World Series, hitting more than 20 homers four times, driving in more than 100 runs once, and batting over .300 twice during his time in Atlanta. One of the franchise's all-time leaders in slugging percentage and OPS, McGriff earned three All-Star selections, two top-10 finishes in the NL MVP voting, and one Silver Slugger as a member of the Braves, before splitting his final seven years in the majors between three other teams.

Born in Tampa, Florida, on October 31, 1963, Frederick Stanley McGriff grew up just four blocks from Al López Field, the longtime spring training home of the Cincinnati Reds. Developing a love for baseball at an early age, McGriff said, "I can't remember going to my first game. I mean, I was always at a baseball game. I lived at ballgames. I always loved the game."

After getting his start in organized ball in the West Tampa Little League, McGriff eventually tried out for the Jefferson High School team, failing to earn a roster spot as a sophomore, before making the squad his junior year after experiencing a growth spurt. First attracting the attention of pro scouts at Jefferson High, McGriff hit a mammoth home run off Hillsborough High School's Dwight Gooden, who told the *Los Angeles Times* in 1992, "I swear, that's still one of the longest home runs I've ever given up."

Offered an athletic scholarship to the University of Georgia, McGriff instead chose to turn pro when the Yankees selected him in the ninth round of the 1981 MLB Amateur Draft. McGriff subsequently spent a little over one year in New York's farm system, before the Yankees foolishly included him in a five-player trade with the Toronto Blue Jays that netted them little in return.

Gradually establishing himself as one of Toronto's top minor-league prospects over the course of the next four seasons, McGriff made a brief appearance with the parent club in 1986, before arriving in the majors to stay the following year. Serving the Blue Jays primarily as a DH in 1987, McGriff batted .247, hit 20 homers, and knocked in 43 runs, in 107 games and just under 300 official at-bats. Named the team's starting first baseman the following year, McGriff spent the next three seasons assuming that role, batting .300 once and averaging 35 home runs and 87 RBIs from 1988 to 1990, with his 36 homers in 1989 leading the American League.

Commenting on his teammate's prodigious power at the plate, Toronto outfielder Lloyd Moseby stated, "You know that highlight reel that shows the Willie Mays catch and then switches to the fan who grabs his head with his hands in amazement? Fred McGriff does that to you when he hits a home run."

Nevertheless, on December 5, 1990, the Blue Jays traded McGriff and shortstop Tony Fernández to the San Diego Padres for second baseman Roberto Alomar and outfielder Joe Carter. While both Alomar and Carter fared extremely well in Toronto, helping to lead the Blue Jays to back-to-back championships in 1992 and 1993, the Padres benefited from the deal as well, with McGriff totaling 66 home runs and 210 RBIs his first two seasons in San Diego. And by finishing first in the senior circuit with 35 round-trippers in 1992, McGriff became the first player to lead two different major leagues in homers since Harry Stovey topped both the National League and the American Association in that category in the 19th century. However, with the Padres seeking to shed salary after getting off to a poor start in 1993, they traded their star first baseman to the Braves for three prospects on July 18, helping to jump-start the offense of the two-time defending NL champions.

Explaining his reasoning behind making the deal, Braves general manager John Schuerholz said at the time, "The first reason we made it was for our immediate concern—to close the gap on the Giants. . . . If we hadn't made this trade, we would have had to do something internally to breathe some life into our offense."

Braves manager Bobby Cox added, "He can add some excitement to our lineup. He's an impact player. Any club can certainly use a guy like that. We certainly can."

Fred McGriff hit more than 20 home runs four times as a member of the Braves.
Courtesy of George A. Kitrinos

Arriving in Atlanta with the Braves trailing the first-place Giants by nine games, McGriff performed magnificently over the season's final 68 contests, helping his new team edge out San Francisco for the NL West title by hitting 19 homers, driving in 55 runs, scoring 59 times, batting .310, and compiling an OPS of 1.004. McGriff, who concluded the campaign with 37 homers, 101 RBIs, 111 runs scored, and a .291 batting average, ended up earning his third Silver Slugger and a fourth-place finish in the NL MVP voting for his efforts.

In discussing what McGriff's presence meant to the Braves, Bobby Cox said, "Just getting a player like that was an inspirational lift. He put the numbers up right away. . . . Fred relaxed our batting order. He made the difference for us in the race."

Teammate Ron Gant expressed similar sentiments when he told a sportswriter, "He just makes everyone else a better hitter. I hit in front of him. It wasn't that the pitchers were throwing me different pitches. They were throwing me the same pitches, but I was just more of an aggressive hitter with him hitting behind me. He just makes everyone else better."

Meanwhile, author Lang Whitaker wrote in his book, *In the Time of Bobby Cox: The Atlanta Braves, Their Manager, My Couch, Two Decades, and Me,* "With McGriff on the team, the Braves were definitely combustible. Fred McGriff got the Braves red hot."

A true game-changer, McGriff gave the pitching-rich Braves a presence in the middle of their lineup they previously lacked. Although Ron Gant and David Justice both had the ability to deliver the long ball, neither man instilled fear in opposing pitchers to the same degree as the 6'3", 220-pound McGriff, whose size and powerful left-handed swing evoked memories of Willie McCovey. Capable of driving the ball out of any part of the park, McGriff hit many of his homers to center and left-center, although the right field stands at Atlanta-Fulton County Stadium served as his primary target.

Picking up right where he left off the previous year, McGriff hit 34 homers, knocked in 94 runs, scored 81 times, batted .318, and compiled an OPS of 1.012 through the first four months of the 1994 campaign, before a players' strike brought the season to a premature end. Continuing to perform at an elite level when play resumed in 1995, McGriff helped lead the Braves to their first NL East title by hitting 27 homers, driving in 93 runs, scoring 85 times, and batting .280, before homering four times, knocking in nine runs, and batting .333 during their successful postseason run to the world championship.

McGriff had another excellent year for the Braves in 1996, earning his third consecutive All-Star selection as a member of the team by hitting 28 homers, driving in 107 runs, and batting .295. But after McGriff posted solid numbers once again in 1997, finishing the season with 22 homers, 97 RBIs, and a .277 batting average, the Braves sold him to the expansion Tampa Bay Devil Rays on November 18, 1997.

McGriff, who during his four-and-a-half-year stint in Atlanta, hit 130 homers, knocked in 446 runs, scored 383 times, collected 700 hits, 132 doubles, and five triples, batted .293, compiled a .369 on-base percentage, and posted a .516 slugging percentage, ended up spending the next three-and-a-half years playing in front of his hometown fans, hitting 97 homers, driving in 352 runs, and batting .295, before being dealt to the Chicago Cubs just prior to the 2001 trade deadline. After hitting 30 homers, knocking in 103 runs, and batting .273 for the Cubs in 2002, McGriff spent one injury-marred year with the Dodgers, before closing out his career back home as a part-time player with Tampa Bay in 2004. In addition to hitting 493 homers and driving in 1,550 runs over parts of 19 big-league seasons, McGriff scored 1,349 runs, collected 2,490 hits, 441 doubles, and 24 triples, stole 72 bases, batted .284, compiled a .377 on-base percentage, and posted a .509 slugging percentage. A five-time All-Star, McGriff also earned three Silver Sluggers and six top-10 finishes in the league MVP voting.

Yet, despite his outstanding list of accomplishments, McGriff, who has spent much of his retirement serving as a consultant, coach, and scout for some of his former teams, including the Braves, never came close to gaining induction into the Baseball Hall of Fame during his period of eligibility. Expressing his disappointment over his former teammate's omission shortly after he received word of his own election in 2018, Chipper Jones said, "It's very unfortunate. I had a conversation with somebody close to me today about Fred McGriff. I feel like he is one of the guys that during his five years in between him being done playing and when he first hit the Hall of Fame ballot that a lot of people passed him by. And some of those people had clouds of suspicion, and it really kind of made the number 500 (home runs) obsolete."

Jones continued, "Having had this guy as a quote/unquote bodyguard hitting behind me in the lineup, there was nobody I enjoyed hitting in front of more than Fred McGriff. People feared this guy. . . . Whenever he was traded, the event was seismic. This guy was a difference-maker. . . . I think if he had maybe been a little more outspoken, a little flashier, or whatever, you may notice the numbers a little more. He was just a professional. . . . Very little was ever said. I had to go up and ask for help from Freddy, but, when I did, he was always very gracious and gave it to me and took me under his wing."

Jones then added, "I'm a little biased but, ultimately, when you're looking at a guy that hit in the .280s, I don't know exactly what his career batting average was, but upwards of 500 homers and 1,550 RBIs, those are Hall of Fame numbers in my book. Especially when he did it as consistently as he did."

BRAVES CAREER HIGHLIGHTS

Best Season

Although the season ended prematurely due to a players' strike, McGriff posted his best overall numbers as a member of the Braves in 1994, earning All-Star honors and an eighth-place finish in the NL MVP voting by batting .318 and ranking among the league leaders with 34 homers, 94 RBIs, 81 runs scored, a .623 slugging percentage, and a career-best OPS of 1.012.

Memorable Moments/Greatest Performances

McGriff made an immediate impact upon his arrival in Atlanta, hitting a two-run homer off Cardinals starter René Arocha during an 8–5 Braves win in his first game as a member of the team on July 20, 1993.

McGriff followed that up by homering twice and knocking in three runs during a 14–2 rout of the Cardinals the very next day.

McGriff helped lead the Braves to a lopsided 12–5 victory over the Giants on April 26, 1995, by going 4-for-5 at the plate, with two homers, five RBIs, and three runs scored.

McGriff led the Braves to a 10–4 mauling of the Colorado Rockies in Game 4 of the 1995 NLDS by homering twice and knocking in five runs.

McGriff helped lead the Braves to a 7–5 win over the Astros on April 30, 1996, by going a perfect 5-for-5 at the plate, with a homer, two RBIs, and two runs scored.

McGriff capped off a five-hit, two-homer performance by hitting a two-out three-run homer in the bottom of the ninth inning that gave the Braves a 6–5 win over the Cubs on August 24, 1996.

McGriff contributed to a 15–0 blowout of the Cardinals in Game 7 of the 1996 NLCS by going 3-for-4 at the plate, with a homer, triple, four RBIs, and four runs scored.

Notable Achievements

- Hit more than 20 home runs four times, topping 30 homers once.
- Knocked in more than 100 runs once.
- Batted over .300 twice.
- Surpassed 30 doubles once.
- Posted slugging percentage over .600 twice.
- Posted OPS over 1.000 twice.

- Led NL in games played once.
- Led NL first basemen in putouts once.
- Ranks among Braves career leaders in slugging percentage (7th) and OPS (9th).
- Two-time NL champion (1995 and 1996).
- 1995 world champion.
- Three-time NL Player of the Week.
- July 1993 NL Player of the Month.
- 1994 All-Star Game MVP.
- 1993 Silver Slugger Award winner.
- Finished in top 10 of NL MVP voting twice, placing as high as fourth in 1993.
- Three-time NL All-Star selection (1994, 1995, and 1996).
- 1993 *Sporting News* NL All-Star selection.

26

JOHNNY LOGAN

The Braves' starting shortstop for nearly a decade, Johnny Logan spent parts of 11 seasons in Boston and Milwaukee, proving to be an indispensable member of teams that won two pennants and one World Series. One of the NL's top defensive shortstops, Logan led all players at his position in assists four times, fielding percentage three times, and putouts once. A solid offensive performer as well, Logan scored 100 runs once and batted over .280 four times, with his strong all-around play earning him four All-Star selections.

Born in Endicott, New York, on March 23, 1926, John Logan Jr. grew up some 190 miles northwest of New York City, where his Russian immigrant father and Croatian immigrant mother ran a grocery store. Although his parents knew nothing about baseball, Logan developed a love for the game through his older brother, remembering, "I had a brother that taught me baseball, taught me football, taught me the finer points. I was a batboy for his semipro team. They played every week. Then he played for his factory team, Endicott-Johnson Shoe Company. Anytime they had practice, I was there instead of hitting the books. I was playing with older guys. What happened is, I learned sports is a way of surviving. Back in them days, you could get scholarships."

An outstanding all-around athlete, Logan starred in baseball, football, basketball, track, and golf at Union-Endicott High School. Particularly outstanding on the diamond and gridiron, Logan excelled on both sides of the ball in football, performing so well that he received scholarship offers from Syracuse, Colgate, Duke, and Notre Dame. But Logan detested the violence of the game, saying, "I only weighed about 160 pounds then. I'd get crushed by some of them bullies. I never liked football. To me, it was an animal game."

Revealing that baseball remained, far and away, his first love, Logan stated, "When I was 15 or 16, every Sunday I'd take a Greyhound bus 40 miles to Homer, New York, to play semipro ball against college boys from Cortland State Teachers College."

Although Logan continued to compete semiprofessionally through high school, he had to put his playing career on hold after entering the military following his graduation in January 1945, recalling, "I went in the Army right out of high school. I was drafted. I went to Camp Wheeler, Georgia. I met a great man named Bobby Bragan. He was the manager of the Camp Wheeler baseball team. He's the guy that taught me how to play baseball."

Logan ended up serving in the Army for 18 months, spending time in Osaka, Japan, before receiving his discharge. Subsequently eligible for benefits under the G.I. Bill, Logan used those payments to further his education, saying, "I went to college for a year and a half. I was a veteran, an Army boy, with no money. I had the privilege of receiving the G.I. Bill of Rights and going to college and getting $75 a month. I went to an extension college in Endicott, an extension of Syracuse University, the one that became Harpur College."

Approached early in 1947 by Braves scout Dewey Griggs, Logan signed a minor-league contract with the organization, recalling, "I signed my contract for $2,500. In them days, it was big money. The first thing I did was I gave my mother $1,500 and I kept a thousand. My family was conservative. They were poor in them days. A thousand dollars was like a million."

Meanwhile, Griggs remembered, "I knew Johnny was a natural the first time I laid eyes on him. Take a look at his hands. They're big and quick paws, ideal for a shortstop. But then, Johnny excelled in any sport. I remember watching him perform at halfback one year during the New York all-state playoffs. That kid was a wonder at football."

Performing extremely well his first year in the minors, Logan batted .331 for the Braves' Class B affiliate in Evansville, Indiana, earning him an invitation to spring training with the parent club in 1948. But, to make the big-league roster, Logan had to beat out Alvin Dark, who had spent the previous season starring at short for the Triple-A Milwaukee Brewers. Recalling his thoughts at the time, Logan said, "I thought I had a good chance of making the Boston Braves. Seeing Dark and seeing myself, I thought I had a good chance. Unfortunately, Dark was a good hitter. He could hit that ball to right field. I could beat him on defense, but back in the '40s and '50s, everybody was a good defense man."

With Dark eventually earning the starting shortstop job in Boston, Logan took over for him in Milwaukee, where he ended up spending the next three seasons, before splitting the 1951 and 1952 campaigns between

Johnny Logan started for the Braves at shortstop for nearly a decade.

the Brewers and Braves. Appearing in 117 games with the Braves in 1952, Logan batted .283, hit four homers, knocked in 42 runs, and scored 56 times. Emerging as one of the NL's finest all-around shortstops the follow-ing year, Logan hit 11 homers, drove in 73 runs, scored 100 times, batted .273, and led all players at his position in putouts and fielding percentage. Logan subsequently batted over .270 in each of the next four seasons, while also leading all NL shortstops in assists on three separate occasions. Performing especially well in 1955 and 1956, Logan earned All-Star honors in the first of those campaigns by batting .297, hitting 13 homers, driving in 83 runs, scoring 95 others, and amassing a league-leading 37 doubles, before batting .281 and hitting a career-high 15 home runs the following year.

A solid contact hitter who possessed occasional power and excellent bat control, the right-handed-swinging Logan finished in double digits in home runs six times and annually ranked among the NL leaders in sacrifice bunts, topping the circuit with a total of 31 in 1956. Extremely versatile, Logan assumed virtually every spot in the batting order at one time or another, although he typically batted either second, sixth, or seventh. An outstanding clutch hitter, Logan drew the following words of praise from former MLB commissioner Bud Selig, who grew up watching the Braves at Milwaukee's County Stadium: "Of all the great hitters on those Braves teams—Hank Aaron, Eddie Mathews, Red Schoendienst, Joe Adcock—Johnny was one of the best clutch hitters they had. He was a critical part of those teams."

Better known for his defense, though, Logan finished either first or second among NL shortstops in assists six straight times from 1953 to 1958, with his quick hands and good range compensating for a merely average throwing arm.

A fierce competitor as well, the 5'11", 175-pound Logan never backed down from a fight, as the much larger Don Drysdale once learned when Logan charged him on the mound after being struck by a pitch. Of course, Logan knew that he always had the support of the equally feisty Eddie Mathews, who he played alongside for nine seasons, once saying, "I never worried about fights because I had Eddie Mathews playing next to me, and he would end them in a hurry. . . . I would start the fights and he would finish them. We could always handle ourselves."

After suffering through a subpar 1958 campaign during which he batted just .226, Logan rebounded the following year to earn All-Star honors by batting .291 and hitting 13 home runs. However, with the 34-year-old Logan batting just .245, hitting only seven homers, and driving in just 42 runs in 1960, the Braves acquired slick-fielding shortstop Roy McMillan from the Cincinnati Reds during the subsequent offseason. After Logan got off to another slow start in 1961, the Braves traded him to the Pirates for outfielder Gino Cimoli on June 15. Logan, who left Milwaukee with career totals of 92 home runs, 521 RBIs, 624 runs scored, 1,329 hits, 207 doubles, and 40 triples, a batting average of .270, an on-base percentage of .330, and a slugging percentage of .384, spent the next two-and-a-half years assuming a backup role in Pittsburgh, never garnering more than 181 official at-bats. Released by the Pirates after the 1963 season, Logan traveled to Japan, where he ended his career as a member of the Nankai Hawks in 1964.

Recalling his brief stint in the Far East, Logan said, "I liked Japan. They were paying me good money. But it was very difficult to communicate. We only had two minor-league ballplayers, Joe Stanka and another kid. I was the only major leaguer. They thought they had a superstar, but, unfortunately, at 36. . . ."

Following his playing days, Logan entered into a brief career in broadcasting, remembering, "I met Ralph Barnes, the manager of radio station WOKY. It was the main station in Milwaukee back in them days. I had a sports show, getting interviews from all the big celebrities, like Vince Lombardi and Pat Harder, the referee. He played with the Chicago Cardinals. And I sold advertising to Selig Ford."

After leaving the broadcast booth, Logan spent one year working on the Trans-Alaska Pipeline in Anchorage, Alaska, recalling, "I was a welder's helper. It was hard work, rough and tough. We lived in barracks in the wilderness. I was with dope addicts, whiskey men, beer drinkers, hard-working men. I never gambled there, never had a drink while I was there. I was like a saint. . . . I sent all my money home, my checks. My kid said, 'Mommy, how come he's sending so much money home? What's he doing there?' It was tough work, but I didn't go there for the money. All I did was work, eat, sleep, and write postcards home."

Upon his return to the States in 1976, Logan, who lost three bids to become Milwaukee County sheriff, helped create the Milwaukee Braves Historical Association and did some scouting in Wisconsin for the Brewers until his health began to decline in his later years. After experiencing problems with his circulation and kidneys for several years, Logan died at a hospital in Milwaukee at the age of 86, on August 9, 2013.

BRAVES CAREER HIGHLIGHTS

Best Season

Logan had his finest all-around season in 1955, when he earned his first All-Star selection and an 11th-place finish in the NL MVP voting by hitting 13 homers, scoring 95 runs, and establishing career-high marks with 83 RBIs, 177 hits, a batting average of .297, an OPS of .802, and a league-leading 37 doubles, while also amassing more assists in the field (511) than any other player in the league.

Memorable Moments/Greatest Performances

Logan hit two home runs in one game for the only time in his career on April 17, 1954, when he reached the seats twice against Reds starter Corky Valentin during a 5–1 Braves win.

Logan had another big day against the Reds almost exactly one year later, going 5-for-5, with a homer, three RBIs, and two runs scored during a 9–5 Braves victory on April 16, 1955.

Logan helped lead the Braves to a 13–5 thrashing of the Pirates on September 10, 1955, by going 4-for-5 at the plate, with a double, two runs scored, and a career-high six RBIs.

Logan went a perfect 5-for-5 at the plate and knocked in a pair of runs during a 7–4 win over the Giants on July 21, 1957.

Logan gave the Braves an early 2–1 lead in their 4–2 win over the Yankees in Game 2 of the 1957 World Series when he hit a solo home run off Bobby Shantz in the top of the third inning.

Logan delivered the pivotal blow of a 4–2 win over the Phillies on April 18, 1958, when he homered off Jack Sanford with the bases loaded in the top of the sixth inning.

Notable Achievements

- Scored 100 runs once.
- Surpassed 30 doubles once.
- Led NL in doubles once, sacrifice hits once, and games played twice.
- Led NL shortstops in putouts once, assists four times, and fielding percentage three times.
- Ranks among Braves career leaders in sacrifice hits (7th), games played (12th), plate appearances (11th), and at-bats (12th).
- Two-time NL champion (1957 and 1958).
- 1957 world champion.
- Four-time NL All-Star selection (1955, 1957, 1958, and 1959).

27

TIM HUDSON

One of baseball's most consistent winners for more than a decade, Tim Hudson helped anchor the Braves' pitching staff for nine seasons after previously excelling on the mound for the Oakland Athletics for six years. Acquired from Oakland for three nondescript players at the end of 2004, Hudson posted double-digit win totals in each of his seven full seasons with the Braves, amassing at least 16 victories on four separate occasions. A member of Braves teams that made four playoff appearances and won two division titles, Hudson earned one All-Star nomination and one top-five finish in the NL Cy Young voting during his time in Atlanta, before spending his final two seasons back on the West Coast with the San Francisco Giants.

Born in Columbus, Georgia, on July 14, 1975, Timothy Adam Hudson grew up in Salem, Alabama, a rural community on the east-central side of the state not far from Auburn. The son of a plant supervisor at a cereal box factory and a homemaker, Hudson spoke of his small-town upbringing in a 2005 interview with *Sports Illustrated*, remembering, "There's one four-way stop sign in the middle of town. I grew up in the country on five acres of land. Me and kids from the neighborhood, we were always out in the woods or riding bicycles or playing baseball. Not a lot of trouble to get into. We played baseball in a cow pasture."

A huge fan of the Atlanta Braves during his formative years, Hudson got his start on the diamond in a local youth league at the age of eight, making his first mound appearance one year later. Recalling his pitching debut, Hudson said, "I was terrible, but I didn't care. I loved it."

Eventually emerging as a standout athlete at nearby Phenix City's Glenwood High School, Hudson starred at cornerback in football and shortstop, center field, and pitcher in baseball, leading both school teams to a pair of Alabama state championships. Particularly outstanding on the diamond his senior year, Hudson compiled a record of 9-0 and an ERA of 0.46, while also hitting eight homers, batting .475, and stealing 16 bases. But, with most college coaches considering him too small and too light, Hudson received no scholarship offers, forcing him to enroll at Phenix City's Chattahoochee Valley Community College. Establishing himself as one of the nation's top junior college players over the course of the next two seasons, Hudson performed so well that the Athletics selected him in the 35th round of the June 1984 MLB Draft. However, with Auburn University offering him a baseball scholarship, Hudson chose to further his education rather than sign with the A's.

Prior to arriving at Auburn, though, Hudson developed a new pitch that helped pave his way to the big leagues, with baseball writer Eno Sarris revealing in a 2014 story, "The first thing Tim Hudson did to become Tim Hudson was learn the splitter that summer before he went to Auburn. There's no great back story, no grandpa behind the barn. 'I was just messing around in the bullpen one day before a game, threw a couple because I didn't have a change-up, threw it in the game a couple times, and got some swings and misses,' Hudson told me this month. 'I've been throwing it ever since, and it's gotten better every year.'"

Armed with his new weapon, Hudson ended up earning SEC Player of the Year and All-America honors his senior year by compiling a record of 15-2 and an ERA of 2.97. Excelling for the Tigers on offense as well, Hudson, who threw and batted right-handed, gained First-Team All-SEC recognition as an outfielder by hitting 18 homers, driving in 95 runs, and batting .396, with his exceptional all-around play prompting the Athletics to select him again, this time in the sixth round of the June 1987 MLB Draft.

Hudson subsequently spent the next two years advancing through Oakland's farm system, learning how to throw a changeup from then-A's minor-league pitching coordinator Rick Peterson. Recalling how quickly Hudson picked up the pitch, Peterson said that his first offering "was as good as any changeup he's ever thrown in the big leagues," and then added, "Great arm speed, and the bottom fell right out. Timmy turned to me and said, 'How was that?' 'Uhhh, pretty good, Timmy. Pretty good.'"

Promoted to the majors in June 1999, Hudson performed extremely well the final four months of the season, earning a fifth-place finish in the AL Rookie of the Year voting and *Sporting News* AL Rookie Pitcher of the Year honors by going 11-2 with a 3.23 ERA. Hudson followed that up by compiling a record of 20-6 and an ERA of 4.14 for Oakland's 2000 AL West division championship team, earning in the process his first All-Star selection and a runner-up finish to Pedro Martínez in the Cy Young balloting. Continuing to excel on the mound for the A's the next four seasons,

Tim Hudson won at least 16 games for the Braves four times.
Courtesy of Rich Anderson

Hudson earned one more All-Star nomination and another top-five finish in the Cy Young voting by going a combined 61-31, while also compiling an ERA under 3.00 twice.

Nevertheless, with the A's making it a regular practice to deal away their best players as a way of keeping their payroll low, they completed a trade with the Braves on December 16, 2004, that sent Hudson to Atlanta for three lesser-known players, Juan Cruz, Dan Meyer, and Charles Thomas, none of whom ended up amounting to very much.

Claiming that the deal came as quite a shock to both him and his wife, Hudson told *Sports Illustrated*, "My wife, Kim, and I loved Oakland so much: the relationships we built with teammates, with fans. I had a pretty hard time with the trade the first few days. Kim had a really hard time. All the wives were calling her and crying, she was crying. But Atlanta was the one place that, if I was going to get traded, I would be happiest. It makes the transition a little easier."

Once the shock wore off, though, Hudson welcomed the idea of going to Atlanta, later saying, "When I was traded from the Oakland A's to the Atlanta Braves before the 2005 season, a childhood dream was realized. I grew up a Braves fan just a few hours south of Atlanta, and it was hard for me to believe that I was going to actually play for the Atlanta Braves and legendary manager Bobby Cox. . . . I was a huge fan of Bobby Cox, a huge fan of Chipper Jones and John Smoltz. And just those guys. I grew up watching those guys and often wondered early on in my career if I would ever have the chance to play for the Atlanta Braves, and there it was. God kind of answered my prayers."

Joining the team that he rooted for as a youth, Hudson pitched well for the Braves in 2005, helping them capture the last of their 11 consecutive NL East titles by going 14-9, with a 3.52 ERA and 115 strikeouts in 192 innings pitched. Somewhat less effective the following year, Hudson went just 13-12 with a 4.86 ERA, although he recorded more strikeouts (141) and threw more innings (218 1/3). Returning to top form in 2007, Hudson compiled a record of 16-10 and an ERA of 3.33, while also leading all NL hurlers with 27 putouts.

Relying heavily on his sinkerball to retire opposing batters, the 6'1", 185-pound Hudson typically delivered his favorite offering to home plate at a speed that approached 90 mph. He also threw a four-seam fastball at the same speed and a cutter that topped out at 87 mph. When facing left-handed batters, Hudson expanded his repertoire of pitches to include a 75–77 mph curveball and a 78–81 mph splitter. Usually trying to locate his pitches on the inside part of the plate, Hudson explained, "Hitters are too big, too strong, and their bats are too quick. I have to go inside to have success."

Though Hudson proved to be a hard thrower during the early stages of his career, striking out as many as 181 batters one year in Oakland, he gradually altered his approach to pitching, saying, "You feel like a stud out there when people swing and miss. As I've gotten older, I've preached to our young guys that strikeouts are sexy, but outs are outs, man, no matter how you get them. It's a lot cooler for me pitching in the seventh or eighth inning than it is going 5 1/3. Your manager likes it a lot more, too."

Finding catching Hudson very much to his liking, Braves receiver Evan Gattis stated, "He's got a good idea what he wants to do, and he's got great command with all of his pitches. It's tough. I'm glad I'm catching and not hitting him."

Hudson also made an extremely favorable impression on Braves third base coach Fredi González, who said, "Watching him the last couple of years, his fastball cuts and sails and sinks. Being a former catcher, I can understand how hard it is for anybody to catch him."

Hudson again performed well for the Braves over the first four months of the 2008 campaign, compiling a record of 11-7 and an ERA of 3.17 through late July, before missing the season's final two months and most of 2009 as well after undergoing Tommy John surgery. Making a triumphant return to the Braves' starting rotation in 2010, Hudson earned NL Comeback Player of the Year honors by ranking among the league leaders with 17 victories, an ERA of 2.83, and a WHIP of 1.150. Hudson followed that up with two more solid seasons, going 16-10, with a 3.22 ERA and 158 strikeouts in 215 innings of work in 2011, before compiling a record of 16-7 and an ERA of 3.62 the following year.

Unfortunately, after going 8-7 with a 3.97 ERA over the first four months of the 2013 campaign, Hudson suffered a season-ending injury on July 24 at New York's Citi Field when Mets outfielder Eric Young accidentally broke his ankle on a close play at first base. With Hudson having turned 38 years of age, the Braves chose not to aggressively pursue him when he became a free agent at the end of the year, prompting him to sign a two-year deal with the San Francisco Giants. Hudson, who during his time in Atlanta, compiled an overall record of 113-72, an ERA of 3.56, and a WHIP of 1.242, threw nine complete games and five shutouts, and struck out 997 batters in 1,573 innings of work, ended up fulfilling the terms of his contract, going a combined 17-22 for the Giants over the course of the next two seasons, before announcing his retirement following the conclusion of the 2015 campaign, one year after San Francisco won the World Series. Over parts of 17 big-league seasons, Hudson posted a record of 222-133, a winning percentage of .625, an ERA of 3.49, and a WHIP of 1.239, tossed 26 complete games and 13 shutouts, and recorded 2,080 strikeouts over 3,126 2/3 innings, becoming in the process one of only 21 pitchers in the history of the game to win at least 200 games, strike out 2,000 batters, and compile a winning percentage of .600 or better.

In summarizing Hudson's playing career, baseball author Jay Jaffe wrote, "He's not Hall of Fame material, but there's no shame in that. Tim Hudson was a damn good pitcher who contributed to several winning teams that had hard luck in the playoffs, but he stuck around long enough to play a significant role on a championship team and left his mark in all three cities where he pitched."

Inducted into the Braves Hall of Fame in 2018, Hudson received the additional honor of being named to the Alabama Sports Hall of Fame that same year. Known during his playing days as a generous and kind-hearted person. Hudson formed with his wife, Kim, in 2009 the Hudson Family Foundation, which supports children and families in need in Georgia and Alabama. A few years later, the Hudsons donated $200,000 to Chattahoochee Valley Community College's baseball program. When asked about his philanthropic gestures, Hudson told the *Seattle Times*, "You start realizing what is important. It's not winning 20 games; it's not winning the World Series or making the All-Star team. It's making a difference in this world."

In addition to remaining active in his foundation, Hudson, who lives with his wife and their three children in Auburn, currently serves as pitching coach at Auburn University and enjoys spending time on his farm.

BRAVES CAREER HIGHLIGHTS

Best Season

After missing most of the previous season, Hudson pitched his best ball as a member of the Braves in 2010, earning his third All-Star selection, a fourth-place finish in the NL Cy Young voting, and NL Comeback Player of the Year honors by going 17-9, with a 2.83 ERA, a WHIP of 1.150, and 139 strikeouts in 228 2/3 innings of work.

Memorable Moments/Greatest Performances

Hudson excelled in his third start with the Braves on April 18, 2005, yielding just four hits and one walk over the first nine innings of a 1–0, 12-inning victory over the Houston Astros.

Hudson outpitched Tom Glavine on April 19, 2006, allowing just three hits, issuing one walk, and striking out six during a 2–1 complete-game win over the Mets.

Hudson threw a one-hit shutout against the Colorado Rockies on May 1, 2006, surrendering just three walks and a third-inning single by pitcher Jason Jennings during a 2–0 Braves win.

Hudson hurled another gem on May 2, 2008, allowing just three hits, issuing no walks, and recording 10 strikeouts during a 2–0 shutout of the Reds.

Hudson earned a 12–3 victory over the Florida Marlins on August 28, 2010, by working seven strong innings, surrendering six hits, one walk, and one run, while recording a career-high 13 strikeouts.

Hudson turned in a dominant performance on May 4, 2011, yielding just a fourth-inning double and a ninth-inning walk to leadoff hitter Rickie Weeks during an 8–0, one-hit shutout of the Milwaukee Brewers.

Hudson defeated the Toronto Blue Jays almost single-handedly on June 20, 2011, allowing just two hits and recording eight strikeouts over the first eight innings of a 2–0 Braves win, while also knocking in the game's only runs with a two-run homer in the bottom of the seventh inning.

Hudson turned in another outstanding all-around effort during an 8–1 victory over the Washington Nationals on April 30, 2013, that marked the 200th win of his career, yielding just three hits, two walks, and one run in seven innings of work, and helping his own cause by going 2-for-3 at the plate with a homer, double, and two runs scored.

Notable Achievements

- Won at least 16 games four times.
- Posted winning percentage over .600 seven times.
- Compiled ERA under 3.00 once.
- Threw more than 200 innings four times.
- Led NL pitchers in putouts twice, assists once, and starts once.
- Ranks among Braves career leaders in strikeouts (10th) and games started (10th).
- Two-time NL Player of the Week.
- August 2010 NL Pitcher of the Month.
- Finished fourth in 2010 NL Cy Young voting.
- 2010 NL Comeback Player of the Year.
- 2010 NL All-Star selection.
- Member of Braves Hall of Fame.

28

— RALPH GARR —

Nicknamed "The Road Runner" for his tremendous running speed, Ralph Garr spent parts of eight seasons in Atlanta, amassing hits at a record-setting pace his first four years as a starter in the Braves outfield. One of the NL's most difficult men to retire during the first half of the 1970s, the left-handed-swinging Garr surpassed 200 hits and batted over .300 three times each, won a batting title, and finished second in the league two other times, earning in the process one All-Star selection and MVP consideration on three separate occasions. An excellent baserunner as well, Garr scored more than 100 runs once and stole more than 20 bases four times, with his outstanding contributions on offense eventually landing him a spot in the Braves Hall of Fame.

Born in Monroe, Louisiana, on December 12, 1945, Ralph Allen Garr grew up in poverty with his seven siblings, recalling, "Like most of us, when you have big families like that, your aunts and uncles that didn't have no children, maybe a couple would stay with them. . . . We had a little three-bedroom. . . . We just tried to make it work. . . . We were poor, but we were never homeless, so we just didn't think about it a whole lot, and we all just cared and looked out for one another."

Eventually moving with his family some 30 miles west, to the city of Ruston, Garr graduated from Lincoln High School, after which he enrolled at historically Black Grambling State University in nearby Grambling, Louisiana. Gradually developing into a star second baseman in college, Garr helped lead the Tigers to an overall record of 103-11, including a mark of 35-1 his senior year, when he led the NAIA with a .585 batting average.

The success that the Tigers, and Garr in particular, experienced during his tenure there instilled in the young infielder a tremendous amount of self-confidence, with former teammate and future big leaguer Matt Alexander saying years later, "I didn't know Ralph Garr before Grambling, but I got to know him real well. He was the first player I met who could talk trash and then go out and back it up on the field. He taught me a lot about confidence."

Meanwhile, former Grambling assistant baseball coach Wilbert Ellis spoke of Garr's resolve and exceptional athletic ability, stating, "Even at a young age, he had so much determination to be the best. He had great speed and great talent, and all he needed to do was develop it and put it all together. He was a bad-ball hitter who had great hand-eye coordination. He had a real sweet swing, and he was powerful."

Ultimately selected by the Braves in the third round of the 1967 MLB Amateur Draft, Garr later credited Atlanta minor-league catching instructor Clint Courtney for discovering him, claiming that Courtney told the team's farm director, Paul Richards, "You just give me that damn little second baseman," and adding, "Mr. Richards told Clint Courtney, 'I'm going to draft him for you, and you're going to train him. Okay?'"

Garr continued, "So, anyway, I end up being drafted off of just Clint Courtney. He drafted me in the third round, and Mr. Richards gave me to Clint Courtney, and from then on, that's the way I got to the big leagues. When I got to spring training, nobody worked with me but Clint Courtney. He worked with me every day."

Moved from second base to the outfield shortly after he joined the Braves' minor-league affiliate at Double-A Austin, Garr recalled, "I wasn't really that good. Playing second base at Grambling and playing second base in pro ball is a whole different world . . . I was playing second base for a while there, and . . . I made five or six or seven errors in the first three or four games, and Mr. Clint Courtney called Mr. Paul Richards, he said, 'Mr. Richards, I tell you, I don't know about that boy playing second base, if we don't get him out of that infield, he's going to get killed, but he's going to hit.'"

After spending most of the ensuing campaign at Shreveport, Garr made a brief appearance with the Braves late in 1968, batting .286 in 11 games, before being returned to the minors the following year. While with the parent club, though, Garr received some advice from Hank Aaron, who told him, "See the ball, this ain't no different. Whatever you did to get you here, that's what's going to keep you here. . . . You just do what you can do, son, and do your best every time you go to the plate."

Although Garr joined the Braves during the latter stages of each of the next two seasons as well, he continued to work on perfecting his swing at Triple-A Richmond, winning a pair of batting titles with averages of .329 and .386. Arriving in Atlanta with huge expectations surrounding him in 1971, Garr remembered, "When I went to spring training, it was my job to lose. They had given me the job."

Ralph Garr batted over .300 and surpassed 200 hits three times each as a member of the Braves.

Replacing an injured Rico Carty as the Braves' starting left fielder, Garr performed magnificently in his first full big-league season, finishing second to Joe Torre in the NL batting race with an average of .343, while also hitting nine homers, driving in 44 runs, and ranking among the league leaders with 101 runs scored, 219 hits, and 30 stolen bases. Acquiring his famous moniker that year, Garr became known as "The Road Runner" after Braves public relations director Bob Hope asked Warner Brothers for permission to use the name of the well-known cartoon character. From that point on, the Road Runner's image appeared on the scoreboard at Atlanta-Fulton County Stadium every time Garr reached base, with the hometown fans crying out "Beep Beep" in an effort to mimic the famed bird.

Continuing to perform at an elite level the next three years, Garr posted the following numbers from 1972 to 1974:

YEAR	HR	RBI	RUNS	HITS	AVG	OBP	SLG	OPS
1972	12	53	87	180	.325	.359	.430	.788
1973	11	55	94	200	.299	.323	.415	.737
1974	11	54	87	**214**	**.353**	.383	.503	.886

Later crediting teammate Hank Aaron for his outstanding 1974 campaign, Garr said, "I had a good year because everybody was worried about Henry Aaron hitting a home run. They weren't paying much attention to me."

Although Garr, who manned all three outfield positions for the Braves at different times, did not hit many homers, drive in a lot of runs, or draw many bases on balls, he consistently ranked among the NL leaders in batting average, hits, and triples, topping the circuit in all three categories in 1974, after finishing second in the league in batting in 1972 and placing second in hits in 1973. An excellent base-stealer as well, Garr swiped more than 25 bags each year, topping 30 thefts in 1973, although he later revealed that he could have stolen many more bases when he said, "Hank Aaron was batting third on the team. They didn't need no base stealing because Hank Aaron could drive you in from second base or first base as well as he could from third base. . . . When he was batting third, if I got on base, I had done my job . . . and I didn't want to be running all over the place or worried about me stealing a base with him hitting."

Employing a batting style similar to that of Ichiro Suzuki, the 5'11", 185-pound Garr rarely looked to pull the ball and often reached base by legging out slowly hit groundballs and bunts, with well-known *Los Angeles Times* sportswriter Jim Murray once stating, "Ralph Garr hit 'em where they couldn't get 'em. He once had eight straight hits, and four of them never left the infield. If the third baseman played back, he dropped a bunt. If he played in, he chopped it over his head. He went down to first base so fast the first baseman didn't dare play the hole. On balls hit to deep short with no one on, the shortstop threw to second."

Discussing Garr in the November 1974 edition of *Baseball Digest*, former Braves manager Eddie Mathews said, "Ralph is about as aggressive with a bat as anyone I've ever seen. At first, you want to tell him to leave those pitches outside the strike zone alone. That is, until you see how many of them he puts between the outfielders for base hits."

In describing his approach at the plate, Garr said, "I always basically hit everything off of the fastball. A lot of people looked for changeups and curveballs . . . I think Ferguson Jenkins was the only guy that made me look for a changeup."

Garr added, "I was just aggressive. Most of the time, I was consistent, and I didn't walk a lot. . . . It's hard to walk a lot and get hits. I was blessed to even go to bat a lot of times."

Praising Garr for the tremendous success he experienced his first few seasons with the Braves, Jim Murray later wrote, "No one ever bounded into major league baseball with a more resounding hit barrage . . . 813 hits in his first full four years, an annual tattoo of 219, 180, 200, and 214 hits. Only Ty Cobb matched it. (Stan) Musial had 20 fewer for that period. (Willie) Mays, 135 less, and (Hank) Aaron nearly 100. (Ted) Williams was not even close. They were measuring Ralph for a suit at Cooperstown before the ink was dry on his bonus. Even Cobb's lifetime 4,191 hits seemed hardly safe."

Unfortunately, Garr failed to maintain the same level of play the rest of his career, although he had several more good seasons, batting .278, scoring 74 runs, and collecting a league-leading 11 triples for the Braves in 1975, before being included in a five-player trade with the White Sox at the end of the year that sent him and infielder Larvell Blanks to Chicago for outfielder Ken Henderson and pitchers Dick Ruthven and Dan Osborn. Garr, who, during his time in Atlanta, hit 49 homers, knocked in 247 runs, scored 470 times, collected 1,022 hits, 132 doubles, and 40 triples, stole 137 bases, batted .317, compiled a .350 on-base percentage, and posted a .429 slugging percentage, ended up spending most of the next four seasons with the White Sox, hitting exactly .300 for them twice, before ending his big-league career with the California Angels, who released him on June 6, 1980, after he batted just .190 for them in 21 games. Over parts of 13 years in the major leagues, Garr hit 75 homers, drove in 408 runs, scored 717 others, collected 1,562 hits, 212 doubles, and 64 triples, swiped 172 bases, batted .306, compiled an on-base percentage of .339, and posted a slugging percentage of .416. Considered only an average defensive outfielder, Garr committed at least 10 errors in the field on four separate occasions, although his great speed enabled him to lead all players at his position in putouts twice.

After briefly considering attempting a comeback, Garr became part-owner of a doughnut shop in Houston, recalling, "I used to have to get in there every morning and make the doughnuts and serve them." But then Garr heard from his old friend, Hank Aaron, who, as Atlanta's director of player development, offered him a position as a roving scout and minor-league baserunning coach at the 1984 winter meetings. Continuing to serve the Braves as a scout these many years later, Garr currently resides with his wife of more than 50 years, Ruby, in Richmond, Texas.

Looking back fondly on his life and career, the 77-year-old Garr says, "I ain't never went, 'Ralph Garr deserved this, or Ralph Garr deserved that.' Ralph Garr worked hard and wanted the people to respect him . . . I've had so many blessings, so I can't afford to run around and complain."

BRAVES CAREER HIGHLIGHTS

Best Season

Although Garr performed brilliantly in his first full year with the Braves, he had his finest all-around season in 1974, when he earned his lone All-Star nomination and a 12th-place finish in the NL MVP voting by amassing a league-leading 214 hits and establishing career-high marks with 305 total bases, an OPS of .886, 17 triples, and a .353 batting average, with each of the last two figures also topping the senior circuit.

Memorable Moments/Greatest Performances

Garr contributed to an 11–2 thumping of the Reds on September 20, 1970, by collecting four hits, stealing a base, driving in two runs, and scoring three others.

Garr helped lead the Braves to a 5–4 win over the Pirates on April 10, 1971, by going 4-for-5, with three runs scored, tallying the game's winning run after leading off the bottom of the 12th inning with a triple.

Garr hit a pair of huge home runs against the Mets on May 17, 1971, tying the score at 3–3 with a two-out solo homer off Tom Seaver in the bottom of the 10th inning, before giving the Braves a dramatic 4–3 victory by reaching the seats against Ron Taylor two innings later.

Garr delivered the big blow of a 6–1 win over the San Diego Padres on June 24, 1973, when he homered off starting pitcher Steve Arlin with the bases loaded in the top of the eighth inning.

Garr provided most of the offensive firepower during a 3–0 win over the Astros on May 24, 1974, homering twice off Don Wilson with no one on base.

Notable Achievements

- Scored more than 100 runs once.
- Batted over .300 three times, topping .340-mark twice.
- Surpassed 200 hits three times.
- Finished in double digits in triples twice.
- Surpassed 30 doubles once.
- Stole more than 20 bases four times, topping 30 thefts twice.
- Posted slugging percentage over .500 once.
- Led NL in batting average once, hits once, and triples twice.
- Finished second in NL in batting average twice and hits twice.
- Led NL left fielders in putouts twice and assists once.
- Ranks among Braves career leaders in batting average (tied for 6th).
- Two-time NL Player of the Week.
- May 1974 NL Player of the Month.
- 1974 NL All-Star selection.
- Member of Braves Hall of Fame.

29

RICO CARTY

Part of the second wave of outstanding Latin-American ballplayers to arrive in the United States during the early-1960s, Rico Carty joined the Braves during the latter stages of the 1964 campaign following a stellar four-year minor-league apprenticeship during which he established himself as one of baseball's top prospects. A big, strong right-handed batter who drew favorable comparisons to some of the finest hitters in the game, Carty did not disappoint his first few years in the league, hitting more than 20 homers twice, driving in more than 100 runs once, and batting over .300 five times, with his league-leading average of .366 in 1970 representing the franchise's second-highest single-season mark of the modern era. However, even though Carty remained an extremely effective hitter the rest of his career, he never achieved the greatness originally predicted for him due to an unfortunate combination of illness, injuries, ineptitude on defense, and a reputation as a troublemaker.

Born in San Pedro de Macorís, Dominican Republic, on September 1, 1939, Ricardo Adolfo Jacobo Carty grew up with his 15 siblings hoping to escape the poverty of his youth. The son of a midwife and a man who worked in the sugar mill and played club cricket, Rico learned how to play baseball at the ballparks built by the local sugar processing plants.

Recalling how he received his introduction to the game, Carty said, "Boys became ballplayers in the plants. When I was a kid, I never left the ballpark. It was going to school, then the ballpark, and then take a bath at the river. It was my hobby. People all over the eastern region of the country were blessed by the sugar industry and all the ballparks they built. Some of them had golf courses, but all of them had baseball fields."

Carty continued, "Guys became ballplayers naturally, just playing the game and watching others. Even when you made it to the major leagues, you had to show your talent. Nobody was there to help. We started playing different types of ball games in San Pedro, hitting balls made out of socks. That made us good hitters."

Adding that he went against his mother's wishes by spending hours on the ballfield, Carty stated, "My mother wanted me to be a doctor, but I didn't like that. My mother wouldn't let me go to the ball field, but I used to steal time to play. I tell my mother I going to school, but I used to go to the river and swim and play ball instead. I would have ended up in the mill but for baseball."

As much as Carty loved baseball, he briefly considered following in the footsteps of his four uncles by pursuing a career in boxing until, after winning his first 17 bouts as a teenager, he suffered a humiliating defeat. Focusing exclusively on further developing his skills on the diamond from that point on, Carty eventually joined a Dominican team that competed in the 1959 Pan-Am Games in Chicago, where he drew the attention of scouts with his exceptional hitting.

Eventually signed by the Braves, Carty began his professional career as a catcher with the organization's Davenport/Quad Cities team in the Class D Midwest League, where he encountered racial and cultural discrimination for the first time in his life, recalling, "We experienced so many horrible situations in a time when the stench of racism was filling the air..... You couldn't sit in the front of the bus. You had to go to the back. You couldn't use any bathroom. It was the same with restaurants. It wasn't like that on the baseball field—the players and coaches did not discriminate against us."

Further troubled by his unfamiliarity with the English language, Carty found it extremely difficult to adapt to his new surroundings, causing him to struggle somewhat in his first year of minor-league ball. Nevertheless, after batting just .233 in 25 games at Davenport in 1960, Carty spent the following year with Class C Eau Claire, for whom he batted .298. Carty then compiled a .367 batting average for Class B Yakima in 1962, although his season ended prematurely when he pulled a leg muscle while running down to first base. Carty subsequently split the 1963 campaign between Double-A Austin and Triple-A Toronto, batting a combined .313 with 31 homers and 111 RBIs, with his strong performance earning him a late-season callup to the parent club and prompting some scouts to identify him as "the best catching prospect in 10 years." But, with Joe Torre having recently established himself as the Braves' starting receiver, Carty spent much of the year learning how to play the outfield.

After being touted during the following offseason as "the best young hitting prospect in the organization," Carty received further praise in the spring from Braves farm director John Mullen, who compared him to Orlando Cepeda. Living up to his advanced billing, Carty performed extremely well after laying claim to the starting left field job, earning a

Rico Carty led the NL with a .366 batting average in 1970.

runner-up finish to Philadelphia's Dick Allen in the 1964 NL Rookie of the Year balloting by hitting 22 homers, driving in 88 runs, and batting .330, which placed him second in the league to Roberto Clemente.

Plagued by back problems throughout the 1965 campaign, Carty appeared in only 83 games, finishing the season with 10 homers, 35 RBIs, and a .310 batting average. Unhappy over his treatment by manager Bobby Bragan, who he claimed undermined his confidence by removing him for defensive purposes late in contests, Carty displayed for the first time his willingness to speak out against perceived injustices. But, while it could be argued that the slow-footed Carty's occasional fielding lapses justified Bragan's actions, a late-season doctor's discovery that Carty's right leg was slightly shorter than his left quieted those critics who had accused the out-fielder of exaggerating his back pain.

Aided by a new orthopedic shoe, Carty returned to action full-time in 1966, when, starting in left field for the newly transplanted Braves, he hit 15 homers, knocked in 76 runs, scored 73 times, and ranked among the league leaders with a .326 batting average and a .391 on-base percentage. Meanwhile, despite his lack of foot speed and reputation as a below-average outfielder, Carty led all NL left fielders with 218 putouts and a .970 fielding percentage, with his strong all-around play making him extremely popular with the team's new fanbase in Atlanta, which dubbed the left field stands "Carty's Corner."

After Carty garnered a $50 fine for insulting an umpire and sustained minor injuries in a car crash while playing winter ball in the Dominican League the following offseason, he experienced further difficulties when he returned to the States in 1967. In addition to driving in only 64 runs and batting just .255 for the Braves, Carty drew the ire of the hometown fans by engaging in a "brief but heated scuffle" during a team flight with Hank Aaron, who later admitted to calling his teammate a "black slick" after he loafed on a ball hit to the outfield.

Detailing the altercation in his 2012 memoir, *Making Airwaves*, former Braves broadcaster Milo Hamilton wrote: "The fight started as a disagree-ment over word choice. Carty was Dominican, not African American. So, he didn't think he was black and didn't like to be thought of as black. In this instance, Carty called Aaron 'a black son-of-a-bitch,' and Aaron replied, 'You're not exactly pink yourself.' . . . Things just exploded. . . . Carty took care of Aaron with one punch."

Subsequently demonized by the press, which held Aaron in high regard, Carty spent the rest of his time in Atlanta sharing a somewhat contentious relationship with Braves fans, who also sided with their team's best player.

Unfortunately, Carty experienced more misfortune in each of the next two seasons as well. After reporting to 1968 spring training 10 pounds lighter and downplaying teammate Clete Boyer's offseason criticism that he "doesn't give 100 percent," Carty received a diagnosis of tuberculosis that forced him to miss the entire year. Fully recovered by the start of the 1969 campaign, Carty appeared ready to resume his onslaught against NL pitch-ers. However, he ended up spending nearly two months on the disabled list with a dislocated shoulder. Still, in only 104 games and 304 official at-bats, Carty managed to hit 16 homers, knock in 58 runs, and compile a batting average of .342 for the NL West champions.

Entering the 1970 season with high hopes, Braves manager Lum Harris expressed his confidence in his team's ability to perform at a similarly lofty level if Carty remained healthy, stating during a preseason interview with *Atlanta Journal-Constitution* sports editor Jesse Outlar, "They believe they can win the pennant, and I believe they can. . . . There's no telling how many games Rico will win for us with his bat. He is capable of becoming the game's next .400 hitter."

Although the Braves ended up finishing a disappointing fifth in the NL West, Carty had a huge year. Despite missing 26 games with an assortment of injuries that included a sprained wrist, a pulled leg muscle, and a chipped bone in his finger, Carty hit 25 homers, knocked in 101 runs, scored 84 times, and led the NL with a .366 batting average and a .454 on-base percentage, earning in the process a 10th-place finish in the league MVP voting and a starting assignment in the All-Star Game as a "write-in" candidate.

A tremendous natural hitter, the 6'3", 200-pound Carty, who referred to himself as "Beeg Boy," possessed excellent vision, powerful forearms, and an innate ability to anticipate the opposing pitcher's next offering. Displaying good power to all fields, Carty hit the ball with equal authority to left, center, and right, making it extremely difficult for the opposition to devise an effective defensive strategy against him. More patient at the plate than most other Latin-American hitters, Carty said years later when comparing himself to other Dominican sluggers, "You won't see a hitter like me again. I always gave the first strike to the pitcher. I only started to work after the first strike. That was my style."

Despite Carty's exceptional performance in 1970, he had to spend the entire offseason listening to trade rumors after engaging in a fistfight with teammate Ron Reed on August 19. Telling reporters that the scuffle began when he took two bats from Reed's locker, Carty said, "He came over to me and was mad about it. Maybe my temper was a little too fast, I do not know."

Carty's situation in Atlanta became even more tenuous when he missed the entire 1971 season after undergoing surgery to repair a fractured knee and severely damaged ligament he sustained while playing winter ball. Then, on August 24, 1971, Carty all but sealed his fate when he and his young brother-in-law fought with two off-duty Atlanta police officers when Rico objected to a racial slur. Although Atlanta mayor Sam Massell labeled the incident "blatant brutality" and suspended the officers, Carty's inability to control his temper and history of injuries convinced the Braves that the time had come to part ways with one of the league's best hitters.

After Carty missed nearly half of the 1972 campaign with elbow ten-dinitis and a pulled hamstring, the Braves dealt him to the Texas Rangers for pitcher Jim Panther in a trade that both the Atlanta press and the hometown fans criticized greatly. Meanwhile, Carty took the news in stride, saying that he was not surprised because he had experienced problems with new manager Eddie Mathews.

Carty, who left Atlanta with career totals of 109 homers, 451 RBIs, 385 runs scored, 871 hits, 137 doubles, and 14 triples, a .317 batting aver-age, a .388 on-base percentage, and a .496 slugging percentage, ended up splitting the 1973 season between the Rangers, Cubs, and Athletics, hitting only five home runs and batting just. 229, before spending the next four years serving the Cleveland Indians almost exclusively as a designated hitter. Playing his best ball for the Indians in 1975 and 1976, Carty hit 18 homers, knocked in 64 runs, and batted .308 in the first of those campaigns, before reaching the seats 13 times, driving in 83 runs, and batting .310 in the sec-ond. Traded by Cleveland to Toronto prior to the start of the 1978 season, Carty had one more big year left in him, hitting a career-high 31 homers, driving in 99 runs, and batting .282, before retiring a little over a year later when the Blue Jays released him on March 29, 1980. Over parts of 15 big-league seasons, Carty hit 204 homers, knocked in 890 runs, scored 712 times, collected 1,677 hits, 278 doubles, and 17 triples, batted .299, compiled an on-base percentage of .369, and posted a slugging percentage of .464.

Following his retirement, Carty returned to his homeland, where he continued to work for the Blue Jays as a scout in Latin America. Carty also remained active as a player, leading the Dominican team to a third-place finish in the 1988 Men's Senior Baseball League World Series and winning the home-run contest in the 40-plus age bracket. Commenting on Carty's ability to still hit with power at 49 years of age, league founder Steve Sigler said, "He's still an amazing hitter, and he was the only one using a wooden bat."

A study in contrasts, Carty, who, despite his fierce glare at the plate, ill temper, reputation as a troublemaker, and willingness to stand up for his rights, became known for his infectious grin and cheerful banter with fans, has spent most of the last three decades running the foundation he estab-lished in his native San Pedro de Macorís that helps the poor with basic needs such as food, clothing, and medicine.

BRAVES CAREER HIGHLIGHTS

Best Season

Carty had easily the best season of his career in 1970, when, despite missing nearly a month of action, he hit 25 homers, knocked in 101 runs, scored 84 times, collected 175 hits, led the league with a .366 batting average and a .454 on-base percentage, and finished second in the circuit with an OPS of 1.037.

Memorable Moments/Greatest Performances

Carty led the Braves to an 8–4 win over the Cardinals on May 23, 1964, by knocking in five runs with a pair of homers off Roger Craig.

Carty helped lead the Braves to a 12–9 victory over the Phillies on August 24, 1964, by going a perfect 5-for-5 at the plate, with a homer, three doubles, and four runs scored.

Carty again went 5-for-5 just six days later, collecting a homer, double, three singles, and two RBIs during a 7–4 win over the Giants on August 30, 1964.

After failing to reach base in the 1970 regular-season opener, Carty hit safely in each of the next 31 contests, batting .451 (51-for-113), with eight homers, nine doubles, 30 RBIs, 31 runs scored, 20 bases on balls, and just 10 strikeouts from April 8 to May 15.

Carty set the tone for a lopsided 9–2 win over the Cubs on April 30, 1970, by homering off Ferguson Jenkins with the bases loaded in the bottom of the first inning. He finished the contest with three hits, two homers, and five RBIs.

Carty keyed a 6–1 victory over the Giants on May 20, 1970, by going 3-for-5, with a homer, triple, and four RBIs, delivering the game's big blow in the top of the 11th inning, when he homered off Gaylord Perry with two men on base.

Carty led the Braves to a 9–1 win over the Phillies on May 31, 1970, by hitting three homers, knocking in six runs, and scoring four times.

Notable Achievements

- Hit more than 20 home runs twice.
- Knocked in more than 100 runs once.
- Batted over .300 five times, topping .330-mark on three occasions.

- Compiled on-base percentage over .400 twice.
- Posted slugging percentage over .500 three times.
- Posted OPS over .900 three times, topping 1.000 once.
- Hit three home runs in one game vs. Philadelphia Phillies on May 31, 1970.
- Hit safely in 31 straight games in 1970.
- Led NL in batting average once and on-base percentage once.
- Finished second in NL in batting average once and OPS once.
- Led NL left fielders in putouts once, double plays turned once, and fielding percentage once.
- Ranks among Braves career leaders in batting average (tied for 6th), on-base percentage (6th), and OPS (10th).
- May 1970 NL Player of the Month.
- 1970 NL All-Star selection.

30

BOB HORNER

Apowerful right-handed batter who consistently ranked among the NL leaders in home runs during his nine years in Atlanta, Bob Horner combined with Dale Murphy to give the Braves arguably the league's top slugging tandem for much of the 1980s. Despite being plagued by injuries throughout his career, Horner hit more than 30 home runs three times, topped 20 homers four other times, knocked in close to 100 runs twice, and batted over .300 twice, establishing himself in the process as one of the most feared hitters in the senior circuit. Though merely adequate in the field, Horner also did a solid job for the Braves at both third and first base, with his strong all-around play earning him one All-Star selection and NL Rookie of the Year honors in 1978.

Born in Junction City, Kansas, on August 6, 1957, James Robert Horner spent his formative years living in Southern California after moving there with his family at an early age, before relocating once again as a teenager to Glendale, Arizona. A star shortstop at Glendale's Apollo High School, Horner elected to continue his education rather than turn pro when the Athletics selected him in the 15th round of the 1975 MLB Amateur Draft, later saying, "The amount of money they were offering didn't come close to the value of a four-year education."

Choosing to attend Arizona State University on an athletic scholarship, Horner went on to have a storied career at ASU, hitting a then-NCAA record 58 home runs, en route to gaining All-America recognition twice after moving to third base as a sophomore, when he led the Sun Devils to the national championship. Particularly outstanding his junior year, Horner hit 25 homers, knocked in 100 runs, and batted .412, with his fabulous performance earning him a first-place finish in the voting for the Golden Spikes Award, which is presented annually to the nation's top college player.

Subsequently selected by the Braves with the first overall pick of the 1978 MLB June Amateur Draft, Horner went straight to Atlanta, bypassing the minor leagues completely. Making his professional debut at only

20 years of age on June 16, 1978, Horner proved that he belonged in the majors by homering off future Hall of Fame right-hander Bert Blyleven during a 9–4 loss to the Pittsburgh Pirates. Continuing to perform well as the Braves' starting third baseman the rest of the year, Horner hit 23 homers, knocked in 63 runs, scored 50 times, batted .266, and compiled an OPS of .852, in 89 games and 359 total plate appearances, with his prodigious slugging enabling him to edge out Ozzie Smith in the NL Rookie of the Year voting.

After signing for $130,000 (a record at the time for second-year players) in the spring of 1979 following a bitter arbitration hearing, Horner proved his worth by placing near the top of the league rankings with 33 homers, 98 RBIs, a batting average of .314, and a slugging percentage of .552, despite missing close to 40 games due to problems with his shoulder and leg. However, after Horner got off to a slow start the following year, Braves owner Ted Turner, perhaps still upset over losing the arbitration case, tried to demote him to Triple-A Richmond. Horner subsequently caused a huge uproar with the local fans and media when he refused to go to the minor leagues, resulting in an impasse that lasted until the Braves finally relented 10 days later. Once again having the last laugh, Horner eventually found his stroke, finishing the season with 35 homers, 89 RBIs, 81 runs scored, a batting average of .268, and a slugging percentage of .529, even though he ended up missing 37 games due to his brief walkout and chronically sore shoulder and leg.

Employing a short, compact swing, the 6'1" Horner, whose weight fluctuated between 210 and 225 pounds for most of his career, drove the ball with power to all fields, although he pulled most of his homers to left. Blessed with tremendous natural strength, Horner, said Luke Appling, who spent more than a decade serving as a troubleshooter in the Atlanta organization, possessed as much power as any player he ever saw, with the Hall of Fame shortstop adding, "This kid's talent with the bat is 100 percent natural, and basically there is no set way for the pitchers to get him out. I also like him for another reason—his guts. People never write much about it, but even though Bob gets thrown at and knocked down a lot, he never gives any ground. Today, some of these kids want to run and hide in the clubhouse if they even see a brush-back pitch."

Bobby Cox also had high praise for Horner, saying, "There are certain guys who come into this world with the ability to hit, and Horner is one of them. You don't try to teach strike zones or anything so obvious to someone like Bob, because with them it's all instinct anyway. The other thing is

Bob Horner hit more than 30 homers three times as a member of the Braves.
Courtesy of Jim Accardino

his strength. There isn't an opposing pitcher he can't pull most of the time. Even balls he doesn't meet squarely sometimes reach the fences."

In discussing his approach at the plate, Horner stated, "Usually, I don't get many fastballs because, when you're able to time a fastball properly, you've got a good chance of hitting it out of the park. Mostly, I try to stay with balls that are in the strike zone and not do the pitchers any favors."

Although hampered by injuries once again in 1981, Horner posted decent numbers, concluding the strike-shortened campaign with a .277 batting average, 15 homers, and 42 RBIs in just 79 games and 300 official at-bats. Healthy for most of the 1982 season, Horner helped lead the Braves to their first division title in 13 years by hitting 32 homers, knocking in 97 runs, scoring 85 times, batting .261, and compiling an OPS of .851, earning in the process his lone All-Star nomination.

Horner, who struggled with his weight throughout his career, subsequently signed a new contract prior to the start of the 1983 season that included an incentive clause promising to pay him close to $8,000 if he weighed less than 215 pounds on each of 13 selected Fridays. Unfortunately, Horner ended up appearing in only 104 games, hitting 20 homers, driving in 68 runs, scoring 76 times, batting .303, and compiling a career-high OPS of .911, before missing most of the final two months after breaking his right wrist sliding into second base. Sidelined for most of 1984 as well, Horner hit just three homers and knocked in only 19 runs in 32 games. However, he rebounded to hit 54 homers and drive in 176 runs over the course of the next two seasons, despite missing a total of 52 contests.

A free agent at the end of 1986, Horner subsequently became one of the many victims of the collusion scandal of 1986-87 that saw team owners conspire to keep player salaries low. Seeking a five-year deal worth $2 million per season that would have made him one of the 10 highest-paid players in the game, Horner, who had earned $1.8 million in 1986, received an offer from the Braves of only $1.5 million for three years. After Horner refused to accept what amounted to a pay cut, the Braves rescinded their offer, with GM Bobby Cox stating that their next offer would be closer to $1 million per year.

Recalling the puzzling chain of events that transpired, Horner told the *Atlanta Journal-Constitution* in 2004, "At the time, I really didn't know what was going on. But after a few years, you figure it out. It is a shame because it wrecked a lot of careers . . . and for what? It accomplished nothing. I mean, look at the salaries they pay today. I will just say, God bless the players."

Horner continued, "They made a big show of saying they wanted to sign me, but deep down inside I don't think they ever wanted to sign me. Judging from what happened, the Braves never made an honest effort to sign me."

After rejecting a last-minute proposal from the Braves of three years and $3.9 million, Horner chose to sign a one-year, $2 million deal with the Yakult Swallows of Japan on April 10, 1987, telling the *Journal-Constitution* at the time, "I could see the handwriting on the wall with the Braves. On May 1, it was going to be 'play for this or don't play at all.' I would have been at their mercy and would have had to do what they dictated. That's a situation I would have been uncomfortable with."

Performing well for the Swallows in 1987, Horner batted .327, hit 31 homers, and knocked in 73 runs in only 97 games, prompting the team to offer him $3 million to return the following year. But, with his heart still in the States, Horner instead signed with the St. Louis Cardinals for just under $1 million. Plagued by shoulder problems throughout the 1988 campaign, Horner appeared in just 60 games, before announcing his retirement at season's end with career totals of 218 homers, 685 RBIs, 560 runs scored, 1,047 hits, 169 doubles, and eight triples, a .277 batting average, a .340 on-base percentage, and a .499 slugging percentage. In explaining his decision to retire when he did, Horner said, "When you get up in the morning and know you need help, it's time to call it a day. It was no way to live."

Some 15 years later, Horner, who currently lives in Irving, Texas, and has spent his retirement focusing on his wife, Chris, their two sons, and their four grandchildren, received more than $7 million from the lawsuit the players filed against the owners for their illegal actions in keeping salaries down.

BRAVES CAREER HIGHLIGHTS

Best Season

Horner had a big year for the Braves in 1982, gaining All-Star recognition for the only time by hitting 32 homers, driving in 97 runs, scoring 85 times, batting .261, and compiling an OPS of .851. He also performed extremely well in 1980, earning a ninth-place finish in the NL MVP voting by finishing second in the league with 35 homers and a .529 slugging percentage, knocking in 89 runs, scoring 81 others, and batting .268. But Horner posted the best overall numbers of his career in 1979, when, in addition to hitting 33 homers and driving in 98 runs, he batted .314, compiled a slugging percentage of .552, and posted an OPS of .898.

Memorable Moments/Greatest Performances

Horner led the Braves to a 4–3 win over the Reds on October 3, 1981, by homering twice, knocking in three runs, and scoring three times, with both of his homers coming off Tom Seaver.

Horner collected five hits in one game for the only time in his career on June 12, 1982, going a perfect 5-for-5 at the plate with two doubles during a 10–5 win over the Giants.

Horner proved to be the difference in an 8–6 victory over the Padres on July 28, 1982, driving in five runs with a single and a pair of homers.

Horner helped lead the Braves to a lopsided 13–5 victory over the Phillies on July 13, 1985, by going 4-for-5, with a homer, two doubles, three RBIs, and four runs scored.

Horner continued his assault on Philadelphia pitching the following day, homering twice, knocking in five runs, and scoring three times during a 12–3 Braves win on July 14, 1985.

Although the Braves suffered an 11–8 defeat at the hands of the Montreal Expos on July 6, 1986, Horner had the most productive day of his career at the plate, hitting four home runs and driving in six runs, with his first three homers coming off starter Andy McGaffigan and his last off closer Jeff Reardon. Looking back on his epic performance years later, Horner said, "I remember that game for a lot of reasons, but what I remember most about it is we lost the game."

Notable Achievements

- Hit at least 20 home runs seven times, topping 30 homers on three occasions.
- Batted over .300 twice.
- Posted slugging percentage over .500 five times.
- Posted OPS over .900 once.
- Hit four home runs in one game vs. Montreal Expos on July 6, 1986.
- Finished second in NL in home runs once and slugging percentage once.
- Led NL first basemen in putouts once and double plays turned once.
- Ranks among Braves career leaders in home runs (8th), slugging percentage (11th), and sacrifice flies (6th).
- 1978 NL Rookie of the Year.
- Four-time NL Player of the Week.
- July 1980 NL Player of the Month.
- 1982 NL All-Star selection.

31

VIC WILLIS

One of the most durable pitchers of his era, Vic Willis spent eight seasons in Boston, completing more than 30 of his starts five times and throwing more than 300 innings on six separate occasions. Surpassing 20 victories four times between 1898 and 1905, the right-handed-throwing Willis served as the ace of Boston's pitching staff for most of his eight-year stint in Beantown, despite losing more games than he won three times due to poor run support. A league-leader in ERA, strikeouts, shutouts, and complete games at various times, Willis proved to be a key figure on the Beaneaters' last pennant-winning team of the 19th century, before spending his last several years in Boston pitching for mostly losing teams. Finally granted a reprieve when the Beaneaters traded him to the Pittsburgh Pirates following the conclusion of the 1905 campaign, Willis won more than 20 games in each of the next four seasons, with his total body of work eventually earning him a place in Cooperstown.

Born in Cecil County, Maryland, on April 12, 1876, Victor Gazaway Willis grew up some 17 miles northeast, in Newark, Delaware, where his father, James, supported the family as a carpenter and his mother, Mary, ran the household. After getting his start in baseball on the sandlots of his hometown, Willis began to make a name for himself as a star pitcher at Newark Academy. From there, he moved on to the University of Delaware, where he continued to excel on the mound, before joining the professional ranks in 1895 as a member of the Harrisburg club in the nearby Pennsylvania State League.

Faring extremely well at Harrisburg, Willis pitched in 16 of the team's 37 games, before the club folded in June, prompting him to sign with Lynchburg in the Virginia League for the rest of the year. Willis subsequently spent the next two seasons with Syracuse of the Eastern League, compiling an overall record of 31-22, before the Beaneaters acquired him for catcher Fred Lake and the sum of $1,000 on September 15, 1897.

Arriving in Boston with huge expectations surrounding him, the 22-year-old Willis joined a starting rotation that also included 26-game-winner Fred Klobedanz, 21-game-winner Ted Lewis, and Hall of Fame hurler Kid Nichols, whose 31 victories the previous season had led the pennant-winning Beaneaters to an extraordinary record of 93-39-3. Willis also had to try to live up to the hype provided by one local sportswriter, who wrote, "The 'Wolf,' as he is termed, ought to be a great winner for Boston."

Acquitting himself extremely well as a rookie, Willis helped lead the Beaneaters to a record of 102-47-3 and their second straight pennant by compiling a record of 25-13 and an ERA of 2.84, throwing 311 innings and 29 complete games, and finishing third in the league with 160 strikeouts. Although the Beaneaters failed to capture their third consecutive league championship in 1899, Willis performed even better, going 27-8 with a league-leading 2.50 ERA and five shutouts, tossing 342 2/3 innings and 35 complete games, and finishing third among NL hurlers with a WHIP of 1.150.

Plagued by elbow soreness and a lack of command on his pitches, Willis subsequently suffered through a dismal 1900 campaign during which he went just 10-17 with a career-high 4.19 ERA, threw only 236 innings, and completed just 22 of his starts. But, despite the struggles of the Beaneaters as a team the next two seasons, Willis rebounded to win a total of 47 games (he also lost 37 times) and rank among the league leaders in ERA, strikeouts, shutouts, complete games, and innings pitched both years. Particularly outstanding in 1902, Willis compiled a record of 27-20, an ERA of 2.20, and a WHIP of 1.154, threw four shutouts, and led the league with 225 strikeouts, 410 innings pitched, and 45 complete games.

A big man for his time, the 6'2", 205-pound Willis had long fingers, which allowed him to throw a sharp-breaking curveball that the *Boston Sunday Journal* described thusly: "Willis has the most elusive curves. His 'drop' is so wonderful that, if anyone hits it, it is generally considered a fluke."

Employing a straight overhand delivery, Willis also possessed an outstanding fastball, which, combined with his sweeping curve and effective changeup, helped make him one of the era's top strikeout pitchers.

After toying with the idea of jumping to the newly formed American League one year earlier, Willis agreed in principle to a two-year contract with the Detroit Tigers in 1902 that would have paid him the then-exorbitant sum of $4,500 per season. However, Willis decided to stay in Boston when the Beaneaters matched Detroit's offer, with his services subsequently remaining in dispute until the end of the season, when he was awarded to Boston as part of the peace settlement between the two leagues.

Vic Willis surpassed 20 victories on four separate occasions during his time in Boston.

Perhaps causing Willis to regret his decision, the Beaneaters finished near the bottom of the NL standings in both 1903 and 1904, winning a total of only 103 games over the course of those two seasons. And, with Willis receiving very little in the way of run support, he finished just 12-18 in 1903, before going 18-25 the following year. Nevertheless, Willis pitched better than his won-lost record would seem to indicate, compiling an ERA under 3.00 both seasons, throwing a total of 68 complete games and 628 innings, and finishing second in the league with 196 strikeouts in 1904.

Willis once again flirted with the idea of leaving Boston when the Beaneaters reduced his salary to $2,400 prior to the start of the 1905 campaign. But, after expressing displeasure with his drastic salary cut by threatening to jump to an outlaw league in Pennsylvania, Willis eventually returned to Boston, where, backed by the league's worst offense, he won just 12 of his 41 decisions, with his 29 losses representing the highest single-season total in the history of modern (post-1900) baseball.

Given a new lease on life when the Beaneaters traded him to Pittsburgh for three players on December 15, 1905, Willis sent a letter to Pirates owner Barney Dreyfuss in which he expressed his approval of the trade and happiness to be leaving Boston, also telling his new employer, "Don't believe those tales you hear about my being all-in. Wait until you see me in action for your team and then form your opinion of my worth to your team. I assure you that I am delighted to be a Pirate and that I will do my best to bring another pennant to the Smoky City."

Pitching some of the best ball of his career over the course of the next four seasons, Willis helped lead the Pirates to one pennant and two second-place finishes by compiling an overall record of 89-46 and a composite ERA of 2.08, while also ranking among the league leaders in complete games and innings pitched each year. Particularly outstanding in 1906 and 1908, Willis went 23-13 with a 1.73 ERA, six shutouts, 32 complete games, and 322 innings pitched in the first of those campaigns, before posting a mark of 23-11 and an ERA of 2.07, tossing seven shutouts, and throwing 25 complete games and 304 2/3 innings in the second.

Nevertheless, with Willis experiencing personal differences with Pittsburgh manager Fred Clarke, the Pirates waived him before the start of the 1910 season, allowing the St. Louis Cardinals to claim him. After the *Sporting News* reported that Willis "should have a year or two of high-class work left in him if he will behave himself," the 34-year-old right-hander went just 9-12 for the seventh-place Cardinals, before being released at the end of the year. Subsequently claimed off waivers by the Cubs, Willis elected to retire rather than start anew in Chicago, ending his career with a record of 249-205, an ERA of 2.63, a WHIP of 1.209, 1,651 strikeouts in 3,996 innings of work, 50 shutouts, and 388 complete games. In his eight seasons with the Beaneaters, Willis compiled a record of 151-147, an ERA of 2.82, and a WHIP of 1.258, registered 1,161 strikeouts in 2,575 innings, and threw 26 shutouts and 268 complete games.

Following his playing days, Willis returned to his hometown of Newark, where he purchased and operated the Washington House Hotel. Willis also remained active in baseball, managing a semipro team, and coaching at the youth and college levels for several years. In his spare time, Willis enjoyed playing golf and raising dogs until he passed away on August 3, 1947, at the age of 71, after suffering a stroke. Willis gained induction into the Baseball Hall of Fame 48 years later, with the members of the Veterans Committee electing him in 1995.

BRAVES (BEANEATERS) CAREER HIGHLIGHTS

Best Season

It could be argued that Willis pitched his best ball for the Beaneaters in 1902, when, in addition to finishing second in the NL with 27 wins and compiling an ERA of 2.20, he set a 20th-century record by throwing 45 complete games. However, Willis posted slightly better overall numbers in 1899, when he went 27-8, led the NL with a 2.50 ERA and five shutouts, and ranked among the league leaders with 342 2/3 innings pitched, 35 complete games, and a WHIP of 1.150.

Memorable Moments/Greatest Performances

Although accounts in both the *Washington Post* and the *Boston Globe* suggest otherwise, Willis threw what is believed to be the last no-hitter of the 19th century against the Washington Senators on August 7, 1899. While both newspapers credited Washington pitcher Bill Dinneen with a sixth-inning infield single after his slowly hit groundball down the third base line eluded Boston third sacker Jimmy Collins, wire service accounts and box scores that spread across the nation claimed that Willis did not allow any hits during his 7–1 victory, prompting MLB to include it on its official list of no-hitters.

Although Willis yielded 12 hits and five runs during a 9–5 win over Cincinnati on June 10, 1901, he drove in a pair of runs with the only home run of his career.

Willis tossed a two-hit shutout on August 26, 2001, allowing just two singles and three walks during a 2–0 win over the Brooklyn Superbas (Dodgers).

Willis hurled another gem on September 13, 1901, when he yielded just one walk and a harmless single by third baseman Charlie Dexter during a 1–0 victory over the Chicago Orphans (Cubs).

Willis dominated Chicago's lineup once again on September 20, 1901, allowing just three hits during a 7–0 win, while also going 3-for-3 at the plate, with a triple and one RBI.

Willis recorded a career-high 13 strikeouts during a 1–0 win over the Giants on May 28, 1902, also surrendering six hits and issuing two bases on balls during the contest.

Willis turned in his last dominant performance for the Beaneaters on September 2, 1905, when he yielded just three hits and recorded eight strikeouts during a 1–0 win over Brooklyn.

Notable Achievements

- Won at least 20 games four times, surpassing 25 victories on three occasions.
- Posted winning percentage over .600 twice, topping .700-mark once.
- Compiled ERA under 2.50 three times.
- Recorded more than 200 strikeouts once.
- Threw more than 300 innings six times, tossing more than 400 frames once.
- Threw more than 20 complete games eight times, completing more than 30 of his starts five times.
- Led NL pitchers in ERA once, strikeouts once, shutouts twice, innings pitched once, complete games twice, saves once, putouts three times, and starts once.
- Ranks among Braves career leaders in wins (8th), ERA (tied for 9th), strikeouts (8th), shutouts (7th), complete games (3rd), innings pitched (7th), and games started (8th).
- 1898 NL champion.
- Elected to Baseball Hall of Fame by members of Veterans Committee in 1995.

32
JAVY LÓPEZ

The Braves' primary starter behind the plate for a decade, Javy López spent parts of 12 seasons in Atlanta, proving to be one of the best-hitting catchers in the game much of that time. A three-time NL All-Star who also earned one Silver Slugger and one top-five finish in the league MVP voting, López hit more than 20 homers five times, knocked in more than 100 runs twice, and batted over .300 three times, in helping to lead the Braves to four pennants and one world championship. Yet, despite his contributions on offense, López's defensive shortcomings prevented him from ever gaining the trust of Greg Maddux, who insisted on throwing to someone else on those days he pitched.

Born in Ponce, Puerto Rico, on November 5, 1970, Javier Torres López grew up with his four siblings in modest means, learning the value of hard work at an early age from his father, Jacinto, an auto-parts dealer, and mother, Evelia, a former bank teller and teacher who left the workforce to better care for her children. After first displaying his fondness for the game that eventually became his livelihood by hitting a bucket of rocks off the roof of his house into a vacant lot across the street with an old bat, López began playing baseball with his friends at the age of seven on a nearby concrete field with a rubber ball. Whenever a bat or tape to make a ball could not be found, Javy and his friends improvised with broomsticks and soda-bottle caps.

Taking note of his son's affinity for the sport, López's father brought him to a recreational league, where he spent the next few years honing his skills under several different coaches while competing for various teams. A good hitter from the start, López finally found a home behind the plate at the age of 13, after previously failing to display the agility to play shortstop or the swiftness to assume one of the three outfield positions. Blessed with a strong throwing arm, López worked hard on improving his fundamentals, enabling him to gradually evolve into a capable receiver.

After further developing his skills at Academia Cristo Rey High School, López found himself being pursued by several major-league teams as he approached his 17th birthday. Ultimately choosing to sign with the Braves for $45,000, López rejected far more lucrative offers from the Yankees, Padres, and Expos. In explaining his son's decision, Jacinto López said, "TBS used to be the only station that showed games here, so we were Braves fans."

Meanwhile, Javy later revealed that even more teams attempted to sign him after he inked his deal with the Braves. But he remained true to his word, recalling that he said to himself, "You know what? Forget it! I'm going to be in Atlanta, on TBS!"

López subsequently spent five long years advancing through the Braves' farm system, before earning a late-season callup to the parent club in 1992 by hitting 16 homers, driving in 60 runs, and batting .321 in 115 games at Double-A Greenville. Appearing in nine games with the Braves during the season's final two weeks, López collected six hits in 16 trips to the plate, giving him a batting average of .375. Returned to the minors the following year, López hit 17 homers, knocked in 74 runs, and batted .305 at Triple-A Richmond, before once again joining the Braves during the season's later stages. Acquitting himself extremely well down the stretch, López helped the Braves edge out San Francisco for the NL West title by homering once, driving in a pair of runs, and batting .375.

Anointed the Braves' starting catcher prior to the start of the strike-shortened 1994 campaign, López finished the season with decent numbers, hitting 13 homers, knocking in 35 runs, and batting .245 in 80 games, although he also led all NL receivers with 10 passed balls. Emerging as one of the better-hitting catchers in the game the following year while sharing playing time with veteran backstop Charlie O'Brien, the right-handed-swinging López hit 14 homers, drove in 51 runs, and batted .315 in 352 total plate appearances, before helping the Braves advance to the World Series by batting .444 against Colorado in the NLDS and .357 against Cincinnati in the NLCS. Although López subsequently batted just .176 against Cleveland in the Fall Classic, he delivered the decisive blow of the Braves' 4–3 win in Game 2 when he homered off Dennis Martínez in the bottom of the sixth inning with one man aboard.

The Braves' regular catcher in each of the next two seasons, López totaled 46 homers and 137 RBIs from 1996 to 1997, while also posting batting averages of .282 and .295, with his strong performance in the second of those campaigns gaining him All-Star recognition for the first time in his career. Earning that distinction again in 1998, López had his finest season to date, finishing the year with 34 homers, 106 RBIs, and a .284 batting average, while also leading all NL receivers with a .995 fielding percentage.

López's 43 homers in 2003 represent a single-season franchise record for catchers.

Praising López for his outstanding all-around play, Braves coach Ned Yost stated, "I still think Javy's underrated. He's the total package. You can count total package catchers on one hand. He's one of them. He's everything you want in a baseball catcher. He plays hard, gives you everything he's got. And he's tough."

Nevertheless, beginning in 1995, López rarely found his name entered on the lineup card on those days that Greg Maddux took the mound, causing many theories to surface as to why arguably the league's best pitcher chose not to throw to the team's number one receiver. Several articles appearing in the local newspapers suggested that, at least on some level, a rift had developed between the two men. Others claimed that Maddux felt that López did not call a good game. Attempting to dispel such notions, longtime Braves backup catcher Eddie Pérez, a personal favorite of Maddux, explained that López simply needed a day off now and then. But the fact remains that López hardly ever caught Maddux, even in the postseason, when it would have been advantageous to the Braves to have his bat in the lineup. And after his career ended, López admitted that his omission from the team's lineup in several critical postseason contests still bothered him.

Experiencing a considerable amount of adversity in 1999, López lost his mother to a stroke, helped see his father through quadruple bypass surgery, and had to come to terms with his failing marriage and his sister Elaine's pending divorce from Rangers outfielder Juan González. Meanwhile, on the playing field, López suffered a torn ACL in late July that limited him to just 65 games, 11 homers, and 45 RBIs, although he finished the season with a .317 batting average.

Healthy again by the start of the 2000 season, López hit 24 homers, knocked in 89 runs, and batted .287. But after he hit just 17 homers, drove in only 66 runs, and batted .267 in 2001, the growing fear that he might become estranged from his two sons while going through a contentious divorce settlement caused López to experience a further decline in offensive production.

However, after hitting just 11 homers, driving in only 52 runs, and batting just .233 in 2002, López entered the ensuing campaign with a new attitude, revised batting stance, and revamped conditioning program. Arriving at spring training weighing a svelte 210 pounds after spending his first several years in the league carrying close to 250 pounds on his 6'3" frame, López kept himself in top condition the entire year by lifting weights. He also opened his stance a bit, helping him to make more consistent contact with the ball. Conveniently making these changes in a contract season, López caused many to wonder if the use of performance-enhancing drugs had contributed greatly to his improved physique, creating further suspicion by giving coy responses to questions during interviews. And during a 2010 interview, López admitted as much, saying, "Well, everybody saw players getting big, hitting the ball harder, home runs and stuff. All of a sudden— boom—they got the big contract and everybody's like, 'You know what, he did that, it worked for him, why not do it?'. . . I mean, how can I explain this? It's like if you're going to race cars, if you're going to race a car and some people are using nitro in the fuel and you see them winning all the time, and you're using regular gas— you know what? If they're using nitro and they've been winning, well, I'd be stupid enough not to use nitro, too."

Whatever the reason for his improved play, López posted easily the best numbers of his career in 2003, earning the last of his three All-Star selections and a fifth-place finish in the NL MVP voting by ranking among the league leaders with 43 homers, 109 RBIs, a batting average of .328, a slugging percentage of .687, and an OPS of 1.065, with his home-run total establishing a new single-season major-league record for catchers. Recalling his banner year, López said, "People don't give me a lot of credit for my defense, but I also had a good season that year behind the plate. That year everything just seemed to come into place both at the plate and behind it. I always was able to hit, and I knew I wasn't the best defensive catcher, but I also wasn't the worst. I think I proved that year how complete I could be."

A free agent at the end of the year, López never received a contract offer from the Braves, remembering, "I knew when they traded Kevin Millwood for Estrada that they had him as their future catcher. John Schuerholz called me right after the season and thanked me for the years and said he really appreciated everything, but that they were not going to offer me a contract. I did appreciate the call."

Choosing to sign with the Baltimore Orioles, López performed well for his new team in 2004, hitting 23 homers, knocking in 86 runs, and batting .316, before experiencing a steep decline in offensive production the next two seasons. Dealt to the Red Sox during the latter stages of the 2006 campaign, López spent the rest of the year in Boston, before signing with the Rockies when the Red Sox released him. Unable to earn a roster spot in Colorado, López sat out all of 2007 and then retired early in 2008 after an attempted comeback with the Braves failed.

Looking back on his decision to retire when he did, López said, "I think it is like everything else, when you know it is time, you stop. I was very happy with what I did in baseball. I feel good about my accomplishments, and it came with an organization that was the best in baseball when I was playing."

Over parts of 15 big-league seasons, López hit 260 homers, knocked in 864 runs, scored 674 times, collected 1,527 hits, 267 doubles, and 19 triples, batted .287, compiled a .337 on-base percentage, and posted a .491 slugging percentage. During his time in Atlanta, López hit 214 homers, drove in 694 runs, scored 508 others, amassed 1,148 hits, 190 doubles, and

14 triples, batted .287, compiled an on-base percentage of .337, and posted a slugging percentage of .502.

After retiring as an active player, López remained connected to the game by founding Bones Bats, a company that made hardwood bats. López, who currently lives with his second wife and their two young sons in Suwanee, Georgia, occasionally travels to Florida to help coach the Braves young players during spring training. Inducted into the Braves Hall of Fame in 2015, López also keeps himself busy by competing in charity golf tournaments and participating in his longtime hobby of flying remote-control airplanes.

BRAVES CAREER HIGHLIGHTS

Best Season

López posted easily the best numbers of his career in 2003, when he won his lone Silver Slugger and earned a fifth-place finish in the NL MVP voting by hitting 43 homers, knocking in 109 runs, scoring 89 times, batting .328, finishing second in the league with a slugging percentage of .687, and placing fourth in the circuit with an OPS of 1.065.

Memorable Moments/Greatest Performances

López led the Braves to a 6–1 win over the Giants on April 14, 1994, by driving in four runs with a pair of homers.

Though not known for his defense, López made a huge play in the field in Game 2 of the 1995 World Series, when, with the Braves holding a 4–3 lead over the Indians with one man out in the top of the eighth inning, Manny Ramírez on first base, and Jim Thome at the plate, he delivered a perfect throw to Fred McGriff to pick off Ramírez. With Thome subsequently walking, the play became even more significant, helping the Braves hold on to their slim one-run lead. Recalling arguably the biggest defensive play of his career, López said, "I know a lot of people don't look at me as a great defensive catcher. But a lot of people remember that play."

López delivered the decisive blow in a 2–1 win over the Dodgers in Game 1 of the 1996 NLDS when he led off the top of the 10th inning with a home run off Antonio Osuna.

López continued his clutch hitting in the 1996 NLCS, earning Series MVP honors by going 13-for-24 (.542), with two homers, five doubles, six RBIs, eight runs scored, and an OPS of 1.607. Particularly outstanding in Game 5, López led the Braves to a 14–0 rout of the Cardinals by going 4-for-5, with a homer, two doubles, and four runs scored.

After homering earlier in the contest, López gave the Braves a 6–2 win over the Mets on June 28, 2001, when he hit a grand slam home run off Armando Benítez in the bottom of the 10th inning.

López helped lead the Braves to a 14–8 win over the Expos on April 17, 2003, by homering twice, driving in six runs, and scoring three times, with his grand slam home run off Rocky Biddle in the top of the 10th inning highlighting a six-run rally that provided the winning margin.

Notable Achievements

- Hit more than 20 home runs five times, topping 40 homers once.
- Knocked in more than 100 runs twice.
- Batted over .300 three times.
- Posted slugging percentage over .500 four times, topping .600-mark once.
- Posted OPS over 1.000 once.
- Finished second in NL in slugging percentage once.
- Led NL catchers in assists once and fielding percentage once.
- Ranks among Braves career leaders in home runs (9th) and sacrifice flies (tied for 10th).
- Four-time NL champion (1992, 1995, 1996, and 1999).
- 1995 world champion.
- 1996 NLCS MVP.
- July 27, 2003, NL Player of the Week.
- 2003 NL Comeback Player of the Year.
- Finished fifth in 2003 NL MVP voting.
- 2003 Silver Slugger Award winner.
- Three-time NL All-Star selection (1997, 1998, and 2003).
- 2003 *Sporting News* All-Star selection.
- Member of Braves Hall of Fame.

33

RAFAEL FURCAL

A solid hitter, superior baserunner, and outstanding defensive shortstop, Rafael Furcal spent six seasons serving as the offensive catalyst for Braves teams that won six consecutive division titles. Hitting out of the leadoff spot in the batting order virtually his entire time in Atlanta, the switch-hitting Furcal provided a spark at the top of the lineup, batting over .290 twice, scoring more than 100 runs three times, and stealing more than 40 bases twice. A well-above-average defender as well, Furcal led all players at his position in putouts and assists once each, with his strong all-around play earning him NL Rookie of the Year honors and one All-Star nomination. Yet, despite the integral role that Furcal played in any success the Braves experienced from 2000 to 2005, the team did not learn his true age until shortly before he departed for Los Angeles.

Born in Loma de Cabrera, a small village in the Dominican Republic near the Dajabón River, on October 24, 1977, Rafael Furcal learned how to play baseball from his father, Silvino, a former standout outfielder in the Dominican Leagues who made his living by driving a cab. Developing into an excellent player himself as a teenager, Furcal starred on the diamond while attending Jose Cabrera High School. An outstanding student as well, Furcal initially planned to enroll in engineering school upon his graduation. However, he chose to pursue a different career path when a Braves scout spotted him at a tryout in Santo Domingo and subsequently signed him as an amateur free agent for a mere $5,000 on November 9, 1996.

After using his signing bonus to purchase a car for his parents, Furcal spent his first two years in the minor leagues playing second base, performing especially well at Danville in 1998, where he earned Appalachian League All-Star and Danville Player of the Year honors by batting .328 and stealing 60 bases in only 66 games. Furcal subsequently split the 1999 campaign between two different teams at the Class A level, batting .337 and stealing 73 bases in 83 games at Macon, and batting .293 and swiping 23 bags in 43 games at Myrtle Beach, with his 96 steals leading all of minor-league baseball. Making a successful transition to shortstop as well, Furcal gained recognition as the Braves Minor League Player of the Year and a *Baseball America* First-Team All-Star. Yet, even as Furcal continued his ascension through the Braves' farm system, he experienced heartbreak off the playing field, losing two of his three older brothers, with José Furcal committing suicide and Manuel Furcal dying in an accident.

Despite the tragic events of his personal life, Furcal made the improbable jump from A ball to the major leagues in 2000, after initially attending spring training as a non-roster invitee. And, with veteran shortstop Walt Weiss suffering an injury prior to the start of the regular season, Furcal soon established himself as the starter at that position, earning NL Rookie of the Year honors by batting .295 and leading all first-year players with 87 runs scored, 40 stolen bases, 73 walks, and a .394 on-base percentage. Commenting on his early success at one point during the season, Furcal said, "I'm so young. When I made the team, it was a big surprise for me."

Furcal subsequently missed much of the following year with a dislocated shoulder he sustained while attempting to steal a base in early July. Limited to just 79 games and 359 plate appearances, Furcal finished the season with four homers, 30 RBIs, 39 runs scored, 22 stolen bases, and a .275 batting average.

Although Furcal arrived at spring training in 2002 fully recovered from his injury, he faced another obstacle when, after being arrested for driving under the influence during the latter stages of the previous campaign, he found himself being accused of lying about his age when HBO's *Real Sports with Bryant Gumbel* showed a photo of his birth certificate that it had obtained from a government office in his hometown of Loma de Cabrera. Accused of shaving two years off his actual age of 24, Furcal told reporters, "You're crazy." Meanwhile, Braves general manager John Schuerholz stated, "If it is true that there is a different age than he is believed to be, he won't be the first, nor will he be the 100th."

Eventually admitting that he had given the Braves his incorrect date of birth, Furcal told the *Atlanta Journal-Constitution* that he had done so on the advice of a youth coach, stating, "He said, 'If you want to play baseball, you have to change your age.' So that's what I did. I wanted to play."

However, when police again arrested Furcal for drunk driving in 2004, reports surfaced that the birth certificate originally shown on *Real Sports* contained incorrect information and that Furcal had actually been born nearly four years earlier, listing his actual date of birth as October 24, 1977.

Putting aside all the distractions, Furcal went on to have a solid year for the Braves in 2002, helping them capture their eighth straight division

Rafael Furcal stole more than 20 bases in each of his six seasons with the Braves.
Courtesy of Kenji Takabayashi

title by hitting eight homers, driving in 47 runs, scoring 95 times, finishing second in the league with eight triples, stealing 27 bases, and batting .275. Improving upon those numbers the following year, Furcal earned his lone All-Star selection as a member of the Braves by hitting 15 homers, knocking in 61 runs, collecting 35 doubles, stealing 25 bases, batting .292, leading the league with 10 triples, and ranking among the leaders with 130 runs scored and 194 hits.

A prototypical leadoff hitter, the 5'8", 195-pound Furcal knew how to work the count, possessed outstanding speed, and hit the ball well from both sides of the plate, making him an excellent table-setter for middle-of-the order sluggers Chipper Jones, Andruw Jones, and Javy López. Capable of upsetting opposing defenses once he got on base, Furcal received praise from Braves outfielder Brian Jordan, who said, "As far as quickness, I don't think there's anyone better. This guy gets started as quick as I've ever seen. You don't think he's going to tag up, and he takes off like he's shot out of a gun. Pretty exciting to watch."

Braves dugout coach Pat Corrales, a former catcher who played against Maury Wills and Lou Brock, suggested, "Brock was faster; this guy is quicker. It's his acceleration, more than anything. He can do things when there are no bats."

Meanwhile, Chipper Jones said of his teammate, "He's made himself into probably the best leadoff hitter in the game. A lot of hits, a high average, high on-base percentage, and wreaking havoc on the bases, that's Raffy."

Although Furcal committed the second-most errors of any player at his position on four separate occasions, his exceptional quickness allowed him to get to many balls other players could not reach, making him one of the NL's better defensive shortstops. Consistently ranking extremely high among players at his position in most defensive categories, Furcal led all NL shortstops in range factor three times and finished either first or second in putouts five times.

Furcal spent two more years with the Braves, hitting 14 homers, driving in 59 runs, scoring 103 times, stealing 29 bases, and batting .279 in 2004, before hitting 12 homers, knocking in 58 runs, scoring 100 others, swiping 46 bags, and batting .284 the following season. A free agent at the end of 2005, Furcal received a three-year, $39 million offer from the Dodgers that prompted him to bid farewell to Atlanta.

Upon announcing his decision to sign with the Dodgers, Furcal said, "The Braves were very good to me, and I hoped to stay. But it's a business. I hoped the Braves would match the offer."

Furcal, who left Atlanta with career totals of 57 home runs, 292 RBIs, 554 runs scored, 924 hits, 160 doubles, 38 triples, and 189 stolen bases, a .284 batting average, a .348 on-base percentage, and a .409 slugging percentage, ended up spending five-and-a-half years with the Dodgers, re-signing with them at the end of 2008 after seriously considering a return to Atlanta. Earning one more All-Star nomination during his time in Los Angeles, Furcal played his best ball for the Dodgers in 2006, when he hit 15 homers, knocked in 63 runs, scored 113 times, batted .300, and stole 37 bases. Dealt to the Cardinals in July 2011, Furcal spent the next year-and-a-half in St. Louis, before announcing his retirement after appearing in only nine games with the Miami Marlins in 2014. Over parts of 14 big-league seasons, Furcal hit 113 homers, knocked in 587 runs, scored 1,063 times, amassed 1,817 hits, 311 doubles, and 69 triples, stole 314 bases, batted .281, compiled an on-base percentage of .346, and posted a slugging percentage of .402.

Since retiring from baseball, Furcal, who resides with his family in Santiago, Dominican Republic, has continued his philanthropic work that he began in 2008, when, after re-signing with the Dodgers, he arranged to have the Los Angeles Fire Department donate a fire truck to his hometown of Loma de Cabrera, which, until then, did not have a fire department. In addition to contributing to several other worthy causes in his homeland, Furcal has arranged to pay the hospital bills of Loma de Cabrera residents.

BRAVES CAREER HIGHLIGHTS

Best Season

Furcal played his best ball for the Braves from 2003 to 2005, having his finest all-around season for them in 2003, when he earned All-Star honors by hitting 15 homers, knocking in 61 runs, batting .292, swiping 25 bags, leading the league with 10 triples, ranking among the leaders with 130 runs scored and 194 hits, and accumulating more assists in the field (481) than any other player in the league.

Memorable Moments/Greatest Performances

In addition to scoring three runs during a 4–2 win over the Florida Marlins on April 21, 2002, Furcal accomplished the rare feat of collecting three triples in one game.

Furcal contributed to a 15–3 rout of the Reds on May 28, 2003, by homering twice and scoring four times.

Although the Braves lost to the St. Louis Cardinals by a score of 3–2 on August 10, 2003, Furcal recorded just the 12th unassisted triple play in major-league history in the bottom of the fifth inning, when, with runners on first and second and nobody out, he made a leaping catch on a line drive hit by Woody Williams, stepped on second base to retire Mike Matheny, and then ran down Orlando Palmeiro as he tried to return to first base.

Furcal helped lead the Braves to a 12–6 win over the Colorado Rockies on August 24, 2003, by going 4-for-6 at the plate, with a homer, double, two RBIs, and four runs scored.

Furcal starred in defeat on July 9, 2004, driving in all six runs the Braves scored during a 7–6 loss to the Phillies with a pair of three-run homers off Philadelphia starter Eric Milton.

Although the Braves ended up losing the 2004 NLDS to the Houston Astros in five games, Furcal gave them a dramatic 4–2 victory in Game 2 when he homered off Dan Miceli with two out and one man aboard in the bottom of the 11th inning.

Furcal contributed to a lopsided 11–4 victory over the Phillies on April 15, 2005, by going 3-for-4, with a pair of solo homers, a walk, and four runs scored.

Notable Achievements

- Scored more than 100 runs three times.
- Finished in double digits in triples twice.
- Surpassed 30 doubles three times.
- Stole more than 20 bases six times, topping 40 thefts twice.
- Led NL with 10 triples in 2003.
- Led NL shortstops in putouts once and assists once.
- Ranks 10th in franchise history with 189 stolen bases.
- 2000 NL Rookie of the Year.
- July 11, 2004, NL Player of the Week.
- 2003 NL All-Star selection.

34

RONALD ACUÑA JR.

An extraordinarily gifted young player with Hall of Fame potential, Ronald Acuña Jr. has excelled for the Braves in all phases of the game since he first arrived in Atlanta in 2018. Blessed with a rare combination of power and speed, Acuña has surpassed 20 homers three times and 30 steals once, while also topping 100 RBIs and 100 runs scored once each. An outstanding outfielder as well, Acuña possesses a strong throwing arm and superb instincts that have helped him gain widespread acclaim as one of the most complete players in the game. A member of Braves teams that have won five division titles, one pennant, and one World Series, Acuña has already earned three All-Star selections, two All-MLB nominations, and one top-five finish in the NL MVP voting before reaching his 26th birthday.

Born in La Guaira, Venezuela, on December 18, 1997, Ronald Jose Acuña grew up some 65 miles east of Caracas, in the tiny coastal town of La Sabana, where baseball is an important part of everyday life. In discussing the environment around which his son spent his formative years, Ronald Acuña Sr. said, "La Sabana is all about drums and music, about baseball, rivers, and beaches. That's who we are. There are five families here, all related, who live for baseball."

Acquiring his love of the game from his father, who spent eight years toiling in the minor leagues, his cousin, Kelvim Escobar, a former pitcher for the Blue Jays and Angels, and another cousin, Alcides Escobar, a big-league infielder for the past 13 seasons, Ronald had many advantages growing up, as his dad suggested when he stated, "Ronald Jr. has the lineage. Like a good rum, he has a fancy pedigree. Not only have I mentored him; he's also benefited from his cousins, older brothers of sorts who have advised and guided him during his journey to the major leagues."

Ronald Sr. added, "He was born with talent. But the little things that you do to polish that talent, he learned from all of us."

Ultimately signed by the Braves as an international free agent for $100,000 in July 2014, Acuña made his professional debut with the Gulf Coast Braves at only 17 years of age in the spring of 2015, before being promoted to the team's minor-league affiliate in Danville after just 37 games. Competing in a total of 55 contests in his first year of pro ball, Acuña finished the season with four homers, 18 RBIs, 41 runs scored, 16 stolen bases, and a .269 batting average. Hampered by injuries the following year, Acuña hit just four homers, knocked in only 19 runs, scored 28 others, and batted .312 in his 42 games at Rome in the South Atlantic League. Acuña subsequently spent the 2017 campaign advancing through three different levels of the Braves' farm system, posting a composite batting average of .325 and totaling 21 homers, 82 RBIs, 88 runs scored, and 44 steals, with his outstanding play prompting *Baseball America* to accord him a number one ranking on its list of MLB's top prospects heading into the 2018 season.

Called up by the Braves early in 2018 after beginning the year at Triple-A Gwinnett, Acuña ended up earning NL Rookie of the Year honors and a 12th-place finish in the league MVP voting by hitting 26 homers, driving in 64 runs, scoring 78 times, stealing 16 bases, batting .293, and compiling an OPS of .917. Hitting primarily out of the leadoff spot in the batting order his first year in Atlanta, Acuña drew high praise from former Braves leadoff hitter, Ender Inciarte, who told David O'Brien of *The Athletic*, "He's the best leadoff hitter I've ever seen. He's the best player I've ever seen."

After signing an eight-year contract extension with the Braves worth $100 million on April 2, 2019, Acuña received a vote of confidence from Atlanta manager Brian Snitker, who said, "If you're asking me if Ronald can handle all this, my answer is yes. He's actually the last guy I would worry about in this position. He has so much talent, it's almost mind-boggling, but none of it has gone to his head. That's what makes him special."

Rewarding the Braves for the faith they placed in him, Acuña earned his first All-Star selection, his first Silver Slugger, and a fifth-place finish in the NL MVP voting by hitting 41 homers, driving in 101 runs, batting .280, and leading the league with 127 runs scored and 37 stolen bases, although he also placed second in the circuit with 188 strikeouts.

Commenting on Acuña's exceptional performance, Brian Snitker told Bob Nightengale of *USA Today* late in the season, "I was with Chipper Jones when he was 18. I was with Andruw Jones when he was 16. They were solid, just really talented ballplayers, with Chipper, of course, going to the Hall of Fame. But this kid. This kid's talent is on a different level."

Ronald Acuña Jr. earned NL Rookie of the Year honors in 2018.
Courtesy of Keith Allison

Claiming that Acuña also possessed a tremendous amount of poise for such a young player, Snitker added, "This is his playground. I don't think I've seen Ronald nervous in a game, no matter how big the situation is. That's saying a lot for a 21-year-old."

Freddie Freeman also spoke highly of his young teammate, saying, "Ronald has a chance to be the best player in the game. He's already on the way. I mean, I'm in the dugout watching him, and I feel like a fan. He's that good."

Big, strong, and extremely fast, the 6-foot, 205-pound Acuña possesses both tremendous natural talent and a keen understanding of the game. A powerful right-handed hitter who drives the ball well to all parts of the ballpark, Acuña has had his batting style likened to that of Roberto Clemente by Sean Casey, who notes that he similarly keeps the knob of the bat pointing down at home plate and uses his natural core power and rotational torque to hit without a backswing. Meanwhile, on the basepaths, Acuña starts off like an infielder with a more upright stance that prevents the opposition from learning his intentions.

Although Acuña is separated from his English-speaking teammates somewhat by the language barrier and relies on a translator to communicate with the American media, he is making progress in that area, saying in 2019, "I'm learning, I'm practicing. I try to talk to the guys here as much as I can. I make mistakes, but it's the only way to learn."

Far more comfortable with Spanish-speaking reporters and TV crews, Acuña seems more himself when speaking with them, revealing his boisterous and outgoing personality that often surfaces on the playing field when he does something out of the ordinary. Known for his swagger between the white lines, Acuña perhaps irritates the opposition more than anyone else in the game with the way he flips the bat after hitting a home run.

Acuña followed up his outstanding 2019 season by hitting 14 homers, driving in 29 runs, scoring 46 times, and batting .250 during the pandemic-shortened 2020 campaign, earning in the process his second Silver Slugger and a 12th-place finish in the NL MVP balloting. But, after getting off to a tremendous start in 2021, Acuña tore the ACL in his right leg while trying to field a flyball during a 5–4 win over the Miami Marlins on July 10, bringing his season to a premature end. Acuña, who finished the year with 24 homers, 52 RBIs, 72 runs scored, 17 stolen bases, and a .283 batting average in 82 games, did not return to action until April 28, 2022, after which he hit 15 homers, knocked in 50 runs, scored 71 times, stole 29 bases, and batted .266 in 119 games over the next five months, while working his way back into top condition. Accorded All-Star honors in each of the last two seasons despite his somewhat limited playing time, Acuña will enter the 2023 campaign with career totals of 120 home runs, 296 RBIs, 394 runs scored, 550 hits, 102 doubles, seven triples, and 107 stolen bases, a .277 batting average, a .370 on-base percentage, and a .517 slugging percentage.

CAREER HIGHLIGHTS

Best Season

Acuña had easily his finest season to date in 2019, when he earned a fifth-place finish in the NL MVP balloting and the first of his two All-MLB nominations by ranking among the league leaders with 41 homers, knocking in 101 runs, batting .280, and topping the circuit with 127 runs scored and 37 stolen bases.

Memorable Moments/Greatest Performances

Acuña contributed to a 7–4 win over the Reds on April 26, 2018, by going 3-for-4 at the plate and hitting the first home run of his career off Homer Bailey with no one on base in the top of the second inning.

Acuña delivered the decisive blow of a 5–3 victory over the Yankees on July 2, 2018, when he homered off David Robertson with one man aboard in the top of the 11th inning.

Acuña homered in five straight games from August 11 to August 14, 2018, reaching the seats six times during that stretch, which included a dominant performance against Miami on August 13, when he led the Braves to a doubleheader sweep of the Marlins by going 5-for-8, with two homers, a double, two walks, five RBIs, and five runs scored. By leading off both games of the twinbill with a home run, Acuña became just the fourth player in MLB history to accomplish the feat.

Acuña led the Braves to a 6–5 win over the Dodgers in Game 3 of the 2018 NLDS by homering off Walker Buehler with the bases loaded in the bottom of the second inning.

Acuña helped lead the Braves to a 29–9 mauling of Miami on September 9, 2020, by collecting three hits, walking three times, homering once, knocking in five runs, and scoring four times.

Acuña displayed his tremendous power at the plate during an 8–7 win over the Red Sox on September 25, 2020, when he led off the bottom of the first inning with a 495-foot home run that proved to be the longest hit in the majors all year.

Acuña gave the Braves a 5–4 win over the Mets on May 19, 2021, when he led off the bottom of the ninth inning with his 13th home run of the year.

Acuña led the Braves to an 8–7 win over the Colorado Rockies on June 5, 2022, by going 4-for-5 at the plate, with a homer, stolen base, and three runs scored.

Notable Achievements

- Has hit more than 20 home runs three times, topping 40 homers once.
- Has knocked in more than 100 runs once.
- Has scored more than 100 runs once.
- Has stolen more than 20 bases twice, topping 30 thefts once.
- Has compiled on-base percentage over .400 once.
- Has posted slugging percentage over .500 four times.
- Has posted OPS over .900 three times.
- Ranks among Braves career leaders in slugging percentage (tied for 5th) and OPS (6th).
- 2021 NL champion.
- 2021 world champion.
- 2018 NL Rookie of the Year.
- Three-time NL Player of the Week.
- April 2021 NL Player of the Month.
- Two-time NL Silver Slugger Award winner (2019 and 2020).
- Finished fifth in 2019 NL MVP voting.
- Three-time NL All-Star selection (2019, 2021, and 2022).
- Two-time All-MLB Second-Team selection (2019 and 2020).

35

DAVID JUSTICE

One of the talented young players who helped restore the Braves to prominence during the early 1990s, David Justice overcame early questions about his attitude and a strained relationship with the media to establish himself as a key figure on teams that won four pennants and one World Series. A member of the Braves for parts of eight seasons, Justice hit more than 20 homers five times, knocked in more than 100 runs once, and batted over .300 twice during his time in Atlanta, earning in the process one Silver Slugger, two All-Star nominations, one top-five finish in the NL MVP voting, and an eventual place in the Braves Hall of Fame. Continuing to excel in the American League after leaving Atlanta, Justice played for teams in Cleveland and New York that won three pennants and one world championship, before ending his career with the Oakland Athletics in 2002.

Born in Cincinnati, Ohio, on April 14, 1966, David Christopher Justice essentially grew up in a single-parent household, being raised by his mother, Nettie, a housekeeper and caterer, after his father left the family shortly after he turned four years of age. In discussing his father, Justice said, "I really wasn't fazed when my daddy left. And I'm not bitter now, never was. The only reason I don't have a better relationship with him is because I think it would be a slap in my mom's face. She was probably hurt by him—It's only natural. We don't talk about him. We don't care about him."

Justice added, "I grew up great and had everything I wanted, so I never missed my father. I do feel like he missed me, though. He missed a son I think he would've been proud of."

An outstanding all-around athlete, Justice starred in football and basketball at Covington Latin High School, a Catholic school located in nearby Covington, Kentucky, that did not have a baseball team. Especially proficient on the hardwood, Justice earned Catholic All-America High School honors his senior year by averaging a school-record 25.9 points per game. Excelling in the classroom as well in a school known for its academic excellence, Justice graduated at the age of 16 after skipping the seventh and eighth grades, recalling, "The school was not for the weak. Everyone was smart. As a 13-year-old sophomore, you take Latin, German, chemistry, computer science, biology, history, and English. And every teacher treats you like his class is the only one you have, so the homework is unbelievable."

Since he graduated at such a young age, Justice, who played American Legion baseball over the summers during his high school years, garnered little interest from college recruiters, forcing him to ultimately accept a full basketball scholarship from tiny Thomas More University, an NAIA school situated in Crestview Hills, Kentucky. Although Justice competed on the diamond as well in college, he admitted that basketball remained his first love, stating, "I didn't love baseball back then." Nevertheless, the Braves selected him in the fourth round of the June 1985 MLB Amateur Draft.

Choosing to sign with the Braves rather than pursue a career in basketball, Justice began his pro career as a first baseman with the Pulaski Braves of the rookie-level Appalachian League. Quickly moved to the outfield after he spent much of his first practice session belaboring the team's third baseman with one hard throw after another, Justice remembered, "I was killing the guy. Knocking him down. They said, 'Justice, go to centerfield.' So, I go to centerfield, and I'm laying down even more ropes. I never saw first base again."

Justice ended up spending parts of the next five seasons advancing through the Braves' farm system, performing especially well in 1986 at Class A Durham, where he hit 22 homers, knocked in 105 runs, and batted .290. Ranked by *Baseball America* as the number-nine prospect in the International League after batting .261 and hitting a team-high 12 homers at Triple-A Richmond in 1989, Justice earned a brief callup to the parent club, before arriving in the major leagues to stay the following year. Appearing in a total of 127 games in his first full big-league season, Justice earned NL Rookie of the Year honors by hitting 28 homers, driving in 78 runs, scoring 76 times, batting .282, and ranking among the league leaders with an OPS of .908, while splitting his time between first base and right field.

His confidence buoyed by his outstanding rookie campaign, Justice reported to 1991 spring training driving a Mercedes-Benz with a vanity plate that read "Sweet Swing" and wearing gaudy gold jewelry that included necklaces, bracelets, rings, and earrings. Feeling that the 25-year-old displayed far too much cockiness for someone who had accomplished so little, several of Justice's teammates began to question his attitude and dedication to his profession. Further troubled by his insistence on being called "David"

David Justice hit more than 20 home runs for the Braves five times.
Courtesy of George A. Kitrinos

instead of "Dave," his refusal to sign autographs, his rudeness to others in the clubhouse, and his tendency to park his car wherever he pleased, including no-parking zones, Justice's teammates listed their grievances to reporters, who subsequently portrayed him as the prototypical spoiled and entitled modern-day athlete in their newspaper articles.

In response, Justice lashed out at virtually every reporter who attempted to interview him and further separated himself from his team-mates, later admitting, "Anger had taken over my personality. My attitude was, 'Hey, these people don't give a damn about me, so why should I give a damn about them?' And that was the wrong attitude to take. That was my mistake."

Despite his personal problems, Justice performed well for the Braves over the first four months of the 1991 campaign after being named the team's full-time starting right fielder, hitting 21 homers, knocking in 87 runs, scoring 67 times, and batting .275, before a stress fracture in his lower back forced him to miss the season's final two months.

Unfortunately, Justice suffered further damage to his reputation the following spring when his involvement in a contract dispute with team management caused him to refuse to pose for individual pictures in uniform. Having grown weary of listening to Justice complain about his situation, veteran team leader Terry Pendleton pulled his friend aside one day during stretching exercises and told him, "Dave, you're going to need to get with the program, or you're going to have to pack up your stuff. Now, I'll go in there and help you pack it. It's plain and simple— there's no maybe, maybe not. The only reason I'm sitting you down and talking to you is because I think Dave Justice can be one of the greatest players to ever play this game, but he's not going to be that with this attitude. The only way you're going to get over these obstacles is to go out and bust your tail. If you have to put blindfolds on, then do so, because if you go between the lines and do your job, they don't have a choice but to pay you."

Heeding the advice of his friend and teammate, Justice played hard and eventually emerged as a team leader himself, playing some of the best ball of his career over the course of the next few seasons. After hitting 21 homers, driving in 72 runs, scoring 78 times, and batting .256 in 1992, Justice took his game up a notch the following year, earning All-Star honors and a third-place finish in the NL MVP voting by hitting 40 homers, driving in 120 runs, scoring 90 times, and batting .270, while also leading all NL right fielders in putouts.

Employing a smooth, left-handed swing that afforded him excellent plate coverage, the 6'3", 210-pound Justice drove the ball with power to all fields and displayed a keen batting eye, drawing more than 75 bases on balls on six separate occasions, while never striking out as many as 100 times in a season. Claiming that Justice altered his approach at the plate somewhat over time, manager Bobby Cox stated, "What I first liked about him was his swing. It was major league, real smooth. Now, he's more upright, and he kicks his leg higher, which he didn't do in those days. He's going more with a modern swing. But I think that first one, it was natural. Probably had it since Little League."

Continuing his outstanding play during the strike-shortened 1994 campaign, Justice gained All-Star recognition once again by batting .313, hitting 19 homers, driving in 59 runs, and scoring 61 times, before play ended on August 11. Although Justice failed to perform at the same lofty level the following year, finishing the season with 24 homers, 78 RBIs, 73 runs scored, and a .253 batting average, he delivered probably the biggest hit of his career in Game 6 of the World Series, when his solo homer in the bottom of the sixth inning provided the winning margin in a Series-clinching 1–0 victory over the Cleveland Indians.

In addition to serving as the game's pivotal blow, Justice's homer silenced the boo-birds at Atlanta-Fulton County Stadium, who objected to earlier remarks he made that appeared in that day's *Atlanta Journal-Constitution*. Criticizing the hometown fans for their lack of loyalty and somewhat apathetic nature, Justice asked Braves beat writer I. J. Rosenberg, "What happens if we don't win? When's the parade then? They'll run us out of Atlanta."

Justice continued, "If we don't win, they'll probably burn our houses down. We've got to win. And if we win, it's for the 25 guys in here, the coaches and Bobby (Cox). It is for us. . . . It's us against the world. I'm the only guy that will sit here and say it, but there are a lot of people that feel this way. . . . If we get down 1-0 tonight, they will probably boo us out of the stadium. You have to do something great to get them out of their seats. Shoot, up in Cleveland, they were down three runs in the ninth inning, and they were still on their feet."

Although the hometown fans eventually forgave Justice for his remarks, the two sides soon parted ways. After Justice sustained a shoulder injury that limited him to just 40 games in 1996, the Braves traded him and center fielder Marquis Grissom to the Indians for center fielder Kenny Lofton and reliever Alan Embree on March 25, 1997.

Justice, who left Atlanta with career totals of 160 home runs, 522 RBIs, 475 runs scored, 786 hits, 127 doubles, 16 triples, and 33 stolen bases, a .275 batting average, a .374 on-base percentage, and a .499 slugging percentage, ended up having three-and-a-half extremely productive seasons with the Indians, playing his best ball for them in 1997, when he earned a fifth-place finish in the AL MVP balloting by hitting 33 homers, driving in 101 runs, and ranking among the league leaders with a batting average of .329 and an OPS of 1.013. Dealt to the Yankees midway through the 2000 campaign, Justice helped lead them to the division title and their third straight world championship by hitting 20 homers, knocking in 60 runs, and batting .305 in the final 78 games of the regular season, which he concluded with 41 home runs, 118 RBIs, and a .286 batting average. Justice spent one more year in New York, before ending his career as a part-time player with the Oakland Athletics in 2002. Over parts of 14 big-league seasons, Justice hit 305 home runs, knocked in 1,017 runs, scored 929 times, collected 1,571 hits, 280 doubles, and 24 triples, stole 53 bases, batted .279, compiled an on-base percentage of .378, and posted a slugging percentage of .500.

After retiring as an active player, Justice briefly worked as a broadcaster at ESPN, before taking a job as a pre-and postgame analyst for the Yankees on their YES television network. Leaving his post in 2008 after the 2007 California wildfires destroyed his family's home in San Diego County, Justice subsequently spent the next few months denying claims that he used performance-enhancing drugs when the Mitchell Report identified him in December 2007 as one of many players who previously used steroids to give themselves an unfair advantage over their opponents. Justice, who divorced his first wife, actress Halle Berry, in June 1997, now lives a quiet life with his second spouse, Rebecca Villalobos, and their three children in San Diego, California.

BRAVES CAREER HIGHLIGHTS

Best Season

Justice compiled his most impressive stat-line as a member of the Braves in 1993, when he earned his first All-Star selection, a spot on the *Sporting News* NL All-Star team, and a third-place finish in the NL MVP voting by batting .270, scoring 90 runs, and finishing second in the league with 40 homers and 120 RBIs.

Memorable Moments/Greatest Performances

Justice contributed to a 3–0 victory over the Astros on September 19, 1989, by hitting the first home run of his career off Mike Scott in the bottom of the fourth inning with no one on base.

Justice helped lead the Braves to an 8–6 win over the Montreal Expos on June 9, 1991, by homering twice and driving in four runs.

Justice led the Braves to an 8–3 victory over the Giants on September 9, 1991, by hitting a pair of homers, knocking in five runs, and scoring three times.

Justice led the Braves to a lopsided 14–5 victory over the Minnesota Twins in Game 5 of the 1991 World Series by knocking in five runs with a homer and single.

Justice contributed to a 15–3 rout of the Colorado Rockies on May 16, 1995, by going 4-for-5 at the plate, with a homer, two doubles, four RBIs, and two runs scored.

Justice's solo home run off reliever Jim Poole in the bottom of the sixth inning of Game 6 of the 1995 World Series gave the Braves the only run they needed to record a 1–0 victory over the Indians that gave them their first world championship in 38 years.

Notable Achievements

- Hit more than 20 home runs five times, topping 40 homers once.
- Knocked in more than 100 runs once.
- Batted over .300 twice.
- Compiled on-base percentage over .400 twice.
- Posted slugging percentage over .500 five times.
- Posted OPS over .900 three times.
- Finished second in NL in home runs once, RBIs once, and walks once.
- Led NL right fielders in putouts twice.
- Four-time NL champion (1991, 1992, 1995, and 1996).
- 1995 world champion.
- August 12, 1990, NL Player of the Week.
- Two-time NL Player of the Month.
- 1990 NL Rookie of the Year.
- Finished third in 1993 NL MVP voting.
- 1993 Silver Slugger Award winner.
- Two-time NL All-Star selection (1993 and 1994).
- 1993 *Sporting News* All-Star selection.
- Member of Braves Hall of Fame.

36

BILL BRUTON

solid hitter and outstanding baserunner, Bill Bruton spent much of the 1950s batting leadoff and patrolling center field for the Braves, adding the important element of speed to the powerful Milwaukee teams of that period. The son-in-law of Negro League legend Judy Johnson, Bruton did an excellent job of setting the table for sluggers Hank Aaron, Eddie Mathews, and Joe Adcock, scoring more than 100 runs twice, finishing in double digits in triples four times, and leading the NL in thefts in each of his first three seasons. Making good use of his exceptional speed in center as well, Bruton consistently placed near the top of the league rankings in outfield putouts, with his strong all-around play making him a key contributor to Braves teams that won two pennants and one World Series.

Born in Panola, Alabama, on November 9, 1925, William Haron Bruton grew up in the segregated South with little to no access to organized baseball. Able to compete only on the local sandlots since none of his schools fielded teams, Bruton nevertheless developed a love for the sport by watching Birmingham Black Barons games, where he witnessed the exploits of Negro League stars such as Satchel Paige and Josh Gibson.

After graduating from Birmingham's Parker High School in 1944, Bruton spent nearly four years in the Army, doing a six-month tour of duty in the Far East, before moving in with relatives in Wilmington, Delaware, when he returned to the States in 1947. Having honed his skills on the diamond by playing on several community teams, Bruton subsequently began competing at the semipro level under the watchful eye of his girlfriend's father, Judy Johnson, who used his connections to arrange for a tryout for his future son-in-law with the Boston Braves.

Invited by the Braves to their minor-league spring-training camp in 1950, Bruton made enough of an impression on those in attendance to be offered a contract. Sent to the team's minor-league affiliate in the Class C Northern League, the left-handed-hitting Bruton, who experimented with switch-hitting in his earlier days, earned Rookie of the Year honors by batting .288, scoring 126 runs, and topping the circuit with 66 stolen bases. Bruton followed that up by batting .303, scoring 104 runs, and collecting a league-leading 27 triples at Class B Denver in 1951, prompting Braves general manager John Quinn to proclaim that he expected the speedy out-fielder to be playing center field for the parent club before long.

After getting off to a slow start at Triple-A Milwaukee in 1952, Bruton turned his season around, with the help of manager Charlie Grimm and veteran teammate Jim "Buster" Clarkson. Bruton, who ended up batting .325 and leading the American Association with 211 hits, later claimed that Grimm's patience proved to be critical to his development, saying, "I doubt if I'd even stayed up in Triple-A ball last year if someone besides Charlie was managing Milwaukee. I was no help at all to the club. I didn't hit at all, the first two and a half to three months. But Charlie kept me in the lineup. He stuck with me."

Meanwhile, Bruton credited former Negro Leaguer Clarkson for help-ing him to improve his overall game dramatically, stating, "All I know about baseball, I owe to Bus Clarkson. He taught me a lot."

Promoted to the big leagues in 1953, the 27-year-old Bruton started in center field and batted leadoff in all but a handful of games for the Braves in their inaugural season in Milwaukee, earning a fourth-place finish in the NL Rookie of the Year voting by driving in 41 runs, scoring 82 times, batting .250, finishing second in the league with 14 triples, and topping the circuit with 28 stolen bases. Bruton subsequently scored 89 runs, batted .284, and led the league with 34 steals in 1954, before hitting nine homers, driving in 47 runs, scoring 106 times, collecting 175 hits, batting .275, and leading the league with 25 stolen bases the following year, while also amassing more putouts (412) than any other NL outfielder.

A line-drive hitter with occasional power, the 6-foot, 170-pound Bru-ton tended to drive the ball more to the gaps than over the outfield fences, accumulating far more triples than homers during his time in Milwaukee. Unlike most leadoff hitters, Bruton did not display much patience at the plate, never drawing more than 44 bases on balls in any season as a member of the Braves. Nevertheless, Bruton's tremendous running speed made him an effective top-of-the-order hitter since he did an excellent job of upsetting opposing pitchers and intimidating opponents into making bad throws and fielding mistakes.

Bruton's great speed also enabled him to track down long flyballs, charge in for potential bloop hits, and cut off balls hit to the outfield gaps. In describing his fielding philosophy, Bruton, who played a shallow center field, said that he had "no problems" going back to catch long flies, adding

Bill Bruton led the NL in stolen bases three straight times.

that, "If somebody hit a line drive to the center field fence, he deserved a base hit. If it wasn't a line drive, I knew I was going to catch it."

In addition to performing well for the Braves on the field, Bruton played an important role in sustaining baseball's initial integration process. Quiet, thoughtful, and articulate, the deeply religious Bruton carried himself with grace and dignity, always conducting himself in a professional manner. Claiming that Bruton served as an excellent role model for him, Hank Aaron once characterized his former teammate as "like a father to everyone. He really saw what needed to be done. . . . Just keep playing baseball and the system would change."

After hitting eight homers, driving in 56 runs, scoring 73 times, batting .272, stealing only eight bases, and leading the league with 15 triples in 1956, Bruton missed significant portions of each of the next two seasons with a torn ligament in his right knee he sustained when he collided with shortstop Félix Mantilla while diving for a ball in the outfield.

Re-establishing himself as the Braves' full-time starting center fielder in 1959, Bruton scored 72 runs and batted a career-high .289, before having arguably his finest season in 1960, when, in addition to hitting 12 homers and driving in 54 runs, he batted .286, stole 22 bases, and topped the senior circuit with 112 runs scored and 13 triples.

Despite Bruton's strong performance, the Braves included him in a six-player trade they completed with the Tigers on December 7, 1960, that netted them second baseman Frank Bolling. Bruton, who, in his eight years in Milwaukee, hit 48 homers, knocked in 327 runs, scored 622 times, collected 1,126 hits, 167 doubles, and 79 triples, stole 143 bases, batted .276, compiled an on-base percentage of .323, and posted a slugging percentage of .391, ended up spending four years in Detroit, hitting a career-high 17 homers and scoring 99 runs his first season there, before announcing his retirement at the end of 1964 after receiving an offer to work for the merchandising staff at Chrysler Corporation. In making his decision known to the public, Bruton, who ended his career with 94 homers, 545 RBIs, 937 runs scored, 1,651 hits, 241 doubles, 102 triples, 207 stolen bases, a .273 batting average, a .328 on-base percentage, and a .393 slugging percentage, said, "A chance like this doesn't come too often."

Meanwhile, Tigers vice president Rick Ferrell expressed the belief that the 38-year-old Bruton still had a lot left, stating, "Bruton is the best player I've ever seen retire. Usually, you have to cut the uniform off a guy to make him quit. Billy can still run and throw and hit the ball."

Following his playing days, Bruton spent the next 23 years serving as an executive at Chrysler, working in sales, customer service, promotion, and financing, primarily in the company's Detroit headquarters, before retiring to private life in 1988. Returning with his wife to Delaware, Bruton continued his work with several churches and charitable organizations until he died of an apparent heart attack while driving near his home on December 5, 1995. State police reported that they found the 70-year-old Bruton slumped over the wheel of his car, which had hit a pole.

BRAVES CAREER HIGHLIGHTS

Best Season

Ironically, Bruton's final season in Milwaukee proved to be his finest. In addition to hitting 12 homers, driving in 54 runs, stealing 22 bases, and batting .286 in 1960, Bruton led the NL with 13 triples and a career-best

112 runs scored, while also setting career-high marks with 180 hits and an OPS of .758.

Memorable Moments/Greatest Performances

Bruton helped the Braves christen Milwaukee County Stadium on April 14, 1953, with a solo home run in the bottom of the 10th inning that gave them a 3–2 win over the Cardinals in the very first game played at the new ballpark.

Bruton led the Braves to a 7–0 win over the Phillies on June 25, 1954, by going 4-for-5 at the plate, with a triple, stolen base, three RBIs, and two runs scored.

Bruton helped lead the Braves to a 10–1 rout of the Reds in Cincinnati on April 17, 1955, by going 4-for-6, with a homer, double, three RBIs, and three runs scored.

In addition to hitting safely in three of his other four trips to the plate, Bruton delivered the key blow in a 7–4 win over the Cubs on September 23, 1956, when he homered with the bases loaded in the bottom of the sixth inning.

Bruton led the Braves to an 8–5 win over the Dodgers on June 13, 1957, by homering twice in one game for the only time as a member of the team.

Although the Braves lost the 1958 World Series to the Yankees in seven games, Bruton experienced a pair of memorable moments in the first two contests, delivering an RBI single in the bottom of the 10th inning in Game 1 that gave his team a 4–3 victory, before setting the tone for a 13–5 rout of the AL champions in Game 2 by leading off the first inning with a home run. Bruton finished the Fall Classic with a batting average of .412 (7-for-17), an on-base percentage of .545, and a slugging percentage of .588.

Bruton contributed to an 11–5 win over the Cardinals on August 2, 1959, by driving in a career-high six runs with a pair of bases-loaded triples.

Bruton led the Braves to a 5–4 win over the Phillies on May 1, 1960, by going 5-for-5 at the plate, with a homer, double, and three runs scored.

Notable Achievements

- Scored more than 100 runs twice.
- Finished in double digits in triples four times.
- Surpassed 30 doubles once.

- Stole more than 20 bases four times, topping 30 thefts once.
- Led NL in runs scored once, triples twice, and stolen bases three times.
- Led NL outfielders in putouts once, assists once, and double plays turned once.
- Led NL center fielders in assists twice, double plays turned twice, and fielding percentage once.
- Ranks fifth in franchise history with 79 triples.
- Two-time NL champion (1957 and 1958).
- 1957 world champion.

37

RON GANT

Plagued by injuries and once described as being "too self-absorbed" to be a star player, Ron Gant failed to take full advantage of the exceptional athletic ability that enabled him to become one of only seven players in major-league history to surpass 30 home runs and 30 stolen bases in consecutive seasons. Nevertheless, Gant managed to carve out an extremely successful 16-year career during which he slugged 321 homers, stole 243 bases, knocked in more than 1,000 runs, and scored more than 1,000 times as an outfielder for eight different teams. Having most of his finest seasons for the Braves from 1987 to 1993, Gant helped lead them to two league championships by hitting more than 30 homers three times, knocking in more than 100 runs twice, and batting over .300 once. A one-time NL All-Star, Gant also earned one Silver Slugger and two top-10 finishes in the league MVP voting, before a motorcycle accident brought his time in Atlanta to a premature end.

Born in Victoria, Texas, on March 2, 1965, Ronald Edwin Gant performed well both in the classroom and on the athletic field while growing up in the rapidly desegregating South. The son of George Gant, a chemistry professor, and Alice Hardeman, a special education teacher, Gant learned the value of studying hard at an early age, although he also found time to compete in several sports. An excellent all-around athlete, Gant starred in football and baseball at Victoria High School, with his outstanding play on the diamond prompting such notable schools as Texas and Oklahoma to offer him athletic scholarships. However, Gant elected to forgo a college education when the Braves selected him in the fourth round of the 1983 MLB Amateur Draft.

Gant subsequently spent nearly five years advancing through the Braves' farm system, playing all over the infield, before finally being called up by the parent club during the latter stages of the 1987 campaign after being named the organization's Minor League Player of the Year the previous season. Starting 19 games at second base for the Braves during the month of September, Gant homered twice, knocked in nine runs, scored nine times, and batted .265.

Impressed with Gant's solid play and superior athletic ability, the Braves named him their starting second baseman in 1988, although he also saw some action at third. Despite committing a total of 31 errors in the field and striking out 118 times, Gant earned a fourth-place finish in the NL Rookie of the Year voting by hitting 19 homers, driving in 60 runs, scoring 85 times, stealing 19 bases, and batting .259 for a Braves team that finished last in the NL West with a record of just 54-106.

Moved to third base in 1989, Gant struggled so terribly at the plate and in the field, batting just .171, striking out 51 times in 204 plate appearances, and committing 16 errors in his first 53 games, that the Braves optioned him to Class A Sumter on June 21 in the hope that he might regain his batting eye and successfully transition to the outfield. In addressing Gant's woes, Braves executive Hank Aaron, who spent some time working with the slumping youngster, said, "He is lost." After two weeks at Sumter, Gant spent two months at Triple-A Richmond, before finally returning to Atlanta late in the year. Appearing in another 22 games with the Braves, Gant finished the season with a disappointing nine homers, 25 RBIs, and .177 batting average.

Bouncing back in a big way in 1990 after being shifted to center field, Gant had a huge year for a Braves team that finished last in the division for the third straight time, gaining recognition from the *Sporting News* as that publication's NL Comeback Player of the Year by hitting 32 homers, knocking in 84 runs, scoring 107 times, stealing 33 bases, batting .303, compiling an OPS of .896, and reducing his strikeout total to just 86. Gant followed that up with another outstanding season, helping the Braves capture the division title and the league championship by hitting 32 homers, driving in 105 runs, scoring 101 others, swiping 34 bags, and batting .251, with his 32 homers and 34 steals allowing him to join Willie Mays and Bobby Bonds as the only players in MLB history to that point to reach the 30-mark in both categories two straight times.

Emerging as an excellent clutch hitter in 1991 after struggling at times with men on base earlier in his career, Gant received praise during the latter stages of the campaign for his ability to drive in runs from teammate Terry Pendleton, who said, "This guy would be batting .400 if he didn't put so much pressure on himself. He's so talented. He's the kind of guy you want at the plate with men on base. He's stuck in there, even though he's been through a lot."

Ron Gant hit more than 30 homers three times and knocked in more than 100 runs twice for the Braves.

Although Gant posted less impressive numbers in 1992, concluding the campaign with 17 homers, 80 RBIs, 74 runs scored, 32 stolen bases, and a .259 batting average, he gained All-Star recognition for the first time, before earning a fifth-place finish in the NL MVP voting the following year by batting .274, stealing 26 bases, finishing fifth in the league with 36 homers, and placing third in the circuit with 117 RBIs, 113 runs scored, and 309 total bases. Continuing to show support for his teammate in an article that appeared in the September 20, 1993, edition of the *New York Times*, Terry Pendleton stated, "Ron Gant might have always put up impressive numbers and never got the respect or notoriety because he always seemed to be doing it quietly. But he's not doing it quietly anymore. He's got 35 homers, and I swear 20 of them have been big and late."

Possessing a much sought-after combination of power and speed, the right-handed-swinging Gant, who gradually added some 15 pounds of muscle onto the lean 6-foot, 172-pound frame he possessed when he first arrived in Atlanta, had the ability to hit the ball out of any part of the ballpark, even though he pulled most of his homers to left field. Although Gant's big swing made him susceptible to the strikeout, he developed a good eye at the plate over time, drawing more than 70 bases on balls on four separate occasions over the course of his career. Meanwhile, Gant's exceptional running speed made him a constant threat on the basepaths, especially his first few years in the league.

Unfortunately, the 1993 season ended up being Gant's last in Atlanta. On February 28, 1994, just one week after he signed a non-guaranteed, one-year deal with the Braves worth $5.5 million, Gant suffered fractures to both bones in his lower right leg in a dirt-bike accident. Subsequently released by the Braves, who paid him a $901,639 buyout, Gant sat out the entire 1994 season, before signing with the Cincinnati Reds prior to the start of the ensuing campaign.

Gant had a solid year for the Reds in 1995, earning All-Star honors by hitting 29 homers, driving in 88 runs, scoring 79 times, stealing 23 bases, and batting .276. But he never again performed at an elite level while splitting the next eight seasons between the Cardinals, Phillies, Angels, Rockies, Athletics, and Padres. A full-time player only in St. Louis and Philadelphia, Gant averaged 24 homers and 70 RBIs for the Cardinals from 1996 to 1998, although he also posted a composite batting average of just .238 and struck out a total of 352 times. Meanwhile, Gant hit 37 homers, knocked in 125 runs, and batted .257 over parts of two seasons with the Phillies, before assuming a part-time role in Anaheim, Colorado, Oakland, and San Diego the next four years.

Choosing to announce his retirement after the Athletics released him midway through the 2003 campaign, Gant ended his career with 321 home runs, 1,008 RBIs, 1,080 runs scored, 1,651 hits, 302 doubles, 50 triples, 243 stolen bases, a .256 batting average, a .336 on-base percentage, and a .468 slugging percentage. During his time in Atlanta, Gant hit 147 homers, knocked in 480 runs, scored 515 times, collected 836 hits, 158 doubles, and 27 triples, stole 157 bases, batted .262, compiled a .326 on-base percentage, and posted a .466 slugging percentage.

Since retiring as an active player, Gant, who currently resides in the Atlanta area, has worked in television, first as a color commentator for the

Braves on TBS in 2005, and, later, as an analyst on SportSouth and the MLB Network. Since 2012, Gant has served as co-host of the morning show *Good Day Atlanta* that airs weekdays on the Fox-owned-and-operated station WAGA-TV.

BRAVES CAREER HIGHLIGHTS

Best Season

Although Gant earned his only *Sporting News* All-Star nomination two years earlier, he had his finest all-around season in 1993, when he earned a fifth-place finish in the NL MVP balloting by batting .274 and placing near the top of the league rankings with 36 homers, 117 RBIs, 113 runs scored, and 309 total bases.

Memorable Moments/Greatest Performances

Gant starred in defeat on July 5, 1990, going 4-for-5, with two homers, a double, six RBIs, and three runs scored during a 9–8 loss to the Mets.

Gant gave the Braves a 3–2 victory over the Dodgers on September 14, 1991, when he knocked in the winning run with a two-out bases loaded single to deep left field in the bottom of the 11th inning.

Gant provided further heroics 11 days later, when he gave the Braves a 2–1 victory over the Reds on September 25, 1991, by delivering a line-drive single to center field that drove home Terry Pendleton from second base with the winning run in the bottom of the 10th inning.

Gant led the Braves to a 9–7 win over the Cardinals in 12 innings on July 21, 1992, by going 4-for-6, with a homer, triple, four RBIs, and four runs scored.

Gant led the Braves to a 13–1 rout of the Padres on September 11, 1993, by going 3-for-5, with a homer, six RBIs, and three runs scored.

Gant experienced probably his most memorable moment as a member of the Braves on September 15, 1993, when he hit a game-winning three-run homer off Cincinnati closer Rob Dibble with one man out in the bottom of the ninth inning, capping off a five-run rally that enabled the Braves to turn a 6–2 deficit into a 7–6 victory.

Notable Achievements

- Hit more than 30 home runs three times.
- Knocked in more than 100 runs twice.
- Scored more than 100 runs three times.
- Batted over .300 once.
- Surpassed 30 doubles twice.
- Stole more than 30 bases three times.
- Posted slugging percentage over .500 twice.
- Finished third in NL in home runs once, RBIs once, runs scored once, and total bases twice.
- Two-time NL champion (1991 and 1992).
- August 26, 1990, NL Player of the Week.
- Finished in top 10 of NL MVP voting twice.
- 1991 Silver Slugger Award winner.
- 1991 *Sporting News* All-Star selection.
- 1992 NL All-Star selection.

38

OZZIE ALBIES

One of the best second basemen in the game today, Ozzie Albies has contributed significantly on both offense and defense to Braves teams that have won five division titles, one pennant, and one World Series. A solid hitter, Albies has surpassed 20 homers three times, driven in more than 100 runs once, and amassed at least 40 doubles three times, en route to winning two Silver Sluggers. An excellent baserunner, Albies has also scored more than 100 runs three times and stolen 20 bases once. Outstanding with the glove as well, Albies consistently ranks among the top players at his position in putouts, assists, double plays turned, and fielding percentage, with his strong all-around play earning him two NL All-Star selections and one All-MLB nomination.

Born in Willemstad, Curacao, on January 7, 1997, Ozhaino Jurdy Jiandro Albies grew up on the same tiny island that former Braves great Andruw Jones calls home. Like most boys on the island, Albies gravitated toward baseball as a youngster, learning how to play the game at the age of six. Discovered by Curacao-based scout Dargello Lodowica some 10 years later, Albies signed with the Braves as an international free agent for $350,000 on July 2, 2013, less than six months after he celebrated his 16th birthday. Unfortunately, that same year, Albies lost his father, who died of a heart attack at only 40 years of age.

After beginning his professional career as a shortstop with the Gulf Coast Braves in 2014, Albies received a midseason promotion to the parent club's minor-league affiliate in Danville. Performing well for both teams while appearing in a total of 57 games, Albies hit one homer, knocked in 19 runs, scored 41 others, stole 22 bases, and batted .364, prompting *Baseball America* to rank him as the fifth-best prospect in the Braves' farm system. Continuing his ascent through the minors the next three seasons, Albies excelled at Single-A Rome, Double-A Mississippi, and Triple-A Gwinnett, with his outstanding play at Mississippi earning him praise from manager Luis Salazar, who said, "The first time I saw him was when he was 15. I saw something in this kid—he has all the ingredients and the talent to be special. The one thing you cannot teach is the speed, the defense, and the one thing he does best is he's so smart on the bases, so smart at the plate."

Salazar continued, "You see this kid in the major-league camp, really impressed the major-league staff. The way he handled himself. That's one of the things they recognize in Albies is he's a very tough kid. Two solid seasons and he made the jump from Low-A to Double-A, and I think he's going to be OK."

Summoned to Atlanta on August 1, 2017, Albies, who gradually transitioned to second base in the minors, ended up starting 57 games at that post for the Braves over the season's final two months, committing just three errors in the field and hitting six homers, driving in 28 runs, scoring 34 times, and batting .286. Replacing veteran Brandon Phillips as the full-time starter at second the following year, Albies emerged as one of the league's best players at his position, earning All-Star honors by homering 24 times, knocking in 72 runs, scoring 105 others, and batting .261, while also leading all NL second sackers in assists.

Extremely pleased with the 22-year-old Albies's performance, the Braves signed him to a team-friendly seven-year, $35 million contract extension on April 11, 2019, just nine days after they inked 2018 NL Rookie of the Year Ronald Acuña Jr. to a $100 million, eight-year deal. Choosing financial security for his family in Curacao over several big paydays via arbitration and free agency, Albies explained, "I look at it as it's not just for money. Because I'm not playing for money. I'm playing for my career. And I took it because I want my family to be safe."

Adding that his love for the organization and his closest friend on the team, Ronald Acuña Jr., impacted his decision as well, Albies stated, "We're more than best friends. We're brothers to each other. I didn't choose this just because of him. I love everybody on the team. I love being part of the Braves, and I want to be a Brave for the rest of my life."

Meanwhile, Braves general manager Alex Anthopoulos expressed his happiness over signing Albies to a long-term deal, saying, "I know he's young in his career right now, but I like if we look a few years from now that he's going to be someone who leads by example day in and day out."

Continuing his outstanding all-around play for the Braves in 2019, the switch-hitting Albies helped lead them to their second straight division title by hitting 24 homers, driving in 86 runs, scoring 102 times, batting .295, compiling an OPS of .852, leading the league with 189 hits, and placing third in the circuit with eight triples and 43 doubles, earning in the process his first Silver Slugger. Albies also committed just four errors in 158 games

Ozzie Albies has helped lead the Braves to five division titles and one world championship.
Courtesy of Keith Allison

at second base, en route to compiling the highest fielding percentage and amassing the most putouts of any player at his position.

Appearing in only 29 of the 60 games the Braves played during the pandemic-shortened 2020 campaign, Albies finished the season with just six homers, 19 RBIs, 21 runs scored, and a .271 batting average. Making up for lost time the following year, Albies earned All-Star honors, his second Silver Slugger, and a 13th-place finish in the NL MVP voting by hitting 30 homers and batting .259 for the eventual world champions, while also ranking among the league leaders with 106 RBIs, 103 runs scored, seven triples, 40 doubles, and 20 stolen bases, and leading all NL second sackers in assists for the second time.

An extremely aggressive hitter, the 5'8", 165-pound Albies rarely walks and strikes out fairly often, fanning more than 100 times three times to this point in his career. A much better hitter from the right side of the plate, Albies boasts a lifetime batting average of .340 and an OPS of .948 as a right-handed batter. Meanwhile, his marks stand at only .250 and .748 from the other side. Despite that disparity, though, Albies's quickness on the basepaths, surprising power for a man of his proportions, and ability to drive the ball to the outfield gaps make him a highly effective and versatile contributor on offense. Capable of hitting virtually anywhere in the lineup, Albies has spent most of his time batting either leadoff, second, or fifth, although he has also assumed other spots in the batting order at times. As his career has progressed, Albies has also taken on more of a leadership role, even taking it upon himself to openly chastise friend and teammate Marcell Ozuna on the playing field for his failure to hustle during a 6–3 win over the Texas Rangers on April 29, 2022.

Forced to undergo surgery after fracturing his left foot during a game against the Washington Nationals on June 13, 2022, Albies ended up missing the next three months, before finally returning to action on September 16. However, in just his second game back, Albies fractured his right pinky finger, forcing him to miss the rest of the season. Albies, who finished the year with just eight homers, 35 RBIs, and a .247 batting average, will enter the 2023 campaign with career totals of 98 homers, 346 RBIs, 401 runs scored, 674 hits, 153 doubles, 25 triples, and 63 stolen bases, a lifetime .271 batting average, a .322 on-base percentage, and a .470 slugging percentage. Hopefully, a return to full health will enable him to add to those numbers significantly in the coming years.

CAREER HIGHLIGHTS

Best Season

Although Albies also posted excellent numbers in 2021, he had his finest all-around season to date in 2019, when, in addition to leading all NL second basemen in putouts, double plays turned, and fielding percentage, he hit 24 homers, knocked in 86 runs, scored 102 times, stole 15 bases, and established career-high marks with 43 doubles, 189 hits, a batting average of .295, and an OPS of .852.

Memorable Moments/Greatest Performances

Albies proved to be the lone bright spot during a 7–4 loss to the Dodgers on August 3, 2017, homering off Tony Cingrani with two men on base in the bottom of the ninth inning for his first big-league hit.

Albies contributed to a lopsided 9–2 victory over the Miami Marlins on May 10, 2018, by homering with the bases loaded for the first time in his career.

After doubling twice earlier in the contest, Albies gave the Braves a 5–4 victory over the Reds on June 25, 2018, by leading off the bottom of the 11th inning with a home run.

Albies gave the Braves an 8–7 win over the Pirates on June 12, 2019, when he drove home Austin Riley from first base with an RBI double to center field in the bottom of the 11th inning.

Albies led the Braves to a 20–2 rout of the Mets on June 30, 2021, by going 5-for-6, with a pair of homers, a stolen base, seven RBIs, and four runs scored.

Albies gave the Braves a dramatic 8–6 victory over the Reds on August 11, 2021, when he hit a three-run homer off Lucas Sims with two men out in the bottom of the 11th inning.

Albies delivered the big blow of a 10–4 win over the Pirates on June 11, 2022, when he homered with the bases loaded during an eight-run bottom of the seventh inning.

Notable Achievements

- Has hit more than 20 home runs three times, topping 30 homers once.
- Has knocked in more than 100 runs once.
- Has scored more than 100 runs three times.
- Has surpassed 40 doubles three times.
- Has stolen 20 bases once.
- Has posted slugging percentage over .500 once.
- Has led NL in hits once and at-bats once.
- Has led NL second basemen in putouts once, assists twice, double plays turned once, and fielding percentage once.
- 2021 NL champion.
- 2021 world champion.
- July 4, 2021, NL Player of the Week.
- Two-time NL Silver Slugger Award winner (2019 and 2021).
- Two-time NL All-Star selection (2018 and 2021).
- 2021 All-MLB Second-Team selection.

39
FELIPE ALOU

The most prominent member of one of baseball's most notable families of the late 20th century, Felipe Alou is perhaps known best by younger fans of the game for the 14 years he spent managing the Montreal Expos and San Francisco Giants. Prior to that, though, Alou carved out an extremely successful playing career that lasted 16 seasons. The first Dominican to play regularly in the major leagues, Alou spent most of his peak seasons with the Giants and Braves, hitting more than 20 home runs, batting over .300, and collecting more than 200 hits twice each during his six years in Milwaukee and Atlanta. A three-time NL All-Star, Alou garnered that honor twice as a member of the Braves, while also earning one *Sporting News* All-Star selection and two top-10 finishes in the NL MVP race, before splitting his last four seasons between three different teams.

Born a few miles from Santo Domingo, in Bajos de Haina, Dominican Republic, on May 12, 1935, Felipe Rojas Alou grew up in modest means with his seven siblings, two of whom, younger brothers Matty and Jesús, later played with him in the major leagues. The son of a carpenter and blacksmith who built the family's small four-room house and many of the other houses in the vicinity, Felipe spent much of his youth swimming and fishing in the nearby ocean, while also working on his uncle's farm and assisting his father with his carpentry business.

After spending six years in local schools, Alou attended high school in Santo Domingo, often making the 12-mile trip on foot. An outstanding student, Alou proved to be an excellent athlete as well, serving as a member of the Dominican national track team, for whom he ran sprints and competed in the discus and javelin throws. While in high school, Alou also played baseball for several local amateur teams.

Eventually enrolling in the University of Santo Domingo as a pre-med student, Alou continued to excel in sports while in college, batting cleanup for the team that won the 1955 collegiate championship, while also starring in track and field. Still planning to pursue a career in medicine, Alou changed his mind when, after both his father and uncle lost their jobs, he received an offer to sign with the New York Giants on the recommendation of his college coach, Horacio Martínez, who also scouted for that National League team.

Alou subsequently spent the next two-and-a-half years advancing through the Giants' farm system, experiencing racism for the first time in his life while playing for their minor-league affiliates in the South, before finally being promoted to the parent club midway through the 1958 campaign. Just the second Dominican-born player to compete in the major leagues, Alou performed fairly well for the Giants over the course of the next three seasons, although he did not become a full-time starter until 1961 due to the team's surplus of outfielders.

After hitting 18 homers, driving in 52 runs, and batting .289 in 1961, Alou earned NL All-Star honors the following year by hitting 25 homers, knocking in 98 runs, scoring 96 times, and batting .316 for the pennant-winning Giants. Praising Alou for his outstanding play, manager Alvin Dark ranked him as the league's second-best outfielder, stating, "After you get past Willie Mays, he's as good as anyone."

However, Alou, who returned home every October throughout his big-league career to play in the Dominican Winter League, drew the ire of baseball commissioner Ford Frick at the end of 1962 when he competed in a series of games arranged by the Dominican government between his countrymen and a touring team of Cuban players after the assassination of dictator Rafael Trujillo resulted in the cancellation of the regular 1962-63 season. With Frick declaring the series of contests "unauthorized," he fined Alou and the rest of the players under his jurisdiction $250 each. Speaking for his compatriots, Alou aired their grievances, suggesting that Latin players have a representative in the commissioner's office who understood their culture, politics, and extenuating circumstances.

After initially stating, "They do not understand that these are our people and we owe it to them to play for them," Alou expounded further on the thoughts of his fellow Latin-American players when he told *Sport* magazine later that fall, "When the military junta 'asked' you to do something, you did it. If I had not played, I would have been called a Communist."

Alou also claimed that Latin players, most of whom came from impoverished backgrounds, needed to earn extra money in the offseason to feed their extended families. He then went on to call the United States a "wonderful country," but added that he considered the Dominican Republic his home. Alou also revealed that Latin players competing in the United States typically found themselves being isolated from their teammates by language

Felipe Alou earned two All-Star selections and a pair of top-10 finishes in the NL MVP voting as a member of the Braves.

and claimed that they were often discouraged, or even disciplined, for speaking Spanish amongst themselves.

Subsequently praised by writer Rob Ruck, who wrote, "Nobody had ever spoken so eloquently or forcefully about Latin ballplayers, much less prescribed how baseball could and should address their unique concerns," Alou became a hero to players from a similar background, with fellow Dominican Juan Marichal later saying, "Everybody respects Felipe Alou. He was the leader of most of the Latin players."

Meanwhile, Santo Domingo native Manny Mota recalled, "Felipe was really the first, the guy who cleared the way. He was an inspiration to everybody (in the Dominican Republic). He was a good example."

But, while Alou's words inspired many, they did not sit particularly well with Giants management, which, after he hit 20 homers, knocked in 82 runs, and batted .281 in 1963, included him in a seven-player trade they completed with the Braves in December of that year that netted them, among others, catcher Del Crandall and pitcher Bob Shaw. Looking back on the deal years later, Juan Marichal said, "I think that was one of the biggest mistakes the Giants ever made."

Fortunately for the Braves, San Francisco's loss proved to be their gain. After an injured knee limited Alou to just 121 games, nine homers, 51 RBIs, and a .253 batting average in 1964, he bounced back the following year to hit 23 homers, drive in 78 runs, score 80 times, and bat .297, while splitting his time between first base and the outfield. With the Braves moving to Atlanta in 1966, Alou took advantage of the warmer climate and more favorable dimensions at the team's new home ballpark, earning his second All-Star nomination and a fifth-place finish in the NL MVP voting by hitting 31 homers, driving in 74 runs despite hitting primarily out of the leadoff spot in the batting order, finishing second in the league with a .327 batting average, and topping the circuit with 218 hits, 122 runs scored, and 355 total bases. Meanwhile, Alou again did whatever the Braves asked of him in the field, manning first base and all three outfield positions at different times during the season.

Named team MVP by the Atlanta writers, Alou drew high praise from several of his teammates, with Joe Torre stating, "I've never seen anyone stand out head and shoulders the way Felipe did."

Hank Aaron added, "I've never seen anyone hit so consistently well all season long."

Known throughout his career for his consistency, the right-handed-hitting Alou rarely entered into prolonged slumps, due in large part to the fact that he stayed within himself at the plate. Although Alou, who stood 6 feet tall and weighed close to 200 pounds, possessed good power, he hardly ever swung for the fences, preferring instead to drive the ball into the outfield gaps. More of a contact hitter than a pure slugger, Alou employed a short, compact swing that enabled him to hit with authority to all fields. Capable of assuming any spot in the batting order, Alou hit anywhere from first to sixth during his time in Atlanta, although he spent most of his time batting leadoff. An excellent all-around player, Alou also ran the bases well and did an outstanding job wherever he played in the field.

Plagued by bone chips in his elbow in 1967, Alou hit 15 homers, knocked in only 43 runs, and batted just .274, before rebounding the following year to earn a 10th-place finish in the NL MVP balloting and his final All-Star selection by driving in 57 runs, finishing third in the league with a .317 batting average, and topping the circuit with 210 hits, while patrolling center field for the Braves under new manager Lum Harris. Alou subsequently got off to a fast start in 1969, batting well over .300 through May. However, after missing two weeks with a broken thumb he sustained on June 2, Alou spent the remainder of the year being platooned in center with Tony González. Finishing the season with only five homers, 32 RBIs, and a batting average of .282, Alou became expendable in the eyes of the Braves, who traded him to the Oakland Athletics for pitcher Jim Nash the following offseason.

Alou, who left the Braves having hit 94 homers, driven in 335 runs, scored 464 times, collected 989 hits, 163 doubles, and 20 triples, stolen 40 bases, batted .295, compiled a .338 on-base percentage, and posted a .440 slugging percentage as a member of the team, ended up spending just one year in Oakland, batting .271 and knocking in 55 runs for the A's in 1970, before being dealt to the Yankees during the early stages of the ensuing campaign. Performing well for the Yankees in a part-time role the next two seasons, Alou posted batting averages of .289 and .278. But, when he batted just .236 in 93 games with New York in 1973, the Yankees placed him on waivers. Claimed by the Montreal Expos on September 6, Alou spent the rest of the year playing north of the border, before closing out his career with a three-game stint with the Milwaukee Brewers early in 1974. Announcing his retirement following his release by the Brewers on April 29, Alou said that he would "have to get used to the life of a man who can't play baseball."

Alou, who over parts of 17 big-league seasons, hit 206 homers, knocked in 852 runs, scored 985 times, collected 2,101 hits, 359 doubles, and 49 triples, stole 107 bases, batted .286, compiled a .328 on-base percentage, and posted a .433 slugging percentage, initially returned to the Montreal organization as an instructor in 1976. However, he ended up taking a yearlong leave of absence after his eldest son, Felipe Jr., lost his life when he jumped into a shallow pool and drowned. Rejoining the Expos in 1977, Alou spent the next 15 years serving the organization, first as a minor-league batting instructor and manager, then as the Expos' bench coach, before assuming the managerial reins in Montreal in 1992. Named NL Manager of the Year in 1994, Alou remained in Montreal until 2001, after which he piloted the Giants for four years. Since retiring as Giants manager after the 2006 season, Alou has remained with the organization as a special assistant to the general manager.

A deeply religious man who did not drink, smoke, or socialize much during his playing days, Alou has nevertheless been married four times and fathered 11 children. In trying to explain that incongruity of sorts, Alou stated in 1995, "People ask how a man who likes to be home with his family gets married four times. All the evils that go on in life, the evils of the life of a traveling ballplayer, I wasn't immune to that. But I loved all my wives and children. . . . I've been a lucky man. I had two children in my 50's, and God gave us other Felipes."

One of the most respected figures in baseball, Alou has proven to be an inspiration to his fellow Dominicans, who consider him a hero. But Alou has also garnered tremendous respect from everyone else with whom he has come into contact, with former Braves first baseman Gene Oliver, a white teammate who lost his starting job to Alou, once saying, "He is the kind of man you hope your kid will grow up to be."

BRAVES CAREER HIGHLIGHTS

Best Season

Alou earned one of his two All-Star selections as a member of the Braves in 1968, when, in addition to hitting 11 homers, driving in 57 runs, and scoring 72 times, he amassed a career-high 37 doubles, led the league with 210 hits, and finished third in the circuit with a .317 batting average. But, in addition to earning a spot on the NL All-Star team in 1966, Alou gained *Sporting News* All-Star recognition by knocking in 74 runs, leading the league with 122 runs scored and 218 hits, and ranking among the leaders with 31 homers, 32 doubles, a batting average of .327, and an OPS of .894, with his stellar play also earning him a fifth-place finish in the NL MVP voting.

Memorable Moments/Greatest Performances

Alou led the Braves to a 12–7 win over the Phillies on June 15, 1965, by collecting three hits, homering twice, and driving in a career-high six runs.

Alou contributed to a lopsided 11–3 victory over the Giants on April 26, 1966, by going 5-for-5 at the plate, with two homers, two doubles, two RBIs, and three runs scored.

After hitting safely in three of his previous four trips to the plate, Alou gave the Braves a 3–1 win over the Giants on July 2, 1966, by hitting a two-run homer off righty reliever Frank Linzy in the top of the 10th inning.

Alou starred in defeat on May 13, 1967, going 5-for-5, with a home run during a 10-inning, 6–5 loss to the Pirates at Forbes Field.

Alou gave the Braves a 5–3 win over the Cubs on April 18, 1968, when, after homering earlier in the contest, he hit a two-out, two-run homer off reliever Pete Mikkelsen in the bottom of the ninth inning.

Notable Achievements

- Hit more than 20 home runs twice, topping 30 homers once.
- Scored more than 100 runs once.
- Batted over .300 twice.
- Surpassed 200 hits twice.
- Surpassed 30 doubles twice.
- Posted slugging percentage over .500 once.
- Led NL in hits twice, runs scored once, and total bases once.
- Finished second in NL in batting average once.
- Finished in top 10 of NL MVP voting twice, placing as high as fifth in 1966.
- Two-time NL All-Star selection (1966 and 1968).
- 1966 *Sporting News* All-Star selection.

40

DICK RUDOLPH

An extremely intelligent pitcher who relied on his wits, great curveball, and superb control to navigate his way through opposing lineups, Dick Rudolph spent parts of 11 seasons in Boston, serving as a key member of the Braves' starting rotation from 1913 to 1919. A two-time 20-game winner who also compiled an ERA under 2.50 four times, threw more than 300 innings three times, and tossed more than 20 complete games on five separate occasions, Rudolph proved to be one of the National League's most reliable pitchers in his prime, which, unfortunately, lasted only a few seasons due to his relatively late arrival in the big leagues. Nevertheless, nearly a century after he threw his last pitch for the Braves, Rudolph continues to rank among the franchise's all-time leaders in several pitching categories, with his huge contributions to Boston's 1914 world championship ballclub making him an important figure in team annals.

Born in the Bronx, New York, on August 25, 1887, Richard Rudolph developed an affinity for baseball at an early age, spending most of his youth dreaming of one day pitching in the major leagues. After failing to receive a response to a letter he sent to Cincinnati Reds owner Garry Herrmann in the summer of 1905 requesting a tryout, Rudolph enrolled at Fordham University, where he spent the following spring playing baseball, before leaving school and splitting the next two seasons between Ruland of the "outlaw" Northern League and New Haven of the Connecticut State League. Switching locales once again in 1907, Rudolph traveled north of the border to Canada, where he spent the next four years amassing a total of 77 victories for the Toronto Maple Leafs of the Eastern League, prompting the New York Giants to purchase his contract during the latter stages of the 1910 campaign. Praising the young hurler just prior to his departure for New York, Toronto manager Joe Kelley said, "He has terrific speed, good control, is a quick thinker, and mixes up his assortment as well as any twirler in the big leagues. I look for him in a few years to be even or as great as [Christy] Mathewson."

Things did not turn out for Rudolph the way Kelley had predicted, and, after pitching poorly in his four appearances as a member of the Giants, he found himself back in Toronto early in 1911. Continuing to dominate Eastern League hitters the next two seasons, Rudolph won a total of 43 games, with his 25 victories in 1912 convincing the 25-year-old right-hander that, if he had any hope of making it back to the major leagues, he needed to do so quickly.

A master of self-promotion, Rudolph took it upon himself to champion his cause, as Fred Mitchell, third base coach of the Boston Braves at the time, recalled year later: "I was going south in 1913 to join the Braves, who were training at Macon, Georgia, that season. A young fellow got on the train in New York. Apparently, he knew me, but I didn't know him. After a while, he came over to my seat and asked me if I was a ballplayer. I told him I was a coach for the Braves. He told me he was Dick Rudolph of the Toronto club but was thinking about quitting if he wasn't sold to the major leagues. 'I know I can pitch better than some of those fellows in the Big League,' said Rudolph, 'if I only get the chance. But if I don't, I'm quitting anyway.' Well, I had a talk with him and found he had a good record in Toronto, but that John McGraw had not given him much of a look. I told him not to be too hasty about quitting. I advised him to get in shape and maybe (the Braves) would be interested in his services. He did as he was instructed. After he was beaten by the Newark club 1-0 in his opening game, he turned in his uniform and said he was through. He then got in touch with me again. I got in touch with Jim McCaffrey, the owner of the Toronto club, and asked what he wanted for Rudolph. Jim (for whom I had previously played) said, 'Oh, he'll be back in a couple of days.' I told him he wouldn't, and he better sell him to the Braves. Well, after a couple of days when Rudolph failed to return, McCaffrey got in touch with us and agreed to let us have him for $5,000 and a pitcher named Brown. That was one of the greatest bargains that (Braves owner) James Gaffney ever got in his life."

Performing well his first year in Boston, Rudolph compiled a record of 14-13 for the fifth-place Braves, while also posting an ERA of 2.92, throwing 249 1/3 innings, and completing 17 of his 22 starts. Taking his game up a notch in 1914, Rudolph helped lead the Braves to the NL pennant by going 26-10 with a 2.35 ERA, with his 26 victories placing him second in the league to Philadelphia Phillies Hall of Fame right-hander Grover Cleveland Alexander. Rudolph also ranked among the circuit leaders with six shutouts, 31 complete games, 336 1/3 innings pitched, and a WHIP of 1.038.

Combining with Lefty Tyler and Bill James during the championship campaign of 1914 to give the Braves a formidable "Big Three" at the top

Dick Rudolph made huge contributions to Boston's 1914 world championship ballclub.

of their starting rotation, Rudolph posted 12 consecutive victories at one point during the regular season, before defeating the Philadelphia Athletics twice in the World Series. Called the "bellwether of the pitching staff" by Fred Mitchell, the 5'9 1/2", 160-pound Rudolph inspired Tyler and James to greater heights, according to the Braves coach, who suggested, "Being a little fellow, I believe his success had much to do with big Bill James and George Tyler putting out that little extra effort to keep pace with the cocky kid from the Bronx."

Although Rudolph did not throw as hard as either James or Tyler, relying primarily on his sharp-breaking curveball and brilliant control to retire opposing batters, Mitchell claimed that his tremendous cunning made him the most effective of the three, stating, "He was one of the smartest pitchers who ever toed the rubber. He wasn't fast but had a good curveball, which he mixed with a spitball, and he could almost read the batter's mind. I've often sat on the bench with him and heard him tell whether a batter would take or hit. He made a real study of the profession."

Continuing to perform at an elite level the next two seasons, Rudolph concluded the 1915 campaign with a record of 22-19, an ERA of 2.37, 30 complete games, and a career-high 147 strikeouts and 341 1/3 innings pitched, before compiling a record of 19-12 and an ERA of 2.16, finishing second in the league with a WHIP of 0.974, and placing third in the circuit with 27 complete games and 312 innings pitched the following year.

After posting less impressive numbers in 1917 (he finished 13-14 with a 3.41 ERA, 22 complete games, and 242 2/3 innings pitched), Rudolph developed arm problems that limited him to just nine wins, 15 complete games, and 154 innings pitched the following season. Although Rudolph rebounded in 1919 to rank among the league leaders with an ERA of 2.17, 24 complete games, and 273 2/3 innings pitched, poor run support from his Braves teammates relegated him to a record of just 13-18.

Aging and worn out by the start of the 1920 campaign, Rudolph never again made much of an impact on the fortunes of the Braves over the course of the next eight seasons, a period during which he served the team more as a coach than a pitcher. Officially announcing his retirement as an active player at the end of 1927, Rudolph ended his career with a record of 121-109, an ERA of 2.66, a WHIP of 1.158, 786 strikeouts, 27 shutouts, 172 complete games, and 2,049 innings pitched, compiling virtually all those numbers as a member of the Braves.

Following his playing days, Rudolph joined his brother in a Nyack, New York, undertaking business for a few years, before eventually returning to baseball as supervisor for Stevens Brothers Concessionaires at Yankee Stadium and the Polo Grounds. Rudolph later became a volunteer freshman baseball coach at Fordham University, a position he held until he died of a heart attack at the age of 62, on October 20, 1949.

BRAVES CAREER HIGHLIGHTS

Best Season

Although Rudolph also performed extremely well for the Braves in 1915 and 1916, he made his greatest overall impact in 1914, when he helped lead them to the pennant by compiling an ERA of 2.35 and finishing in the league's top three with 26 wins, a .722 winning percentage, a WHIP of 1.038, six shutouts, 336 1/3 innings pitched, and 31 complete games, earning in the process a seventh-place finish in the NL MVP balloting.

Memorable Moments/Greatest Performances

Rudolph allowed just two hits and one walk during a 2–0 shutout of the Cardinals on July 31, 1914, surrendering only a single to second baseman Miller Huggins and another to shortstop Dots Miller.

Rudolph tossed another two-hit shutout in his next start, allowing only singles to right fielder Zip Collins and legendary shortstop Honus Wagner during a 1–0 victory over the Pirates on August 4, 1914.

Rudolph set the tone for a stunning four-game sweep of the heavily favored Philadelphia Athletics in the 1914 World Series by recording eight strikeouts and surrendering just five hits, three walks, and one unearned run during a 7–1 complete-game victory in Game 1. Commenting on Rudolph's effort afterward, Braves second baseman Johnny Evers said, "Dick pitched one of the smoothest and nerviest games that I ever saw delivered in a World Series, or any other."

Returning to the mound four days later, Rudolph completed the sweep by registering another seven strikeouts and allowing seven hits and just one run during a 3–1 Braves win.

Rudolph dominated the Chicago Cubs on July 24, 1915, yielding just two hits and one walk during a 1–0 Braves win.

Rudolph experienced one of the most memorable moments of his career on September 14, 1915, when he drove in three runs with the first of his two career homers during a 7–1 win over the Cubs.

Rudolph won an 11-inning 1–0 pitchers' duel with Cardinals right-hander Lee Meadows on August 1, 1916, going the distance and surrendering just four hits.

Rudolph shut out the Cubs on just three hits on August 25, 1916, also issuing two walks and recording six strikeouts during a 1–0 Braves win.

Rudolph topped that performance on June 10, 1918, yielding just one hit and one walk during a 1–0 win over the Reds, whose only hit came on a single by first baseman Hal Chase.

Notable Achievements

- Won more than 20 games twice, surpassing 25 victories once.
- Posted winning percentage over .600 twice, topping .700-mark once.

- Compiled ERA under 2.50 four times.
- Posted WHIP under 1.000 once.
- Threw more than 300 innings three times.
- Threw more than 20 complete games five times, completing at least 30 of his starts twice.
- Led NL pitchers in strikeouts-to-walks ratio, putouts, and assists once each.
- Finished second in NL in wins, WHIP, innings pitched, and complete games twice each.
- Ranks among Braves career leaders in ERA (6th), WHIP (6th), shutouts (6th), complete games (9th), and innings pitched (12th).
- 1914 NL champion.
- 1914 world champion.
- Finished seventh in 1914 NL MVP voting.

41

FÉLIX MILLÁN

A steady contact hitter who rarely struck out, Félix Millán spent parts of seven seasons in Atlanta, starting at second base for the Braves in five of those. Extremely reliable, both at the bat and in the field, Millán batted over .300 once, scored more than 95 runs twice, and fanned just 150 times in almost 3,400 total plate appearances during his time in Atlanta, while also consistently ranking among the top players at his position in putouts, assists, and fielding percentage. A three-time NL All-Star, Millán also won two Gold Gloves before the Braves dealt him to the New York Mets after the 1972 season in what is generally considered to be one of the poorer trades in team annals.

Born in Yabucoa, Puerto Rico, on August 21, 1943, Félix Millán grew up in the barrio of El Cerro del Calvario, where he learned how to do without. Often forced to attend school barefoot, Millán lived in constant fear of his teacher calling him to the front of the classroom, typically hiding his feet from the other students by stretching them as far under his seat as possible. Hoping to earn a little money, Millán worked several odd jobs, such as shining shoes or picking a grass called *coitre*, which he sold for 10 cents a bag to people who raised rabbits.

Recalling the poverty of his youth, Millán said, "Yes, growing up was tough, but our faith in God sustained my family and me. I prayed to God that I could make enough money to help my parents."

Adding that he hoped to one day escape his poor upbringing through baseball, Millán stated, "When I was a kid, I always dreamed to be a big leaguer. And I say no matter what happens to me I'm going to try to make it. . . . I never saw him play, but the story of Lou Gehrig was my great inspiration."

After receiving his introduction to the sport as a youngster by batting a ball of string with a guava branch, Millán began playing baseball in grade school in a league sponsored by the Yabucoa police department, before competing for a local amateur team while in high school, remembering, "In

Yabucoa, I played 'barrio' baseball . . . I played in high school . . . I played the top caliber of amateur ball with my hometown team. Finally, Kansas City A's scout Felix Delgado signed me to a professional contract in 1964 with Daytona in the Florida State League."

Prior to signing with Kansas City, though, Millán spent some time in the US Army, where his unfamiliarity with the English language made him feel lonesome and homesick until he found a sanctuary on his base's baseball team. Then, following his discharge from the military, Millán joined Puerto Rico's Double-A professional league, where Delgado spotted him for the first time.

After signing with the A's, Millán spent a year playing second base for the team's Class A affiliate in the Florida State League, before the Braves claimed him in the 1964 Rule 5 Draft. Advancing rapidly through their farm system, Millán joined the parent club in June 1966, batting .275 and scoring 20 runs in 37 games, before being sidelined for the rest of the year by a broken finger.

Returning to the Braves in 1967, Millán seemed poised to win the starting second base job, manning that post for much of the first six weeks of the campaign, before being resigned to a spot on the bench for a month after stretching his Achilles tendon. Ultimately sent down to Richmond to play himself back into shape, Millán ended up earning minor-league Player of the Year honors by batting .310 for the International League champions, with his exceptional play making an extremely favorable impression on manager Lum Harris, who took over as Braves skipper the following year.

Bringing Millán with him to Atlanta, Harris had high praise for the man who acquired the nickname "The Cat" for his tremendous quickness in the field, saying during his introductory press conference in the winter of 1968, "Millán is going to replace Bill Mazeroski as the best second baseman in this league, and I don't mean that as a knock against Maz. But Maz is 31 years old, and Félix already has as much range as Maz ever had."

After supplanting Woody Woodward as the Braves' starting second baseman, Millán performed relatively well in his first full big-league season, batting .289, scoring 49 runs, and finishing third in the league with 14 sacrifice bunts. Improving upon his overall numbers in 1969, Millán earned the first of his three straight All-Star selections by hitting six homers, driving in 57 runs, scoring 98 times, and batting .267, while also winning his first Gold Glove by leading all players at his position in putouts, assists, and fielding percentage.

Commenting on Millán's stellar all-around play, noted sportswriter Gary Ronberg wrote, "He can hit, he can hit and run, bunt for a hit,

Félix Millán won two Gold Gloves for his outstanding defensive work at second base.

sacrifice, and finagle a base on balls. He can run and slide, and he can scramble back up and run some more."

Meanwhile, Lum Harris continued to sing the praises of his young second baseman, saying, "He's the type of player that you never realize is around until the game is over. Then, you look up and he's got two hits, an RBI, a stolen base, and he's been in on two double plays."

Harris added, "The most fantastic thing about him is his quickness. I can name you about five balls hit to him this year that took bad hops at the last possible second. His hands were down there to field the ball—and then suddenly he was jumping in the air, catching the ball above his head."

Spending most of his time hitting out of the number two spot in the batting order, the 5'11", 172-pound Millán proved to be a significant contributor on offense as well, doing an excellent job of moving runners along and helping to set the table for middle-of-the-lineup sluggers Hank Aaron, Rico Carty, and Orlando Cepeda. A right-handed hitter who employed a short, compact swing and choked up on the bat nearly a third of the way, Millán sprayed the ball to all fields and hardly ever struck out, making it extremely difficult for him to enter into any kind of prolonged slump.

In discussing Millán's hitting style, Braves coach Jim Busby stated, "It's a perfect swing. It's a compact snap, and he's smart enough to control it with a heavy, bottle-handled bat. He's as liable to kick up chalk down the right-field line as he is to drill it inside third base. And he can bunt. Ohhh, is he a beauty."

Meanwhile, Millán described his approach at the plate thusly: "I was simply a contact hitter. I choked up on the bat in a way not regularly seen . . . but it was comfortable for me."

Continuing to perform well for the Braves in 1970 and 1971, Millán batted .310 and scored 100 runs in the first of those campaigns, before batting .289 in the second, earning in the process another two All-Star nominations. But, after Millán batted just .257 and scored only 46 runs in 1972, the Braves traded him and left-handed starter George Stone to the New York Mets for pitchers Gary Gentry and Danny Frisella.

Millán, who, during his time in Atlanta, hit 14 homers, knocked in 221 runs, scored 391 times, collected 874 hits, 118 doubles, and 26 triples, stole 56 bases, batted .281, compiled an on-base percentage of .319, and posted a slugging percentage of .349, ended up spending the next five seasons starting at second base for the Mets, helping them advance to the World Series in 1973 by batting .290, scoring 82 runs, and accumulating 185 hits. However, Millán's major-league career ended abruptly on August 12, 1977, when he suffered a devastating injury during an altercation with Pirates catcher Ed Ott at Pittsburgh's Three Rivers Stadium. Upset over being bowled over at second base by a hard-sliding Ott, Millán shouted at the Pittsburgh receiver and hit him in the jaw with the ball in his hand. Ott, a former wrestler, responded by picking up Millán and body-slamming him to the ground, causing him to be carried off the field on a stretcher with a broken clavicle and dislocated shoulder.

Released by the Mets at the end of the year, Millán accepted an offer to play for Japan's Yokohama Taiyo Whales, with whom he spent the next three seasons, compiling a batting average of .346 in 1979 that made him the first foreigner to win the Japanese batting title. Millán subsequently spent one season playing in the Mexican League for the Mexico City Red

Devils, before announcing his retirement following the conclusion of the 1981 campaign.

Remaining close to the game after retiring as an active player, Millán worked as an infield instructor for the Mets' rookie league in Port St. Lucie, Florida, during the 1980s, and for a time worked as the coordinator for Latin America in the team's minor-league system. He also continued to be involved for many years with the Félix Millán Little League that he first established in New York in 1977. Now fully retired, Millán currently resides in his homeland of Puerto Rico.

BRAVES CAREER HIGHLIGHTS

Best Season

Millán had an excellent year for the Braves in 1969, earning All-Star honors for the first of three straight times by scoring 98 runs, collecting 174 hits, stealing 14 bases, establishing career-high marks with six homers and 57 RBIs, and leading all NL second basemen in putouts, assists, and fielding percentage. But he posted slightly better overall numbers the following season, concluding the 1970 campaign with 100 runs scored, 183 hits, 16 steals, and a career-best .310 batting average and .732 OPS.

Memorable Moments/Greatest Performances

Millán starred in defeat on September 28, 1967, going 4-for-4 and hitting the first home run of his career during a 9–1 loss to the Reds.

Millán helped lead the Braves to a 5–3 win over the Cardinals on August 11, 1968, by going 5-for-5 at the plate, with a double, one RBI, and one run scored.

Millán became the first Braves player to collect six hits in one game when he went 6-for-6, with a triple, double, four singles, four RBIs, and two runs scored during a 12–4 win over the Giants on July 6, 1970.

Exactly one month later, on August 6, 1970, Millán led the Braves to a 4–1 win over the Dodgers by going 5-for-5, with a pair of doubles and two RBIs.

Millán gave the Braves a dramatic 7–5 victory over the Dodgers on May 1, 1971, when he homered off right-handed reliever Sandy Vance with two men out and one man aboard in the bottom of the ninth inning.

Millán contributed to a 5–3 win over the Astros on September 5, 1972, by going a perfect 5-for-5 at the plate and scoring a run.

Millán tripled, singled, and drove in a career-high five runs during a 13–6 victory over the Astros on September 20, 1972, with the Braves oddly enough scoring all their runs in the second inning.

Notable Achievements

- Scored 100 runs once.
- Batted over .300 once.
- Had six hits in one game vs. San Francisco Giants on July 6, 1970.
- Led NL second basemen in putouts, assists, and fielding percentage once each.
- Two-time Gold Glove Award winner (1969 and 1972).
- Three-time NL All-Star selection (1969, 1970, and 1971).

42

BOB BUHL

A hard-throwing right-hander who intimidated opposing batters with his dark features, cold stare, and willingness to throw inside, Bob Buhl joined Warren Spahn and Lew Burdette in giving the Braves a formidable "Big Three" at the top of their starting rotation for nearly a decade. Spending nine of his 15 big-league seasons in Milwaukee, Buhl posted double-digit win totals six times, winning as many as 18 games twice, while also compiling an ERA under 3.00 three times and throwing more than 200 innings on four separate occasions. A member of teams that won two pennants and one World Series, Buhl played a huge role in the Braves' successful run to the 1957 NL championship, earning MVP consideration by ranking among the league leaders in wins and ERA, before gaining All-Star recognition for the only time in his career three years later.

Born in Saginaw, Michigan, on August 12, 1928, Robert Ray Buhl grew up during the Depression and war years, deriving most of his pleasure as a youth by playing baseball on the local sandlots. Recalling the affection for the game that he developed during his formative years, Buhl said, "When I was a kid, I used to ride my bike around in the winter with my glove hooked onto the handlebars. There was always snow around, but I wanted to be ready just in case one of my friends had a ball."

Although Buhl also competed in basketball and football at Saginaw High School, baseball remained his first love. However, even his favorite sport ended up taking a backseat to the responsibilities he had to assume his senior year after his father passed away, with Buhl remembering, "My father died when I was a senior in high school. I had to get a job from 2:30 to 10:00 each day. I had to drop part of my schoolwork and go back the following semester (in the fall of 1946)."

Prior to graduating, though, Buhl made enough of an impression on those in attendance at a Chicago White Sox tryout camp in Saginaw that the team signed him as an amateur free agent. Then, after Buhl completed his classes in the fall, the team re-signed him to a minor-league contract.

Beginning his professional career in the spring of 1947, Buhl excelled at Madisonville in the Class D Kentucky-Illinois-Tennessee League, finishing among the circuit leaders with 19 wins and a 3.00 ERA. But, when the White Sox offered him a contract worth just $200 a month and a promotion to Class C at season's end, an insulted Buhl sent a letter to MLB commissioner Happy Chandler notifying him that Chicago had illegally signed him to a contract prior to his graduation from high school. Subsequently declared a free agent following an investigation by Chandler, Buhl signed an $800-a-month minor-league deal with the Braves that also included a new car as a bonus.

Initially assigned to the Saginaw Bears of the Class A Central League, Buhl came to regret pitching for his hometown team, later saying, "Pitching in my hometown turned out to be a big mistake on my part. Fans expected too much."

Struggling on the mound throughout the 1948 campaign, Buhl compiled a record of 11-12 and an ERA of 5.22, registered 152 strikeouts, and issued 145 bases on balls in 224 innings of work, recalling, "I used to strike out as many as I walked. I just threw fastballs and tried to throw a curve."

Although Buhl went just 8-8 with a 4.43 ERA for the Hartford Chiefs of the Class A Eastern League the following year, he began to develop into more than just a thrower, later saying, "Hartford was like a baseball school, and I started to learn about fundamentals."

After earning a spot on the roster of the Triple-A Milwaukee Brewers in the spring of 1950, Buhl grew increasingly impatient with his lack of playing time, stating, "I wasn't used. I got disgusted and told the manager, Bob Coleman, to send me someplace where I'd pitch."

Subsequently sent to the Dallas Eagles, an unaffiliated team in the Double-A Texas League, Buhl compiled a record of 8-14 and an ERA of 3.47, before having his contract purchased by the Braves at the end of the year. But just as it appeared that Buhl was ready to begin his major-league career, he entered the military, missing the next two seasons while serving as an Army paratrooper stationed in Fort Campbell, Kentucky, during the Korean War.

Joining the Braves after he received his discharge early in 1953, Buhl made a favorable impression on manager Charlie Grimm, who commented during spring training, "The guy has everything but control. He throws as hard as any pitcher I ever saw."

Although Buhl continued to struggle somewhat with his control, he had a solid rookie season, going 13-8, with a 2.97 ERA and 83 strikeouts in 154 1/3 innings pitched, while serving the Braves as a spot starter and

Bob Buhl won 18 games for the Braves twice.

long reliever. Still, Buhl remained dissatisfied with his overall performance, recalling, "Sometimes, I was so tired that I didn't feel like going to the park. My fastball didn't move."

Buhl subsequently suffered through a horrendous 1954 season during which he went just 2-7 with a 4.00 ERA while working primarily out of the bullpen. However, after finally earning a regular spot in the starting rotation the following year, Buhl compiled a record of 13-11 and an ERA of 3.21, struck out 117 batters in 201 2/3 innings pitched, and threw 11 complete games. Establishing himself as one of the NL's better pitchers over the course of the next two seasons, Buhl concluded the 1956 campaign with a record of 18-8, an ERA of 3.32, 13 complete games, and 216 2/3 innings pitched, before helping the Braves capture the 1957 pennant by going 18-7 and ranking among the league leaders with a 2.74 ERA and 14 complete games.

The 6'2", 190-pound Buhl, who relied almost exclusively on a hard fastball that the *Sporting News* called the best on the Braves and a rather mediocre curve during the early stages of his career, attributed his later success to pitching coach Bucky Walters, who helped him develop a slider that he claimed, "looked like a fastball, but would break real quick down and away from a righthanded hitter."

Buhl also benefited from the reputation he developed as someone who was not afraid to pitch inside or knock down opposing hitters that crowded the plate. Admitting that he had a nasty streak in him, Buhl said, "I was mean on the mound." Buhl's occasional wildness, bushy black eyebrows, and tendency to glare at batters from the mound made him that much more intimidating, especially to the Brooklyn Dodgers, who he defeated eight times in 1956 alone, earning in the process the nickname "Dodger Killer."

In explaining his dominance over "The Boys of Summer," Buhl stated, "I showed them I was the boss. They knew I'd brush them back. I'd pitch Hodges wide and throw him a lot of curves. I'd throw Campanella nothing but inside fastballs. I'd pitch Duke Snider high and tight."

Meanwhile, Buhl described his delivery to home plate thusly: "I had a herky-jerky motion. I was a short-armed pitcher and, instead of moving way back and way forward, I'd let loose tighter to my body."

Buhl appeared to be on his way to another outstanding season in 1958, winning four of his first five starts, with his early success prompting new Braves pitching coach Whit Wyatt to comment, "I never noticed how well Buhl spotted his pitches. He hits the outside corner like he owns it." However, Buhl ended up starting just five more games the rest of the year due to a sore shoulder that first began troubling him the previous season, later saying, "It wasn't fun throwing the ball. I couldn't even lift my arm to put on a jacket."

After failing to respond to treatment administered to him at the Mayo Clinic in Minnesota, Buhl ironically overcame his malady during the latter stages of the campaign with the help of his neighbor, a dentist who, after discovering he had serious nerve problems in two of his teeth, removed them. Looking back on his recovery, Buhl said, "Two weeks later, I was pitching with no pain. I was very fortunate. A dentist saved my career."

Arriving at spring training in 1959 fully healthy for the first time in three years, Buhl announced that he had altered his pitching motion somewhat during the offseason, saying, "I used to be straight up and deliver the ball with a snap. Now, I bend over more and get my body, as well as my arm, into the pitch. It gives me more on my breaking stuff."

Agreeing with his teammate's assessment, Braves catcher Del Rice stated, "He throws more overhanded now. His curve is a lot sharper. His delivery is smoother, too."

Returning to top form in 1959, Buhl compiled a record of 15-9, led all NL pitchers with four shutouts, and posted an ERA of 2.86 that placed him third in the league rankings. Buhl followed that up with another outstanding season, earning his lone All-Star nomination in 1960 by going 16-9 with a 3.09 ERA, throwing 11 complete games, and tossing a career-high 238 2/3 innings. But after Buhl experienced differences with new Milwaukee manager Birdie Tebbetts in 1961, the Braves traded him to the Chicago Cubs for 24-year-old pitcher Jack Curtis during the early stages of the ensuing campaign.

Recalling the circumstances surrounding his departure from Milwaukee, Buhl said, "I had stopped having fun. Birdie told me I'd be a spot starter and would work in the bullpen. I didn't want that."

Buhl, who left the Braves having compiled a record of 109-72, an ERA of 3.27, and a WHIP of 1.390, registered 791 strikeouts in 1,600 innings of work, thrown 83 complete games, and tossed 16 shutouts as a member of the team, subsequently spent four years in Chicago, posting an overall record of 51-52 for the Cubs, before retiring early in 1967 after going 6-8 for the Philadelphia Phillies the previous season. Over the course of 15 big-league seasons, Buhl went 166-132, with an ERA of 3.55, a WHIP of 1.373, 1,268 strikeouts in 2,587 innings pitched, 111 complete games, and 20 shutouts. A notoriously weak hitter, Buhl also posted a lifetime batting average of just .089, failing to hit a home run in 857 official at-bats.

Following his playing days, Buhl settled with his wife and four children in the northern Michigan community of Mio, where he became involved in youth baseball and later coached the baseball team at Hillman High School. Eventually retiring to Titusville, Florida, Buhl lived until February 16, 2001, when he died from emphysema at the age of 72. Two days later, his former roommate and longtime friend Eddie Mathews passed away.

BRAVES CAREER HIGHLIGHTS

Best Season

Although Buhl won the same number of games and compiled a slightly lower WHIP the previous season, he pitched his best ball for the Braves in 1957, when, despite being sidelined by shoulder problems for three weeks, he led all NL hurlers with a .720 winning percentage and ranked among the leaders with 18 victories, a 2.74 ERA, and 14 complete games, with his excellent mound work earning him a 14th-place finish in the league MVP voting.

Memorable Moments/Greatest Performances

Buhl turned in an outstanding all-around effort on June 14, 1953, allowing just two hits and walking four batters during an 8–0 shutout of the Pirates, while also going 3-for-4 at the plate, with one RBI and one run scored.

Buhl displayed his determination during a 14-inning, 2–1 win over the Cubs on August 22, 1953, working all 14 innings and yielding five hits and six walks, while striking out seven.

Buhl earned a 7–1 complete-game victory over the Phillies on July 14, 1955, surrendering five hits and issuing four bases on balls, while recording a career-high 12 strikeouts.

Although Buhl issued five walks during a 10–0 shutout of the Phillies on July 20, 1956, he yielded just two hits, which came on a pair of harmless singles by center fielder Richie Ashburn and shortstop Granny Hamner.

Buhl won a 1–0 pitchers' duel with Philadelphia's Curt Simmons on July 23, 1957, allowing just two hits and walking four batters, while recording six strikeouts.

Buhl surrendered just three hits and one walk during a 6–0 shutout of the Cardinals on July 31, 1959.

Buhl issued five walks but allowed just one hit during a 2–1 complete-game win over the Cardinals on July 29, 1961, with the Redbirds' only hit coming on a seventh-inning single to left by third baseman Ken Boyer.

Notable Achievements

- Won 18 games twice.
- Posted winning percentage over .600 six times, topping .700-mark twice.
- Compiled ERA under 3.00 three times.
- Led NL pitchers in winning percentage once and shutouts once.
- Finished third in NL in wins once and ERA three times.
- Two-time NL champion (1957 and 1958).
- 1957 world champion.
- 1960 NL All-Star selection.

43

DARRELL EVANS

dentified by noted baseball statistician Bill James as "the most underrated player in baseball history," Darrell Evans earned that distinction with his ability to deliver the long ball, outstanding patience at the plate, and high on-base percentage. A powerful left-handed hitter who played multiple positions for three different teams over the course of 21 big-league seasons, Evans hit a total of 414 homers, knocked in 1,354 runs, and drew 1,605 bases on balls, with the last figure allowing him to reach base 36 percent of the time even though he compiled a lifetime batting average of just .248. A member of the Braves for parts of nine seasons, Evans surpassed 20 homers and 100 walks three times each during his time in Atlanta, reaching the 40-homer plateau once. The team's primary starter at third base from 1972 to 1975, Evans also did a creditable job in the field, leading all NL third sackers in putouts twice and assists once, with his strong all-around play earning him one All-Star nomination.

Born in Pasadena, California, on May 26, 1947, Darrell Wayne Evans grew up in a baseball-oriented family. The son of a sheet-metal worker at an aircraft factory who had played semipro ball and the former star of a women's professional softball team, Evans knew at an early age that he wanted to become a major leaguer, recalling, "I got my first baseball uniform when I was four or five years old. It's what I always wanted to be."

Eventually establishing himself as a star in multiple sports at John Muir High School, Evans excelled in baseball and basketball despite his poor vision, which he corrected with glasses and, later, contact lenses. Continuing to star on both the diamond and hardwood at Pasadena Junior College after choosing not to turn pro when the Chicago Cubs selected him in the 13th round of the 1965 MLB Amateur Draft, Evans led the school to California junior college championships in both sports, becoming in the process a much-sought-after commodity. Also drafted by the Yankees, Phillies, and Tigers over the course of the next two seasons, Evans remained in college until he signed with the Kansas City Athletics as a third baseman after they selected him in the seventh round of the 1967 June Draft. However, after Evans performed well for three different teams while advancing through Kansas City's minor-league system in 1967, he tore ligaments in his right shoulder the following year, causing both his hitting and fielding to suffer. Subsequently left unprotected in the Rule 5 Draft, Evans became the property of the Braves when they claimed him from the A's.

Fully recovered from his ailing shoulder by the start of the 1969 season, Evans hit nine homers, knocked in 59 runs, and batted .338 while splitting the campaign between Double-A Shreveport and Triple-A Richmond, earning in the process a late-season callup to the Braves. But, with Clete Boyer firmly entrenched at third in Atlanta, Evans spent most of the next two seasons at Richmond, before finally laying claim to the Braves' starting third base job when differences between Boyer and general manager Paul Richards prompted the team to release the veteran third sacker in June 1971.

Acquitting himself fairly well at the plate during the second half of the 1971 campaign, Evans hit 12 homers, drove in 38 runs, and batted .242, in just over 300 total plate appearances. However, he struggled terribly in the field, committing 14 errors in just 67 starts at the hot corner, prompting his teammates to nickname him "Clank." Determined to improve his defense, Evans, who also acquired the moniker "Howdy Doody" due to his resemblance to the popular television puppet of the same name, subsequently spent hours on end working with Braves coach and future manager Eddie Mathews, recalling that the Hall of Fame third baseman told him, "I was just like you when I first came up. I couldn't catch the ball, and I couldn't throw either."

Evans continued, "Eddie would hit hard liners and grounders to me at third, then, as I got better, he would gradually move up the line and hit them even harder."

Although Evans also saw some action at first base the next few seasons, he spent most of his time at third, gradually developing into one of the league's better defenders at that position. Meanwhile, after hitting 19 homers, driving in 71 runs, scoring 67 times, batting .254, and drawing 90 bases on balls in 1972, Evans emerged as a true force on offense the following year, gaining All-Star recognition by raising his batting average to .281, ranking among the NL leaders with 41 homers, 104 RBIs, 114 runs scored, and an OPS of .959, and topping the circuit with 124 walks.

A dead-pull hitter, the 6'2", 200-pound Evans learned quickly how to take advantage of the favorable dimensions and wind currents at Atlanta-Fulton County Stadium, often launching balls high in the air that carried over the right field fence. But, in addition to his ability to drive

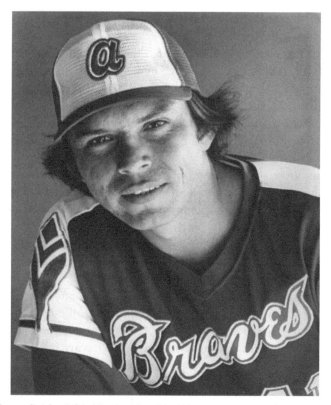

Darrell Evans finished third in the NL with 41 home runs in 1973.

the ball with power, Evans possessed a keen batting eye that made him extremely effective at working the opposing pitcher. Typically placing near the top of the league rankings in walks, Evans drew more than 100 bases on balls on five separate occasions over the course of his career, doing so three straight times for the Braves from 1973 to 1975.

Evans followed up his outstanding 1973 campaign with a somewhat less productive 1974 season, hitting 25 homers, driving in 79 runs, and batting just .240. Nevertheless, he ranked among the league leaders with 99 runs scored and topped the circuit with 126 bases on balls, compiling in the process the third-highest single-season total in franchise history. One of the few bright spots on a Braves team that won only 67 games in 1975, Evans hit 22 homers, knocked in 73 runs, scored 82 times, and finished third in the league with 105 walks, while also leading all NL third basemen in putouts, assists, and double plays turned. Yet, despite his solid play at the hot corner, Evans moved to first base the following year to make room at third for hot prospect Jerry Royster, who the Braves acquired from the Dodgers during the offseason.

Perhaps affected by his move across the diamond, Evans got off to a terrible start in 1976, hitting just one homer, driving in only 10 runs, and batting just .173 through mid-June. Recalling his struggles at the plate, Evans said, "It was the one time in my career when I really doubted myself. I couldn't seem to do anything right. I couldn't see the ball very well, and I wasn't being patient at the plate. Then, I'd take a pitch and it would be right down the middle."

Having grown impatient with Evans's lack of production, the Braves included him in a six-player trade they completed with the Giants on June 13, 1976, that netted them, among others, colorful first baseman/outfielder Willie Montañez. Happy to be returning home to his native California, Evans eventually came out of his slump, after which he went on to perform well for the Giants over the course of the next seven-and-a-half years, hitting 142 homers, driving in 525 runs, scoring 534 times, and batting .255, while splitting his time between first base, third base, and the outfield. Particularly effective in 1983, Evans earned his second All-Star nomination by hitting 30 homers, knocking in 82 runs, scoring 94 times, and batting .277.

Nevertheless, with Evans having turned 36 years of age during the early stages of the 1983 campaign, the Giants displayed little interest in re-signing him when he became a free agent at season's end. As a result, Evans signed with the Detroit Tigers, with whom he spent the next five years playing some of the best ball of his career. After hitting 16 homers and driving in 63 runs for Detroit's 1984 world championship team, Evans knocked in 94 runs and led the AL with 40 homers the following year, becoming in the process the first player to hit 40 or more home runs in each league. Two years later, at the age of 40, Evans earned a 12th-place finish in the league MVP balloting by hitting 34 homers, driving in 99 runs, and scoring 90 times.

But after Evans failed to produce at the same level in 1988, the Tigers released him, allowing him to re-sign with the Braves as a free agent. Evans subsequently spent the 1989 campaign assuming a part-time role in Atlanta, before being released by the Braves at the end of the year. Discussing his feelings with the Associated Press at the time, Evans said, "It's happened to a lot of my friends, and it's not easy. I guess when it slaps you in the face, you don't know how to feel. I don't know what to expect because I've never been in this situation before."

Announcing his retirement shortly thereafter, Evans ended his playing career with 414 homers, 1,354 RBIs, 1,344 runs scored, 2,223 hits, 329 doubles, 36 triples, 98 stolen bases, 1,605 bases on balls, a .248 batting average, and an OPS of .792, with his 1,605 walks placing him eighth on the all-time list at the time. As a member of the Braves, Evans hit 131 homers, knocked in 424 runs, scored 453 times, collected 712 hits, 98 doubles, and 16 triples, stole 31 bases, batted .246, and posted an OPS of .794.

After retiring as an active player, Evans briefly coached for the Yankees and worked as a minor-league instructor for the Tigers and Red Sox, before beginning a lengthy career as a manager in the minor leagues and independent leagues that lasted nearly two decades. In the mid-2000s, Evans also worked as a consultant for Netamin Corporation in the development of its Ultimate Baseball Online multiplayer game. Now 75 years old, Evans currently resides with his wife, LaDonna, in Long Beach, California.

BRAVES CAREER HIGHLIGHTS

Best Season

Evans had easily his best season for the Braves in 1973, when he gained All-Star recognition for the only time as a member of the team by finishing third in the NL with 41 homers, 104 RBIs, 331 total bases, a slugging percentage of .556, and an OPS of .959, topping the circuit with 124 bases on balls, and ranking fourth with 114 runs scored.

Memorable Moments/Greatest Performances

Although the Braves suffered an 8–7 defeat at the hands of the St. Louis Cardinals on May 29, 1971, Evans collected three hits and hit the first home run of his career off Bob Gibson with one man aboard in the top of the third inning.

Evans gave the Braves an 8–7 win over the San Diego Padres on July 21, 1971, when he homered off Al Severinsen with one man out and no one on base in the bottom of the 11th inning.

Evans homered twice in one game for the first time in his career during a 9–6 win over the Dodgers on September 18, 1971, finishing the contest with three hits, three RBIs, and three runs scored.

Evans led the Braves to a lopsided 9–3 victory over the Mets on June 4, 1972, by driving in five runs with a homer and single.

Evans contributed to an 11–5 win over the Phillies on September 1, 1972, by going 3-for-4, with a homer, four RBIs, and three runs scored, with his homer coming with the bases loaded.

Notable Achievements

- Hit more than 20 home runs three times, topping 40 homers once.
- Knocked in more than 100 runs once.
- Scored more than 100 runs once.
- Drew more than 100 bases on balls three times.
- Compiled on-base percentage over .400 once.
- Posted slugging percentage over .500 once.
- Posted OPS over .900 once.
- Led NL in walks twice.
- Led NL third basemen in putouts twice, double plays turned twice, and assists once.
- Ranks among Braves career leaders in walks (9th) and sacrifice flies (tied for 10th).
- 1973 NL All-Star selection.
- 1973 *Sporting News* All-Star selection.

44

RYAN KLESKO

big, strong left-handed hitter who played multiple positions for the Braves over parts of eight seasons, Ryan Klesko is remembered most by fans of the team for his exceptional performance in the 1995 World Series, when he homered against Cleveland in three straight games. However, Klesko accomplished a good deal more during his time in Atlanta, hitting more than 20 home runs four times and batting over .300 twice, despite often being platooned by manager Bobby Cox. A regular member of the Braves' starting lineup from 1995 to 1999, Klesko made significant contributions to teams that won four pennants and one World Series, before being dealt to the San Diego Padres, with whom he earned his lone All-Star nomination.

Born in Westminster, California, on June 12, 1971, Ryan Anthony Klesko grew up hardly knowing his father, who spent most of his time away from home working in the Southern California oil fields. Fortunately for young Ryan, his mother, Lorene, who worked at an aerospace parts company in nearby Santa Ana, took an interest in his athletic development, enrolling him in pitching school and donning catcher's gear three times a week to help him practice on the mound she dug for him in the backyard.

Later crediting his mother for the success he eventually experienced on the diamond, Klesko recalled, "When I was a kid, my mom would watch baseball on TV and say to me, 'See those guys? You're going to be one of them someday.' I never thought it was possible, but she always believed in me."

Klesko continued, "I went to Ron LeFebvre's pitching school eight years. At first, I was going for fun. But, after a certain point, I was good enough that I knew I would do something in baseball after high school. I thought it would be pitching."

Developing into a top pitching prospect at Westminster High School, Klesko drew the attention of scouts with his 92-mph fastball that enabled him to compile a record of 13-6 and strike out 138 batters in just under

100 innings of work in his first three seasons as a member of the varsity squad. However, after straining a ligament in his elbow late in his junior year, Klesko spent his remaining time at Westminster playing first base, saying, "I was always a pretty good hitter, too. When I was a freshman and sophomore at Ron's school, I started batting against college pitchers and I did fine. I knew I could make it as a hitter, too."

Offered a baseball scholarship to Arizona State University, Klesko initially signed a letter of intent to play for the Sun Devils. However, he elected to turn pro instead when the Braves selected him in the fifth round of the 1989 MLB Amateur Draft.

Just days after signing with the Braves, Klesko took part in a batting practice session held at Dodger Stadium prior to the start of a three-game series between the two NL West rivals. Believing that he made an extremely favorable impression on everyone in attendance, Klesko stated, "A lot of teams came to see me when I was in high school. They thought only of me as a pitcher. It had everything to do with how hard I threw. That is what they wanted. I was a good hitter in high school, but they weren't focused on anything else, and I played in an awful big park, so it was hard to hit it out. It all worked out after hitting with the Braves at Dodger Stadium. I think they really realized then just how good I could hit and the power I had."

Subsequently assigned to the Braves' minor-league affiliate in the rookie Gulf Coast League, Klesko developed an immediate dislike for Florida, recalling, "I remember getting to Bradenton, and it was hot as crap and hot and rainy at the same time. There were also these big mosquitoes. I went in and told the coach I hated it, was depressed, and wanted to go home. I said, 'How do I get out of here?' He said, 'Hit.' So, I did, and I was gone very quickly."

Promoted to Sumter (South Carolina) of the Class A South Atlantic League after batting .404 with one home run and 16 RBIs in 17 games at Bradenton, Klesko continued to advance through Atlanta's farm system the next four seasons, performing well at every stop, before finally being called up to the majors late in 1992. Appearing in 13 games with the Braves, mostly as a pinch-hitter, Klesko failed to get a hit and struck out five times in 14 official plate appearances. Returned to the minors the following year, Klesko spent most of the season with Triple-A Richmond, hitting 22 homers, driving in 74 runs, and batting .274, before rejoining the Braves in early September. Faring much better in his second tour of duty with the club, Klesko batted .353, homered twice, and knocked in five runs in 17 official trips to the plate.

Ryan Klesko played for Braves teams that won four pennants and one World Series.
Courtesy of George A. Kitrinos

Arriving in the majors to stay in 1994, Klesko earned a third-place finish in the NL Rookie of the Year voting by hitting 17 homers, driving in 47 runs, scoring 42 times, batting .278, and posting an OPS of .907, while platooning in left field with the right-handed-hitting Dave Gallagher for much of the season. Although Klesko shared playing time in left with Mike Kelly the following year, he increased his offensive production dramatically, batting .310, compiling an OPS of 1.004, hitting 23 homers, and driving in 70 runs, in only 100 outfield starts and fewer than 400 at-bats. Klesko subsequently performed brilliantly for the Braves during the 1995 post-season, batting .467 against Colorado in the NLDS, before batting .313, homering three times, and knocking in four runs during their six-game victory over Cleveland in the World Series, with his home runs in Games 3, 4, and 5 making him the first player in the history of the Fall Classic to reach the seats in three consecutive road games.

The Braves' full-time starter in left field in 1996, Klesko posted his best overall numbers as a member of the team, finishing the season with 34 homers, 93 RBIs, 90 runs scored, and a .282 batting average, despite finishing sixth in the league with 129 strikeouts. Klesko placed near the top of the league rankings in that category once again in 1997, fanning 130 times, although he also led the Braves with 24 homers, knocked in 84 runs, and batted .261.

Employing a long, looping swing geared toward delivering the long ball, the 6'3", 220-pound Klesko left himself vulnerable to the strikeout. But, when he connected, he had as much power as anyone on the team, with the exception of Fred McGriff. Learning to shorten his swing over time, Klesko eventually reduced his strikeout total, making him a better overall hitter.

However, Klesko, a natural first baseman who, due to the presence of McGriff, spent most of his time in Atlanta playing left field, never developed into anything more than a marginal defensive outfielder. Lacking superior running speed and agility, Klesko displayed limited range and below average instincts, leading all players at his position in errors on three separate occasions. Nevertheless, Klesko worked hard at improving himself defensively and always put forth a 100 percent effort.

Despite missing more than two weeks of action in 1998 after undergoing an emergency appendectomy, Klesko had another solid season, hitting 18 homers, driving in 70 runs, batting .274, and striking out only 66 times. Posting slightly better overall numbers the following year while splitting his time between first base and left field, Klesko hit 21 homers, knocked in 80 runs, and batted .297, before being included in a six-player trade the Braves completed with the Padres at season's end that sent him, second baseman Bret Boone, and pitching prospect Jason Shiell to San Diego for first baseman Wally Joyner, outfielder Reggie Sanders, and second baseman Quilvio Veras.

Recalling his feelings upon learning of the deal, Klesko said, "I was upset at first because the Braves were so good. But [Padres manager] Bruce [Bochy] brought me in and said I was going to be an everyday player. . . . I remember when [Braves general manager] John [Schuerholz] told me about the trade. He said, 'Ryan, I think you are going to be happy.' I knew then that I was going to San Diego, Anaheim, or Los Angeles. It was fun going back home, and I had good seasons there. I cut down on my swing and stride and things worked out."

Klesko, who left Atlanta with career totals of 139 home runs, 450 RBIs, 374 runs scored, 684 hits, 140 doubles, 18 triples, and 26 stolen bases, a .281 batting average, a .361 on-base percentage, and a .525 slugging percentage, ended up spending the next seven seasons in San Diego, playing some of the best ball of his career for the Padres. After hitting 26 homers, driving in 92 runs, scoring 88 times, stealing 23 bases, and batting .283 in 2000, Klesko earned All-Star honors the following year by hitting 30 homers, knocking in 113 runs, scoring 105 times, swiping another 23 bags, and batting .286. Klesko had one more big year for the Padres, hitting 29 homers, driving in 95 runs, scoring 90 times, and batting .300 in 2002, before injuries began to take their toll on him. After missing all but the final two weeks of the 2006 season with an injury to his throwing shoulder, Klesko spent the ensuing campaign assuming a part-time role in San Francisco. A free agent at the end of 2007, Klesko chose to announce his retirement, ending his career with 278 home runs, 987 RBIs, 874 runs scored, 1,564 hits, 343 doubles, 33 triples, 91 stolen bases, a .279 batting average, a .370 on-base percentage, and a .500 slugging percentage.

When asked about spending the early portion of his career being platooned by Bobby Cox, Klesko said, "Bobby and I were always good, but I wanted to play every game. I think he would want any player to want to be out there every day. What it came down to is, I played for two of the best managers in the game in Bobby Cox and Bruce Bochy. I did get to hit a lot more against lefties under Bruce, but the Braves gave me my chance, and we won big there."

Since retiring as an active player, Klesko, who now lives with his wife near Macon, Georgia, has made a fortune investing in real estate. The owner of 17 rental homes and more than 7,000 acres of land in several states, Klesko also currently serves as a pregame and postgame analyst for the Braves on Fox Sports South.

BRAVES CAREER HIGHLIGHTS

Best Season

Although Klesko compiled a higher batting average, on-base percentage, and OPS in two or three other seasons, he had his most productive year for the Braves in 1996, when, in addition to hitting a career-high 34 homers, he knocked in 93 runs, scored 90 times, batted .282, and posted an OPS of .894.

Memorable Moments/Greatest Performances

Klesko had a big day against the Cubs on June 6, 1995, going 4-for-5, with two homers and six RBIs during a 17–3 Braves win, homering once with the bases loaded.

Klesko had an outstanding 1995 postseason for the Braves, batting .467 and scoring five runs during their four-game victory over Colorado in the NLDS, before homering three times, knocking in four runs, and batting .313 against Cleveland in the World Series.

Klesko contributed to a 15–10 win over the Florida Marlins on July 14, 1996, by homering twice and knocking in six runs.

Klesko led a 10–2 rout of the Mets on September 17, 1997, by going 4-for-5, with a homer and four RBIs, all of which came on a first-inning grand slam off New York starter Bobby Jones.

Klesko had a similarly productive day against New York's other team on July 16, 1999, going 4-for-5, with two homers and four RBIs during a 10–7 win over the Yankees.

Notable Achievements

- Hit more than 20 home runs four times, topping 30 homers once.
- Batted over .300 twice.
- Posted slugging percentage over .500 four times, topping .600-mark once.
- Compiled OPS over 1.000 once.
- Ranks among Braves career leaders in slugging percentage (4th) and OPS (tied for 7th).
- Four-time NL champion (1992, 1995, 1996, and 1999).
- 1995 world champion.
- April 7, 1996, NL Player of the Week.

45

MAX FRIED

The ace of the Braves' pitching staff the last few seasons, Max Fried has excelled on the mound ever since he became a regular member of Atlanta's starting rotation in 2019. A significant contributor to teams that have won five division titles, one pennant, and one World Series, Fried has won at least 14 games three times, en route to posting the third-highest winning percentage in franchise history. Fried has also compiled an ERA under 3.00 three times, earning in the process one All-Star nomination, two All-MLB selections, and a pair of top five finishes in the NL Cy Young voting. An excellent fielder and solid hitter as well, Fried has won two Gold Gloves and one Silver Slugger, with his total body of work making him arguably the senior circuit's top left-handed pitcher.

Born in Santa Monica, California, on January 18, 1994, Max Dorian Fried grew up in a moderately religious Jewish family, recalling, "I grew up fairly observant. We went to synagogue on High Holidays, and I had my bar mitzvah. So, all that good stuff." The middle son of Carrie and Jonathan Fried, Max first made a name for himself at the 2009 Maccabiah Games, where he served as a member of the Team USA Juniors baseball team that won a gold medal in Israel.

An outstanding all-around athlete, Fried starred in baseball, football, and basketball at Montclair College Preparatory School, in Van Nuys, Los Angeles, performing especially well on the diamond, where he earned All-California Interscholastic Federation Division V First-Team honors as a sophomore by going 10-3 with a 1.81 ERA. Even better his junior year, Fried gained recognition as the 2011 Southern California Jewish Sports Hall of Fame Male High School Athlete of the Year by compiling a record of 7-3 and an ERA of 1.31, while also hitting four homers, driving in 30 runs, and batting .360 as a part-time outfielder.

With Montclair Prep abandoning its baseball program prior to the start of his senior year, Fried transferred to Harvard-Westlake High School in Los Angeles, where he won eight of his 10 mound decisions, compiled an ERA of 2.02, and recorded 105 strikeouts in 66 innings pitched. Paying homage to his childhood hero, Sandy Koufax, by wearing #32 at Harvard-Westlake, Fried said, "Growing up in L.A., being left-handed, and also Jewish, made Sandy Koufax a really good role model. It didn't hurt that he was also one of the best pitchers of all time. Those are some big shoes to fill, though."

After accepting a baseball scholarship to UCLA, Fried chose to put his college education on hold and sign with the San Diego Padres for $3 million when they selected him with the seventh overall pick of the June 2012 MLB Draft. Fried subsequently spent the next two seasons performing well at the lower levels of San Diego's farm system, before undergoing Tommy John surgery after injuring his elbow during the early stages of the 2014 campaign. Although the Braves knew that Fried would not be available to them for quite some time, they completed a deal with the Padres on December 19, 2014, that sent him and three other minor leaguers to Atlanta for outfielder Justin Upton and pitching prospect Aaron Northcraft.

After missing nearly two whole years, Fried returned to action in 2016 with Class A Rome in the South Atlantic League, where he spent the season strengthening his arm and working on his mechanics. Invited to spring training by the Braves the following year, Fried told reporters, "Last year, I went through a phase where I was relearning myself. Taking a couple of years off due to an injury isn't the most ideal situation. Then, trying to go out and compete when you haven't done that in a long time is definitely tough. During the second half I started to feel like myself and really got comfortable on the mound."

Spending most of 2017 with Double-A Mississippi in the Southern League, Fried pitched poorly, compiling a record of just 2-11 and an ERA of 5.54. Called up by the Braves late in the year, Fried performed somewhat better, going 1-1 with a 3.81 ERA in his four starts and five relief appearances. Although Fried spent most of the ensuing campaign at Triple-A Gwinnett, he joined the Braves again at one point during the season, compiling a record of 1-4 and an ERA of 2.94, while also striking out 44 batters in 33 2/3 innings of work.

Arriving in Atlanta to stay in 2019, Fried helped lead the Braves to their second straight division title by going 17-6, with an ERA of 4.02 and a team-high 173 strikeouts. Having established himself as arguably the Braves' top starter, Fried received a vote of confidence heading into 2020 from teammate Freddie Freeman, who predicted that he would be "phenomenal, better than last year." Although the pandemic that gripped the nation limited Fried to just 11 starts, he performed just as well as Freeman had predicted, earning All-MLB First-Team honors and a fifth-place finish

Max Fried currently holds the third-highest winning percentage of any pitcher in franchise history.
Courtesy of Ian D'Andrea

in the NL Cy Young voting by going a perfect 7-0, with an ERA of 2.25 and a WHIP of 1.089. By leading all MLB pitchers in assists for the second straight time, Fried also won his first Gold Glove and the Fielding Bible Award as the best fielding pitcher in the game.

Fried followed up his outstanding 2020 campaign by compiling a record of 14-7 and an ERA of 3.04, tossing a pair of shutouts, and striking out 158 batters in 165 2/3 innings pitched in 2021, before winning the final game of the World Series by throwing six shutout innings against the Houston Astros. Meanwhile, Fried once again led all MLB pitchers in assists and compiled a batting average of .273 at the plate, earning in the process Gold Glove and Silver Slugger honors.

Primarily a fastball/curveball pitcher prior to 2020, the 6'4", 190-pound Fried has since added a slider, sinker, and changeup to his repertoire of pitches. Fried's four-seam fastball, which typically registers somewhere between 94 and 96 mph on the radar gun, remains his swiftest offering, although his sinker often approaches the plate at 93 mph. Fried also throws an 84-mph slider, an 84-mph changeup, and two types of a 74-mph curveball, both of which break in an 11–5 direction. However, while one curve is designed to induce slowly hit grounders, the other breaks from about the waist of the hitter to his mid-shin, causing him to frequently miss it entirely.

Extremely impressed with Fried's arsenal of pitches and the way he handles himself on the mound, veteran left-hander David Price said, "He's a special pitcher. He's one of the guys that I really enjoy watching."

Continuing to perform at an elite level in 2022, Fried earned All-Star honors for the first time by going 14-7, with a 2.48 ERA and 170 strikeouts in 185 1/3 innings pitched. Heading into the 2023 campaign, Fried boasts a career record of 54-25, a lifetime ERA of 3.09, a WHIP of 1.167, and 617 strikeouts in just over 632 innings of work.

CAREER HIGHLIGHTS

Best Season

Although Fried won more games in 2019, he had his finest all-around season in 2022, when, in addition to posting 14 victories and finishing third in the NL with a 2.48 ERA, he recorded 170 strikeouts and established career-best marks in WHIP (1.014) and innings pitched (185 1/3).

Memorable Moments/Greatest Performances

Fried recorded a career-high 11 strikeouts during an 11–4 win over the Cardinals on June 30, 2018, allowing four hits and three walks over 6 2/3 shutout innings.

Fried performed brilliantly during the first six innings of a 9–4 victory over the Cubs on April 4, 2019, striking out five and allowing only right fielder Mark Zagunis to reach base via a sixth-inning single, before turning the game over to the Braves bullpen in the seventh.

Fried turned in a similarly dominant performance on September 5, 2019, throwing seven shutout innings, yielding just one hit, issuing no walks, and recording nine strikeouts during a 4–2 win over the Washington Nationals.

Fried excelled in his first postseason start, working seven shutout innings against Cincinnati in the 2020 NL Wild Card Game, which the Braves ultimately won by a score of 1–0 in 13 innings.

One of the league's better-hitting pitchers, Fried gave the Braves an 8–7 victory over the Miami Marlins on July 4, 2021, when he delivered a game-winning pinch-hit RBI single to center field with the bases loaded and two men out in the bottom of the 10th inning.

Fried threw the first complete-game shutout of his career on August 20, 2021, when he surrendered four hits, issued no walks, and recorded four strikeouts during a 3–0 win over the Orioles.

Fried tossed another shutout a little over one month later, yielding just three hits, issuing no bases on balls, and striking out four during a 4–0 blanking of the Padres on September 24, 2001.

A huge contributor to the Braves' successful run to the world championship in 2021, Fried allowed just three hits and recorded nine strikeouts over the first six innings of a 3–0 win over the Milwaukee Brewers in Game 2 of the NLDS.

Fried subsequently came up big for the Braves against Houston in Game 6 of the 2021 World Series, yielding just four hits and striking out six batters over the first six innings of the 7–0 series clincher. Commenting on Fried's performance afterward, Astros' three-time batting champion José Altuve stated, "He was almost unhittable."

Fried earned his first win of the 2022 campaign on April 19, when he allowed just two hits and recorded eight strikeouts over seven shutout innings during a 3–1 win over the Dodgers.

Although Fried did not figure in the decision, he turned in another dominant performance on June 3, 2022, yielding just two hits and surrendering no runs over the first eight innings of a 3–1 victory over the Colorado Rockies.

Fried dominated Pittsburgh's lineup on August 23, 2022, recording seven strikeouts and allowing just three hits and one run over the first eight innings of a 6–1 win over the Pirates.

Notable Achievements

- Won 17 games in 2019.
- Has posted winning percentage over .600 four times, finishing with mark of 1.000 in 2020.

- Has compiled ERA under 3.00 three times.
- Has led NL pitchers in winning percentage once, shutouts once, and assists three times.
- Has finished second in NL in wins twice.
- Ranks among Braves career leaders in winning percentage (3rd), WHIP (8th), and strikeouts-to-walks ratio (4th).
- 2021 NL champion.
- 2021 world champion.
- September 2021 NL Pitcher of the Month.
- 2021 Silver Slugger Award winner.
- Two-time Gold Glove Award winner (2020 and 2021).
- 2022 NL All-Star selection.
- 2020 All-MLB First-Team selection.
- 2021 All-MLB Second-Team selection.

46

SAM JETHROE

The first African-American player to don a Braves uniform, Sam Jethroe arrived in Boston in 1950 at the age of 33 after starring in the Negro Leagues for nearly a decade. Despite already being in the latter stages of his career, the speedy Jethroe proved to be a productive player for the Braves for three seasons, leading the NL in stolen bases and scoring at least 100 runs twice each, before his skills began to diminish. Although Braves fans likely never got to see the very best of Jethroe, his strong play, tremendous popularity, and historical significance earned him a place on this list.

Born in Columbus, Mississippi, on January 23, 1917, Samuel Jethroe grew up in East St. Louis, Illinois, where he learned how to play baseball from his father at an early age. Often competing against next-door neighbor and future New York Yankees outfielder Hank Bauer during his youth, Jethroe recalled, "His backyard touched my backyard, and we'd play games, Hank Bauer's team and my team."

Eventually establishing himself as a star in multiple sports at Lincoln High School, Jethroe excelled in softball, football, basketball, boxing, and track. Competing semiprofessionally as well while in high school, Jethroe played for both the East St. Louis Colts and the St. Louis Giants, remembering, "I would play doubleheaders for the East St. Louis Colts, then head over to St. Louis for a night game . . . those teams were all black . . . and I made hardly nothing."

Jethroe also briefly caught for the Indianapolis ABCs of the Negro American League in 1938, before disappearing into the world of semipro baseball, declining offers from several Negro League teams so that he might care for his ailing mother. Returning to the professional ranks after his mom passed away in late 1941, Jethroe spent seven seasons starring in center field for the Cleveland Buckeyes, earning four All-Star nominations, winning a pair of batting titles, and becoming the NAL's top base-stealer. Particularly outstanding in 1945, Jethroe, who did not serve in the military during

In 1950, Sam Jethro became the first African American to play for the Braves.
Courtesy of Boston Public Library, Leslie Jones Collection

World War II due to a physical deferment, led the NAL with a batting average of .393.

Recalling his years in Black baseball, Jethroe said, "When I played in the Negro Leagues, I enjoyed it. I loved to play ball, and baseball was fun then. I played against Don Newcombe, Monte Irvin, Henry Thompson, 'Double Duty' Radcliffe, Gentry Jessup, and many others."

Impressed with Jethroe's exceptional athletic ability and outstanding all-around play in Cleveland, Dodgers general manager Branch Rickey considered signing him to a minor-league contract in 1946, before ultimately choosing to integrate the game with Jackie Robinson instead. Reflecting back on Rickey's decision, Jethroe, who acknowledged during his interview with the Dodger GM that he smoked and drank, stated, "He [Robinson] had everything Mr. Rickey wanted. He was a college man who had experienced the white world, and I wasn't."

Two years later, though, Rickey purchased Jethroe from the Buckeyes and assigned him to the Dodgers' minor-league affiliate in Montreal. Appearing in 76 games with the Royals in 1948, Jethroe batted .322 and scored 52 runs, before emerging as arguably the International League's best player the following year, when, in addition to hitting 17 homers, driving in 83 runs, and batting .326, he topped the circuit with 154 runs scored, 207 hits, 19 triples, and 89 stolen bases.

Aside from his exceptional hitting, Jethroe became known during his time in Montreal for his tremendous running speed, with *New York Times* sportswriter Arthur Daley reporting during spring training that the players took part in "thousands of foot races" and that Jethroe "was easily the fastest man in the camp." Daley also noted that, on one occasion, Jethroe scored from second base—standing up—on an infield dribbler.

Don Newcombe said of his former Royals teammate, "He was the fastest human being I've ever seen."

And, with Jethroe posting a time of 5.9 seconds in a 60-yard sprint, scholar James A. Riley later wrote in *The Biographical Encyclopedia of the Negro Baseball Leagues*, "His time during one of those foot races was close to a world record."

Nevertheless, with Duke Snider firmly ensconced as the starting center fielder in Brooklyn, Rickey dealt Jethroe to the Braves for three players and $150,000 at the end of 1949, in what he later said, "might be the biggest mistake I ever made in baseball."

Finally making his big-league debut on April 18, 1950, nearly three months after he celebrated his 33rd birthday, Jethroe went on to earn NL Rookie of the Year honors by hitting 18 homers, driving in 58 runs, scoring 100 times, batting .273, and topping the circuit with 35 stolen bases, while also amassing more assists (18) than any other center fielder in the league. Jethroe followed that up with a similarly productive 1951 season, concluding the campaign with 18 home runs, 65 RBIs, 101 runs scored, a batting average of .280, and a league-leading 35 steals.

Although Jethroe encountered some racism his first two years in the league, especially in those cities that had yet to accept integration, he found himself being welcomed with open arms by the fans of Boston, with *Boston Globe* sportswriter Bob Holbrook writing, "Jethroe's box-office appeal amazed even the Braves' front office, who knew they had acquired a good outfielder but never guessed the staid Boston fans would adopt him as their favorite National League player and murmur with excitement every time he reached base."

While the 6'1", 180-pound, switch-hitting Jethroe's ability to drive the ball with power from both sides of the plate contributed greatly to his tremendous popularity, it was his blinding speed that truly made him a fan favorite, with longtime Braves supporter Mort Bloomberg remembering years later, "A wave of excitement rose from the stands when he stepped to the plate because he was our hometown answer to Jackie Robinson—a self-assured threat to steal one or more bases each time he reached first. . . . Boos when he came to bat? Never. We just wanted to see Sammy run."

Jack Barnes, who worked as a vendor at Braves Field during Jethroe's tour of duty with the club, addressed the manner with which the outfielder's relationship with the fans crossed racial lines when he stated, "We never had too many full houses at Braves Field—maybe there'd be 10 or 12,000 of us there—but the racial question, I'm gonna tell you, there was never anybody booing or hissing Sam. We loved him. Everybody would chant, 'Go, Sam, go.' Sam the Jet at Braves Field was a hero. Everybody loved to see Sam run. He brought some life to the ball team. We weren't a very fast team, and he was a breath of fresh air to us. I went to a lot of games when Sam was playing and I never heard anybody . . . I never heard any racial slurs, or anything but admiration for Sam the Jet."

Recalling how the hometown fans readily accepted him, Jethroe said, "The people in Boston were crazy about me. Everyone crowded around me for autographs after my first game. There was this woman who wanted to take me to dinner. A white woman. I didn't do it because I figured that was one of the reasons they didn't want us in the majors to begin with."

Jethroe continued, "I loved the Boston fans. They used to chant, 'go, go, go,' every time I got on base. Never had a problem in Boston. . . . I was lucky. Everywhere I went I seemed to have the fans on my side. They kidded me about my fielding, but I didn't have rabbit ears. The fans could say what they wanted. The only confrontations I had were on the playing field."

Capable of using his great speed to track down long flyballs, the right-handed-throwing Jethroe nevertheless struggled at times in the field, leading all NL outfielders in errors three straight times. Eventually, though, Jethroe developed into a solid defender after he began using eyeglasses, telling writer John Gillooly in 1952, "I'm ashamed I didn't get to the eye-doctor before I did."

After undergoing intestinal surgery during the early stages of the 1952 campaign, the 35-year-old Jethroe experienced a decline in offensive production, finishing the season with just 13 homers, 58 RBIs, 79 runs scored, a .232 batting average, and a career-high 112 strikeouts, although he still managed to finish second in the league with 28 stolen bases. Aside from his subpar performance and advancing age, Jethroe found himself faced with the unenviable task of trying to cultivate a relationship with new Braves manager Charlie Grimm, who he claimed once called him "Sambo," later telling the *Boston Globe*, "Charlie Grimm was a prejudiced man, and he didn't like me."

Not too surprisingly, the Braves optioned Jethroe to their Triple-A affiliate in Toledo, Ohio, just prior to the start of the 1953 regular season. Although Jethroe hit 28 homers and batted .309 at Toledo, the Braves never recalled him, instead trading him, along with five other players, to the Pittsburgh Pirates for infielder Danny O'Connell at the end of the year. Released by the Pirates in April 1954 after appearing in just two games with them, Jethro subsequently spent the next five seasons with the minor-league Toronto Maple Leafs, before announcing his retirement following the conclusion of the 1958 campaign.

Jethroe, who hit 57 homers, knocked in 264 runs, scored 397 times, collected 638 hits, 123 doubles, and 39 triples, stole 134 bases, batted .275, compiled an on-base percentage of .345, and posted a slugging percentage of .435 in his three years with the Braves, settled in Erie, Pennsylvania, following his playing days. After briefly working in a factory and playing semipro baseball with the Pontiacs in the city's Glenwood League, Jethroe opened a steakhouse he called Jethroe's Bar and Restaurant, which did well for several years until the city's redevelopment authority forced him to sell the property in 1994. Forced to take out a loan and purchase another business located in a seedy part of town, Jethroe experienced significant financial loss that made it necessary for him to sell off his Rookie of the Year award for $3,500.

Jethroe lived until June 16, 2001, when he died of a heart attack at the age of 84 while recovering from pacemaker surgery he underwent two weeks earlier. Quoting Jethroe on his inability to play in the major leagues until he reached his 30s, Richard Goldstein wrote in a piece that appeared in the June 19, 2001, edition of the *New York Times*, "I'm not the type of person to be bitter. I was honored to play. I'm thankful that I was able to do what I did."

BRAVES CAREER HIGHLIGHTS

Best Season

With Jethro posting extremely similar numbers in 1950 and 1951, either of those seasons would make a good choice. But, since he knocked in seven more runs (65 to 58), batted seven points higher (.280 to .273), and compiled a considerably higher OPS (.816 to .780) in 1951, we'll go with that as his finest season.

Memorable Moments/Greatest Performances

In addition to making history on April 18, 1950, by becoming the first Black player to appear in a game for the Braves, Jethroe homered, singled, and knocked in two runs during an 11–4 win over the Giants in New York's Polo Grounds.

Jethroe led the Braves to a 15–6 win over the Pirates on June 17, 1950, by homering once, knocking in four runs, and scoring three times, with his three-run homer in the bottom of the eighth inning highlighting a 10-run rally by the home team.

Jethroe gave the Braves an 8–5 victory over the Giants on April 18, 1951, by hitting a three-run homer off reliever Dave Koslo in the bottom of the ninth inning.

Jethroe displayed his outstanding all-around ability during a 13–12 win over the Giants on April 19, 1951, going 3-for-5, with two homers, a walk, a stolen base, and three RBIs.

Jethroe's two-out, two-run homer off reliever Clyde King in the top of the ninth inning proved to be the decisive blow of a 6–5 victory over the Dodgers on April 25, 1951.

Jethroe delivered the big blow of a 7–6 win over the Cubs on June 8, 1952, when he homered off starter Bob Rush with the bases loaded in the top of the second inning.

Jethroe turned in an exceptional all-around effort during a 9–3 win over the Phillies on August 13, 1952, going 3-for-3, with two homers, a double, two walks, a stolen base, four RBIs, and four runs scored.

Notable Achievements

- Scored more than 100 runs twice.
- Finished in double digits in triples once.
- Stole more than 30 bases twice.
- Led NL in stolen bases twice.
- Led NL center fielders in assists twice.
- 1950 NL Rookie of the Year.

47
DUSTY BAKER

Much like Joe Torre and Felipe Alou, two of the men who preceded him on this list, Dusty Baker is known primarily to younger fans of the game for the success he experienced as a manager after his playing days ended. However, prior to guiding five different teams to a total of nine division titles, Baker proved to be a hard-hitting outfielder who manned all three outfield positions at various times during a career that covered parts of 19 seasons. Playing his best ball for the Braves and Dodgers from 1972 to 1983, Baker hit at least 20 homers six times, knocked in more than 90 runs twice, and batted over .300 three times, earning in the process two All-Star nominations and two top-10 finishes in the NL MVP voting. A member of the Braves from 1968 to 1975, Baker surpassed 20 homers twice, scored more than 100 runs once, and batted over .300 once during his time in Atlanta, while also doing an excellent job of patrolling center field.

Born in Riverside, California, on June 15, 1949, Johnnie B. Baker Jr. acquired his familiar nickname at an early age, recalling, "We had a big backyard that my dad planted, had grass everywhere. It was like a football field, and then there was one dirt spot in the middle, and that's where I seemed to like to play. My mom didn't want to call me 'Dirty,' so she called me 'Dusty.'"

The son of a professor and a defense industry worker who spent his evenings moonlighting as a salesman at Sears, Baker developed a strong sense of responsibility early on, often being called upon to manage his four younger siblings while his parents worked during the day. Growing up in an extremely structured environment, Baker typically adhered to the wishes of his mother, who determined what courses he took in school and insisted that he take piano lessons, with Baker saying, "I wanted to be Little Richard or Jerry Lee Lewis. She wanted me to be Liberace. Did I have a choice? That wasn't a word in our house. She told me that I was going to have culture whether I wanted it or not. Love is discipline. I had plenty of both."

Developing a fondness for baseball as well during his formative years, Baker learned how to play the game from his father, who remembered, "Dusty said he wanted to play baseball, so I hit him hundreds of balls. By the time that he was 12, he was a very good player."

Nevertheless, Baker's road to success on the diamond proved to be a long and arduous one, as he revealed when he stated, "My dad cut me from his Little League team three times. He said I had a bad attitude. I had a bad, horrible temper. I threw my bat up against the wall one time. He cut me. The next time, I threw my glove down, and he cut me."

Adding that he seriously considered quitting and getting a paper route after being overlooked for an all-star team, Baker said, "Thankfully, my father wouldn't let me. . . . My dad said that no son of his is going to quit. He said, 'If you want to quit at the end of the season, that's fine, but you ain't quitting even before we really get started.' He said if I could take that bad attitude and put it in a positive direction, that I could be something one day."

Eventually emerging as a star in multiple sports at Del Campo High School in Sacramento, California, after his family moved there from Riverside when his father lost his job in 1963, Baker excelled in baseball, basketball, football, and track, competing in the latter as a sprinter, long-jumper, and broad-jumper. Claiming that his basketball skills exceeded his abilities on the diamond during his teenage years, Baker said, "I was good in baseball, but I wasn't great in baseball. I played in the spring with the school team, and, in the summer, I would play with the American Legion, Little League, or Pony League. I came all the way up. I was skilled in all departments, but I just wasn't strong."

After receiving a scare in 1966 when a benign heart murmur was misdiagnosed as a significantly more serious condition that likely would have ended his career in sports, Baker resumed his athletic pursuits his senior year, performing well enough on the hardwood that Santa Clara University offered him a basketball scholarship. However, just before Baker committed to Santa Clara, the Braves, who had selected him in the 26th round of the 1967 MLB Amateur Draft, offered to fly him and his mother down to Los Angeles to meet members of the team, who were in town to play the Dodgers.

Influenced tremendously by Hank Aaron, who, in his own words, "promised my mother he'd take care of me as if I were his son once I got to Atlanta," Baker chose to sign with the Braves on the spot, inking his deal with them on the hood of a car in the Dodger Stadium parking lot. Revealing that he also based his decision on his parents' recent divorce, which

Before beginning a lengthy career in managing, Dusty Baker played for the Braves for eight seasons.

made him feel as if he needed to provide for his family, Baker recalled, "I said, 'Well, I gotta do what I gotta do.'" Although his father attempted to nullify the contract since he wanted his son to go to college, Baker and his mother ignored his wishes, causing Dusty and his dad to stop speaking to one another for several years.

Beginning his pro career with the Double-A Austin Braves, Baker struggled at first, forcing him to split the 1968 campaign between the organization's Single-A affiliates in West Palm Beach, Florida, and Greenwood, South Carolina. Experiencing a considerable amount of racism off the playing field in both cities, Baker recalled, "I couldn't eat where the white players ate. I couldn't live where they lived." Nevertheless, Baker eventually won the hearts of the hometown fans in Greenwood by batting .324, with an article appearing in an August edition of the local newspaper quoting the team's manager as saying, "Dusty's very popular with the players and the fans. They cheer him every time he comes to bat—and I guess you could say that's a little unusual in the South, the fans cheering a Negro boy."

Rising through the Braves' farm system the following year, Baker spent time at both Double-A Shreveport and Triple-A Richmond, performing well at both stops, while also beginning a six-year stint as an auto mechanic in the US Marine Corps Reserve. Looking back at his time in the service, Baker said, "It turned out to be one of the best things that ever happened in my life. It helped me a lot. I came home more disciplined."

Remaining at Richmond in 1970 and 1971, Baker posted batting averages of .325 and .311, earning him late-season callups to the parent club both years. Joining the Braves for good in 1972, Baker laid claim to the team's starting center field job during the early stages of the campaign, after which he went on to hit 17 homers, drive in 76 runs, score 62 times, and finish third in the league with a .321 batting average. Meanwhile, as Baker rose to prominence, he developed a symbiotic relationship with Hank Aaron, who fulfilled his earlier promise to the rookie's mother, with Baker recalling, "He made me go to church. I ate with him every night."

Improving upon his overall numbers in 1973, Baker hit 21 homers, knocked in 99 runs, scored 101 times, stole 24 bases, and batted .288, while also leading all NL outfielders with 390 putouts. Touted by the local media as "the next Hank Aaron," Baker also received praise from Braves manager Eddie Mathews, who commented, "He has super tools. Maybe he doesn't have the power that Hank has, but he has everything else. He's a tremendous athlete."

The right-handed-hitting Baker, who stood 6'2" and weighed close to 190 pounds, did indeed possess outstanding athletic ability. Blessed with excellent speed, Baker ran the bases well and covered a lot of ground in the outfield. He also displayed good power at the plate and hit the ball with authority to all fields. However, even though Baker proved to be a very good player for several years, he never quite attained the level of excellence originally predicted for him, causing many to view his playing career as something of a disappointment.

Regressing somewhat in 1974, Baker hit 20 homers but knocked in only 69 runs and batted just .256. Posting extremely similar numbers the following year, Baker homered 19 times, drove in 72 runs, and batted .261. With Baker expressing a desire to play elsewhere at the end of the year, the Braves granted his request, including him in a six-player trade they completed with the Dodgers on November 17, 1975, that sent him and infielder Ed Goodson to Los Angeles for top prospect Jerry Royster, outfielder Jim Wynn, and utilitymen Lee Lacy and Tom Paciorek.

Expressing his happiness over acquiring Baker after completing the deal, Dodgers general manager Al Campanis stated, "He can run, throw, field, and hit for power. And it's our feeling that he has yet to reach his peak."

Baker, who left Atlanta with career totals of 77 home runs, 324 RBIs, 311 runs scored, 616 hits, 111 doubles, eight triples, and 58 stolen bases, a .278 batting average, a .351 on-base percentage, and a .440 slugging percentage, ended up spending the next eight seasons manning left field for the Dodgers, helping them win three pennants and one World Series by surpassing 20 homers four times and batting over .300 twice. Particularly outstanding in 1977 and 1980, Baker hit a career-high 30 homers, knocked in 86 runs, and batted .291 in the first of those campaigns, before earning a fourth-place finish in the NL MVP voting in the second by hitting 29 homers, driving in 97 runs, and batting .294.

Nevertheless, with Baker's name being included in unsubstantiated rumors of drug use during the 1983 season, the Dodgers placed him on waivers at the end of the year. Baker subsequently signed with the Giants on April 1, 1984, but only after he signed his waiver release, saying at the time, "I knew the only way to clear my name and feel good with myself was to be performing out in the field. Even if I got a chance to play next year, then there always would be a shadow hanging over my head."

When asked about his purported drug use, Baker said, "I'm afraid to do something illegal. I have a nice life. I have a nice family."

Baker split the next three seasons between the Giants and Oakland Athletics, serving both teams as a part-time player, before announcing his retirement following the conclusion of the 1986 campaign with career totals of 242 home runs, 1,013 RBIs, 964 runs scored, 1,981 hits, 320 doubles, 23 triples, and 137 stolen bases, a .278 batting average, a .347 on-base percentage, and a .432 slugging percentage.

Following his retirement, Baker briefly worked as a stockbroker in Los Angeles, before returning to the game in the fall of 1987 as first base coach of the Giants. After fulfilling that role for one season, Baker spent the next four years serving as the team's batting coach, all the while refusing a managerial assignment in the organization's farm system. In explaining his stance during an interview in 1992, Baker said, "I think that minor league experience is overrated. I always thought I was bright about baseball from the start. I was always told that I played older than my age. I've been a so-called student of the game. As a player, I managed in my mind."

Promoted to manager of the Giants in 1993, Baker spent the next 10 years in that position, before piloting the Chicago Cubs from 2003 to 2006, the Cincinnati Reds from 2008 to 2013, the Washington Nationals from 2016 to 2017, and the Houston Astros from 2020 until now. One of the most successful managers in baseball for much of the last three decades, Baker has guided his teams to 11 playoff appearances, nine division titles, three pennants, and one World Series championship, winning in the process Manager of the Year honors on three separate occasions. The first MLB manager to reach the playoffs and win a division title with five different teams, Baker is also one of only nine skippers to win a pennant in each league.

In discussing the qualities that have made Baker such a successful manager, former Giants pitcher Kirk Rueter stated, "He made you feel like you could do anything on the field. He was always positive. You always felt like he was in your corner, and he cared about you. He became a father figure when you were struggling because he wanted you to do so well."

Baker, who made a full recovery from a ministroke he suffered in 2012, has taken a brief break from managing three different times. During one of those hiatuses, he returned home to be closer to his family, recalling, "When my dad was ill, I came back to help take care of him. He had dementia. I was here that year, and it's one of the best things I ever did in my life."

Baker, whose father suffered a stroke one year later and passed away in 2009, continued, "The toughest thing that people do in life is to forgive each other. And I can hold a grudge, man. But you've got to work on yourself."

BRAVES CAREER HIGHLIGHTS

Best Season

Although Baker finished third in the NL with a .321 batting average in 1972, he proved to be a more productive offensive player the following year, concluding the 1973 campaign with 21 homers, 99 RBIs, 101 runs scored, 24 stolen bases, and a .288 batting average.

Memorable Moments/Greatest Performances

Baker led the Braves to a 7–4 win over the Giants on September 17, 1972, by going 4-for-4, with a walk and two RBIs.

Baker contributed to a 9–3 victory over the Pirates on August 11, 1973, by homering twice and knocking in four runs.

Baker gave the Braves a 6–5 victory over the Giants on September 11, 1973, by driving home Ralph Garr with the winning run with a single to center field in the bottom of the 11th inning.

Baker proved to be the difference in a 7–5 win over the San Diego Padres on May 13, 1974, going 4-for-5, with a homer and four RBIs.

Baker helped lead the Braves to a 12–0 rout of the Giants on September 15, 1975, by going 4-for-5, with a triple, two doubles, five RBIs, and two runs scored.

Notable Achievements

- Surpassed 20 home runs twice.
- Scored more than 100 runs once.
- Batted over .300 once.
- Surpassed 30 doubles once.
- Stole more than 20 bases once.
- Posted slugging percentage over .500 once.
- Finished third in NL with .321 batting average in 1972.
- Led NL outfielders in putouts once.

48

JEFF BLAUSER

A versatile player who manned every infield position but first base during his 11 years in Atlanta, Jeff Blauser overcame injuries and bouts of inconsistency in the field to establish himself as one of the better middle infielders in franchise history. After spending his first few seasons with the Braves assuming the role of a utility man, Blauser served as the team's primary starter at shortstop from 1990 to 1997, a period during which he earned two All-Star nominations and one Silver Slugger. Though somewhat erratic in the field, Blauser made up for his defensive shortcomings by batting over .300 twice and scoring more than 100 runs once, making him a significant contributor to Braves teams that won four pennants and one World Series.

Born in Los Gatos, California, on November 8, 1965, Jeffrey Michael Blauser grew up some 125 miles northeast, in the city of Auburn, where he got his start in organized baseball as a pitcher for the Placer Savers Little League team. After throwing two no-hitters in a three-week span at the age of 12, Blauser gradually transitioned to shortstop while attending Placer High School, earning All-CAL honors his senior year by batting .347, collecting 33 hits, driving in 19 runs, and stealing 19 bases. A star on the gridiron as well, Blauser excelled as a wide receiver, safety, kicker, and punter, once scoring 18 of his team's 24 points in a 1982 game against Woodland High.

After going undrafted by all 26 teams in the June 1983 MLB Draft, Blauser accepted a baseball scholarship to Sacramento City College, where he spent the summer and winter months improving his speed while competing in unofficial games against other colleges. Subsequently selected by the St. Louis Cardinals with the eighth overall pick in the January phase of the 1984 Amateur Draft, Blauser remained in school until the end of the season, batting .383 and driving in 26 runs, before re-entering the June draft when he and the Cardinals failed to come to terms on a contract. This time selected number-four overall by the Braves, Blauser elected to turn pro, spurning in the process scholarship offers from such notable institutions as Miami, Arizona State, and USC.

Expressing his glee over signing Blauser to a deal, Braves scout Bill Wight said at the time, "He was our first choice all the way around. He's really come on in the last year, and I think he'll make the big leagues within three or four years."

After beginning his pro career in the rookie-level Appalachian League with the Pulaski Braves, Blauser graduated to Low-A Sumter in the South Atlantic League, where, despite stealing 36 bases in 1985, he batted just .235 and committed 35 errors in 117 games at shortstop. Although Blauser continued to struggle somewhat in the field the following year, committing 25 errors at High-A Durham, he began to turn heads with his offensive production, hitting 13 homers, amassing 27 doubles, scoring 94 runs, and batting .286. Meanwhile, Hank Aaron, then the Braves' director of player development, praised Blauser for his baseball acumen, describing him as a "very intelligent player," and adding, "You don't have to tell him anything twice."

Joining the Braves midway through the 1987 campaign after spending the season's first few months at Double-A Greenville and Triple-A Richmond, Blauser received a vote of confidence from manager Chuck Tanner, who told the *Atlanta Constitution*, "I love the kid. I don't care if he played in the North County League last year. He can play in the major leagues right now at second or short. There's no question about it."

Starting 50 games for the Braves at shortstop the rest of the year, Blauser batted .242, homered twice, knocked in 15 runs, and committed nine errors in the field, while sharing playing time with Andrés Thomas and Rafael Ramírez. With Ramírez laying claim to the starting shortstop job in Atlanta in 1988, Blauser spent most of the season at Richmond, before arriving in the major leagues to stay when rosters expanded in September. Assuming an important role on the Braves the following year, Blauser saw a significant amount of action at second, short, and third, appearing in 142 games, and batting .270, with 12 homers, 46 RBIs, and 63 runs scored, in just over 500 total plate appearances.

Despite being plagued by injuries in each of the next three seasons, Blauser remained a regular member of the Braves' starting lineup, averaging 122 games played, 11 homers, 46 RBIs, and 52 runs scored from 1990 to 1992, while posting batting averages of .269, .259, and .262. Fully healthy in 1993, Blauser had his finest season to date, earning All-Star honors by hitting 15 homers, driving in 73 runs, stealing 16 bases, batting .305, and

Jeff Blauser played all over the infield during his time in Atlanta.

ranking among the league leaders with 110 runs scored and 182 hits, while playing shortstop exclusively for the first time in his career.

A solid hitter, the right-handed-swinging Blauser, who stood 6-foot and weighed 170 pounds, displayed occasional power at the plate, finishing in double digits in home runs on seven separate occasions. Blauser also gradually learned how to work the pitcher, drawing as many as 85 bases on balls one season. But, with slightly below average range and questionable hands, Blauser was never able to distinguish himself with the glove, forcing his managers to often replace him in the field during the latter stages of contests.

Unable to replicate his outstanding 1993 performance in any of the next three seasons, Blauser suffered through a particularly poor 1995 campaign during which he batted just .211 and knocked in only 31 runs. Blauser subsequently batted just .245 and committed 23 errors in only 79 games at shortstop the following year, while being sidelined much of the time by an injured right knee and a broken left hand he sustained when Montreal's Jeff Juden hit him with a pitch. However, Blauser returned to top form in 1997, earning his second All-Star nomination and his lone Silver Slugger by hitting 17 homers, driving in 70 runs, scoring 90 times, and batting .308.

A free agent at season's end, Blauser signed with the Cubs for two years and $8.4 million on December 9, 1997, some three weeks after the Braves inked veteran shortstop Walt Weiss to a three-year, $9 million deal. Lamenting the loss of Blauser, who, during his time in Atlanta, hit 109 homers, knocked in 461 runs, scored 601 others, collected 1,060 hits, 201 doubles, and 28 triples, stole 61 bases, batted .268, compiled a .355 on-base percentage, and posted a .415 slugging percentage, Braves manager Bobby Cox said, "It's hard to part with guys like that because they've helped us so much, and they can still play. But it's like everything else in baseball. You adjust. We're still going to have a good ballclub, period."

Blauser ended up serving the Cubs as a part-time player for two years, before announcing his retirement at the end of 1999 with career totals of 122 home runs, 513 RBIs, 691 runs scored, 1,187 hits, 217 doubles, 33 triples, and 65 stolen bases, a .262 batting average, a .354 on-base percentage, and a .406 slugging percentage.

After retiring as an active player, Blauser spent three years working as a roving instructor in the Braves' minor-league system and another managing in the minor leagues, before leaving the game. He currently lives with his family in the Atlanta area, where he holds the position of senior partner at StaffMetrix HR, a human resources firm.

BRAVES CAREER HIGHLIGHTS

Best Season

Blauser earned one of his two All-Star nominations in 1997, when he knocked in 70 runs, scored 90 times, and established career-high marks with 17 home runs, 31 doubles, a batting average of .308, and an OPS of .886. But he compiled slightly better overall numbers in 1993, hitting 15 homers, driving in 73 runs, stealing 16 bases, batting .305, posting an OPS of .837, and placing in the league's top 10 with 110 runs scored, 182 hits, 85 walks, and a .401 on-base percentage.

Memorable Moments/Greatest Performances

Blauser led the Braves to a 5–3 win over the Cubs on August 26, 1989, by going 3-for-4, with a pair of solo homers.

Blauser homered twice and knocked in three runs during a 9–8 win over the Cubs on May 7, 1990, with his two-run blast off reliever Mitch Williams in the top of the ninth inning providing the margin of victory.

Blauser starred during a 9–5 win over the Phillies on June 4, 1991, knocking in six runs with a homer and a pair of doubles.

Blauser led the Braves to a 7–4 victory over the Cubs on July 12, 1992, by hitting three homers and knocking in five runs.

Blauser contributed to a 13–5 win over the Colorado Rockies on May 7, 1993, by going 3-for-3, with two homers, a double, four RBIs, and three runs scored.

Blauser punctuated a four-hit, three-RBI performance with a two-run homer off reliever Jeff Brantley in the bottom of the ninth inning that gave the Braves a 6–5 win over the Reds on June 17, 1994.

Blauser led the Braves to an 11–3 rout of the Phillies on May 11, 1996, by homering twice and knocking in a career-high seven runs, with one of his homers coming with the bases loaded.

Although the Braves suffered an 8–3 defeat at the hands of the Mets on June 10, 1996, Blauser had the only five-hit game of his career, going a perfect 5-for-5 on the day.

Notable Achievements

- Scored more than 100 runs once.
- Batted over .300 twice.
- Surpassed 30 doubles once.
- Compiled on-base percentage over .400 twice.
- Hit three home runs in one game vs. Chicago Cubs on July 12, 1992.
- Four-time NL champion (1991, 1992, 1995, and 1996).
- 1995 world champion.
- Two-time NL Player of the Week.
- 1997 Silver Slugger Award winner.
- Two-time NL All-Star selection (1993 and 1997).
- 1997 *Sporting News* All-Star selection.

49

SID GORDON

Nicknamed the "Solid Man" for his sturdy and consistent play, Sid Gordon spent 13 years in the major leagues, manning multiple positions for three different teams over the course of his career. A member of the Braves from 1950 to 1953, Gordon proved to be one of the National League's top sluggers and run producers during his time in Boston and Milwaukee, surpassing 20 homers three times and 100 RBIs twice, while also batting over .300 once. Displaying a keen batting eye as well, Gordon drew a total of 306 bases on balls and struck out only 152 times in his four years with the Braves, en route to establishing himself as one of the franchise's all-time leaders in on-base percentage and OPS. Meanwhile, whether playing left field, right field, or third base, Gordon fielded his position well, consistently compiling one of the highest fielding percentages in the league for players who manned his post.

Born in the Brownsville section of Brooklyn, New York, on August 13, 1917, Sidney Gordon grew up in a Jewish family whose patriarch, Morris, a plumber and coal miner, emigrated to the United States from Russia. Eventually moving with his family to the borough's Flatbush section, Gordon attended Samuel Tilden High School, where he made a name for himself as a standout baseball player.

After an unsuccessful tryout with the Dodgers in 1936, Gordon signed with the Giants as an amateur free agent two years later when team scout George Mack offered him a contract after seeing him play sandlot ball. Subsequently assigned to the Milford (Delaware) Giants in the Class D Eastern Shore League, Gordon nearly chose not to report and instead carry on the family business when his father died suddenly. However, his mother insisted that he pursue his dream, offering to run the business herself.

Gordon subsequently spent the next five years advancing through the Giants' farm system, performing well at every stop while splitting his time between third base and the outfield. He also received brief callups to New York in 1941 and 1942, before joining the Giants for good in 1943. Posting

Sid Gordon finished second in the NL with 109 RBIs in 1951.
Courtesy of Boston Public Library, Leslie Jones Collection

decent numbers his first full season in the majors while shifting back and forth between first base, third base, and left field, Gordon hit nine homers, drove in 63 runs, scored 50 times, and batted .251. However, with World War II raging, Gordon ended up missing the next two seasons while serving in the US Coast Guard.

Returning to the Giants after the war, a more physically mature Gordon laid claim to the starting left field job in New York, concluding the 1946 campaign with five homers, 45 RBIs, 64 runs scored, and a .293 batting average. Gordon followed that up with another solid season, hitting 13 homers, driving in 57 runs, scoring 57 times, and batting .272 in 1947, before emerging as more of a power threat after Giants coach Red Kress tinkered with his batting style prior to the start of the ensuing campaign. Taking note of the right-handed-hitting Gordon's powerful 5'10", 190-pound frame, Kress helped turn his pupil into more of a pull hitter, enabling him to establish himself as one of the league's top sluggers. In easily his finest season as a member of the Giants, Gordon earned All-Star honors for the first of two straight times and a fourth-place finish in the NL MVP voting in 1948 by hitting 30 homers, knocking in 107 runs, scoring 100 times, batting .299, and compiling an OPS of .927. Meanwhile, after being shifted to third base, Gordon led all players at his position with a .948 fielding percentage.

After holding out for more money the following spring, Gordon ended up signing for $2,500 less than he originally demanded. He then went out and hit 26 homers, drove in 90 runs, scored 87 others, batted .284, and compiled an OPS of .909. Nevertheless, with new Giants manager Leo Durocher wanting more speed and a good double-play combination, he traded Gordon and three other players to the Braves for middle infielders Alvin Dark and Eddie Stanky on December 14, 1949. Unhappy over having to part ways with one of his team's most popular players, Giants owner Horace Stoneham told Gordon that "it broke my heart to let you go," and sent him a check for $2,500.

Continuing his outstanding slugging in Boston, Gordon hit 27 homers, knocked in 103 runs, batted .304, compiled an on-base percentage of .403, and finished fourth in the league with a slugging percentage of .557 and an OPS of .960 in 1950. Also doing a good job with the glove after being moved back to left field, Gordon, who lacked great speed but caught almost everything within his reach, finished second among NL outfielders with a .990 fielding percentage. Gordon had another big year in 1951, hitting 29 homers, driving in 109 runs, scoring 96 times, batting .287, and compiling an OPS of .883, before posting somewhat less impressive numbers the following season, when he homered 25 times, knocked in 75 runs, scored 69 others, and batted .289.

As he had done in New York, Gordon soon became extremely popular in Boston, with his friendly disposition making him a well-liked person wherever he traveled. But even though Gordon did not encounter nearly as much prejudice as Hank Greenberg, the game's first great Jewish player, he did experience at least one case of anti-Semitism, which occurred one day in St. Louis when Cardinals players spent much of the afternoon hurling ethnically related insults at him. In trying to diffuse the situation afterward, Cardinals manager Eddie Dyer said, "Sid is a friend of mine," and went on to explain that the outfielder had been attacked not because he was Jewish, but because he was a good player and "the good ones receive the attention of bench jockeys." Although Dyer's explanation rang hollow, Gordon chose to take the high road, ignoring the alleged anti-Semitic remarks and forcing his detractors to begrudgingly give him the respect he deserved.

Gordon spent one more year with the Braves, hitting 19 homers, driving in 75 runs, scoring 67 times, and batting .274 for them after they moved to Milwaukee in 1953, before being included in a multiplayer trade with the Pittsburgh Pirates on December 26, 1953. Gordon, who left the Braves having hit 100 homers, driven in 362 runs, scored 310 times, collected 582 hits, 105 doubles, and 11 triples, batted .289, compiled an on-base percentage of .385, and posted a slugging percentage of .500 as a member of the team, subsequently hit 12 homers, knocked in 49 runs, and batted .306 as a part-time player with Pittsburgh in 1954, before splitting the ensuing campaign between the Pirates and Giants. Announcing his retirement at the end of 1955, Gordon ended his career with 202 home runs, 805 RBIs, 735 runs scored, 1,415 hits, 220 doubles, 43 triples, a .283 batting average, a .377 on-base percentage, and a .466 slugging percentage.

Following his playing days, Gordon remained in baseball briefly, serving as a coach with the International League's Miami Marlins for a few years, before becoming a life insurance underwriter with the Mutual of New York Insurance Company. A good family man and solid citizen, Gordon made certain that his children received a Jewish education and helped various Jewish groups by lending his name to their causes. Taken from us far too soon, Gordon died of a heart attack he suffered while playing softball in New York's Central Park on June 17, 1975. He was only 57 years old at the time of his passing.

BRAVES CAREER HIGHLIGHTS

Best Season

Gordon had an outstanding year for the Braves in 1951, hitting 29 homers, finishing second in the NL with 109 RBIs, scoring 96 times, batting .287, and compiling an OPS of .883. But, despite playing in 16 fewer games and making close to 80 fewer official plate appearances the previous season, Gordon posted slightly better overall numbers, concluding the 1950 campaign with 27 home runs, including four grand slams, 103 RBIs, 78 runs scored, a .304 batting average, and a career-best 33 doubles, .557 slugging percentage, and .960 OPS.

Memorable Moments/Greatest Performances

Gordon helped lead the Braves to a 10–6 win over the Giants on April 19, 1950, by driving in five runs with a pair of homers, one of which came with the bases loaded.

Gordon contributed to a 14–2 rout of the Pirates on June 1, 1950, by collecting three hits and knocking in four runs with a first-inning grand slam.

Gordon continued his assault on Pirates pitching two days later, homering twice and driving in seven runs during a 10–6 Braves win, with one of his home runs coming with the bases loaded.

Gordon gave the Braves a 12–9 win over the eventual NL champion Phillies on July 4, 1950, when he homered off ace reliever Jim Konstanty with the bases loaded and two men out in the top of the ninth inning, tying in the process the then single-season record for most grand slams (4).

Gordon starred in defeat on September 6, 1952, collecting a career-high five hits and driving in a run during a 7–6 loss to the Phillies in 17 innings.

Notable Achievements

- Hit more than 20 home runs three times.
- Knocked in more than 100 runs twice.
- Batted over .300 once.
- Surpassed 30 doubles once.
- Compiled on-base percentage over .400 once.
- Posted slugging percentage over .500 twice.
- Compiled OPS over .900 once.
- Finished second in NL with 109 RBIs in 1951.
- Led NL outfielders in fielding percentage once.
- Ranks among Braves career leaders in on-base percentage (tied for 8th) and OPS (tied for 7th).

50

EARL TORGESON

A tall, bespectacled left-handed-hitting first baseman who possessed good power, excellent speed, and outstanding patience at the plate, Earl Torgeson arrived in Boston in 1947 with huge expectations surrounding him after spending three years serving in the military during World War II. Proving to be a solid player for the Braves the next six seasons, Torgeson hit more than 20 homers and compiled an on-base percentage over .400 twice each, while also leading the NL in runs scored once. Nevertheless, with Torgeson never quite living up to the standards others set for him, his 15-year major-league career is generally considered to be something of a disappointment.

Born in Snohomish, Washington, on January 1, 1924, Clifford Earl Torgeson spent his youth living on and off with each of his parents, who divorced early in his childhood. Growing up in the small lumber town, Torgeson came to idolize former Snohomish resident Earl Averill, the Cleveland Indians Hall of Fame center fielder whose nickname he adopted when he became known as the "Earl of Snohomish" during his teenage years.

An outstanding all-around athlete, Torgeson excelled in baseball and football at Snohomish High School, performing so well on the diamond that the city's residents petitioned the football coach to make him surrender his spot on the team so that he might focus exclusively on further developing his baseball skills. After also competing semiprofessionally in the area for a few years, Torgeson signed with the Seattle Rainiers of the Pacific Coast League at only 17 years of age, leaving school to train with the Rainiers in the spring of 1941. Optioned to Wenatchee of the Class B Western International League shortly thereafter, Torgeson began his pro career in fine fashion, ranking among the circuit leaders with a batting average of .332, before nearly losing his life later in the year in an automobile accident that killed his aunt and seriously injured his mother.

Promoted to Seattle in 1942, Torgeson had another excellent year, batting .312 and stealing 32 bases. But Torgeson had to temporarily put

Earl Torgeson led the NL with 120 runs scored in 1950.
Courtesy of Boston Public Library, Leslie Jones Collection

his playing career on hold when he entered the military to serve his country during World War II. Drafted into the Army toward the end of 1942, Torgeson spent all of 1943 at Fort Lewis and Fort Lawton in Washington State, before seeing action the next two years in the Aleutians, France, and Germany, where he suffered an injury when a shell that landed in his platoon exploded. Fortunate to escape with only minor wounds, Torgeson spent his last several months in the Army playing baseball with the 70th Division team following the German surrender in May 1945, before receiving his discharge early in 1946.

Returning to Seattle following his discharge, Torgeson batted .285, knocked in 53 runs, and stole 20 bases in just over 100 games with the Rainiers in 1946, before missing the final two months of the campaign with a dislocated shoulder. Acquired by the Braves for five players at season's end, Torgeson received a vote of confidence prior to his departure for Boston from Rainiers' vice president Torchy Torrance, who said, "He can't miss. He can hit, run, field, and think, and what else do you have to do? Wait and see what this kid does to big league pitching. . . . I have been looking at young players for quite a few years, and I am making this prediction—this boy is destined to be one of the great first basemen of the decade."

After being playfully labeled "a poor man's Ted Williams" by new Braves teammate Red Barrett due to his West Coast roots, tall, lanky physique, and long left-handed swing, the 6'3", 180-pound Torgeson initially struggled at the plate upon his arrival in Boston. However, he found his stroke before long, driving in 36 runs in his first 30 games, prompting the local media to begin comparing him to The Splendid Splinter, who also wore the number 9. In response, Torgeson stated, "I didn't ask for it. I didn't know until the City Series that Ted Williams also wore that number."

Torgeson ended up having a solid rookie season for the Braves, hitting 16 homers, driving in 78 runs, scoring 73 others, batting .281, compiling an on-base percentage of .403 and a slugging percentage of .481, and finishing fifth in the league with 11 stolen bases. Somewhat less productive during the Braves' championship campaign of 1948, Torgeson hit 10 homers, knocked in 67 runs, scored 70 times, batted .253, and posted an OPS of .770, although his 19 steals again placed him fifth in the league rankings.

Torgeson subsequently missed most of the 1949 season due to a left shoulder separation he sustained while trying to break up a double play at second base. But he rebounded the next two years to post the best numbers of his career, concluding the 1950 campaign with 23 homers, 83 RBIs, 119 bases on balls, 15 stolen bases, a league-leading 120 runs scored, a batting average of .290, and an on-base percentage of .412, before hitting 24 homers, driving in 92 runs, scoring 99 times, stealing 20 bases, drawing 102 walks, batting .263, and compiling an on-base percentage of .375 the following year.

Although Torgeson proved to be a solid offensive performer for the Braves, especially after he added some much-needed bulk onto his lean frame, he never developed into the true home-run threat others expected him to become when he first arrived in Boston. Nevertheless, Torgeson's size generally prompted Braves managers Billy Southworth and Tommy Holmes to assign him a spot somewhere toward the middle of the batting order, even though his keen batting eye and speed on the basepaths perhaps made him better suited to hit leadoff.

In discussing Torgeson's outstanding running speed, Detroit Tigers coach Bill Sweeney, who saw him play in the Pacific Coast League, said, "I'll wager today that he's the fastest man in the National League."

Braves first base coach Ernie White added, "I see the best runners in our league tear down the line. And take my word for it, Torgy gets down here the quickest."

Meanwhile, Torgeson did an excellent job of working the count, twice drawing more than 100 bases on balls and compiling an on-base percentage over .400.

Possessing a fierce competitive spirit and an unbridled passion for the game that belied his somewhat studious appearance, Torgeson also became known as one of the game's great brawlers, engaging in (according to Bruce Nash and Allan Zullo's *Baseball Hall of Shame*) an estimated 50 fights, fracases, and melees over the course of his career. Perhaps the most notable of those confrontations occurred on July 1, 1952, when Torgeson battled it out with New York Giants catcher Sal Yvars, one of his better friends in baseball.

To summarize the events that transpired that day, Torgeson warned Yvars several times to give him more space in the batter's box. But Yvars, who liked to set up close to the plate, refused, causing Torgeson to resort to flinging his bat backward after hitting the ball as a means of getting his point across to the New York catcher. After getting nicked a few times, Yvars threatened to break Torgeson's bat the next time he tossed it in his direction. Things finally came to a head when, prior to reaching first base via a single, Torgeson caught Yvars on his shin guard with his backswing. Following through on his promise, Yvars picked up the bat and whacked it on home plate until the handle split, all the while staring defiantly at Torgeson as he stood watching from first base. The next inning, Torgeson removed his cap and glasses, trotted out of the Boston dugout, and bolted across the diamond, where, after reaching the Giants bench, he wheeled Yvars around as he was strapping on his catching gear, struck him in the face, knocking him down, and gave him a sound pummeling. In explaining his actions afterward, Torgeson said, "Sal and I always have been good friends. But breaking a guy's bat is like slapping him in the face. We may be in seventh place, but we don't have to take that insult."

Still, Torgeson possessed a very different personality away from the playing field, as Braves teammate Roy Hartsfield acknowledged when he stated, "Torgy is actually a very humorous fellow, and enjoys a practical joke. But not after the game starts. Then he's fiercely competitive."

Experiencing a precipitous decline in offensive production in 1952, Torgeson hit just five homers, knocked in only 34 runs, and batted just .230, prompting the Braves to include him in a complicated four-team trade they completed with the Phillies, Dodgers, and Reds on February 16,

1953, that netted them Joe Adcock and backup outfielder Jim Pendleton. Torgeson, who left Boston with career totals of 82 homers, 377 RBIs, 428 runs scored, 657 hits, 116 doubles, 19 triples, and 80 stolen bases, a batting average of .265, an on-base percentage of .385, and a slugging percentage of .427, ended up spending the next two-and-a-half years in Philadelphia, before splitting his final six-and-a-half big-league seasons between the Tigers, White Sox, and Yankees, serving as a part-time player most of that time. Announcing his retirement following the conclusion of the 1961 campaign, Torgeson ended his playing career with 149 homers, 740 RBIs, 848 runs scored, 1,318 hits, 215 doubles, 46 triples, 133 stolen bases, a .265 batting average, a .385 on-base percentage, and a .417 slugging percentage.

After retiring from baseball, Torgeson briefly worked as a stockbroker with Mitchell Hutchins in Chicago, then operated a sports camp for boys in Westfield, Wisconsin, for two years. Returning to Washington in 1965, Torgeson took a job as parks director for Snohomish County. After four years in that post, Torgeson spent two years managing in the farm system of the expansion Seattle Pilots, before serving as a county commissioner in Snohomish from 1972 to 1975. Failing to gain re-election on two separate occasions, Torgeson went to work for a timber company and eventually became the Snohomish County director of emergency management, a position he held for eight years. Diagnosed with leukemia in the fall of 1990, Torgeson died six weeks later after undergoing unsuccessful chemotherapy, passing away at the age of 66, on November 8, 1990.

Following his passing, county executive Willis Tucker said, "If you had Earl Torgeson for a friend, it was 100 percent, it was unqualified, and it was forever."

Longtime friend Charlie Poier added, "He would never flaunt the fact he was a big leaguer. He would never talk about it unless you'd ask questions. Then he'd go on forever."

Looking back on his playing career some years earlier, Torgeson said, "Unlike my boyhood hero, Earl Averill, I'll never be voted into the Hall of Fame. But I had 15 enjoyable years and accomplished things that most players would like to achieve. Even though we lost the 1948 World Series to the Indians, I led both teams in hitting with a .389 average. And I played in three World Series in three different decades—with the Braves in 1948, the White Sox in 1959, and the Yankees in 1961."

When asked about his reputations as a brawler, Torgeson said somewhat wistfully, "I regret some of the things I did, and I don't like the reputation I had as a bad guy. I really wasn't a bad guy. I just wanted to win."

BRAVES CAREER HIGHLIGHTS

Best Season

Although Torgeson hit more homers and knocked in more runs the following year, he had his finest all-around season in 1950, when he hit 23 homers, drove in 87 runs, batted .290, compiled an OPS of .885, and established career-high marks with 167 hits, 30 doubles, 119 walks, and 120 runs scored, with the last figure leading the National League.

Memorable Moments/Greatest Performances

Torgeson led the Braves to a 7–4 win over the Cubs on May 13, 1947, by going 4-for-5 with a homer, two doubles, and five RBIs.

After hitting a solo homer off Ralph Branca earlier in the contest, Torgeson gave the Braves a 5–4 win over the Dodgers on June 28, 1947, when he knocked in Tommy Holmes from second base with a two-out RBI double to right field in the bottom of the ninth inning.

Torgeson contributed to a 9–1 rout of the Reds on July 29, 1950, by driving in three runs with a pair of homers and a triple, walking once, and scoring three times.

Torgeson proved to be a thorn in the side of the Reds once again on September 17, 1950, homering twice and knocking in three runs during a 6–2 Braves win.

Torgeson homered twice and knocked in a career-high seven runs during a 19–7 rout of the Giants on June 30, 1951, homering off Sal Maglie with the bases loaded in the seventh inning, before reaching the seats off Al Gettel with two men on base in the ensuing frame.

Torgeson contributed to a 14–2 mauling of the Dodgers on September 25, 1951, by driving in six runs with a homer, double, and single.

Notable Achievements

- Hit more than 20 home runs twice.
- Scored more than 100 runs once.
- Surpassed 30 doubles once.
- Stole 20 bases once.
- Drew more than 100 bases on balls twice.
- Compiled on-base percentage over .400 twice.
- Led NL with 120 runs scored in 1950.

- Led NL first basemen in assists once.
- Ranks among Braves career leaders with .385 on-base percentage (tied for 8th).
- 1948 NL champion.

SUMMARY

Having identified the 50 greatest players in Braves history, the time has come to select the best of the best. Based on the rankings contained in this book, the members of the Braves all-time team are listed below. Our squad includes the top player at each position, along with a pitching staff that features a five-man starting rotation and a closer. Our starting lineup also includes a designated hitter.

STARTING LINEUP

Ozzie Albies 2B
Chipper Jones DH
Hank Aaron RF
Eddie Mathews 3B
Dale Murphy LF
Freddie Freeman 1B
Andruw Jones CF
Brian McCann C
Rabbit Maranville SS

PITCHING STAFF

Warren Spahn SP
Greg Maddux SP
Tom Glavine SP
John Smoltz SP
Phil Niekro SP
Craig Kimbrel CL

GLOSSARY

ABBREVIATIONS AND STATISTICAL TERMS

1B. First baseman.

2B. Second baseman.

3B. Third baseman.

AVG. Batting average. The number of hits divided by the number of at-bats.

C. Catcher.

CF. Center fielder.

CG. Complete games pitched.

CL. Closer.

DH. Designated hitter.

ERA. Earned run average. The number of earned runs a pitcher gives up, per nine innings. This does not include runs that scored as a result of errors made in the field and is calculated by dividing the number of runs given up by the number of innings pitched, and multiplying the result by 9.

HITS. Base hits. Awarded when a runner safely reaches at least first base upon a batted ball, if no error is recorded.

HR. Home runs. Fair ball hit over the fence, or one hit to a spot that allows the batter to circle the bases before the ball is returned to home plate.

IP. Innings pitched.

LF. Left fielder.

OBP. On-base percentage. Hits plus walks plus hit-by-pitches, divided by plate appearances.

OPS. On-base plus slugging (the sum of a player's slugging percentage and on-base percentage).

RBI. Runs batted in. Awarded to the batter when a runner scores upon a safely batted ball, a sacrifice, or a walk.

RF. Right fielder.

RUNS. Runs scored by a player.

SHO. Shutout. A complete game in which a pitcher does not allow the other team to score a run.

SLG Slugging percentage. The number of total bases earned by all singles, doubles, triples, and home runs, divided by the total number of at-bats.

SO. Strikeouts.

SP. Starting pitcher.

W-L. Win-loss record in a season for a pitcher.

WHIP. The sum of a pitcher's walks and hits divided by the number of innings pitched.

BIBLIOGRAPHY

Books

Berger, Walter Anton, with George Morris Snyder. *Freshly Remember'd*. Redondo Beach, CA: Schneider McGuirk Publishing, 1993.

Caruso, Gary. *Braves Encyclopedia*. Philadelphia: Temple University Press, 1995.

DeMarco, Tony, et al. *The Sporting News Selects 50 Greatest Sluggers*. St. Louis, MO: The Sporting News, a division of Times Mirror Magazines, Inc., 2000.

McConkey, Matthew. *Never Say Die: The 1914 Braves*. Morrisville, NC: Lulu Press, 2013.

Nash, Bruce, and Allan Zullo. *Baseball Hall of Shame: The Best of Blooperstown*. Guilford, CT: Lyons Press, 2012.

Shalin, Mike, and Neil Shalin. *Out by a Step: The 100 Best Players Not in the Baseball Hall of Fame*. Lanham, MD: Diamond Communications, Inc., 2002.

Thorn, John, and Pete Palmer, eds., with Michael Gershman. *Total Baseball*. New York: HarperCollins, 1993.

Whitaker, Lang. *In the Time of Bobby Cox: The Atlanta Braves, Their Manager, My Couch, Two Decades, and Me*. New York: Scribner Publishing, 2011.

Williams, Ted, with Jim Prime. *Ted Williams' Hit List*. Indianapolis, IN: Masters Press, 1996.

Videos

Sports Century: Fifty Greatest Athletes—Hank Aaron. ESPN, 1999.

The Glory of Their Times. Cappy Productions, Inc., 1985.

The Sporting News' 100 Greatest Baseball Players. National Broadcasting Co., 1999.

Websites

Bio Project, SABR.org
(www.sabr.org/bioproj/person).

Historical Stats, MLB.com
(https://www.mlb.com/stats/all-time-totals).

The Players, Baseball-Almanac.com
(www.baseball-almanac.com/players/ballplayer.shtml).

The Players, Baseball-Reference.com
(www.baseball-reference.com/players).

The Players, Retrosheet.org
(www.retrosheet.org/boxesetc/index.html#Players).

The Teams, Baseball-Reference.com
(www.baseball-reference.com/teams).